THE SUPRACONSCIENCE OF HUMANITY

Edward H. Strauch

University Press of America,® Inc.
Lanham · Boulder · New York · Toronto · Plymouth, UK

Copyright © 2010 by
University Press of America,® Inc.
4501 Forbes Boulevard
Suite 200
Lanham, Maryland 20706
UPA Acquisitions Department (301) 459-3366

Estover Road
Plymouth PL6 7PY
United Kingdom

All rights reserved
Printed in the United States of America
British Library Cataloging in Publication Information Available

Library of Congress Control Number: 2010924020
ISBN: 978-0-7618-5159-2 (clothbound : alk. paper)
ISBN: 978-0-7618-5160-8 (paperback : alk. paper)
eISBN: 978-0-7618-5161-5

∞™ The paper used in this publication meets the minimum
requirements of American National Standard for Information
Sciences—Permanence of Paper for Printed Library Materials,
ANSI Z39.48-1992

Other Books by the Author

A Philosophy of Literary Criticism. A Method of Literary Analysis and Interpretation. Exposition UniversityPress. Jericho, NY. 1974.

How Nature Taught Man to Know, Imagine, and Reason. How Language and Literature Recreate Nature's Lessons. American University Studies. Linguistics. New York. Peter Lang Publ. 1995.

Creative Writing for Africans. How to Write Descriptions, News Reports, Explanations, Essays and Original Stories. Lanham, MD. University Press of America. 1995.

Beyond Literary Theory. Literature as a Search for the Meaning of Human Destiny. Lanham, MD. University Press of America. 2001.

The Creative Conscience of Humanity. American University Studies. Philosophy. New York. Peter Lang Publ. 2004.

BD
493
.S87
2012

Table of Contents

Preface   *vii*

Part One: *The Psyche's Struggle for Survival*
Chapter One: Conscience versus Subconscience   3

Part Two: *The Beginning of the Supraconscience*
Chapter Two: The Afterlife as World View:
                     The Subconscience versus Supraconscience   27
Chapter Three: Myth, Ritual, Cosmologies and Theism   45
Chapter Four: Four Archetypes of the Emerging Supraconscience   73
                     A.   *Sōphrosynē* (Temperance)   74
                     B.   The Great Chain of Being   77
                     C.   The Bible: Four Levels of Significance   80
                     D.   The Divinity   86

Part Three: *The Bible as Evidence of Humanity's*
                 Evolving Supraconscience
Chapter Five: The Old Testament: The Law and Historical Books   95
Chapter Six: The Old Testament: The Poetical and Prophetic Books   107
Chapter Seven: The New Testament   129

Part Four: *The Supraconscience: Historical and Modern*
Chapter Eight: Mystics and Mysticism   147
Chapter Nine: A Twenty-First Century Version of Heresy   185

Part Five: *The Inferior versus Superior Destiny of Humankind*
Introduction   211
Chapter Ten: The Conflict between the Inferior and
                  Superior Human Nature   213
Chapter Eleven: Psyche's Journey Through Time   231

Glossary   251
Bibliography   263
Index   267

Preface

This book introduces original terms unique to its argument. The preface undertakes to make clear the purpose of the argument and the method used to investigate the powers of the evolved psyche. There is little replication of the well known psychological terminology of the past two centuries.

The familiar vocabulary of specialists has hitherto failed to take into account the cultures and civilizations which energized and accelerated the evolution of psyche itself. Therefore, the philosophical aim of this text is to suggest a more complete understanding of psyche and of human evolution.

Much of human history illustrates that superstitious interpretations of human nature are destructive. The pervasive superstition that our kind are congenitally evil demeans the good in man and ignores the great potentials in humankind.

Challenging the fatalistic judgment that man's inferior nature will forever dominate his life, the history of human culture over the last seven millennia is proof that our species is evolving a superior human nature.

Hence previous theories of psyche prove incomplete in so far as they neglect the philosophical effect of culture and civilization on the evolution of the psyche. To help rectify that incomplete understanding, it has been necessary to probe the significance of psyche's transformation from pre-history to modern man and woman. Humankind's accelerated evolution is the outcome of psyche's evolving exponential powers.

For readers prepared to advance their knowledge of psyche's metamorphosis over time, *The Supraconscience of Humanity* recapitulates our species' mental journey. To begin this odyssey, we need to first understand three central terms: *subconscience*, *conscience*, and *supraconscience*. Through their dialectical interaction, they made possible psyche's evolution over 5,000 generations of humankind.

During prehistoric times, man's instinct-intuition was largely a *subconscience*. It was *sub* by being underdeveloped, incomplete and unintegrated. In the prehistoric age, we survived daily life-and-death situations. The constant threat of man-eating predators surely brutalized, maimed and wounded the minds of the survivors.

Our nature-born conscience emerged to restrain the more savage emotions of the subconscience. Moreover, from predators, man learned stalking skills, watchful patience and cunning. This conscience, born-in-nature, helped man realize two basic truths: first, ignorance endangered one's life; and second, new skills and accurate knowledge of the real world made tomorrow possible. Beyond these lessons in survival, the mystery and majesty of the primeval earth calmed and reassured him. Mentored by our primordial conscience, the life instinct of the subconscience made possible our survival.

Over time, man's intuitive creativity oriented him toward the fantastic and the spiritual. Within savage nature, he began to sense the presence of supernatural powers. As imagination quickened, it created a multitude of gods and goddesses. They seemed everywhere in nature. Man learned to look deeper into nature and within to discover his own spirit.

In the next stage of human evolution, mythical imagination became mystical conscience. It gradually transformed man's raw survival instincts into a belief in benign supernatural beings. At times, people felt serenity through trust in a higher spirit power.

Eventually, humankind learned to perceive the summer and winter solstices as well as the seasonal cycle of the stars. Gradually, it dawned on mystics and thinkers that a Supreme Deity had created the universe. This belief led conscience to focus its powers of perception and to concentrate the mind in elementary forms of logic.

Belief in the omniscience of the Deity eventually made conscience aware of its own limitations. Fear of ignorance thus spurred humankind to learn all that could be learned. Commitment to more knowledge and to keener understanding led mankind to foster innate potentials. Across the millennia, learning in some form or another transformed our species to present day humanity.

Through religious ritual, prophets and Holy Scripture, our kind evolved stages of spiritual conscience. In time, mystics converted orthodox teaching into a superior conscience. It expressed mankind's spiritual nature: our religious supraconscience.

When the prefix *supra* is used, it generally means the following: over, above, beyond any previous understanding of conscience; more comprehensive, more inclusive, more universal in scope; superior in complexity, intricacy and exponential powers.

Concurrently, through the creation of cultures and civilizations, man evolved a secular conscience. This conscience guided him in the development of innovative crafts and skills. Man also discovered the benefit of hygiene, sanitation and irrigation. And, he amassed useful knowledge. Gradually, his myriad mental activities made clear psyche's endowments. To reason soundly and skillfully, to create significant ideas and systems of thought became psyche's purpose in life.

Through architecture and engineering, medicine and science, psyche's capacity for ingenious creation and intricate integration of projects enabled man to change. He became ever more conscious his intelligence was developing exponentially by bringing forth never-before-seen wonders. Yet, beyond practical accomplishments, self-expression through the arts, literature, philosophy and history taught him the nobler meanings of humanity's common heritage. These accomplishments reveal the secular destiny of man. Culture and civilization revealed man's secular supraconscience.

In sum, man has evolved both a religious and a secular supraconscience which fulfill spiritual and intellectual needs. It is hoped that this book will introduce the reader to his or her own superior nature, and thereby lead to greater awareness of the powers of the supraconscience.

Part One

The Psyche's Struggle for Survival

Chapter One

Conscience versus Subconscience

History quite accurately provides us with solid evidence of the confrontation between various life philosophies and their continuous oscillation between the extreme actions they recommend.

Already in early civilization, conscience implied sharing and co-operation, which meant increasing the chances of survival. Today, biology writes of the mutually beneficial association between animals and organisms. This survival principle was relied upon by members of a group, race or religion. Despite human differences, the common bond between families and diverse peoples helped assure their mutual survival. Thus at the root of humankind's original conscience was sharing and cooperation.

Of course, at successive stages of evolution, man became aware of other forms of conscience. At the hunting/gathering stage, hunters were recognized by the tribe for their knowledge of animal habits and skill in pursuing and capturing prey. On the other hand, women became skilled in finding food sources among plants as well as herbs to be used for healing and curing. To be sure, female resourcefulness included the invention of cooking, baking, distilling, and using potions and cathartics. So, conscience meant the application of intelligence in the practical uses of the resources which the natural environment offered.

Of course, early man experienced periods of feast and famine. Hence hindsight fostered foresight and so led to the invention of various methods of food storage and preservation. These periods also taught people self-restraint, self-discipline, and, to a degree, self-denial. Ignoring conscience could lead to starvation and death.

However, the dark side of man's predatory skills led to the practice of capturing members of other tribes to enslave them, especially women. At its worst, (as with the Aztecs in Meso-America), such captives were ritually used as human sacrifices.

When small populations gathered together to form villages and towns, land ownership became a "necessity" to protect what was one's own--fertile ground, grazing areas for domestic animals, shelters for the women and their children. The defense of property justified the use of violence, and ownership came to be viewed as a natural right. This development added a new dimension to conscience.

Various ancient civilizations developed new levels of understanding in the face of widespread cruelty and inexplicable death. Ancient Egyptian culture, for example, became obsessively preoccupied with death. There emerged a presentiment that the moral quality of one's life on earth would decide one's life after death. Over 4,000 years ago, the Egyptians believed in a form of divine judgment that weighed the deceased's moral behavior.[1] This capacity to visualize the afterlife in heaven or hell established the basis for the moral code and conscience of Western humankind for thousands of years to come. Maat, the Egyptian goddess of universal justice, made truth, virtue and goodness enduring qualities of conscience.

These have continued to be the triadic elements of a moral life on earth. As early as 2400 BC, a testament read "A good man is one who gives bread to the hungry, water to the thirsty, and clothing to the naked." To any member of the Jewish, Christian and Muslim faith today, this is a fundamental moral maxim.

In several myths which have come down to us from antiquity, the hero of many cultures is renowned not only for his epic exploits, but also for his determination to merit a worthy afterlife. This meant that he conscientiously performed his duty as protector of his people and also set the example of a noble life for his descendents. Such a life philosophy became a memorable trait of human conscience.

On the other hand, humankind's tendency to violence and genocide led men to conceive of natural disasters as punishment for crimes against humanity—thus wakening a sense of collective sin.

Over time, the moral code of Middle Kingdom Egypt had declined and the wealthy by-passed their obligation to the ritual of Osiris (god of the underworld) by buying dispensations.[2] So here we have clear evidence of cynicism about belief in justice or any kind of divine retribution. Such cynicism arose as a result of the sardonic influence of humankind's primitive subconscience, which yields to no power or authority other than its own.

The harshness and cruelty characteristic of the ethic of Babylon saw to the drowning of adulterers and the incestuous as well as the castration of homosexuals. Yet, injuring a slave was an act that was fined, and reasonable men held women in esteem. Babylonians held no belief in an afterlife.[3] Thus the excessive punishment they meted out reveals the enduring power of the subconscience.

Other ancient civilizations demonstrated traits of cruelty and compassion.

An interesting exception to the emphasis on severity was the Minoan Golden Age on the island of Crete. Basically, the Minoans were a people involved in trade throughout the Mediterranean. Yet, this society also enjoyed games, acrobatics and communal dance. Their statuettes of bare-breasted snake goddesses revealed a lust for life and a place in their conscience for play and creativity. This revealed a philosophy that seemed to worship life itself.

As the centuries unfolded, evidence of a higher level of human moral development came to the fore accompanied by the ingenuity of vice and psychological sickness. Humankind may have become more contemplative, but, still, a variety of vices became the staple of a degenerate side of ancient conscience: gambling, alcoholism, coerced prostitution of women, and sadism on a vast scale.

Moral deterioration in any culture calls for comment. Such degeneration can be counteracted, in measure, by the practice of some form of introspection, which can guide intelligence, mind and psyche toward honest self-evaluation. Introspection can aid the individual in identifying what is most important in one's survival.

On the other hand, vices are often an escape from honest self-evaluation. The individual who gives in to his biological urges may also believe irrational superstitions, or misplace confidence in his inimitable shrewdness at gambling. For example, one often puts trust in fantastic good luck and loses a fortune. On the other hand, the vice of sadism inflicts pain on those who cannot respond in kind. Vices often undermine man's otherwise healthful gift of creativity. In the final analysis, they originate in the unconscionable subconscience.

In ancient Egypt, during Akhenaton's (Ikhnaton's) reign (1360-1340 B.C.), the pharaoh introduced the moral virtues of truth, racial equality and family responsibility. During his time, women were well treated, had equal rights to property and filial duty was extolled.

By contrast, during the time of Ramses II (1293-1292 B.C.), torture was widely used and war glorified. It was he who brutalized the Hebrew slaves and initiated the infanticide of their males.

As an ex-slave, the Hebrew prophet Moses (c. 1300-1220 B.C.) gave Western civilization the Ten Commandments, what we know as the core principles of Old Testament theology (Exodus 20 and Deuteronomy 5). These religious injunctions required observance of the Sabbath and honor of parents. They also listed prohibitions governing human relations. One must not kill, commit adultery, steal, bear false witness, or covet another's wife or property. The Ten Commandments were obeyed in recognition of God's deliverance of the Hebrew people out of bondage in Egypt. They condemned the worship of any gods other than Yahweh.

Moses' instructions as to human comportment regulated marriage, sexual hygiene and prostitution. Adultery was punishable by stoning to death, and homosexuality was considered an abomination. One's daughters were not to be sold into whoredom.

Here again we see the admixture of sensible practices advised by an enlightened conscience and excessive punishment urged by the severity of the subconscience.

In the *Book of Joshua* (c. 1250-1200 B.C.) we see the Hebrew conscience, afflicted by what was still the subconscience, when Joshua obeyed Jehovah's command to exterminate the population of Jerusalem. Apparently, Jewish brutality did not hesitate to eliminate other populations from the promised land. According to secular history, prisoners of war were slaughtered and elders of the defeated were beaten to death with thongs for refusing to accept the Jews as victors. Indeed, many Jewish heroes in the Old Testament appear ruthless and sadistic.

Unfortunately, such ruthlessness and sadism is quasi-universal in most of the world's early cultures. The twentieth century itself offers abundant evidence of the fact that man's inhumanity to man has not subsided. There is essentially no race or religion that has not been involved in some form of genocide. Though the human psyche has certainly evolved beyond its initial stage as subconscience, that subconscience remains a threat to human sanity and to the sound conscience which humankind needs to survive.

No race on the face of the earth has the moral high ground because history reveals all too starkly the continual struggle between our evolved conscience and the paranoia, violence and murderous mentality of our primeval subconscience–that which motivated our ancestors' struggle to survive in a world of ever-present death.

The great prophets of the ancient Hebrews reveal the steady evolution of Israeli wisdom. Of special note was Micah's "Do justly, love mercy, walk humbly with God." Then there was Isaiah's unforgettable "Nation shall not raise sword against nation."

Of course, the story of Job (c. 580 B.C.) is a lesson for all humankind who lose faith in any justice on earth or in the universe. God permitted Satan to torture Job with all forms of material deprivation, physical sickness and mental anguish. Nevertheless, Satan could not destroy his faith in God: Satan failed. As a consequence, God restored all Job had lost and more.

Yet, the story haunts us to this day because it does not explain away the evil in the world. If God is omnipotent, then why does He allow evil things to happen? The story fails to account for injustice and affliction of the innocent who themselves have committed no offence to man or God.

By contrast, in the heroic age of ancient Greece (850-800 B.C.), Homer's *Iliad* and *Odyssey* represent the birth of the heroic conscience. The age expected men to be fearless and truthful, strong and courageous. Yet, the greatest vices of the age were treachery, perjury and cowardice. It was despicable for the strong to harm the helpless and old. On the other hand, the victor was to respect the vanquished enemy. These noble traits were intertwined with the belief that reward and punishment received in the hereafter were retribution for one's decisions and acts. These characteristics summed up the noble Greek conscience. Thus out of this Mediterranean civilization arose a code of morality which did everlasting honor to the ancient Greeks.

Greece is also remembered for the great tragedies of, e.g. Aeschylus, Sophocles and Euripides. Tragic figures found themselves entangled or trapped in circumstances virtually beyond their control. And, despite the fact that they were unable to extricate themselves from their fate, each was found responsible for the consequences of his decisions and acts.

In his classical treatise on tragedy (*Poetics*), Aristotle defines the essence of conscience. "Character is that which reveals moral purpose, showing what kind of things a man chooses or avoids." "The important thing is that he or she must be good--that is, manifest a moral purpose of any kind." Otherwise, characters who evince arrogance (*hybris*) or blindness to the consequences of their actions (*hamartia*) end up as tragic figures. Hence modesty, temperance, or *sōphrosynē* are the indications of right-minded kind of character. In other words, he admires most those who display conscience tempered by philosophy and wisdom. This is the timeless legacy which the ancient Greeks bequeathed to mankind.

Early Man and the Subconscience

In our description of early man's psyche, we must not forget that instinctively he reacted to nature as a spiritual environment.

We tend to ignore the fact that, for him, raw nature and existence itself was full of mysteries. Wherever there was movement, for example, wind through the trees or a rush of running water, invisible powers seemed to be present. The habits and activities of every insect, snake, bird, and animal seemed to disclose the presence of the special spirit of the environment.

Every recurring pattern of nature such as rain, drought, storms and seasons, as well as the shifting constellations and brightest stars in the night sky, seemed to reveal supernatural powers watching over man and pondering the reality of his being. He himself became preoccupied with the intention, mystery and meaning of spiritual presences that existed in their own realm.

Eventually, man's common sense understood that the wind and flowing water were simply natural to the earth. Yet, the "cause" of the germination, growth, and flowering of plants, followed by their withering and dying, remained an enigma too great for him to comprehend. Millennia later, the emergence of the sciences of biology, botany, zoology, and ecology unveiled the secret processes that animate visible nature.

That early spiritual vision of existence still lingers in our psyche's imagination, and it continues to exert an influence on personal myths, beliefs, and religious interpretations of life. We still seem to feel as if our soul is on a spiritual journey through life. As a poetic way of looking at life, this has its own beauty, truth and meaning.

However, the murky side of our primeval imagination appeared when we subconsciously and instinctively feared the presence of unreal predators. This age-old anxiety eventually became the fear of demons and devils. Such deeply rooted superstitions made our ancestors and even our forefathers vulnerable to mental anguish, foreboding and terror.

In our time, it behooves us to resist telling "boogeyman stories" to our children, even if our intent is humorous. Such threats are all too real to the impressionable minds and vulnerable hearts of the young. Rather, from childhood on, our children should be taught "Get thee behind me, goblin!" Aside from Halloween Night, there are no spirits or ghosts abroad in the night. And like the imaginary monsters in our nightmares, they are simply the subconscience re-dreaming its primeval life and remembering the putrid breath of death from millennia past.

More on the Subconscience

As we have seen, history reveals that humankind is cursed with destructive impulses as if the psyche were still held in thrall to its primitive environment. This mental state contributed to the male's psychic sense of the "law of the jungle". In fact, the world over, the human species was at a physical disadvantage when faced with carnivores.

The female must have shared this same general anxiety, but because of her mammalian nature, giving birth and suckling her new born, the mother's instinct, deeper than her fear, was to protect her offspring. In this role, she could show tenacity and even ferocity. However, when she and her child were not threatened, her energies were concentrated on nurturing her young. The tenderness and love she felt for them and her spouse humanized the entire family.

So, male and female formed a bond that allowed them to rise above the more coarse tendencies of aggression toward other tribes and peoples. In other words, although the goal of the primitive subconscience was self-preservation and survival, that fierce need was somewhat mollified by the initial phase of development of human conscience.

Nevertheless, throughout history the subconscience has driven men to murder, torture and terrorize so as to establish their "superiority" over others. This fact became evident in the ancient Middle East where the defeated were slaughtered en masse, or it led to the brutal treatment of the conquered.

The history of the slave trade in Africa demonstrates this fact. For over one thousand years, the Arabs made slaves of the black populations. They often killed the males and kept the women and children as chattel. The Spanish exercised a similar type of sadistic power over the natives of Latin America. At least Northern European slave traders gave up the trans-Atlantic slave trade eventually and the young American navy hunted down slave ships as part of an effort to re-settle blacks in Liberia. True, the Atlantic slave trade went on for some time, but finally the teachings of Judaism and Christianity humanized men sufficiently to confront the injustice of it. Hence upon occasion, religious conscience could, and did, overcome the darker powers of the subconscience and counter its disregard for human life.

However the historical fact remains that inflicting pain on other human beings was an accepted practice among those who dominated others. Moreover, the scope of this practice exceeded any limited law that might attempt to curb or control such atrocities.

The subconscience also used man's ingenuity to invent all forms of humiliation and abuse of the weak and defenseless. Indeed, certain periods of history show how far genius can go when controlled and guided by an unsound subconscience which is able to wantonly maim, torture and murder. As if that were not enough, the subconscience invented all sorts of self-punishing addictions. It practiced self-mortification and seemed to relish abandoning any pretext at being human.

Fortunately, the human psyche finally became nauseated by its own cruelty and senseless killing. There followed a recurrent need to re-assert self-control, to cleanse the conscience, to re-instate family values and sensible virtues. It is probable that woman's maternal, compassionate nature put an end to excesses, orgies, and senseless living. Thus women proved their intelligence, authority and value to mankind beyond the role of mate and child-bearer.

Indeed, archeologists tell us that womankind actually established agriculture, and invented pottery and devised weaving. They not only taught themselves a whole range of ways to cook raw meat and vegetables but also developed methods for conserving food in various climates. Most assuredly they were the first apothecaries, nurses and doctors to care for the family's hurts, wounds and illnesses and to ensure their children survived through adolescence.

As periods of peace lasted longer, woman's maternal nature modified the spirit of aggression and competition between males. Her humane attitudes led to greater co-operation between families, tribes and peoples. Ultimately, charity in understanding others reached out to all in need. And, curiously, in some societies, this charitable understanding turned into its own form of superiority. It often shamed the selfish, the greedy, the unscrupulous and the pitiless into becoming more human.

Competition, rather than warfare, led to the sublimation of the more aggressive instincts. Through games, sports, and contests of all sorts, competitors established a scale of superiority and inferiority. Inadvertently, such competition led to the improvement of skills, the origin of innovative game strategies, the building of unusual strength, and the sharpening of mental abilities--all in order to win.

In other words, peaceful rivalry effected a marked change in the subconscience, such that conscience gained a sensible advantage over it, and thus could become superior. The relationship between the two became less a matter of controlling primeval instincts than of transforming and sublimating them into beneficial, educational activities which subdued, and to a degree, morally converted the sub-conscience. This shift made possible the astonishing creative achievements of later civilization.

On the other hand, throughout much of human history, the primitive subconscience has been responsible for the disrespect and abuse of women and children because the abusers were exempt from punishment, and no thought was given to the fact that the victim deserved some form of consideration or humane justice. Often, regard for the abused was blunted by the fact that such victimization had been so widely practiced for so many generations. Ironically, those who considered themselves superior felt no need to feel anything for those whom they viewed as inferior.

In other words, both compassion and humanity's emotional intelligence can be numbed, anesthetized, even paralyzed by too much familiarity with injustice, crime and killing. Ancient Roman practices were particularly appalling. For the entertainment of the public, gladiators fought to the death, and early Christians were martyred by inciting hungry lions to attack, tear apart and eat their victims. Today, American television itself is overly preoccupied with the horror of daily rape and murder of women and children. It seems the primitive subconscience is alive and well in modern America. Of course, European and Asian history is itself replete with recurrent periods of mutual slaughter characteristic of the unsoundness of the subconscience.

Yet, the American media are themselves clearly in need of a cathartic dose of conscience. The endless pulpit preachments offered through television bore and benumb us. The wearisome repetition of religious truths finally converts them into platitudes. Self- serving evangelism gives one cause for dismay and appalls us. Such programming offers little evidence of original thought about the implications of Scripture on modern life. Those who have already been "saved" seem to possess a limitless sense of self-righteousness. There is no place in this schema for the outsider, the unbeliever, the "lost sheep". The ostracized have been cast aside and forgotten—tossed into the dumpster with the rest of human trash. Whatever happened to the authentic faith of our grandparents and the enduring commitment to democracy of our forefathers? Sucked into the oblivion of TV.

Judaism, Christianity and Islam were born out of human suffering and need. These faiths created moral systems which still guide one-third of the world's population. Yet much of humanity suffers from want and exists at the edge of starvation. How does such a 'salvation' religion help "save" the sick and starving of the world?

Many people of the Third World are faced with the fact that the quantity of arable land available to them is diminishing, their food sources are disappearing and they have limited access to potable water. In many regions, women and children do not live in safety or have the security of the humblest home. These impoverished areas of the world show us the urgent need for a more effective, universal morality, one that transcends human cultural and religious differences.

Ironically, the life enjoyed in early agrarian communities was like Eden before the superstitious invention of sin and Satanic evil. In that pristine age, we lived in a tamed nature. We believed the earth was benign, bountiful, succoring and maternal. The husbandman was the most respected of men and his wife was a fount of home-loving wisdom. Or at least so it seems in our "civilized" memory of that early age.

Yet, today we have an extensive scientific knowledge of farming and husbandry. Scientists have come a long way in fathoming the secrets of soil, animal feed, weather, season and climate. With good will and a true sense of humanity, we can still feed much of the world, if the most technically advanced nations undertake to help the disadvantaged regions.

But, in addition to this, the world needs a third millennium moral system based on a vocational, secular, and non-denominational system of education. If it were to focus on multi-racial/religious understanding, practical know-how and secular knowledge, such a system of worldwide education would enable individuals, communities, societies, and nations to live with human dignity.

This world model could provide a means of healing, curing and metamorphosing our primeval subconscience into a more productive, humane collective conscience; it could lead to a higher stage of human evolution. Basic to such an international, humanitarian code would not only be compassion, but also mutual education in the religions and cultures of ethnic groups and different religions of the world. When we truly try to understand others, they will be willing to understand us.

Indeed, the earth is only a tiny island of life in a vast ocean of what may prove to be lifeless space. Unlike our migratory ancestors, there seems little prospect that the human race will be able to migrate to some other eco-niche in space to live out our destinies in another self-contained world.

For now, and for at least the rest of the third millennium, it is all but certain that humankind needs to learn to live together in peace. We also need to help one another survive with dignity, with true respect for human rights and, on the practical level, with food shortage problems having been sufficiently solved so that all members of the race can help themselves and ensure that their children have a future.

Ancient Gnosticism and Early Conscience

The cult of Gnosticism, which was active for a few centuries before and after the life of Christ, believed man was torn between opposing powers. According to the Gnostic, Marcion (2nd - 3rd cent. A.D.), this dualism was evident in the opposition between the theological doctrines of the Old and New Testament. He described how the Old Testament revealed the God of Creation to be a tyrant commanding Joshua to kill the populations of the cities conquered by the Jews. This was a God who expected His Chosen People to carry out His Justice without pity. Marcion thus considered the God of the Old Testament inferior; by contrast, the New Testament reflected, in his view, a superior concept of God.[4]

Of particular interest to our study of psyche is the Gnostic view that conscience had passed through two stages. If the earlier form of conscience passed severe judgments and dealt out merciless justice, the later one preached charity and forgiveness. Its superiority lay in the fact that it made man peace-loving and compassionate.

Possibly these two concepts of God arose from Marcion's childhood memories of his own father and mother. Traditionally, fathers mete out punishment to discipline the young. By contrast, mothers generally forgive and embrace the child. This seems to be a universal experience and could explain the Gnostic conception of what God's justice should be.

Though we respect the strength and authority of the father, our memory of motherly love remains and influences our lives perhaps more because we feel ashamed at doing wrong and hurting her feelings. Instinctively, the child knows her love must be deserved.

Similarly, the Deity who judges severely and punishes erratically may arouse respect, fear and command silence, but a more compassionate Divinity inspires devotion, gratitude and commitment to a gentler wisdom.

The ancient Gnostics envisioned human destiny in cosmic terms. Fixated by the opposition between a lifetime in light or darkness, above and below, they believed human existence revealed superior and inferior destinies. For the Gnostics, the God of eternity was not the God who created the material earth and life which ended in death. Hence gnosis or esoteric knowledge became the secret path to transcending death. That knowledge would enable the individual to survive death as an inferior being. As a superior soul, one could enter an afterlife with the eternal God. Thus though there were, in their view, two orders of reality, the study of spiritual reality could free the person from an ignoble death.

Gnostics sought to free themselves from the relentless flow of time. Release could be achieved in a single life. Otherwise, those who lived an inferior life would undergo countless, futile reincarnations. In the end, they would disappear into the vast, inscrutable mystery of the cosmos. While time on earth meant delusion and despair for the inferior soul, the gnostic could ultimately achieve the freedom of mind and material plenitude associated with a higher plane of existence. To become one of the Elect, the individual could commit self to attaining knowledge of the noumenal world and thereby assure his or her spiritual destiny. A lifetime of study would eventually enable the seeker to reach the highest stage of self-perfection.[5]

In sum, in our early conscience, the ancient Gnostics discovered the endless potential of human intuition: Mankind's higher mental power was, for them, an intimation that humankind was evolving toward a higher nature or superior psyche.

Conscience and Subconscience in Conflict

Judging by history's major events and the biographies of great men, humankind lived in conflict between a sound conscience and recurrent unsound emotions. Though we are well aware of the world's moral traditions, in the recent twentieth century, we witnessed: an upsurge of skepticism and cynicism regarding morality, a virtual outbreak of domestic violence and an eruption of wars within and between nations.

Though strife and turmoil may be attributed to unresolved economic and social issues, and though cultural differences are often cited as "justifying" regional conflicts, human violence and aggression has a deeper source. Its ultimate cause is probably older than history.

The real reason is to be found in our prehistoric struggle for survival. Especially in times of perceived danger, the psychological origin of our mutual distrust and outbursts of rage is the subconscience. Characteristic of our prehistoric subconscience was its extreme readiness to respond to any danger, and that psychic state aroused our vigilance and provoked rage against any sort of threat, imagined or actual. That is, throughout history, when our survival was challenged, our entire being was called upon: We did or died.

An ancient myth also dramatized the struggle for survival. It described the cosmos as an arena of infinite powers of good and evil confronting one another for all eternity. So humans had to choose to fight on behalf of one or the other of these powers, to align themselves spiritually with either light or darkness. Thus all mankind was divided between those who were good and those who were evil: "We" were good, "they" were evil.

Another fatalistic explanation was that human life was ruled by karma. Hindus and Buddhists believe in reincarnation, or the transmigration of a soul from the present life to one's next existence. One's good or evil actions inevitably have moral consequences: they define one's next life. The notion of karma was used to explain suffering, sorrow or tragedy experienced in this life as due to the unclean passions and despicable acts done in previous lifetime(s).

Even if both the imaginative myth of a cosmos in conflict and the belief in the poetic justice of karma illuminate the creative genius of different cultures, they are still not really acceptable explanations.

The psychological reason for periodic emotional upheavals is the traumatic existence experienced by our prehistoric kin. That age, marked by its ongoing struggle for survival, left an indelible scar on our primeval psyche. It accounts for murderous acts of violence that the evolved conscience could never condone.

These reactions occur whenever we unexpectedly find our lives endangered. In such instances, our evolved psyche reverts to primitive instincts forgotten over hundreds of generations of humankind. In an instant, we can revert to the primal subconscience which kept us alive in a world filled with predators.

Due to the savage conditions of prehistoric life, the survival of the individual depended on vigilance, strength, and skill in defense and offense. This threatening environment required our senses to be alert and the body constantly prepared for life-and-death struggles. Stress would have exhausted the weaker humans, but for the survivors, stress sharpened the senses and improved the ability to think through emergencies. The primitive subconscience must have undergone times of paranoia countered by the determination to survive.

Since prehistoric times, consciousness of nature's ferocity and the daily threat to human life deeply affected the human brain. Its effect was reflected in psyche's imagining gods who had dual natures subject to unpredictable fits of rage. The conflict between human fear and courage confirmed the sense that there existed, within ourselves, powers of evil and good.

In terms of the evolutionary movement toward the supraconscience of humanity, this condition of mental turmoil became the origin of the perennial struggle between our subconscience and the beginnings of a religious conscience.

In fact, the superstitious belief in supernatural good and evil spirits predominated through much of human history. Judging others we mistrusted and hated as evil beings, made it easier to commit atrocities against them. Belief in the evil nature of others "justified" the mass execution of innocents and heretics for some 400 years of European history. It also condoned the slaughter of conquered peoples when they refused to convert to the conqueror's religion. Judaism, Christianity and Islam have all committed heinous crimes against humanity in the name of their one and only God.

This moral schizophrenia not only characterized all three "salvation" religions, but also marked the split in the collective conscience of Near Eastern and Western civilizations.

Long-held superstitions have serious consequences. They have scarred the human conscience with unfounded prejudices and persistent hatred. As Christians are aware, our conscience finds itself doubting the purity and integrity of our religious mentors and sometimes of the faith itself. Some desperate disbelievers embrace atheism as the only viable alternative.

Hence religious conscience is tormented by both indecision and fear of making the wrong decision. The twentieth century was confronted by a series of horrific wars during which religion seemed unable to exert any sane influence over men's fanatical acts of mutual extermination. Both friend and foe claimed God was on their side; each group considered their cause to be "just." As a consequence, organized religion has lost much of its credibility. To those who felt the betrayal most deeply, moral values were ignored, by-passed or discarded.

Promises of rewards in an afterlife came to be scorned or ridiculed. With the exception of sects legally deprived of their rights, fundamentalist groups were seen as crazed fanatics who used their religion to justify the murder of the condemned and apostates. On the other hand, the truly conscientious faithful were seen as mindlessly obeying beliefs and dogmata which had lost all moral meaning.

By contrast, the positive power of religious conscience educated us to responsibility, determination, dependability, and honorableness in our relationships. Conscience also taught us dutifulness, commitment to our word, and the need for the application of practical measures to meet collective goals.

The sadistic gratification of our primeval subconscience must appear morally repugnant to us today, yet human history and pre-history provide evidence to the contrary. Apparently the subconscience took keen pleasure in revenge, in tricking other human beings or trapping them as prey. There was satisfaction to be had in making a kill, in vanquishing a foe, in enslaving the weak, and tyrannically controlling the helpless—a sense of power came with rape, with unpunished crime, with duping the innocent and trusting. In short, some of our primitive ancestors surely enjoyed victimizing those who could not defend themselves. Moreover, the satisfaction that accompanied such vile, subhuman, homicidal acts has been displayed throughout human history and continues to be today.

Over time and in all cultures with a moral code, human conscience has judged and condemned such subhuman behavior. Dishonesty, deceit, entrapment, crime and homicide are considered immoral, damnable, vicious, and inhumane. Yet often the perpetrator of such acts derives a secret, sadistic thrill from his craftiness or skill in stalking his prey—such rapacity represents the lowest form of human gratification. It epitomizes a subhuman state of psyche.

As commonly understood, conscience represents a more evolved, advanced stage of human intelligence and moral character than does subconscience. Originally, it existed at the tribal level where the chief exercised final authority over the life and death of members of the tribe. That is why the Yahweh of early Judaism was basically a tribal lord with all the characteristic mood swings, irascibility, strictness, justice and injustice that were also characteristic of His final judgments.

Influenced by the dualism of Zoroastrianism and Manichaeism, Judaic and Christian conscience began to openly do battle with the subversive power of the primeval subconscience.

Most often, this struggle takes place deep within the individual and meets with no clear resolution. It may continue over years and decades through a lifetime of self-torment. But the fear of punishment in an eternal hell requires an ultimate decision. The here and now which determines the quality of the afterlife usually moves conscience to obedience.

For many followers of a traditional religion, the incessant struggle with conscience determines the tenor and meaning of one's entire life. Conscience is torn between absolute good and absolute evil. Good is what is acceptable, proper, decent, and moral. Bad is made up of evil acts against one's own kind--family, community, race, religion. They can range from acts of betrayal and disloyalty to one's clan, race, or country to indiscriminate crime and murder.

Over time, finding a medium between these extremes seems to be an impossible task. Either some degree of inner peace and serenity must be recovered or some form of insanity will seize the individual and communal psyche.

Fortunately, with the steady, secular education of humankind, the relentless fanaticism spawned by the subconscience began to give way; little by little; it began to become transformed. From the earliest stages of the human species, there was a natural hunger and thirst for the simple joys of life. Moreover, our natural maternal and paternal instincts introduced kinder, succoring, protective attitudes not only to our own kin but also to the innocent and defenseless of other people. Gentler gods began to appear as consorts of goddesses who awarded supplicants with fertility and maternal love. They rewarded the male with love and companionship in place of paternal punishments and authoritarian justice.

In other words, these human instincts eventually displaced, in part, the dualistic vision of good versus evil, right versus wrong, life versus death. Over time, altruism overcame egotism, noble self-sacrifice supplanted ritual sacrifice of the innocent. A form of moral conscience came to govern, in part, our immoral subconscience.

Yet, there is more to say about the subconscience in daily life. Our efforts to live a morally conscientious life often lead us, as individuals, to despondency and harsh self-judgments. This is not evidence of keenness of conscience; to the contrary, such self-mortification may actually arise from our subconscience. Or it may be characteristic of the continual struggle between our inferior, archaic self and what we sense is superior in us.

Then again, conscience may experience periods of exhaustion when the struggle itself seems pointless. At times, civilization's crimes, murders, violence and wars, seem to make modern life increasingly meaningless in the virtual absence of effective justice for all or any acceptable moral code for all.

Another reason for the continual re-emergence of the sub-conscience is that too strict a religious life often urges followers to deny their natural passions. The clerical condemnation of carnality should not be confused with the expression of our natural passions. What may appear condemnable to those who have sworn their lives to chastity and abstinence cannot be sensibly accepted as law for the laity. To the contrary, the denial of a normal sex life is what probably accounts, at least in part, for the sexually obsessed individuals who commit rape, murder and sadistic crimes of passion.

Moreover, early history itself contradicts the sense of such an edict. In the earliest ages when humankind migrated across continents, few sexual partners were available to the explorers. Then again in primitive times, mates were often killed by predators. Furthermore, throughout history many women died in childbirth, and many children died of disease or became easy prey to predators. In any migratory group there may have been few partners of the opposite sex available. Far removed from the religious concept of carnality, natural sex was absolutely vital to the survival of the species. Rather, it was a precious pleasure in the midst of ever-present danger and uncertainty about whether one would be alive another day.

On the other hand, long ago religion came to emphasize chastity in order to prevent the infection that results from crippling or deadly venereal disease. (Consider that today there are estimated to be 35,000,000 individuals worldwide infected with HIV or AIDS.) However, this historical injunction proved impossible to many because physical love is a natural response to human need. Indeed, the demand for absolute chastity and abstinence only aroused instinctive rebellion. To humankind still struggling to stay alive, the clergy seemed to deny life's simplest yet most meaningful pleasure. For the "masses", sexual love is an escape from the meaninglessness of life that ultimately ends with death.

This instinctive urge in us is telling us something. It is as if those yet-to-be-born are urging us from within to make it possible for them to come into life, to know all the joys and sorrows of being alive.

From the discussion of subconscience and conscience thus far, some readers may feel the need for clarification of how the human psyche integrates the two spheres of the brain. An appropriate analogy for this may be the growth of the bulb of an onion, which takes place in concentric layers around the germinal seed. (Like the lily, hyacinth, and tulip, the onion is formed underground and creates its buds within overlapping membranes). Its underground germination is imperceptible much as the psyche itself grows invisibly in the physical brain.

The outermost layers of psyche would be those of conscious life, those which reflect what we learn in a lifetime. As we grow mentally in life, successive layers of experience accrue. As we grow mentally, we mature by learning the meaning of our experiences. With that understanding comes self-knowledge. Gradually, spheres of significance important to us guide us to choose a destiny.

However, let us bear in mind that the growth comes out of the germinating center of the brain, our deepest psychic sphere. It is entirely possible that the spheres closest to the growth center represent the initial phases of psychic growth from our primeval beginnings. As such, they still exert their primeval influence on us as the psyche matures and acquires ever more layers of experience, knowledge and wisdom.

Although we tend to ignore and neglect these innermost orbs of memory, they are probably the source of many of the spontaneous impulses of feeling and imagery that we usually do not understand.

How far-fetched is the analogy between the growth of this form of life and the entelechial growth of the human psyche? Both illustrate forms of germinating life, embryo and seed. Similarly, the human fetus adds cells to create tissue, bone, organs and muscle.

The brain's neurological development may follow a similar pattern as well. Though the shapes differ, they seem to undergo comparable processes of growth, completion and perfection. Correlatively, the spheres of practical and theoretical knowledge that man used to create cultures and civilizations served to expand and mature mind. Our powers of abstract reasoning and our emotional intelligence both seem enhanced in much the same manner.

If this insight is apt, then the primeval psyche first developed in the darkness of our age of survival. As our subconscience gradually became aware of life-nurturing powers and benign elements in the world, it began to seek beyond the obscurity of the self; and this search was the beginning of human conscience. As it experienced paternal and maternal love, the infant conscience felt the nurture of family and caring kin--like a gentle rain, soft sunlight. Thus the dawning awareness of the beginning of life.

The birth of our natural conscience was very much like our physical birth. When we emerged, we heard tender words, dimly saw friendly faces, and felt a loving breast—all to protect us. When later we became aware of mutual feelings and love of one's own kind, psyche began to feel the first stirrings of a higher conscience in us. So experience upon experience developed the primitive psyche. Humankind was beginning to evolve: a superior form of conscience was emerging. But it was not yet the future.

We had yet to go through periods of struggle between the subconscience and the conscience. Indeed, the torments of conscience seemed clear evidence of the savage, primate power of the subconscience as it lashed out at conscience for trying to tame it. Conscience tried to calm and restrain it with intuitive advice and sane precautions against rash and self-destructive acts.

Perhaps the clearest evidence of the power of the subconscience emerged centuries after religious conscience had been established. In the European Middle Ages (A.D. 500-1500), Christianity had come to govern much of life. The monastic life attracted those who found the realities and injustices of the world too great to bear. Poverty, plagues, and repeated wars drove many to try to escape from the world by finding solace and consolation in the religious life of prayer.

History provides us with stories of mystics who practiced asceticism, self-discipline, and self-mortification so as to be worthy of the love of Christ. The pain that some of them underwent to humiliate their own bodies was already symptomatic of some type of mental aberration. There was a passion to be forgiven by God for one's sins. Many believed their sinful lives were the cause of the calamities and disasters afflicting mankind. In the course of their excessive self-punishment, they engaged in pathological practices which are an indication of a wounded subconscience.

Mystics sought martyrdom in the misguided belief that the torturous path through life led to sainthood. In his work, *Varieties of Religious Experience*,

William James discusses sainthood. He enumerates the dangers of devotional excesses which he defines as varieties of religious insanity. Carrying self-starvation and self-flagellation to the point at which one risks death was believed to lead to saintly ecstasy. To the sober-minded conscience, it must have seemed that the rebellious subconscience was determined to humiliate and destroy religion itself because religion had condemned it as Satan's hold on the human soul. But the subconscience had the power to mercilessly torture the religious conscience and so reasserted itself and made clear its power over the human mind. Once again, psyche reminded us of the danger of the unnatural, of emotional excesses, and of blindness to the fatal consequences possible in committing insane acts.

On the other hand, to the authentic mystic, holy experiences could bring to the individual startling revelations, such that at times he or she seemed to transcend rational consciousness and attain to numinous truths. Such experiences could motivate the individual to begin to live a more spiritual life beyond the demands of mundane responsibilities and expectations.

Yet, our third millennium must beware of succumbing to the delusion that mankind is doomed to the oncoming triumph of the Antichrist among us. The terror this expectation has aroused seems to be spreading like a panic. The belief that the world is coming to an end is clearly symptomatic of mass hysteria and borders on insanity. Such excesses of religious fervor and such evangelical credulity seem inspired by a new outbreak of the power of the primitive subconscience among us. The Antichrist is a Satanic phantom spawned by a delirious subconscience.

We can still believe in the moral idealism of religion. Such hope is not based on hysteria. Religion inspires reverence, reflection and reconciliation--it is a source of refuge. Faith in a Supreme Being ensures restoration, renewal, regeneration and re-creation of the human spirit.

We can also have faith that humankind's evolution has some ultimate purpose. If we heed the insights which we come to in secular life and respect the epiphanies that we experience, we may yet achieve a noble destiny--one worthy of all the good we have done and may still do. In fact, we may learn why we are here on earth.

The Incarnation of Conscience

We have used the term *conscience* in various historical contexts, some of them unfamiliar, hence some further clarification is in order here. We rarely think of how conscience came to be, but most of us would accept the dictionary definition of it: "the sense of consciousness of the moral goodness or blameworthiness of one's own conduct, intentions, or character together with a feeling of obligation to do right and be good." Or again, "sensitive regard to fairness or justice." [6]

While this definition is certainly concise and commendable, it is a reflection of the universally accepted vision of conscience as a conflict between good and evil, right and wrong. Virtually all readers would ask "What more do you need?" Not only is it a worthwhile definition. For as long as there have been salvation religions, conscience meant we must learn to decide between good and evil, then act according to what was true, just and wise.

Such reasoning may be perfectly sound for believers in Judaism, Christianity and Islam, but how did our ancestors develop a conscience suitable to agrarian life and living in rough-hewn homes in an untamed wilderness?

Early human communal life was largely determined by the seasons. From the very beginning, the cultivation of crops taught people important lessons. Timing was basic to survival. Each season, the land required a different type of care and commitment, if the people were to produce enough to survive the winter. There was a time to nurture the soil, a time to plant and to attend to the nurslings, a time to protect them from insects, birds and rodents, and a time to bring in the harvest.

The cycle of life had it truth. Planting, growing and harvesting taught humankind that steadfast attention was necessary if there were to be a reward for their conscientious work. Peasants and farmers learned that nature took her time to complete and perfect what she brought to life.

The seasons brought the appearance and disappearance of life from the land. Life was cyclical because nature created time in the birth and death of all living creatures. This meant that in the persistence and renewal of life, an underlying wisdom was to be learned. That awakening was probably the beginning of humankind's natural conscience.

In *Ecclesiastes*, the wisdom of natural time is defined. "For everything its season, and for every activity under heaven its time."

> a time to be born and a time to die;
> a time to plant and a time to uproot;
> a time to kill and a time to heal;
> a time to pull down and a time to build up;
> a time to weep and a time to laugh;
> a time for mourning and a time for dancing;
> a time to seek and a time to lose;
> a time to keep and a time to throw away;
> a time to tear and a time to mend;
> a time for silence and a time for speech;
> a time for love and a time for hate;
> a time for war and a time for peace.

Ecclesiastes (3:18-19) goes on to say it is God's purpose to test men and to see what they truly are. However, if they have no sense of past and future, they have "no comprehension of God's work from beginning to end." (3:10)

Hence one of the most fundamental lessons humankind learned was to work in tandem with the rhythms of nature. First and foremost, we became conscious that life itself had its beginning, its seasons, and its end. Mother Earth was there to teach us. We must attend to her needs, and we must be careful and responsible in what we do if we are to harvest what life offers us.

So before *Ecclesiastes* could have been written down, our conscience had to understand something about nature. As her children, we imagined we saw fish, animals and human forms in the constellations overhead in the night sky. Natural phenomena seemed like sprites and spirits of all sorts. When natural yearning moved the vivid imagination of women, they saw in nature a goddess of fertility, abundance and motherhood.

In Near Eastern and Mediterranean legends, a young god-lover stood next to the goddess of life. In women's warm hearts, they prayed to the godly couple for love, pregnancy and motherhood. In the depths of woman's gentle being, her conscience was yearning, passionate and maternal.

However, this prayer for love has a deeper meaning. Prayer to the sacred couple was in actuality the worship of nature's powers of renewal. The link between loving and love-making held the promise of new life. To the women, the goddess was mother earth and the young god was eternal youth bringing fresh virility and vitality into the world. Remarkably, this promise seems the eternal purpose of evolution itself.

But there is more. New love is the discovery of new knowledge of what it means to be human in the most natural way. This transforms itself into the wisdom of knowing who and what you are simply as a lover of life. So at the center of psyche and our natural conscience is a being free to create a new soul of its own.

In a later stage of human evolution, the memory of natural man and our evolution--to be free, free to love, free to create--is essential to discovering the resourceful self each of us is meant to be in this life. It is the ultimate source of man's creativity, innovation and self-creation. It also opens us to the investigation of life and its significance and invites us to glean the harvest of our own life experience, our purpose in life and our personal wisdom.

But eventually the young god of legend and myth will become a sovereign power, superior to all lesser men and gods. The worship of the lordly man reveals the instinctive hierarchy in nature where one animal becomes the alpha male and among men he becomes the king, the sage living in the deepest forest, or the wise man meditating on the highest mountain.

What does this fable or myth tell us about conscience and the world of imagination? Humans were becoming aware that nature revealed hierarchies of strength and power as well as stages of development and perfection in all living beings. Nature evinced grades of inferiority and superiority in all its creatures.

That truth also applied to our decisions, actions and life goals.

This scale of awareness then became combined with a new understanding of human responsibility. We had to learn to distinguish between what was wanted and what was, in fact, not needed to complete a given task; also we needed to discern what was truly significant and what was not. We had to determine what had to be done immediately and what could be done later. In short, there was an inferior way to live life and a superior way. Each of us at some time has to estab-- lish a hierarchy of values and decide on ways to reach our goals. These are the simplest, yet the most enduring lessons of nature.

Slowly, by using all these measures in tandem, human conscience matured. Its newly acquired skills enabled it not only to take on new responsibilities, but also to grow in practical wisdom. In sum, it came to understand what life expected of us.

Later, society became so structured that a king became the highest authority, the source of decisions and orders for actions to be taken. He was supposed to know the law and pronounce the soundest judgments, and could so do because he had at his disposal all the knowledge available to human beings and the best advisors to be found in the realm.

In these examples of human social hierarchy, we find another dimension of conscience. It is based on a simple but fundamental insight. If you honor Truth, you can act wisely. However, being absolutely certain that you are in possession of the Truth is quite another matter.

In any event, conviction depended entirely on what proved true and effective in the past. In other words, certainty depends on reliable hindsight, which confirms the commonly held belief that what the past taught us is still true. Thus the mature conscience believes in the truths confirmed by personal experience.

In this review of the perennial conflict between conscience and subconscience, what have we learned from the past? One Truth most certainly: There never has been a universally accepted code of morality in all recorded history. In other words, geographical and cultural differences have led people to believe in the superiority of their own collective conscience. Moreover, different civilizations have probably evolved at different rates.

In addition, the conscience of humanity is not only diverse but also multi-dimensional, multi-religious, and multi-cultural. Different cultures develop distinct conceptions of morality and intelligence as well as different interpretations of life's meaning. Various branches of the human race have probably passed through unique phases of evolution; various peoples are still living in distinct periods of indigenous history. Today, the peoples in various areas of the world still live within their own historical time frames.

Since the dawning of human time, the human conscience has become a repository for the experience of all humanity. Thousands of languages and cultures have evolved in their own eco-niches. For that reason, going back to a time prior to orthodox religions and universal written history to an understanding of primeval man and woman has proved helpful in ascertaining what is truly archetypal in the formation of our primary conscience.

Yet, conscience does not remain fixed in the past, but is aware that it still has much more to learn. It has evolved a process which is the opposite of the use of hindsight, i.e. It draws on the age-old practice of divination, which is defined as "the art or practice that seeks to foresee or foretell future events or discover hidden knowledge usually by the interpretation of omens or by the aid of supernatural powers". Divination is also identified as "unusual insight; intuitive perception".[7]

The traditional prophet or diviner undertakes to predict what will become true at some future time. But what possible connection does prophecy or divination have with the modern tendency of human conscience to focus on the future?

The merit of divination is that it increases the capacities of conscience to grow beyond its present day dictionary definition. Possibly, ancient and medieval divination inspired the induction practiced by dedicated modern scientists. As a matter of fact, the inductive reasoning used by science has already led to whole new worlds of knowledge and generated new forms of knowledge which were heretofore inconceivable.

Furthermore, given that today's sciences are developing the capacity to better predict developments and outcomes, it is reasonable to say that human collective conscience is approaching a level of knowledge which adds the prophetic dimension to the psychological. This relatively new skill in foresight may be due to our continuing cerebral evolution. It is possible that the evolved neo-cortex of the human brain is the source of psychic potential to extrapolate future knowledge.

On the other hand, the ancient Egyptian cult of the dead is a probable source of the incarnation of conscience in humankind. Though generally this cult was intended to venerate worthy and exceptional ancestors, it is likely that its practices affected the way conscience began to both judge life in the present and encourage thoughts about the future. Indeed, honoring the dead naturally leads one to evaluating one's own life. It may prod the individual to foresee what can still be made of one's own. The person may also come to think more deeply about the future consequences of past decisions and acts as they may apply to a possible afterlife. What proved to be of worth in one's past often becomes the moral ideal for the future.

After all, what the afterlife may mean in reality might be in line with the Asian belief in karma. In Hinduism and Buddhism, it is believed there is a force generated by one's actions, one that has a certain moral weight. It perpetuates transmigration into future lives: the moral decisions made in one's present life are affected by those made in a previous life. Though karma usually implies that we live again to cleanse the self of the impurities or bad things done in a past life. that need not be its sole consequence or purpose. From a Westerner's perspective, karma could imply living again in the form of the Buddhist bodhisattvas. Because they saved people from meaningless or dire destinies, they are awarded a new life to further aid humankind.

In any event, knowing that mankind's past conscience has evolved through dimensions of darkness and light leaves us better prepared to comprehend how the human supraconscience is emerging in our secular age.

Notes

1. James, E.O., *The Ancient Gods*, p. 174. All references to James' work are paraphrases. His *History and Diffusion of Religion in the Ancient Near East and the Eastern Mediterranean* provides abundant evidence of early man's supraconscience.
2. James, p.175.
3. James, p. 179.
4. Hutin, S. *Les Gnostiques*, p. 28.
5. Summary of *Les Gnostiques*.
6. Merriam Webster's Collegiate Dict., 10th ed., p. 245.
7. Webster's Dict., 10th ed., p. 339.

Part Two

The Beginning of the Supraconscience

Chapter Two

The Afterlife as Worldview: Subconscience versus Supraconscience

Undoubtedly, there are ancient cultures whose conceptions of the beyond are unknown to us. However, where a geo-cultural area such as the Mediterranean Basin gave rise to a multitude of beliefs about the beyond, we find evidence of the continual confluence of beliefs, monotheisms, gnosticisms and Near Eastern religions. The mutual influence these cultures exercised upon one another probably promoted not only geographical interaction, but a general historical progression from ancient to medieval to modern times. There we can find credible evidence of a mutual cultural, enrichment and possibly also identify successive concepts as evolving world views.

In point of fact, this region has a common history of developing both negative and positive conceptions of life-after-death. Different religions gave rise to antithetical metaphysical claims: Zoroastrianism/Mazdaism, Judaism, Christianity, Neoplatonism and, centuries later, Islam, all arose in roughly the same geographical area.

These cross currents of belief have attributed good and evil to 'the cosmos itself', and, as two streams of human consciousness, they reveal the essential polarity of the human psyche. Historically, extreme points of view have been ascribed to the dualism inherent in existence itself. Contradiction seems to mark the history of the psyche wherever distinct cultures meet.

Let us review some of the cultural beliefs of the past from: Egypt, Persia, Greece, the Etruscans, Romans, the barbarians, Neoplatonism, and early Christian Church Fathers.

Egypt

The ancient Egyptians were an agricultural people who farmed the rich deposits of silt along the Nile River. Their religion centered on the agrarian god Osiris who was killed by his jealous brother Seth and preserved from corruption by his sister-wife Isis. Magically, out of her love for him, she called him back to life.

In time, he was transfigured into a god. According to archeologists, this story introduced the practice of mummification. It was intended to conserve the body of the deceased; at the same time, the soul was prepared for its journey through the underworld. There it faced many tests of its purity and worthiness. Actually, mummification and ritual preparation were carried out to ward off the Egyptian dread of the beyond.

The Egyptian *Book of the Dead* includes magic formulas for deceiving the gods of the underworld and even Death Himself. As pragmatists, the Egyptians showed considerable ingenuity in undertaking such deception, yet their rites and preoccupation with death revealed their conscientious effort to come to terms with the end of this life.[1]

Of special interest was their view of judgment in the after world. In a crucial ritual, the deceased's heart would be weighed in a balance against a feather on the opposite side of a scale. If the feather weighed more, the deceased's purity of heart would bring reward. If the heart were heavier, his or her impurity would bring punishment by one of the forty-two divinities in charge of chastising the impure. Clearly, in the next world, justice reigned—that is, justice based on the principle of retribution.

This myth contains a number of valuable insights. To believe in justice in this world is evidence of a developing conscience. Beyond the earthly realm, one's death meant absolute judgment by the gods. Belief in this purest form of justice in fact reveals a fear of the merciless judgment of one's own primitive subconscience.

By contrast, the vision of some type of supernatural justice, however severe, is an indication that our early, evolving superconscience was capable of attenuating the terror of death. It also enabled us to gain control over ourselves and our worst fears. If one had faith in the ancient myth, the ritual transformed despair at life's inevitable end into a moral philosophy superior to the dread of death itself.

At this stage of the development of the psyche the subconscience still tormented humankind by such nightmarish images as the forty-two divinities, each of which punished a distinct misdeed or crime.

In other words, the subconscience still gratified its need for self-punishment. Nevertheless, the need for a final judgment of one's life became evident in the millennia-long struggle between the primitive subconscience and the emerging supraconscience.

Ancient Persia

Approximately one thousand years before Christ, Zoroaster of Persia created a dynamic religion called alternately Zoroastrianism or Mazdaism. It argued that a cosmic dualism existed between opposing gods. Ormazda is described as the one true and luminous Reality of the universe. Infinitely Wise, He created all good beings. This benevolent god was opposed by Ahriman, the spirit of death, destruction and evil. Zoroaster predicted their struggle would last 12,000 years and would end in the ultimate victory of goodness, light and truth. However, because the war between good and evil was inexorable and unrelenting, its conclusion was forever in doubt.

This struggle can be interpreted as an explanation of humankind's endless wars. In psychological terms, it is more apt to give us a realistic insight into the human psyche. In general, the evil, nihilistic spirit Ahriman seems a personifica tion of our primitive subconscience, whereas the good and wise creator, Ormazda, seems a personification of our supraconscience.

We need to describe and further discuss these polarities of psyche. As we have already learned, our primitive subconscience was unable to free itself from anxieties, fears and the terror of death. In nightmares, the subconscience feels defenseless before obscure phantoms threatening to devour our body and annihilate our hapless soul. It exists in a state of perpetual anguish, convinced that, because of the power of evil in the world and within our very being, our soul, the most divine and enduring element of the self, may itself not survive.

As our ancient subconscience conjured up the evil god Ahriman, our evolving supraconscience conceived of Ormazd. Perhaps in time, the subconscience could be overcome, converted into a life-trusting part of psyche.

Inherent in this metaphysical dualism was the doubt that any ultimate concord could ever be achieved between the different beliefs, principles and convictions held by mankind.

But the archetypal traits of these opposing poles of psyche require further examination-- they call us to probe them more deeply. Judging by its history, the subconscience distrusts itself because it perpetually experiences inner conflict. It is as if it needs to be sick, to suffer, to hate. It expresses spite, envy, and anger to hurt others. It also punishes itself. In psychological terms, the historical subconscience was afflicted by masochism and sadism. To modern man, such intense strife is as real as Hell itself.

Zoroaster's Mazdaism turns out to be an example of the emerging supraconscience teaching humanity the dangers associated with our primeval subconscience. The ancient supraconscience taught the individual he has a personal responsibility to contribute to the ultimate triumph of the good as it was typified by the benevolent Ormazd. In essence, Zoroaster's doctrine embraced notions familiar to Christians: salvation, expiation and reward for fulfilling one's purpose in life.

To believe that one's life can contribute something to shaping the destiny of humanity is certainly a noble ideal. This vision of human purpose is surely worthy of respect. In its own way, it contributed to the evolution of the supraconscience.

By contrast, the average person trapped by indecision or by a moral dilemma may be unable to deal with everyday reality. This inner confusion can re-awaken age-old doubt and fears. That state of anxiety can easily re-evoke the powers of the subconscience and drag one down into a personal hell.

On the other hand, trust in oneself can bring hope and reassurance that ultimately "all will be right with the world". Hence to be realistic in the ideals one holds and to take appropriate action should result in the realization of one's sincerest dreams; and, conversely, to surrender to skepticism and cynicism can defeat the worthiest ideal.

Confidence in deciding one's own destiny is born of our supraconscience. It nurtures our higher passions and inspires men and women to be worthy individuals, worthy of a nobler future.

Further evidence of the existence of the psyche's subconscience and supraconscience is imaginatively described in Zoroaster's portrayal of the afterlife:

> At death, the soul will be judged according to its earthly works. It will first meet its own conscience (a radiant young woman, the incarnation of piety and virtue), or if the life was corrupt and he was a sinner, he will meet a disgusting sorcerer.[2]

The symbolism of this is obvious. The sinful, repulsive sorcerer typifies the deceit that our primeval subconscience uses whereas the radiant young woman incarnates into a life of virtue and wisdom. She personifies the supraconscience at its feminine best.

Thus Zoroaster counsels us to choose wisely. As we pursue an inferior or superior existence on earth, we will merit a corresponding existence in the beyond. The individual is given a choice. Either we descend into baseness, perversion and evil, or we ascend toward the upright, ethical and good. Either we surrender to the lower nature of primitive subconscience, or we decisively strive to realize what is noble and humane in humanity.

Zoroaster also made clear how evil and good individuals end their existence. Hell is described as bitterly cold and dark, a place where the damned are fed putrid food, gnawed on by demons, and exist in total isolation. By contrast, the good no longer fear death and live serenely near God. This hallowed life is lived in three blessed spheres--good thoughts, good works, and good actions.[3]

Why do good works, good thoughts and good actions merit nearness to God and receive His blessings? Because they foster mutual understanding among humankind and encourage the individual to pursue a worthy purpose in life.

In its belief in the dualism of good versus evil, and in its basic moral vision, Zoroastrianism was not only a precursor of Judaism and Christianity. Zoroaster's philosophy helped the human psyche learn to decide between our lower and higher passions. It taught the ancients of Persia to discover higher truths. It also taught the need to judge the experiences one had in life by acknowledging humankind's deeper emotional needs. Eventually the human supraconscience came to create a vision of existence which enabled humankind to decide its future more wisely.

Ancient Greek Mythology

Burial practices among the Pre-Hellenic Greeks provide evidence of rites, cremation and provisions for an after-life.

Homer's *Odyssey* describes Hades, the underworld abode of the dead where judges such as Minos and Rhadamanthus determined the merits and demerits of the dead. The unworthy and ignoble were sent to Tartarus, an infernal region. Tantalus was condemned to this realm for revealing the secrets of the gods. His punishment was to stand up to his chin in water under a tree loaded with fruit. Whenever he tried to satisfy his hunger, a blast of wind whirled the fruit above his reach, and when he tried to satisfy his thirst, the water drained into the ground till it was dry. On the other hand, Sisyphus was condemned forever to roll a big rock uphill, but as he reached the top, some invisible force rolled it down again to the plain below. Both Tantalus and Sisyphus had gravely offended the gods. Thus Tartarus seems an imaginative interpretation of the darker aspect of the afterlife, one inspired by humankind's subconscience.

On the other hand, the worthy and noble souls were sent to Elysium, the residence of the blessed. Later, philosophers were rewarded by a return of their soul to the celestial fields.[4] Hence Elysium seems an imaginative creation of the supraconscience as well.

Though the Greeks were able to understand the unpredictability of their gods, the human being was judged as having brought his fate upon himself. Thus wherever one's arrogance, deceit, treachery, blindness or other crimes offended the gods, one doomed oneself. By contrast, where the individual acted justly, nobly or heroically, he was rewarded with a more noble destiny.

Of particular interest was Orphism, a mystical religion which offered initiates purification of the soul from inborn evil and hence release from the endless cycle of reincarnation. Those who practiced this diligently were thought to eventually live as souls in glorious light, feasting and dancing. [5]

Plato, Socrates and the Human Soul

Plato conceived the soul as both immortal and eternal, a spark of divine fire within the individual. The soul was a prisoner of the body, in exile from the World of Forms. In that realm, ideas, forms and archetypes represent unchanging truths. This world of ours is not what is most real. It is merely an imitation of the World of Ideas. Everything ideal participates in the superior world. Just as its Forms are eternal, so is the individual soul.[6]

One may believe that the soul, conceived as a divine spark, was inspired by the awesome sight of a star falling through the night sky. But why should the soul be a prisoner?

In Plato's *Republic*, Socrates describes human beings as living in a cave, shackled there by their ignorance. They have never emerged into the real world of sunlight. They know only the reality of their own distorted shadows cast on the walls by the firelight. This well known allegory is intended to encourage the human race to go forth from the darkness of their ignorance toward the brilliance of the sunlight, i.e. knowledge of things as they really are. The writhing shadows cast by the flickering fire represent our primitive emotions and imaginings. The irony of the allegory makes clear that only natural sunlight, viz., philosophy, can shed light on the errors to which our beliefs are subject. Plato's allegory of the cave illustrates how our primeval subconscience has kept us in the darkness of superstition and ignorance.

Socrates himself is a clear example of the human supraconscience in antiquity. By using the dialectical method to question those who assumed they possessed knowledge, he uncovered the awkward fact that we usually live by vague half-truths, and he proved the falsity of the sophistry we often use to disguise our ignorance. He sought precise definitions of abstract ideas as virtue and justice. He believed that knowledge coincided with *arêté* (virtue, excellence). Socrates' faith in *arêté* made it possible to foresee the wisest action needed to resolve the ambiguity inherent in any situation. In his dialogues, Plato left us a record of Socrates' inimitable wisdom. Socrates was an incarnation of the supraconscience. Plato himself believed personal dedication to an Ideal was necessary for a soul to become immortal. Only intelligence merited immortality. Since he dedicated his life to philosophy, that meant he had entrusted his existence to his own supraconscience.

How otherwise is personal immortality to be gained? One would need to undertake the study of some serious subject of keen interest or to consecrate oneself to a purpose worthy of commitment. Or, one could ponder the significance of an unforgettable human destiny, as Plato understood Socrates' life. Then one would grasp why the dedicated life is always worth living and remembering.

Thus when an individual lives as a true parent or teacher, when a person devotes him or herself to work, to a faith, or to an ideal, that individual hardly does so for egotistical purposes. The "I, me, myself" have little to do with the love of a parent or the dedication of a teacher. The search for some form of perfection transcends personality and requires decision and determination of character. Only when the psyche is in a supernal state of concentration do the immortal and eternal become clear. This state of mind is experienced beyond all individual limitations, emotions, and intelligence.

Today, we are much too concerned with money, success, reward, and careerism. There is not much virtue in such forms of passion. What is done for its own sake is its own reward. Any sense of true accomplishment is greater than any vanity about success. What the mind conceives transcends the reality of this world. Plato would understand the supraconscience as the total immersion of the psyche in the intelligible reality of the universe.

Aristotle

Aristotle conceived the soul to be a vital activity which dies when the body does. Hence the soul is described as an entelechy, i.e., an inborn directing power which develops the body and regulates its functions. The soul cannot live without the body.

Though a Christian, Jew or Muslim may find this definition of soul disconcerting or disheartening, the secularist would likely find it closer to the biological fact than the belief in an afterlife where the soul might live forever.

Nevertheless, Aristotle's insight into the generative and perfecting power in animate nature, as well as in the human species, invites further thought based on contemporary biological knowledge.

If it be true that the soul generates the embryonic and ontogenetic growth of our bodies, and if, as the power of intelligence in us, it develops through successive stages of maturation, then it may be possible that evolution encourages or fosters the entelechy of the soul over generations of humankind. Perhaps this is the scientific truth behind the belief in the transmigration of souls.

The Afterlife as Worldview

In terms of evolutionary biology, human evolution is largely guided by the interaction between our innate powers of self-transformation and self-integration to create and sustain our intricate life support systems. Moreover, there is the evolution between the individual and the cultural environment. In this context, the transmigration of souls can be re-interpreted. Indeed, humankind's transmigratory evolution could be seen as fostering a supraconscience—a sophisticated, moral and compassionate stage of evolution superior to the self-punishing, fear-ridden conscience often preached by traditional religions.

However, this evolution of psyche demonstrates the reality of cultural complexities. For instance, where there has been a fairly consistent culture across centuries or millennia, as in ancient Egypt, that stability might tend to cause stagnation of mind and spirit as regards conventional beliefs or established religion. Such stagnation of the psyche would primarily occur where traditional conscience pre-dominated, but, wherever creativity was encouraged to innovate and invent, there psyche would evolve.

On the other hand, there is the case of the intersecting cross currents of Taoism, Confucianism and Buddhism in China. These world views were complementary philosophies and so must have effected the co-evolution of these traditions and the reconciliation of their beliefs.

Thus, although Aristotle and modern skeptics may be quite right that the individual's soul appears to die when the body dies, there may be more to this than meets the eye. Does not the same archetypal genetic code pass on into embryonic souls through every generation of humankind?

The seventeenth century believed we are born as a tabula rasa. Or, rather, are we not born with a blueprint of talent and character and with the inherent capacity to create an original life of our own. If that were the case, the individual would be responsible for discovering and defining his or her unique destiny.

Aristotle also spoke of the soul's "superform" identified as intelligence or *nous*. Not only was this mind and reason. It also reflected the intelligent principle and purpose in nature. Neo-Platonism re-interpreted *nous* as the emanation of divine reason into human consciousness. This made the soul of men and women transcendent.

Ever since antiquity, humankind has sought enlightenment through religion. This millennia-long search for supernatural guidance influenced more than the development of a rational, religious conscience. Religious devotion also fostered a superior, transcendental conscience. Correspondingly, the growing conviction that a Supreme Being governs all existence stirred the intuition that humankind is graced with a degree of superhuman emotional acumen. That power appears to be intrinsic to humanity's supraconscience.

Along with this spiritual evolution, substantial archeological and historical evidence attests to the probability that, over deca-millennia, humankind has been developing a superior secular psyche. This evolving intelligence we choose to call the secular supraconscience of humanity.

The Ancient Stoics

Founded by Zeno of Citium about 300 B.C. in ancient Greece, Stoicism taught indifference to pleasure and pain. The wise man should not yield to excesses of grief, joy or passion. Stoics believed a dynamic principle in nature initiated life on earth, whereas a transcendental Being animated all existence: Man's soul was created by the breath of God. A later Stoic, Epictetus (55-135 A.D.), believed man had been co-generated with the divinity. The earlier Stoics believed the soul survived as an impersonal identity, which returned in cycles of succeeding lives.[7]

Though later Stoics came to reject the idea of an afterlife, or the claim that the beyond rewarded a noble life on earth, their resignation did not lead to fatalism or cynicism. They felt virtue was its own reward. One attained virtue by aligning one's life according to the divinely ordained order of existence.

Stoicism was based on common sense. Impassivity in the face of both pain and pleasure and the exercise of self-discipline, courage and integrity meant that one had gained control over one's life. If we were to live up to the noble wisdom of the Stoics, our example would encourage others to appreciate these ancient truths. As wiser men and women, we would be able to face the future with a certain self-mastery.

The teaching of patience, self-moderation and sensible living would restrain the rabid emotionalism of our time. By heeding the call to temperance and the use of common sense of this ancient philosophy, by re-evaluating what it means to be a human being, we ourselves would grow wiser. The practice of stoicism could nurture the evolution of sage psychic powers in humankind.

Neo-Platonism Reborn

Ancient Neo-Platonism derived from Plato's theory that the true world is made of perfect Forms and Ideas. Empirical evidence is a mirage merely reflecting in an opaque way the eternal truth. As developed in third century Rome by Plotinus (A.D. 205-270), Neo-Platonism was a synthesis of ancient Middle Eastern religious doctrines, the Orphic mystic tradition of ancient Greece, Plato's own Idealism, and Christian speculation. For Plotinus, existence represented a gradation from pure being downward to the lowest forms of life. He proposed that there was a transcendent creative force (God or Logos), which conceived everything in a hierarchy of perfection. Since humankind was created by that force, the soul yearns to overcome its earthly, mortal flesh by returning to the realm of original perfection.[8]

Anthropologically speaking, the idea of a pure state in the beginning likely harkens back in actuality to the pristine sea, land and forests of prehistoric man. Geologically, the earth was a cauldron of seething lava, earthquakes and massive volcanic eruptions. In the very beginning, the cosmos itself was a conflagration of gases, plasmas, and infinite forces churning elements through timeless space.

A more realistic view of primeval existence was manifest in the unceasing emanation of millions of species, from which there emerged endless generations of generations.

Moreover, based on the evidence of the evolution of the species which survived the earth's changing environment, the perception that we have moved toward perfection must be revised. Instead of looking back to some period of pure existence at the origin of life, evolution teaches us that some degree of perfection was realized stage by stage. At some future stage of evolution, humankind may finally be converted from their savage beginnings--still evident in our modern history of violence, homicide, murder and wars. Perhaps in some future time, there will reign a stage of mutual respect and the veneration of humanity's geniuses.

In other words, at the summit of our future evolution, mankind may learn to live in universal symbiosis with its environment, and harmony may exist among all its cultures.

Gregoire's *L'Au Délà* sums up the historical significance of Neo-Platonism: "For the first time in Occidental philosophy, we see...the destiny of the soul logically linked with sin, salvation and expiation; after death, each soul goes where it merits to go in terms of the life it has lived. Rewards and punishments...follow a law of exact compensation." [9]

In other terms, though human existence began in savagery and imperfection, the future can be fulfilled by transcending our subhuman nature and furthering our cultural intelligence. Ultimately, to arrive at a higher degree of perfection in this life, we must continue to pursue a destiny that can consummate the evolution of humanity's supraconscience.

The Etruscans and the Romans

From Asia Minor, the Etruscans viewed the afterlife with pessimism, conceiving it as a subterranean realm. Nevertheless, out of need, the early Etruscans, Sabines and Latins developed a cult honoring the dead. Their fear and respect for the deceased also showed reverence for the wisdom of their ancestors. Forbearers who were remembered as having been good served as models for the moral life; those known as evil served to warn the living of the consequence of the immoral life. The cult taught that life should be lived with virtue. In the afterlife, we are rewarded or punished for what we have done in this life.

This twofold anticipation of the afterlife reflects the psyche's polarity between a pessimistic world view offering severe judgments of human fate and an optimistic one based on reassuring prophecies of human destiny. History itself illustrates that the antagonism between these is ever-present in psyche: The unyielding subconscience denies the superiority of the evolving supraconscience.

Decay and decomposition prompt the living to bury the dead or incinerate them as quickly as possible. Not only is that done for practical reasons, but also out of respect for the deceased and what they achieved in this life. During the funeral rites, each individual undertakes to cope with his or her own fear of death.

If one's emotional intelligence has matured, the psyche has reason to hope that the deceased is now in a realm free of pain, sorrow, and regret.

Our intuitive intelligence has learned to accept the inevitable. It transcends loss, self-pity and the realization that death also awaits us. Thus does the supraconscience convert despair to the prospect that the afterlife may be a beautiful dream.

In Book V of the *Aeneid*, the Roman poet Virgil (70-19 B.C.) portrayed the existence of sinners in the infernal region Tartarus. There they were whipped and tortured till they confessed their sins. Misers, perjurers, and adulterers were thrown into a gulf as enemies of the gods. Criminals were tormented and afflicted with sores and various types of illness by the avenging Furies. By contrast, in Elysium, the worthy, good, noble and loyal dwell in a realm of greenery and gentle sunlight, where they enjoy music, dance and sports.[10]

Tartarus or Elysium, which did one deserve? Virgil's examples of poetic justice as punishment or reward in the afterlife reveals how the human psyche visualizes its own possible fate. Between moral impotence and moral virility, between irresolution and determination, human decisions are decisions for all eternity. Our choices result in one sort of afterlife or the other. We can either succumb to fate or grapple with and realize our true destiny.

Nonetheless, at times the demands, passions and excesses of the subconscience seem impossible to resist. There are days when the upsurging of our psychic underworld overwhelms us with fierce desires, fears and nightmares. These upwellings severely test the courage of moral convictions and mock our faith in the fact that we are in control of our lives. Still, the supraconscience, linked directly to the life instinct, knows that we have survived by resisting despair, momentary madness and death. Thus the superconscience urges us to overcome the deceptive message that our primitive subconscience would teach us that we cannot control our baser instincts and that life itself is meaningless.

From millennia-long interaction with its subterranean self, psyche's supraconscience has learned to recognize the subconscience for what it is--ultimately, the source of human fatalism.

From the ancient cultures discussed here, we learned the subconscience and supraconscience were locked in an archetypal struggle for dominance. Yet our ever-evolving psyche urged their reconciliation. In fact, each form of conscience had potentials unknown to the other. The passionate power of the instinctual subconscience proved able to survive whatever challenged its life, whereas the evolving emotional intelligence of the supraconscience intuitively sensed that there existed a higher order and the meaning of life went beyond physical survival.

In time, the supraconscience understood that the prehistoric subconscience had survived through its resourceful and courageous nature. It had overcome its own terror and paranoia. Hence the survival of our species revealed the life instinct could be stronger than fear of death itself. Thus the supraconscience did learn to comprehend the subconscience. The supraconscience sought to heal its brother's wounds and to teach it to confront its schizophrenia.

But the subconscience could never fully trust itself or the predatory world into which it had been born. In surrendering to its passion for heroic action, violence and conquest, it seemed to determine its own fate from one lifetime to the next.

The Celts, German and Gauls

From archeological evidence, the prehistoric Celts, Germans, Nordics and Gauls held fairly common beliefs about the afterlife. Often *the beyond* meant a journey through the underworld or an endless voyage over a limitless ocean. General humanity could expect none of life's joys there. Only the elect would experience pleasures eternally.

In Irish and Welsh sagas and in religious legends, the ancient Druids preached an afterlife in a far away land. There, old lives were exchanged for new ones, old souls were traded for new ones in an endless reciprocal barter between the world of the living and the dead.[11]

In another version of the beyond, Nordic legends of the Scandinavians described an after-world where dead heroes relived noble lives by daily venturing out to fight forces of evil. In Valhalla, those who died valiantly during the day were healed at night to rise again to do battle once more.[12]

Today certain Sub-Saharan tribes in Africa believe that the courageous warrior who exhibits honor toward the fallen enemy has earned such merit that his soul can survive. Yet even after a noble death, his soul has to overcome continuous challenges to secure his stay in the afterworld.

There is wisdom in the warrior code. In the young, not only did it encourage their conduct in battle, but also taught them to defy death. The courage to meet death face-to-face promised the true warrior respect in the afterlife. So, the need to scorn death influenced them to live with valor and act decisively. In the evolution of the human psyche, this code of conduct became inherent in those who survived. Moreover, hope for an honorable afterlife tempered the warrior's fatalism. Over time, the life-instinct's defiance of death created the undaunted character of our psyche.

Yet, recurrent thoughts of death could still arouse a sense of helplessness, despair and frustration at the realization that life had to end in death, a fact which made all hope and effort seem utterly meaningless. Our subconscience continually reminded us of our coming extinction. In nightmares, we dreamed of demons, predators, and maniacs waiting in the dark to seize and murder us. This resulted in the belief that supernatural evil inhabits the world.

To be sure, in the past man did live in a truly savage environment with mountain lions, jungle jaguars, venomous snakes and giant constrictors, all driven to kill in order to survive. Everywhere in nature he faced deadly threats. At times, invading tribes might seek to abduct women, steal property, or even take over home territory. So humankind's fears and nightmares often mirrored reality.

There came a point when the individual had to defend himself. Fear and anxiety turned to anger and the will to strike back: Better to kill than be killed. Thus psyche was overwhelmed by uncontrollable rage. Paranoia was replaced by the determination to survive at all costs. As a consequence, all too often the victim became the victimizer. This decisive shift occurred in the psyche's subconscience.

By contrast, man also knew the good that life could bring because he dwelt in nature. When the lifeless landscape came alive again, lush prairies, trees laden with fruit and nuts, and abundant game were everywhere. Fresh rain showered into streams and lakes to provide sweet water for man and beast. Alternating with storms, the warm sun reawakened the sense that some great, charitable power ruled over the good earth. She gave food to mankind. Many plants proved to be of practical use in making clothes, building temporary shelters and erecting sturdy homes. Despite harsh dangers and seasonal hunger, diseases and unforeseeable death, life was still worth living.

The psyche welcomed the kinder experiences of life. With the rising sun came the feeling of safety and protection. With spring and summer came times of contentment, happiness and abundant food. Yet, the bounty did not leave humankind ungrateful or unmindful of the generosity of life. Over time, they developed rituals and devotions to express their gratitude.

They also respected the dead and prayed to fertility gods and goddesses. Various forms of worship helped mature the still innocent side of psyche. Because the world was yet a great mystery, man's spirit began to intuitively probe beyond what was seen and heard. The earth seemed to camouflage the supernatural meanings of life itself. Humankind was awakening to superhuman powers omnipresent everywhere. To some cultures, the sun became a Deity. In fact, the supraconscience of humankind was becoming aware of its own existence.

Struggling to survive over the millennia, humankind's subconscience had been haunted by terrifying apparitions, by disgusting phantoms of the dead, by nightly specters of death. Now this primitive stage of psychic evolution began to be changed by the hope that a person could ward off these demons. One could merit a better or kinder fate. The individual could be rewarded for courage, for helping others in need, and for sincere gratitude to the gods for the blessings one did have.

Over time, a deeper understanding developed. If the sub-conscience still feared death, the supraconscience came to sense that death was a transition to an after-life where one would rejoin long lost friends and meet time-honored ancestors. This would not only be consolation for life's losses, wounds, pain and tears, but also a reward for fear overcome and battles won. From afar in that distant land, the dead could take comfort in watching their children become men and women. Hence humankind's maturing supraconscience believed the afterlife to be a realm of happiness where the deserving and courageous would live in reward for their devotion to the tribe, kin and their young.

In sum, between despair and hope, the subconscience and supraconscience struggled for control of the psyche. The fatalism of the subconscience was checked by the life-embracing nature of the supraconscience. Slowly it instilled the faith that by living a worthy life, a person would deserve a more certain afterlife. As human beings developed more human characteristics, their understanding of self and others led to greater mutual trust. As the supraconscience grew in strength, the fear, anger and rage of the subconscience lessened. The supraconscience had begun the endless task of humanizing our species.

Gradually, animist superstitions weakened and belief in many gods and goddesses both flourished and withered. All-powerful divinities arose to inspire the imagination of humankind. For millennia, these gods were worshipped, but their dominance could not still explain the ever-present power and destructive effect of the primeval subconscience. Obviously, psyche's providential supraconscience was the sole, sovereign power that could match and transcend the ancient savagery of the subconscience. Hence the supraconscience of humanity emerged not only as a twenty-first century reality, but, as life-force capable of overcoming the fatalistic philosophy of the irrational, psychopathic subconscience.

The Church Fathers and the Supernatural

The Church Fathers offered a striking argument against the skeptics who scoffed at the belief in an afterlife. Tertullian (ca. A.D. 155) summed up his argument by concluding "...the resurrection is no more improbable than procreation." [13]

A thoughtful insight. The Bible tells us that humankind was created from "dead" matter. Today, scientists theorize that life originated out of a cauldron of swirling chemical elements in the oceans where they were impacted by lightning, sunlight and cosmic rays. Could such an original state of primordial nature have brought forth life? Most unlikely. And yet the oceans and earth eventually generated countless life forms over billions of years.

On the other hand, the Church Father Justin (ca 100-ca 150) noted, "You see this flesh, these bones, these nerves, all this substance of man--a few drops of seminal liqueur suffice to form it all. Would you have believed an assertion that this was possible before seeing it?" [14]

A sensible argument for belief in miracles. In the light of evidence from paleontology and evolutionary biology, forms of life appeared over millions of years and then went extinct. All that is left of them is their skeletons. Still, the good Fathers would teach us Christ's Resurrection is proof a human being can come again to life as a disembodied soul.

In addition to the persuasion of the Church Fathers, there is an argument beyond the purely empirical or rational interpretation of the material world. Empiricism claims to provide us with the ultimate truth about the physical universe. It concludes we should accept death for what it is. Nevertheless, empiricism is quite incapable of accounting for man's amazing creativity nor the original ideas that are the source of religion and science, cultures and civilizations.

Though reason may be used to explain the order and design manifest in the world, and though it is a practical means of dealing with problems of survival, it remains unable to cope with the reality of death. Death faces us with the image of our bodily decay and disintegration. Why do we die?

That image can drag the fearful down into total despair; yet, curiously, it can also stimulate higher emotions which play a vital role in our psychic survival. These spiritual passions are the psychic source of our evolving supraconscience.

Our *subconscience* reacts to the reality of death either by striking out at others or by surrendering to the hopelessness of fatalism. By contrast, the *supraconscience* impels us to aid others, to nurture the helpless, to be charitable, to transcend our humiliating fear through heroic thoughts and acts. Over time, the supraconscience enables us to confront our own death with stoic dignity and faith in some higher meaning to human destiny beyond the death of an individual. By trusting psyche's higher nature, we can believe the Supreme Being also is a reality and a fact in our mortal lives.

We have human passion and love to thank for initiating the miraculous event of birth. Let us bear that in mind. Moreover, it is the deeper and higher passions that lead us to hope that God is as real as a new born.

It is a psychological fact that authentic religious experience seems to engulf the devout in a reality far greater than he or she is in real life. It also seems true that the individual who devotes his or her life to creativity and the integration of knowledge and experience appears to be guided by some higher conscience. In times of inspiration, the person senses the presence of a transcendent power.

In a lifetime of learning, the earnest student may ascend through spheres of knowledge and wisdom that fill him or her with an almost religious rapture. Put another way, by studying the secular knowledge and cultural wisdom of humanity, the adept may come to understand God's intention in creating humankind's superior intelligence. The individual who creates sense and value in his or her life has learned that we ourselves create the meaning of our human destiny.

As a consequence of our religious ideals and passion to learn all we can about God's Nature, men and women throughout history who dedicated their lives to this search for life's meaning, heralded the advent of the supraconscience of humanity. While in their religious passion they yearned for a clear sign from the Deity, they studied creation to discern His laws. Vital to their discovery was psyche's search for the significance of human existence.

To recapitulate Father Justin's definition two thousand years ago, we might say, "Do you see this erect creature, man, studying the horizon to discover the yet unknown? How weak he is compared to his predators and the stronger species better framed to survive! Yet long ago he not only mastered fire. Through the obscurity of time, the light in his eyes guided him. Through ages of darkness, he evolved--as priest, magician, alchemist, scientist, philosopher. In each guise, he pondered the nature of Nature, seeking all along to understand the secret of Creation and to learn what God Himself might want of us. Man is God's miracle."

Of What Consequence is Belief in the Afterlife?

Of what consequence to us is the belief in the soul and an afterlife? What influence would that belief have on our superconscience?

The effort to see beyond death--beyond the final end of life--has induced humankind to fantasize about a parallel world with multiple pleasures. Indeed, it offers the pleasures of this life without its sicknesses, disappointments, sorrows, and the tragedies that bring on death.

But besides those misfortunes, there are our failures in life. What are we to make of them? What do they teach us? If we are of sound-mind, they invite us to remember our successes and to think about what it takes to overcome, survive and succeed.

Of course, success in life goes beyond the accumulation of wealth and property. Basic to life is good health. But there is something even more important than these very real concerns. The most important is to guide one's daily life intelligently and with self-discipline. In this way one can master the decades as they arise to challenge us.

Yet, the cynic may argue that death makes a mockery of all of life's purposes, that life is a vain game, based only on delusion, a grand act of self-deception. What is the use of self-discipline if, in the end, we will no longer have the will-power to do what is positive and meaningful?

Perhaps after life there is indeed *nothing*. No use whimpering or crying over that. Anyway, that would only amount to self-pity. What is important is to help ease the ills, hunger and hopelessness of those in need while we are still alive.

Belief in the Beyond

Rather than being merely evidence of superstition, belief in the beyond is probably a sign of humankind's new power of intuition. It reveals that man's inner being has been evolving mentally and spiritually. Mythology expressed the maturing insight of our species' supraconscience. In past cultures, reverence for the dead indicated a new stage in psyche's perception of the self: Belief in the beyond meant conscience was learning the wisdom that death teaches us while we are still living.

Cultural belief in the beyond links this life's decisions and actions to future punishments and rewards. An age-old faith in poetic justice contends that vice is punished and virtue rewarded in a strikingly apt or ironic way. The sense that poetic justice rules life forewarns us that we are accountable for our future. As we live a moral or immoral life, we will be dealt with accordingly.

Characteristic of our belief in the beyond is our respect or reverence for the dead. Our veneration stems from the superstition that they now know the final truth about human fate. But is that feeling awakened solely by the memory of worthy ancestors? Could this sentiment also be an intuition of our future? Does psyche foresee that we should attain some final wisdom as to the value and meaning of our own life?

Though reverence for the dead brings with it recognition of our own fate, it also reminds us that we ought to do something with our lives. We want to be worthy of the chance to live a while longer, to find the purpose of our own lives before it is too late. How many lives are wasted, unused, ruined by ignorance, thoughtlessness and irresponsibility?

Moreover, as a universal belief, faith in the beyond is not only concerned with the afterlife, but also with the future evolution of humanity. Since our prehistoric beginnings, we have undergone an accelerated evolution over the past ten millennia--and it holds promise for the next thousand years.

Each century is a dialectic between the unalterable and irretrievable of the past and the dynamic *now*, between the reality of the present millennium and the fulfillment of our future. Mankind's continued evolution will require further humanization of our prehistoric subconscience and the further evolution of our supraconscience. Each of them needs to be educated as to what is universally human--and humane.

Each culture developed rituals to honor its dead. Each respected death for the lesson it taught concerning life's significance. Cultures which investigated this deeply sought to define ultimate truths.

Commemorating humankind's achievements indicates that the supraconscience records what is meaningful in human history. The act of recalling certain events reveals a need to come to terms with the phenomenon of time. Rituals which honor the dead are spiritual ways of commemorating life itself.

The attainments and breakthrough achievements of the dead make clear the noteworthy stages of the psyche's evolution. Advances in knowledge and wisdom remind us life is not meaningless. Rather, the men and women who used their inborn originality and intelligence to pursue a lifetime goal left their mark on the process of human evolution. They did not allow eternal death to grind them down to meaningless dust.

Defining oneself means coming to terms with what one truly wants out of life as an individual with rights, desires, needs and talents. It also means recognizing the right of others to their own happiness. Beyond intimate relations, all of us need to comfort strangers in times of personal grief and natural disasters. We all need to deflect senseless injustice and to prevent mindless violence.

It is often said that death is the great equalizer, which means that it annihilates the person we were. Yet, the world remembers Socrates, Plato, Aristotle, Moses, Christ, Mohammed, Buddha and Confucius. Moreover, in every age and culture, the good, thoughtful, and responsible are remembered by some of their descendents. They are more than names in a family genealogy. Where there is true culture, children acquire their identity from their parents and grandparents who tell the life stories of relatives or ancestors who achieved something in life.

Perhaps death equalizes all those who wasted their lives, all who gave up on life because they could not find the courage to move beyond its accidents and tragedies. Perhaps it also equalizes the nameless masses who never got the chance to learn what life was all about, and whose only option was to struggle to stay alive another day. Truly those were tragic lives. But the decisive were determined to live life for all it was worth. They placed their courage, ingenuity, and intelligence on the scale of life in an attempt to outweigh senseless death. They were more than equal to fate and mortality.

Rather than equalizing us, death makes clear we are not all the same in striving to come to terms with our purpose in life or with our responsibility to other human beings. Nor are we equal in seeking to create a meaningful destiny.

So, our death leaves behind evidence of how we lived. And, our descendents can judge the value of the life we endeavored to fulfill.

One purpose of *The Supraconscience of Humanity* is to urge the reader to think about many of the generous and ingenious lives of the past. Hopefully readers will then ponder what they most value in life. It may guide them to fulfill their destiny in the time that remains to them.

A concluding remark: It is possible that the soul passes into an afterlife. However, scientifically speaking, it is more credible to believe that our collective psyche evolves toward an ever-wiser supraconscience with each succeeding generation. Wherever sane religion and culture exist, and wherever sound reason and emotional intelligence guide humankind, a superior humanity is to be found.

Notes

1. Grégoire, F. *L'Au Dela/ The Beyond*, p.31. Grégoire's description of pagan and religious views of death and the afterlife are thought-provoking. His work provides a full overview of the subject. Unless otherwise noted, all references drawn from it are paraphrased.
2. Grégoire, p. 35, my translation.
3. Grégoire, p. 36-37
4. Grégoire, p. 39.
5. Grégoire, p. 75.
6. Grégoire, p. 76.
7. Grégoire, p. 79.
8. Grégoire, p. 80.
9. Grégoire, p. 81.
10. Grégoire, p. 42.
11. Grégoire, p. 25.
12. Grégoire, p. 27.
13. Grégoire, p. 119.
14. Ibid.

Chapter Three

Myth, Ritual, Cosmologies and Theism

Ancient Greece and Its Myths

Before the rise of Greek civilization, the ancient Greeks were largely peasant farmers, ploughing, sowing and harvesting the land. Prominent among their crops were corn, barley, wheat, figs, olives and wine. There is evidence that the early Greeks invented agrarian dramas to note the beginning, middle and end of each season.[1]

In the springtime, communal feasts were held to celebrate the reappearance of green vegetation and the return of life. Early in the year, rustic comedies were enacted to encourage the germination and growth of crops. After the harvest, tragedies based on legends marked the disappearance of life and the reappearance of death over the land.[2] Thus, over the centuries, the imaginative Greek mind came to practice rituals which revealed life's deeper meanings.

Related to Greek mythology, rites were performed in honor of Dionysus, the god of wine. Ecstatic and orgiastic, they gave vibrant expression to intense emotions during Dionysian wine festivals.[3] They are believed to be the true origin of ancient Greek drama.

One of the most memorable among these is the myth of Orpheus. A legendary poet and musician, he lost his wife when a venomous snake bite took her to the underworld. When his appeal to the lesser gods failed, he boldly descended into Hades to seek her release.

There in the darkness, the wonderful music of his lyre made even the ghosts weep. The monarch, Pluto himself, was even moved. At last, he freed Orpheus' wife on condition the poet not look back at her till they reached the surface. Dutifully, she followed him upward through dim caverns, but as they reached the entrance, he impatiently looked back to be sure she was there. In that instant, the power of death drew her down again into the eternal realm of the dead.

The myth inspired Orphic initiation rites which became a part of the cult of Dionysus. The Orphic doctrine of the incarnation of the blessed in the Elysian Fields offered hope of immortality. These Eleusinian rites were religious mysteries centered on the worship of Demeter and Persephone who personified the powers of life and death. Under the influence of the Dionysian cult, Orpheus' quest came to epitomize the soul's struggle to free itself from the suffering, mortal body.[4]

Such cults addressed people's emotional needs. The early myths treasured the passion for life whereas the later Greek tragedies revealed that they had learned the irony inherent in human nature. Greek tragedy acknowledged that Fate often brought down and destroyed men and women of exceptional intelligence and noble birth.

As the Dionysian cycle of festivals matured and evolved into great tragic drama, Greek genius discovered the nexus of its own nature. The evolving comprehension of human emotions taught Western civilization the need for down-to-earth wisdom. Transcending myth, ritual and cult, the Greek world view became the foundation of our civilization through the unforgettable achievements of their greatest philosophers.

Myth as Source of Ancient Conscience

Myths illustrate ancient conscience by the expression of noble emotions and passions. As we learned from the ancient Egyptian myth of Osiris, his wife Isis represented what men most admire in woman. The female conscience had long been esteemed for loyalty to brother, mate, husband and father. From the myth of Orpheus, we learn of a husband who loved his wife so deeply that his love drove him to defy the realm of death itself. Thus we remember him as the male conscience most admired by women: fidelity, bravery, grace in action, and resolute decision.

The myth of Adonis offers another insight into ancient conscience. Passionately loved by the goddess of love herself, he was killed while hunting wild boar in a forest. In her grief, Aphrodite could not accept his death, and so she secured his freedom from Hades for at least part of the year. Called Tammuz by the Jews and Syrians, Adonis became the dominant figure in rituals celebrating resurrection of the dead. Though worshippers wept at his death, his return to life filled them with rejoicing. His resurrection became possible only through the supernatural power of love. Later in Rome, Adonis became a god who guided the souls of the dead through the mystery of the beyond.

The unpredictable, immoral behavior of some ancient Greek gods led to their discredit in the eyes of those who later believed in one supreme God. Others endured because of their salutary influence on spontaneous creative imagination. Over the centuries, these imaginative myths, featuring noble characteristics of man and woman, not only developed a deeper emotional wisdom, but furthered our civilized human conscience.

Conscience and Self-Purification

In Orphic and Neo-Platonic teachings, the ignoble soul would be tortured by an infernal divinity. Other less vile souls could be cleansed of their impurities through a rite of dousing, or by fire. The soul could thus recover its original purity through expiation.[5] It could then choose the new earthly body it would bring to life.

The purpose of self-purification is fundamental to many religions. The act of self- examination leads us to perceive how personal weaknesses, base passions and perversions can lead to a loss of self-worth. Humiliation and dishonor not only wound us, but also teach us bitter lessons to be wary of the unpredictable nature of our subhuman self.

By purging and cleansing one's conscience, the individual can realize he still has the power to correct the disgraceful, expunge the shameful and redress the moral mistakes of the past. As a result, conscience gains a new respect for the power of the human mind. It experiences a change from a feeling of inferiority to one of superiority, it gains a new sense of self-respect. The self-converted conscience, now better able to deal with inner conflicts, begins its slow evolution toward a personal superconscience.

Ritual and Its Implications for Human Evolution

Ritual is of two basic types: secular and religious, exoteric and esoteric. Traditionally, it expresses a series of gestures, acts and entreaties to a higher power. Its common purpose is to invoke a supernatural entity for protection and guidance.

In generic terms, rituals reveal a need to gather together to meet a challenge to the group's survival. Such a threat may be a natural disaster, an epidemic, or an invasion by hostile forces. Anything that menaces group safety represents a force that could destroy the family or community.

In life-threatening circumstances, ritual becomes a communal response. Perils arouse our survival instincts and require us to be resourceful in using all we have learned and experienced in life. Impending danger demands courage, steadfastness, and the decision to resist what portends extinction. Gathered in prayer, people appeal to a higher power. A congregation undergoes a transformation--from a collection of isolated individuals to communion of spirit.

Hence beyond being merely a conventional, religious practice, ritual opens to us a deeper insight into faith: Those who pray together to the Almighty can move It to protect all from harm and evil.

Though the ancients prayed to invoke a god (e.g. Osiris, Dionysus, or Orpheus), later supplicants appealed to prophetic figures (Moses, Mohammed, et al) for guidance. Other cultures supplicated a human being who embodied a sacred, archetypal destiny (Buddha, Christ). They could console humanity for tragedies experienced, could uplift the soul to a nobler vision of human life. To supplicants, each wise ancestor was a spiritual hero guiding them through the worst in life. Even faced with defeat and death, ritual instills the hope that the individual soul would survive. In essence, as a symbolic act, ritual endeavors to prove the soul's superiority to fate itself.

We resort to ritual when ordinary means prove inadequate. When endangered, sometimes our reason, common sense and practical counsel cannot alleviate fear, pain or sorrow. At such times, only ritual is able to bring about a clearer awareness of the true meaning of our lives. When ritual is heartfelt in its search for an answer, it can reveal to us how our lives can aspire to a worthier destiny.

Life involves accidents, terminal diseases and unexpected deaths, which defy reason and make life seem senseless. When we are faced with such experiences, ritual provides us with the means to recover from the unpredictability of life, to cope with the pain and senselessness of tragedy. And, it actually embodies the hope of survival bequeathed to us by thousands of past generations of humankind. In a profound sense, ritual teaches us to contemplate anew the purpose of our lives. Hence the practice of ritual seems an early manifestation of humanity's supraconscious wisdom.

A form of sympathetic magic arises among participants in religious rituals. By identifying with the sorrow and suffering of the afflicted, we discover that such sympathy can be healing. Remarkably, ritual also makes us aware of the healing powers of our own bodies. Unfortunately, deadly diseases often gainsay any power in ritual to heal. Realists maintain this belief is nothing more than medieval superstition. Nevertheless, contemporary medicine has found that the body cures itself. Evidence of this is the immune system's response to invading bacteria and viruses. Medical experiments have even proved that life-inspiring images can activate the body's defense system, mitigating sicknesses and healing psyche's wounds.

This recent discovery by Dr. Jeanne Achterberg, *Imagery in Healing: Shamanism and Modern Medicine* (1989), curiously reminds us again of the myth of Osiris. Thanks to the magical powers and wisdom of his sister-wife Isis, he was brought back to life and later underwent an apotheosis. The belief in resurrection reveals an enduring fact about women.

Isis' acts of devotion were acts of healing. Her empathy and resourcefulness epitomizes the love and know-how of endless generations of wives.

Instinctively and intuitively, they have, over time, accumulated great knowledge of nature and the human body itself. Indeed, from time immemorial, they have nursed, healed and cured their men and children. Because of their maternal wisdom, it is probable that womankind have developed a deep faith in the vital and restorative powers of the body and psyche itself. In addition, their commitment to their family's survival steadily evolved their intuitive acumen. Not only did their effective use of herbs and medicines show competence and knowledge. Nursing, healing and curing were a ritual to restore the life of her loved ones.

In general, ritual dramatizes the history of the past. The preservation of significant stories helps us better appreciate the value of culture. Ritual educates psyche as to the meaningful experiences of our ancestors.

Stories illustrate the meanings of life events which allow us to face the future with both greater hindsight and foresight. Some stories and rituals teach courage and faith in one's ability to resolve life's most painful problems. By contrast, from ancient Greek tragedy, we learn the consequences of blindness, arrogance, and rashness: Such excesses can humiliate the most intelligent person or tragically lead him to his death.

Ritual, story and drama represent the essential wisdom of world cultures. They teach us to consolidate life's experiences into personal meaning. Practice in

Myth, Ritual, Cosmologies and Theism

interpreting their significance defines one's own values. Developing skill in interpretation matures and integrates one's character. The identity that a person develops in a lifetime is due to his or her psyche's understanding the past. Over the generations, world cultures have contributed to educating humankind's superior intelligence. Emotional wisdom at the heart of ritual has for millennia been cultivating humanity's supraconscience.

This wisdom evolved as an answer to suffering, loss of heart, and despair that life ends. The purpose of ritual is to teach us not to fear the approach of death. The person who lives to give meaning to life rises above despair. To live for a truth or an ideal is to deflect the fate of living a banal life.

Ritual, myth and literature offer more than the fictitious hope that life has meaning. They make clear that courage, integrity, and compassion are the essence of human nature. As virtues that give life its nobler significance, they confirm the truth and value of living for ideals. By the pursuit of meaning in this life, one can find life just, good and full of grace.

Life itself is a rite of passage, a passing through challenges and crises which test our decision, our honor, and what we value most in life. If we fail its tests, we may change from decisiveness to submissiveness, deteriorate from self-respect to self-scorn, devolve idealism to nihilism. Yet, successfully meeting the tests of life can mean giving up ignorance in exchange for knowledge and transforming innocence to modest wisdom. Success means discovering one's capacity to integrate both intelligence and ideals in the fulfillment of a life purpose.

Before concluding the remarks on the significance of ritual, we need to refer to ritual originating in the Near East.

In ancient Rome, the populace was strongly attracted to the exoticism of Near Eastern cults and religions. From the Greeks, the Romans had adopted the legendary figures of Pythagoras, Orpheus, Heraclitus, Plato and Aristotle. The fact that sanctuaries of the Middle Eastern religions were scattered throughout the Eastern Roman Empire bore witness to the Roman tendency to absorb 'barbarian ways.'

The attraction of the sophisticated Roman Empire to these cults and religions may seem strange. Yet, at the time, famine and pestilence were widespread throughout the Eastern Mediterranean. Hence the salvation promised by these foreign forms of worship must have seemed irresistible. Moreover, their rituals had a strong, passionate appeal. The imaginative, emotional and empathic responded to the gods who had suffered as had the poor people--deprived, cast out and victimized.

It is recorded that these impassioned rituals aroused female hysteria. Clearly, women had need of an emotional outlet. Perhaps the authoritarian laws of the empire and the injustice of social life were too much for the common folk to bear. So, they sought relief, release and escape from daily reality.

They spent their days buying and selling, bartering and trading, lending money and swindling the naive and innocent. They were crowded into unsanitary quarters and squalid living conditions. Most of them had lost their simple life as peasants and farmers, close to the freshness of nature. Civilized living tended to make them forget the emotions natural to human nature, close to the good earth.

But these foreign religions offered yet another attraction. To be initiated into them, one had to first become-immersed in their mysteries. The rituals excited the senses, thrilled the emotions, and fulfilled a passionate need. The experience was an enchantment promising ecstasy. So, the psychological effect freed rapturous emotions and deep mystical passions in the individual.

Hence these religions recognized psyche had its needs—needs which law and order knew nothing about. As Blaise Pascal so wisely said four centuries ago, "The heart has its reasons the Reason knows nothing about."

The psychological importance of ritual is the arousal of the deepest of human feelings, an experience that has little to do with common sense. A mature man knows he should obey reason, yet an age-old instinct urges him to achieve some heroic deed or to surrender himself to some noble, uplifting passion. This is the basis for identification with a god, even one who has been unjustly judged and put to death.

Obviously, the Christian Church recognized humanity's inborn thirst for mystery, ecstasy and spiritual catharsis. Ritual also released common man and woman from the fear of fate. People needed communion with a Deity who offered hope of a kinder afterlife. In addition, from ancient Egypt, there was already the cult of a universal mother who cared for humanity. To Christians, the Egyptian goddess Isis seemed a pagan anticipation of the Madonna.[6]

Another influential myth was founded on the legend of the ancient Persian god of light, Mithra. Many soldiers of the widespread Roman army were adherents of this cult. By the late Roman Empire, Mithraism had become Christianity's main source of competition. The Emperor Aurelian (215-275 A.D.) undertook to merge the divergent groups of the cult of Isis, Christians and Mithraists. This culminated the tendency in ancient Egypt, Mediterranean nature cults and Near Eastern religions to find common ground in their worship.

This instinct to consolidate beliefs and ritual practices into a universal religion seems to be natural to our evolving psyche. There seems a syncretic drive in the psyche which seeks to encompass and comprehend all feelings and all realities. In fact, syncretism reveals the synoptic purpose guiding the evolution of the human psyche. In sum, psyche's use of syncretism is two-pronged: 1) to create a common bond between the races of humanity, and 2) ultimately, to integrate humanity's knowledge and wisdom.

An historical example of incomplete religious syncretism is the affinities between Mithraism and Christianity. These likenesses were also the reason for the keen competition between them. The central act of Mithraic ritual was the sacrifice of a bull, after which a sacrificial meal was shared by the faithful. Mithra himself partook of a feast with the Sun before he ascended on a solar chariot to his throne in heaven--a ritual which reminds Christians of the Last Supper, the blood spilt at the Crucifixion, and Christ's promise of a feast in heaven with God the Father. During their feast, the Mithraists also ate bread and drank wine. They sanctified Sunday as the day of the Sun and the 25th of December as the day the sun began its return. They also named the seven days of the week after seven pagan gods. These facts are well known to students of cultural history. Thus both Christianity and Mithraism adopted and adapted ritual practices aimed at evoking mystical faith in a supreme being.

Rather than be dismayed at this historical evidence of such borrowing, we should realize that such mutual exchange of ideas and practices reveal that ritual, myth and religion are needed to satisfy universal emotional needs.

Understanding that syncretism leads to mutual spiritual enrichment among religious faiths should make us more open-minded, more appreciative of the foreign and more tolerant of mankind's diverse cultures. The driving force behind syncretism seems to be psyche's emotional intelligence.

In so far as any religion predicates its system of beliefs on respect for all humanity, it preaches a sound and humane philosophy of life. The combined virtues of mutual understanding, charity and compassion can subdue our primitive subconscience and humanize it. Emotional wisdom can cure its paranoia, heal mankind's psychological wounds and transfigure present-day fatalism into a new faith in humanity's future.

Ancient Cosmologies
The Subconscience and Supraconscience in Antiquity

In general, fatalistic religions in the ancient world expressed the power of the *subconscience*. This state of mind emerged when whole populations became victims of nature's deadliest forces. In Babylonia, scorching sun, sand storms, brutal heat, floods, drought, and torrential rains made for a struggle for survival for everything that lived. Evil seemed to suffocate existence. These conditions in the Near East bred anew the paranoia of man's subconscience, which had first appeared in prehistoric times when the unpredictable and predatory threatened every life.

Moreover, inexplicable sicknesses and sudden misfortune seemed the work of evil ghosts and demons. Any personal transgression might be an offence against some god or goddess. Supernatural beings brought pain and punishment, and human offences were avenged by irate gods.

Penitence could be obtained when a priest exorcised the demon within the individual. The victim had to answer deeply probing questions. Had the penitent insulted his father or mother, or, taken a neighbor's wife? Shed the blood of one of his own tribe, or offended some god or goddess? Such probing questions were to be echoed in Moses' Ten Commandments. [7]

Whenever the gods forsook the people or brought disaster upon humankind, the sins of the community were believed to be the cause. Yet sometimes the penitent knew not what sin or error he or she had supposedly committed. Bewildered innocents must have suffered under the lash of false accusations many a time. (cf. the afflictions of Job in the Old Testament) Victims of domestic violence or rape could be accused of causing the crime and maligned by moralistic members of a community. The senselessness of such punishment served to reinforce the paranoia of the subconscience, especially in women.

On the other hand, *conscience* can accept guilt when one's own act has brought unhappiness or personal tragedy upon others. But when innocents are made to suffer the acts of malice carried out by those who supposedly represent the will of the gods, such 'justice' mocks the meaning of conscience altogether. (cf. the Spanish Inquisition).

At every stage of our evolution, injustice has fed the subconscience with unfounded suspicion and poisonous words. In the Babylonian world, diseases and fatalities were 'caused' by the intrigues of malignant beings or the schemes of demons. To control these, the Babylonians developed an intricate system of ritual. It aimed to purify the individual, shield him or her from evil, and to propitiate the creatures in the darkness.[8]

In this paranoid atmosphere, the cult of Ea, god of wisdom, was active at Eridu. The holy waters there were used to cleanse the individual's soul and expel the evil spirit, thus preventing him or her from infecting others. These life-giving waters exuded the Power that created the universe. As a god, Ea released the individual from sin and disease and gave him or her the strength to overcome the demoniac. Ea represented sublime knowledge.[9]

The history of Babylonia seems to offer evidence of the beginning conflict between our paranoid/predatory subconscience and the earliest manifestations of humankind's conscience and supraconscience. From the modern perspective, the god Ea was born of human imagination to counter and allay our primitive anxieties and fears which drove men to commit vicious and ruthless acts against their own kind. In its embryonic state, the *subconscience* must have had its origins in the Stone Age, the prehistoric human culture characterized by use of tools and weapons.

In the eighteenth century B.C.E., the Babylonian king Hammurabi published a code of laws. These practical laws regulated the just distribution of food supplies, controlled money lending and debtor's claims, directed public works, transportation and other activities necessary to govern a country justly. Judges determined rights in any breach of contract, and the city elders as magistrates assessed the value of property. The code made no claim of divine approval or authority, and was therefore secular in intent.[10]

Here we have historical evidence of a developing *conscience* based on pragmatic wisdom and clear understanding of the need for justice based on reciprocity. The code proved that humankind could establish law and order by appealing to common sense, an earthly sense of justice, and educating a population to the codification of practices based on social rights and mutual respect. Undoubtedly, Hammurabi's code influenced the regulation of human conduct in neighboring countries. It is evidence that justice and secular wisdom prevailed in a culture some 3000 years ago. In fact, the Hittites and Assyrians also had legal codes.

Egypt

Hollywood has portrayed the ancient Egyptians as inhumane and evil because they believed in gods other than the Yahweh of the ancient Hebrews. This portrayal is a gross misinterpretation of ancient Egyptian culture. As a matter of fact, the Egyptians were preoccupied early on with understanding the moral nature of existence. As agrarian communities developed along the Nile River, they became conscious of the rhythm and order of the natural world.

Gradually, their history reveals a belief in the goddess Maat who personified moral truth, justice and right. She kept order in heaven and earth and brought the deceased before the gods who judged the soul of the dead. It was the duty of the Pharaoh to ensure that Maat's justice was upheld. Maat reigned over the universe and spoke to the conscience of the Pharaoh.

In contrast to the severe forms of justice that prevailed in neighboring countries, the early Egyptians considered the heart as the center of the conscience. It gave all men knowledge of the just and good, right and wrong. The heart heard the voice of God. It understood the mysterious nature of the universe. It told humankind to live in harmony with the celestial order.[11]

These initial observations require comment. Today the 'civilized' man or woman would find it difficult to enter into any direct harmonious relationship with nature or the universe. In general, the average, 'educated' individual is quite out of touch with nature or the natural. In our technological world, we have lost touch with what is natural in us.

Today, astronomy shows us the cosmos. The lifeless worlds in space, the threat of incoming comets, the predicted extinction of our sun, and the scientific calculations of the final entropy of all energy in the cosmos makes it difficult for modern humankind to discern any moral order or 'heart' in our universe. Add to these doomsday prophecies, Darwin's theory of evolution assuredly does not provide comfort when it comes to a notion of justice. Nature is, for him competitive and predatory. Scientifically speaking, there is no moral principle underlying existence, no 'heart' at its center.

By contrast, the ancient Egyptian understanding of the human heart as the seat of mind and conscience held the promise of a form of universal morality. Moreover, their conception teaches us that the good life is to be guided by an ideal or a moral truth.

Even today, belief in the wisdom of the heart energizes us. An inspired person is viewed as possessed of greater life, guided by something far above the demands of daily duties, rules or regulations established by staid, rational society. Noble emotion can be a special form of energy, a power pouring through and from us much as light from the sun. So might the ancient Egyptians have looked upon the goddess Maat whose radiance was felt in the social moral and cosmic order of existence.

Hence during the period of the Middle Kingdom (c. 2000-1780 B.C.E.), the Egyptian ethic was ruled by faith in a divinely ordered existence. Praised were virtues such as honesty, truthfulness, and justice. They opposed the vices of adultery, dishonesty, and violence.[12]

Of particular interest is the Egyptian attitude toward death. *The Book of the Dead.*[13] It described how the deceased must prove his moral character. The judges of the underworld weighed his conscience to see if it was worthy of an afterlife. One's lifetime guilt or innocence decided one's fate. If the deity were to forgive and show mercy, a sinner had to acknowledge his unworthiness. Only through honesty and contrition would the sinner receive salvation. Even the virtuous individual had to prove his innocence.

As the sage Amenemope taught his time, each individual knew in his heart good and evil, so everyone was morally responsible. One had to listen to the voice of the divinity within and do God's will.[14]

The judgment included a detailed scrutiny of all transgressions against the moral order established by the goddess Maat. The heart was weighed against Truth, symbolized by a feather and an image of Maat. The balance revealed whether or not the individual had lived in harmony with divine justice. Hence the Egyptians believed the heart bore witness for or against the deceased. The conscience knew what had been done and what had not.

For those deemed unworthy of an afterlife, at the foot of the scale were predators, hybrid monsters made up of crocodile, hippopotamus, and lion ready to devour whose who failed to reveal a pure moral heart. The description fits our understanding of the horrors of our primeval subconscience.[15]

So despite the later attempt of Egyptians to manipulate the final judgment by talismans and magic formulas, conscience remained the key to the ethic of the Middle Kingdom. In general, social equality and justice maintained balance in society and assured a just relation between the human and cosmic/divine orders. To follow the justice, harmony and equilibrium of Maat was to live in keeping with the highest good. Thus, at this time, Egypt embraced a noble cosmology. One's conduct in this life was determined by how one conformed to cosmic justice. Life beyond the grave depended on obedience to this rule. This sacred conception of morality resulted in a level of civilization above that of any surrounding country.

However, this period of moral idealism inspired by an archetypal intuition of the Supraconscience, came to an end in the next period of Egyptian history. With the invasion of the Asiatics, Egypt was thrown into a chaotic period of turmoil, misery and tragedy. It might be said that people's minds were enslaved and their lives dehumanized. Conscience was garroted.

The Egyptian goddess Maat epitomizes what today we might identify as the cosmic Supraconscience. In point of fact, in the cultural history of mankind, she is an early symbol of the fact that psyche's superior conscience was evolving.

By contrast, the brutality and mercilessness of the Asiatic hordes in Egypt allowed the subconscience to reappear once again. They crushed whatever moral order and humane justice the reign of Maat had secured for ancient Egyptians. Military barbarism ruthlessly undid the world's first collective expression of faith in the goodness of the human heart. This event is recorded in ancient history as a moment in which the primeval, powerful subconscience suffocated the fledgling supraconscience of a people.

Ancient Egyptian morality of this period disintegrated in the grip of subconscience--anarchy and insanity. Once again, this illustrates the struggle between our primate subconscience and our developing, nobler nature.

Ancient Greek Cosmology

Over the centuries, men came to regard ancient paganism as inferior to monotheism. Viewed through the lens of Judaism and Christianity, the ancient pagan gods displayed human weaknesses and passions, and engaged in intrigues unbecoming of any god. Jews and Christians could hardly accept them as deities who had helped create the universe. In fact, not only were they earth-bound in their moral behavior; they were evidence of mankind's uncertain conscience, still skilled in sin, deceit, indecency and blameworthy behavior.

However, the Indo-European Sky-god Zeus (Jupiter) merited some respect. Known as the god of light and the sky, he controlled the fertilizing rains, and when angered, he blasted the other gods and humans alike with thunderbolts. Yet, he was also the god of justice, ruling over the laws and ensuring the welfare of the land.

Conceptually speaking, Zeus assimilated the traditions of various, regional gods, uniting their powers and characteristics into one superior god. In the Greek mind, he embodied the endowment of lesser gods to rule as 'the Father of gods and men'.

Furthermore, not only did the nature of each god and goddess survive in this assimilation, but also transformed into a sovereign being. The psyche was on a journey to find a universal and all powerful divinity.

So, each culture could be inspired by the god(s) of another if belief in that other deity could lessen their suffering or possibly teach them how to survive death. Beyond such practical reasons for adopting the gods of other cultures, the attraction between different peoples revealed a deep desire in the races of humanity to share emotions and to reach lasting, mutual understanding.

Besides encouraging cultural tolerance, an interest in others' cultures and views of life matures the individual. Cultural knowledge guides us away from senseless prejudices. It invigorates us to learn more about mankind. Ultimately it stimulates the mind to integrate a vast range of historic facts, ideas and principles into a coherent, viable world view.

The Olympian Gods

The Greek gods occupied the earth above and below. Some lived in the sacred abode of Mt. Olympus and thus were believed to occupy the heavens. Others lived in the sea, and the dreaded gods dwelt in the infernal underworld. A modern psychologist might find this mythology an apt means of delving into the ancient Greek psyche.

The gods of the infernal region revealed dark fears and dread typical of our primitive subconscience. Superstition and feverish imagination created lurid episodes in which phantoms and ghosts threatened the helpless in Hades.

On the other hand, the fact that the Greeks imagined superhuman gods living among and above mortals on a sacred mountain indicates that those gods embodied human traits and potentials. The elevation of certain gods seemed to express the Greek sense of awe at powers yet unrealized by humankind. An intuition of the superhuman hinted that mankind was on the way to evolving its own superior mental powers.

Otherwise, the mythical middle world was filled with gentle deities who were respected, venerated and revered. This form of conscience displayed an intimate affection for the benign powers of nature. The people worshipped her fertility and expressed gratitude for her motherly nurture. In much of the Mediterranean world, the peasant farmers held seasonal festivals to show their love and gratitude for nature's bounty.

Though many feared the unpredictability of the gods of both the upper and nether realms, the common folk possessed a simple, sane, appreciative conscience of the good in life.

The myth of the Greek goddess of agriculture, Demeter (Ceres) provides a story beautiful in its own right, one that is redolent with psychological meaning. Her daughter Persephone, the maiden of the springtime, was abducted by Pluto, king of the dead. At the behest of Venus, Cupid had shot an arrow into his dark heart. The lord of the underworld had then carried Persephone away in his chariot, drawn by pitch-black steeds, down into the nether world.

In vain, her mother searched for her. In anger and anguish, the goddess withdrew her life-giving bounty from the land. That year became the cruelest humankind could remember. Famine covered the earth.

Though Zeus sent gods to beg her to relent, she refused to listen to their appeals. Then the father of the gods sent Hermes (Mercury) to the lord of the underworld to order Persephone's release. Of course, Pluto had to obey such a command. But before he would let her go, he asked her to eat a pomegranate, knowing she must return if she did so. Eager to return to her mother, Persephone did as she was told.

With great joy mother and daughter were reunited, but Demeter learned that she had to give up her daughter for four months each year. Persephone's fresh loveliness had to disappear again into the world of the dead. Finally, saddened by the desolation of the earth and human kind's suffering, Demeter once more made the fields and trees rich with abundant grain and fruit.

The stories of both Demeter and Persephone are full of sorrow. Demeter must forever watch her daughter die because each year she must return again to live among the dead during the winter. Though Persephone did arise again each year, her bright beauty was darkened by her memory of life among the dead. So, it was in the hour of death that humankind turned to Demeter for compassion; in turn, they felt compassion for the daughter who had to die every year.

To be sure, this lovely, imaginative story of the changing seasons is unforgettable. It shows Greek mythical genius at its best. The Eleusinian mysteries dramatized this myth. The story evoked a mystical communion between those who shared a mother's anguish at the loss of a child. The myth illustrates the instinct of women to unite with those who suffer and to comfort one another for life's tragedies.

As the basis for later Greek drama, Demeter's story helped humanize us. Women's mutual bond and their sisterly compassion fostered the growth of empathy. Such intuitive understanding, when shared, gradually transformed into humanity's emotional acumen.

Clearly, the Greeks contrasted the bounty and joy of life with the tragedy and death we experience in life. There seem cycles of happiness and sadness, joy and sorrow, hope and despair. It takes little intellectual reflection to understand that these fluctuations not only reflect the biorhythms of the human psyche but of the earth herself. It is also obvious that our supraconscience is responsible for much of life's creative joy, its abundant pleasures and its eventual harvests.

By contrast, our subconscience tends to present us with the realities of life's tragedies, which remind us of our own weakness and mortality. Yet the faith expressed in this myth of Demeter is that death is followed by a rebirth of the powers of life. Even in horrifying periods of history (as today), we trust in the creative powers of nature, and we have faith that humankind will be reborn when we have suffered enough.

In sum, benign nature teaches us one of the most fundamental truths about life. If we undergo the loss of love or of a loved one, we learn the meaning of solitude and loneliness. Yet, since we must survive such despair, the heart can be renewed because life generates ever new love and meaning for those who seek it. This wisdom our emotional intuition teaches us.

Moreover, this experience of personal renewal reminds us of the process of continual regeneration in evolution itself: Generations pass away, and new ones emerge to evolve beyond past mistakes and offenses, beyond sorrow and suffering, beyond regret to rejoicing in the happiness life has to offer.

With each actual birth and each spiritual rebirth, life renews itself. Indeed, evolution reveals the sacred power of life: its capacity to resurrect itself.

So, too, with the life-exploring psyche. Much as the life-force itself, our supraconscience pursues a teleological purpose. As humanity's powers of perception and conception increased exponentially, our superior nature undertook to integrate theoretical knowledge with practical wisdom.

Just as evolutionary biology reveals the emergence of ever new species over geologic time, humanity's cultural history evinces transformations of psyche through our evolving ever-new powers of cognition and comprehension.

The life force itself has overcome death in its many forms. So, too, can humanity mitigate the effect of death by mutual understanding, respect and aid. The individual who dedicates his or her life to self-realization and self-fulfillment, as well as to family and humanity, negates the final sorrow of personal death. The dedicated life helps ensure the future. Such unfailing love and perpetual renewal are humanity's destiny.

About 800 B.C.E., the Greek poet Hesiod imagined the cosmos to have originated out of chaos through the creative force of Eros. It is interesting to note how this ancient concept is still used today. As a psychological concept, Eros represents the life-preserving instinct. It sums up the impulses which gratify our basic needs. It describes our sublimated emotions and includes our visceral determination to stay alive.

In psychoanalytical theory, the life instinct, Eros, is contrasted to Thanatos, the death instinct. Supposedly, this death-wish is inborn and explains the aggressive and destructive behavior of humankind. Unconsciously, it can also lead to self-destruction.

Hence we still understand Eros as a universal force, an instinctual drive motivating human decisions and actions. Our acceptance of Eros as the expression of an essential emotion in humankind seems to indicate that our life-creating passion is somehow linked to the central creative power of the universe.

In our definition of humankind's supraconscience, we might regard this creative passion as emanating from the psyche itself. For the ancient Greeks who studied the star-filled sky, Eros brought out the order and beauty of the universe. If we allow ourselves to regard Eros as a real force in the life of modern man, this could be an indication of our evolving supraconscience. If God actually initiated evolution, he gave us the special power to evolve from species into human beings. Acknowledging the full, natural power of Eros would give us the capacity to transcend who we are and to become who we are meant to be.

On the other hand, the psychoanalytical term Thanatos has an obvious, marked resemblance to our term the prehistoric *subconscience.*

Of further interest is the psychological significance of the imagined transformation from chaos to cosmos. The archetype of chaos is ubiquitous in worldwide creation stories—and so psyche's evolution from subconscience to supraconscience indicates a parallel metamorphosis.

The ancient mythical description of chaos appears to depict our mental state prior to the beginning of psyche's evolution. The metamorphosis began with the emergence of the earliest conscience from the maelstrom of the anxieties, fears, and paranoia of the primeval subconscience.

In plain terms, what we conceived as the original chaos was actually the state of our aboriginal psyche prior to our developing a rudimentary conscience.

This change may have been affected by the observation of natural phenomena. At some moment in time, the primitive mind awoke to the regularities and order manifest in nature, perhaps first evident in the flowering of plants, the bearing of fruit in trees, and the ripening of grain in cereal grass. Maybe the germination of seeds was observed to follow the rhythm of rain and sunshine. Finally, the succession and cycle of the seasons revealed that the earth herself followed a rhythm, pattern, and a plan.

This realization may have led womankind to identify with the rhythm of the moon's waxing and waning. Somehow women responded to the moon in their twenty-eight day menstrual cycle. On the other hand, men may have become astronomically interested in the sun's June and December solstices, which marked its nearest and furthest distance from the earth. These solstices determined the bounty and scarcity of food, the time for work and for enjoying the fruits of one's wisdom. Man, woman and child would have been fascinated with the seasonal rotation of the stars across the night sky.

More closely connected to their daily lives was the association of grandparents, parents and children. This relationship made clear the succession of generations, the rhythm of being born, living and dying. Yet through all change, through all stages and sequences of life, the astral cycles seemed beyond temporality. The cosmos and the earth seemed to promise that life itself was eternal. Hence the human psyche grew, with every experience it understood, continually evolving practical knowledge while its emotional intelligence sought some ultimate meaning to life.

Greek mythology left another imprint on the collective memory of Western civilization. The story of Orpheus engendered the Orphic cosmology that held the cosmos to have been created out of an original chaos. In this belief, the Creator Eros generated light and life before even the sun itself was created. Orphic initiation rites undertook to purify the soul from innate evil and to release it from the cycle of reincarnation. They believed an inner light illumined human reason and wisdom. In other words, for the ancient Greeks, reason became the power to convert the chaos of wild, insane emotions into common sense, mental balance and sensible understanding--and ultimately to comprehend the Logos of the universe.

This realization invites further speculation as to the emergence of human consciousness. A parallel between the awakening consciousness of an infant and early man may clarify the similarity of these experiences. Both would have undergone a period of confusion when they first became aware of the world around them. Both would have been bewildered and perplexed. In the beginning, the still underdeveloped mind would have been unable to understand its world.

This initial psychic state was chaotic, an insight that may have been the source of Orpheus' intuition. In the beginning, he sensed that chaos had ruled existence. With time, infant and primate-man began to perceive the world more clearly. Along with more focused perception came recognition of sense and order. The child's maturing mind slowly understood that adults were reasonable and did things with a purpose. Primitive man also gradually grasped the regular the succession of the seasons and the annual movements of the stars. When a tribe initiated adolescents into their traditions, they learned to obey the rules of law and order established by their own people. Most traditional cultures tell a story of how, out of chaos, the cosmos came into being.

Communal life brings together people of all ages. The child would have witnessed the senility of the elderly, and families would have had to deal with the mental disintegration of parents, relatives and friends. Knowledge of the decomposition that comes with death would weigh heavily on the strongest heart. It was not unthinkable that, in the end, the world would plunge anew into chaos and everything would die. For these reasons, the cosmology of Orpheus foreshadows a return to chaos at the end of time.

However, other ancients refuted such fatalism. Two natural phenomena seemed eternal. Overhead in the dark sky, the stars and constellations appeared infinite, permanent and timeless. Similarly, on earth, life was everywhere, and despite the death and disappearance of plants, animals and persons, the generation of life seemed to be everlasting and constant as the celestial bodies themselves. Hence the tragic conclusion of the poet's cosmology could not be universally true.

On the other hand, Orpheus described salvation not so much as a deliverance from sin as the preservation of what is most precious in human life. His belief seems founded on the story of Demeter and Persephone with its lesson that death is followed by a new springtime of life. What is clearly preserved in this story is the eternal truth of parental and filial love. In fact, family love is the salvation of humankind. It is the noble verity that transcends death. As it passes through thousands of generations of humanity, such love never dies. Through all time, love is humanity's salvation. It is intrinsic to our species. As long as we give and receive that love, our cosmos will not die.

Yet, the centuries following the age of myth discovered their own eternal truth. Between 525-460 B.C.E., the Greek writers of tragedy (Aeschylus, Sophocles and Euripides) taught mankind to be wary of their excesses and to avoid arrogance, violent passions and blindness to the consequences of our acts. Together these Greek pagans taught us one enduring moral lesson: Beware of what you may become if you surrender to the fatalism of humankind's subconscience.

Beyond myth and tragic literature, ancient Greek philosophy from 470 to 322 B.C.E. explored the innermost dimensions of the human mind. As presented by Plato, Socrates' ironic dialogues provided his and our time with a method of systematic inquiry. Its initial purpose was to confront the false claims of the Sophists, who denied that there was any ultimate truth. As it developed, Plato's philosophy defined more exactly and completely the knowledge men imagined they possessed. Aptly, Socrates demonstrated the truth about human living: "The unexamined life is a life not worth living." Put another way, the unexamined truth may prove to be a falsehood and so too a lifetime.

On the other hand, Socrates' student, Plato, asserted that the actual things we see in this world are mere copies of the transcendent ideas in which all things participate. True knowledge emerges when we recall the pure Forms from the transcendental world of our true birth.

Plato's student, Aristotle, gave us books on logic, ethics, physics, metaphysics, politics and poetics. These works would influence the history of philosophy for at least two thousand years. His logic (*Posterior Analytics*) provided the knowledge of the syllogism, i.e. the rules for drawing legitimate inferences from major and minor premises. His logic was relied upon until at least the Middle Ages and still serves as the basis for the modern system of quantification logic. It also provided the foundation for scientific investigation. Lastly, and perhaps most importantly, Aristotle was empirically minded. He insisted that theory must follow from fact, and fact could only be gotten at by observing nature directly.

Of enormous interest to contemporary thinking was his perception of the generic, transformational powers present in biological life. He distinguished potentiality from actuality, the former being the inherent power in nature to emerge into a given form, and the latter being the full realization of that form, e.g. a seed and a full-grown plant. That is, until it has come into existence, but not actually done so, a thing remains in a state of potentiality; by contrast, an *entelechy* is a form which has realized its potential or been actualized.

Obviously, throughout *The Supraconscience of Humanity,* when we refer to human evolution or to the evolution of the psyche, we are speaking of its actualization in successive cultures and in the maturing of our emotional acumen.

In sum, these 'pagans' contributed a great deal to the development of modern man's collective conscience and to our contemporary understanding of cosmology.

Ancient Hebrew Cosmology

Though the ancient Hebrews may have adopted the traits of some vegetations gods, they primarily conceived of Yahweh as the Supreme Deity who by *word* and *act* created the cosmos.

The creation story reveals how concepts affected the mind of an ancient people. It identified their awakening conscience and defined their sense of a greater Self. With conscience came a clearer direction and purpose for the whole people. In other words, belief in one God provided a basis for unity and solidarity among them. It consolidated their forms of worship and made conscience their master.

Yahweh's divine law became Hebrew law. A legal decision enacted the will of God. The Pentateuch was believed to reveal the decrees Yahweh gave directly to Moses on the Holy Mountain. Religious, civil and criminal law were one and the same. The *Book of the Covenant, Exodus (xxi-xxiii)* appears to have been modeled, in part on the Code of Hammurabi.[16]

The laws of Yahweh gave unity to Hebrew life. The Torah, i.e. Law, confirmed the covenant between Israel and Yahweh and required absolute obedience to Him.[17] In this respect, the commitment of an entire people signaled the spiritual evolution of a segment of humanity. In that part of the ancient world, Judaic faith showed that humankind was capable of developing a superior conscience by obeying God.

The prophets of the Old Testament spoke in impassioned language of the glories of Creation and the duty to worship the Almighty. They sought to raise Hebrew devotion above the level of mere obedience and pragmatic action. Their passion awakened the devout to a rhapsodic, intimate feeling of God's presence in their world. With the prophecies came a new stage of human spiritual development–that of seeking God's omniscience and yearning for superior wisdom.

The communal psyche acquired deeper confidence in the context of this unity and solidarity, and this, in turn, helped establish a clearer commitment to the Supreme Being. The Israelites emulated Yahweh by implanting justice among themselves and inculcating the principles of morality into the faithful. Parents were responsible to bring order into family life and instill such knowledge in their children.

At the mythological level, Yahweh was viewed as the conqueror of monsters, leviathans and dragons. By conquering Baal and Marduk, He brought order out of chaos.[18] This imaginative interpretation of a cosmological event has a number of implications for the modern mind. Psychologically speaking, Yahweh's conflict with the predators of the primeval abyss may represent the psyche's sane supraconscience emerging to do battle with our primitive, demon-haunted subconscience.

Fiends were fearful imaginings of our primitive psyche still striving to survive in a predatory world. The killers in primeval nature were met again in our nightmares where they lurked in the darkness of our being. So, the subconscience made our ancestors wary of being ensnared by stalkers ready to seize and devour them. In time, they became wary of the demonic others, people in their own tribe.

An event well known in Hebrew history was the deliverance from bondage in Egypt. The event became intertwined with sacerdotal and sacrificial elements of the Passover celebration. Based on historical fact, the story of Exodus came to be elaborated in memory and imagination into an event of cosmic proportions.[19] It is also believed that God made possible the liberation of the Hebrews by the miracle of the parting of the waters of the Red Sea. They were thus able to escape the Pharaoh's revenge.

Acceptance of God's omnipotence, his ability to alter or amend the laws of nature should prepare the true believer to be reconciled to the fact that Yahweh not only commanded that the process of Creation begin, but also foreordained that all forms of life should evolve. Thus evolution would have impelled all archetypes of species to adapt, transform and perfect themselves over time. If this is true, the cosmic Father, who vanquished the demons of chaos, must also have created all species and directed them to evolve beyond their original primitiveness. By the same logic, the Almighty must have predestined human evolution. Moreover, he would have empowered psyche to realize and perfect the potentials of humanity's superior intelligence. Humankind could hence accelerate its own evolution.

Perhaps. But why should God favor our kind? The reason could be to enable us, as a species, to evolve further of our own accord, to transform ourselves. And, conversely, through self-integration and self-transformation, each human being can increase the capacity of his or her natural endowments. As a consequence, with our species maturing stage by stage, humankind could more clearly comprehend the significance of God's omniscience.

Other Biblical passages reveal how their cosmology helped the Hebrews to partially free themselves from their own prehistoric subconscience. They visualized Yahweh as seated on a heavenly throne under the starry dome of our universe. This radiant epiphany may have been their vision of the reality of the Cosmic Supraconscience.

Based on today's knowledge, we may also reinterpret the Hebrew self-portrait as God's 'chosen people'. In the scientific context of evolutionary biology, we may now infer that all humankind is His "chosen species". That judgment would explain humankind's remarkable evolution. The purpose behind our mental and spiritual development would be the evolution of a supraconscience able to apprehend in finite ways the wisdom of the infinite Supraconscience.

In the Old Testament description of creation, God's spirit planed over the sea of chaos to separate the light from the darkness. Then the earth appeared.

In effect, this ancient description may record an event in the history of the human psyche. Perhaps it is the imaginative record of our psychic evolution. Such speculation is suggested on the basis of recent anthropological theory. There is evidence that our species experienced the chaos of a worldwide natural disaster that tragically reduced our kind.

A super-volcano called Toba erupted in Indonesia about 74,000 years ago, causing a volcanic winter. It filled the world's atmosphere with choking ash. Researchers believe the entire human population was reduced to a few thousand people. The pollution and toxic air may have attacked the resilient genes of our species, but those individuals who survived were stronger physically and mentally than ever before. It may have been at this point that we transformed from humanoids to humans.

On the other hand, we could consider the story of Creation as the account of a psychic experience. If we do, how should we understand God's dividing the light from the darkness? Perhaps this is a description of the first appearance of the supraconscience as the power to confront the chaos of the subconscience. Over time, life's experiences taught the supraconscience the value of both foresight and hindsight. It also taught psyche to be unafraid and to trust itself. Since it was born from the life instinct, the supraconscience did not fear death itself.

Practicality and resourcefulness protected humankind from extermination. We survived by learning co-operation and acting with a common purpose. Eventually, experience taught psyche it could think and act with some wisdom.

Belief in the Creation narrative merits further comment. Man is portrayed as having dominion over the earth and all its living creatures. The story persuades us we were created in the image of the Almighty. What do these reassuring images tell us? How do they fit in with our scientific account of life on earth?

In geologic time, the earth is estimated to be about four and a half billion years old. Every schoolchild has some knowledge of evolution. They know that the age of dinosaurs began some 425 million years ago and lasted until their extinction 65 million years ago. That biological break marked the beginning of the earth's largest mammals. About 24 million years ago, the earliest hominids appeared. The earliest members of the human species are charted at about three million years ago.

Evolutionary biologists and anthropologists are unable to account for the remarkable physiological transformation of the species. Psychologically speaking, we must surmise that our accelerated transmutation over time resulted in a comparable mental evolution. We learned that we possessed an intelligence superior to other creatures. This became evident in our increasing ability to prevent predation by carnivores, to grow crops and domesticate animals. In large measure, we utilized our eco-niches intelligently. In time, we came to inhabit virtually all the habitable world--an impressive achievement for any species.

But were we really created in the image of God? To the ancient Hebrews, Yahweh was a replica of humankind. However, since our mental image of the Almighty derives from His omniscience of the All, it follows that humans should devote much of life to accumulating knowledge, using reason, and gaining some sort of wisdom. That could be true if the ideal name for man as *Homo sapiens* were valid, but the mass of humanity can hardly hope to think beyond the needs and demands of everyday.

The creation story invites further comment. God gave us dominion over all the earth and its creatures. Though it means literally having power or sovereignty over others, is there a deeper significance to the word *dominion*?

If we look beyond its general, semantic meaning, the term commends authority over one's own emotions, desires, attitudes, thoughts and actions. Practically speaking, if one wants to be like God, then one must learn self-mastery and self-actualization of one's innate powers.

Yet, God created humankind to illustrate the eternal significance of *decision*. Throughout our history, we have learned that intelligent decisions largely determine the outcome of a single human destiny. That self- knowledge has helped us to fathom God's will. By endowing man with the power of judgment, He enabled man to gain control over his own evolution. Sensible human decisions did indeed guide the direction of our evolution and the realization of our achievements.

With the birth of human conscience, God gave man his earliest form of judgment. The gradual emergence of the human supraconscience suggests that we are learning to use the power that comes with decision more wisely. After millennia in which we sought to discover the strength and purpose of the supraconscience, we are almost ready to decide the future destiny of humankind.

Furthermore, conviction that the Creator called all life into being had its effect on human history. Jehovah's example likely inspired human decision makers to bring their own cultures and civilizations into being.

On the other hand, the certitude of Hebrew trust in divine protection from evil has repeatedly been tested throughout human history. Sadly humankind have themselves called forth violence, war and genocide—none condoned by God. Nor does history prove that humankind is congenitally evil. It is our savage, prehistoric subconscience that is responsible for these wholesale atrocities and disasters, not God.

Skeptics and cynics are, however, quick to point out that today's predators are germs--bacteria and viruses. Though we cannot see them with the naked eye, these microorganisms are able to kill us. Is not God accountable for them, for the disease and death they bring us?

The answer to this chilling question is "No." God is not guilty. His intention was not to create an ever-lasting Eden for humankind. Such threats to racial survival have always driven human evolution to find our purpose in the here and now.

All such challenges force us to come to terms with existence as it is. They require us to search out the meaning and reason for our life. Every creature has a purpose of its own and in the universal scheme of things. The individual is responsible for creating his or her own reason for being. That personal discovery leads one to decide one's destiny. Such self-understanding empowers the psyche with the creative genius to integrate our lives in the same way that God Himself overcame chaos to create and integrate the universe.

The ancient Hebrews believed their history was intricately connected with the process of creation. If God was responsible for our creation, He must also have been responsible for human evolution. Not only did God give all creatures and species the innate power to mutate and achieve degrees of self-perfection. To humankind, he gave the special potential to create its own future.

Is There a Cosmology Behind the Supraconscience of Humanity?

Tenets

1. God, the Supraconscience of the universe, is responsible for setting in motion the evolution of all species as well as that of humankind.
2. The essence and purpose of human evolution is self-realization and self-perfection.
3. God initiated evolution with the purpose of creating a species that could eventually grasp the significance of the universe.
4. Because the creative conscience of nature evolved all creatures through the connected processes of creation and integration, humankind evolved a finite creative conscience of its own.
5. Moreover, He gave humankind a purpose not only to perfect the self but through creativity to transcend the self. This meant humankind became capable of continually evolving a vaster perception and conception of a Supraconscience in Existence. Correspondingly this mental endeavor generated the evolution of humanity's own supraconscience.
6. While the history of humankind has demonstrated that our religious beliefs and faiths became incarnate in conscience, psyche has evinced periodic mental and moral degeneration. Such intermittent disintegration may occur when civilization becomes "too much for us". Perhaps such cyclical collapse is due to "burn out". The reasons

may be: our intelligence is still limited; our moral nature is yet poorly cultivated; our emotions are still unsure of what we are—species or human. Humanity can take just so much of religious obedience, disciplined behavior and otherworldly ideas before nature rebels and must express itself through instincts and passion.

7. At our stage of evolution, man's secular knowledge balances his religious beliefs and faith. But we can continue to expect periods of exhaustion, of rebellion, of surrender to flesh, bone, sinew and nerve. Yet one can anticipate renewal through our readiness to meet the Supreme Being's expectations of us. As an evolved species, we can be sure we have indeed been "chosen".

Theism and its Effect on the Human Psyche

To better understand the influence of theism on the cultural evolution of psyche, let us consider the significance of ancient Egypt's cosmology for human history.

In the ancient Near East, the human imagination created the gods and goddesses; they were thought to be responsible for the generation of life on earth. It was natural for the ancient mind to believe that a primal pair, male and female, generated all living things. These progenitors called into being other divinities to personify nature's many phenomena and processes.

If we translate this mythology into modern terms, we might interpret it as follows. It actually seems to describe the origin and history of human language.

First came the naming of individual things and entities (as mountains, rivers, trees, clouds, and animals of every kind). From that simple beginning came identification of the similarities and likenesses among living creatures (as grass-grazing animals, prey, predators). .In other words, from man's earliest use of intelligence, humankind organized their experiences into meaningful wholes. This was done intuitively and inductively. Over successive generations, the human mind connected impressions, identities and ideas to meld them into concepts.

The ancient Egyptians also believed all creatures were called to life out of the abyss called *Nun*. Psychologically speaking, we might say today that out of the abyss of the primitive mind there emerged the act of the creation of the world as humankind took to identifying what existed in it.

In other words, the original abyss conceived by the ancient Egyptians actually described the chaotic nature of the primitive mind. Fortunately, the actual brain is the neurological nexus of the human body, an intricate organic unity which coordinates and integrates the input of the senses. This body-mind integrity is the probable basis of the intuition that the earth itself is a symbiotic unity, called today a biosphere. Thus originally humankind may have sensed that existence embodied some totality of meaning--if it could but be comprehended. So perhaps, over hundreds of thousands of years, the oneness of our body-mind came to be identified with the wholeness and perfection of the universe.

Of particular interest to us in this connection is the ancient Egyptian image of a self-created father of all the gods. It is he who brought forth life out of the primeval waters. Thinking with his heart and commanding with his tongue, this father of all the gods created the earth and the cosmic order.[20]

Thus did the Creator *Ptah* conceive creation. Anthropologically speaking, the Creator- God was probably the first man or woman who used language by naming, identifying and describing things in the environment. The process required keenness of observation, intelligence, and imagination to name all that was seen, heard, tasted and felt. Moreover, the person was also able to discover the underlying relationships between all things, inert and living. Through the thousands of languages which eventually emerged among humankind, the first man or woman who used language re-created the world. How powerful the mind of the first human must have been who uttered sounds and turned them into words for all things seen, sensed and felt. Clearly the invention of language was the most remarkable manifestation of the mind's power to re-create the world into a cosmic system.

In ancient Egyptian lore, it is especially noteworthy that, whereas other gods created by physical means, *Ptah* created everything through thought and speech. By the Egyptian emulation of this creator, prayer became the way to share thoughts and feelings with Him. *Ptah* was the transcendent power over the earth. With time, the theology that centered on him faded because it was too abstract. During the Old Kingdom (Heliopolis c. 2380 B.C.), *Atum-Re* was the new self-created creator, who personified the sun and its powers.

One noteworthy fact about the conceptions of both *Ptah* and *Atum* is that it took an imaginative human genius to create them. These cosmic imaginings were based on the solid evidence of earthly phenomena and celestial observations. But at the same time, they were the result of people's own mental capacity for meaningful interpretation of experience. This realization of the potency of the human mind leads to further insights which are of value to modern man and woman.

Anyone—artist, writer, thinker, et al--who creates anything noteworthy, truthful, durable, or meaningful is, through his or her creations, genuinely creating a new Self. Such individuals are discovering latent capacities and transforming them into realities by actualizing their inborn powers. Such creativity is the primary way to convert an old self into a new one, shedding past immature identities, possibly past karmic lives. By so doing, the innovative individual emulates the evolutionary creativity in all nature and all humankind.

Hence the ancient Egyptian image of the self-creating god is rooted in both evolutionary fact and in psychologically sound cultural evidence.

It is also important to allude to the role of the Pharaoh. As mediator between Upper and Lower Egypt, he used his divine power to maintain order in this unified nation. In fact, he represented Maat, the female goddess who embodied divine justice. She dispelled disorder and re-established moral order in synchronization with the even measure evident throughout the universe.[21]

The need to restore order and morality reveals the age-old conflict between the primitive subconscience and the Homo sapiens conscience inherent in evolved cultures. Also, the role of the Pharaoh as power to guide the law and order of the land seems to prefigure or foreshadow the evolutionary role the supraconscience will play in human history.

In ancient Hermapolis, another Egyptian god was *Thoth*. As self-created God, he personified omniscience. His creative power came from his divine words. Over time, his thoughts became enduring wisdom. Finally, he became one of the judges of the dead.[22]

This imagined god would seem to be evidence that the human mind was awakening to its own innate powers. Moreover, *Thoth* left a record of the ancients' astonishment and awe at words which came from within humankind as if emanated from an indwelling spirit. Language itself seems the ultimate mystery of psyche. It is inexplicable how words rise up within us to express concealed feelings and buried thoughts. It is a kind of miracle that these consonants and vowels convey meaning from one person to another whether it be in ancient Egypt or across time to the twenty-first century.

In the New Kingdom, Thebes witnessed the absorption of earlier cosmogonies, including the incorporation of the earlier gods into the existing system of religious doctrine. Except during Akhenaton's time (1379-1362 B.C.), no single god had been worshipped until he briefly unified belief under the sun god, *Aton*.[23] The unification of gods under one symbol is significant. It is characteristic of the evolving human psyche to combine different beliefs and practices with the purpose of unifying and harmonizing divergent views and disagreements. The habit of syncretizing beliefs is a well-documented propensity of human nature.

In our age of specialization and fragmentation, there is a great need to integrate humankind's extensive secular knowledge and the mystical wisdom of its many religions. Given the diversity of races and religions on our planet, the pessimists among us are convinced there never can be unity among us. However, the cultures of the world need to educate one another in order to be able to prove our mutual good will and our readiness to learn from each other. In time, that commitment will erase much of the harm done in the past.

Under Amen-Re, Egyptian gods were collected into pantheons, with the Pharaoh being regarded as their incarnation. Hence the various gods, as various cosmic powers, came under the rule and guidance of the single human divinity.

However, after the overthrow and extermination of the monotheist sun worshipping religion that Akhenaton (Ikhnaton) had tried to establish, the old order was restored. Hence the old Egyptian gods were again the creative powers of the universe, but united under Maat's just and compassionate embrace. During Ikhnaton's reign, polytheism had been displaced by a monotheism, but after he died, the former polytheism was reinstated.[24]

This historical reflection on the ancient Egyptian mind reveals how the archetypal psyche can oscillate between two propensities--one toward divergence and variation (polytheism), and the other toward consolidation and integration (monotheism). Otherwise stated, psyche seems to alternate between the need for freedom of expression and the need for self-discipline as dictated by the conscience.

In any event, during Ikhnaton's time as Pharaoh, he undertook to transform the traditional polytheism of his culture into monotheism. Though he did not succeed in this, his vision of the ultimate cause of existence and life was a manifestation of the emerging supraconscience in the ancient world. On the other hand, the polytheistic mode of worshipping specific gods seemed to illustrate the growing need of psyche to discover its special powers.

Ancient Egyptian texts also spoke of the pharaoh as the son of the heavenly father. When the pharaoh died, he passed into a world of eternal bliss. Supposedly, this is the same blessedness later promised by Judaism, Christianity, and Islam. What does such assurance really mean? To visualize eternity as a realm of sensuous/sensual delights in a perfect paradise would seem a childish view of heaven and an immature understanding of Yahweh, God and Allah.

For individuals who have lived to the age of mature adulthood, the afterlife should bring other, more responsible pleasures such as guiding our descendants in any way we can. In the hereafter, the mature soul would find its greatest joy to be to help heal the loneliness, pain and suffering of those left behind in this all-too-real world. At times, life on earth can become unbearable for the living.

Let us remember the goddess Maat, who represented divine justice. The ancient Egyptians knew womankind as just and compassionate. We recall how the deceased's heart was weighed for its purity and innocence. The Egyptians understood the heart was the seat of emotions. Hence humankind was to be judged by their emotional honesty and wisdom. If this is correct, then a significant role for the soul to play in heaven would be to heal the sorrowful heart of loved ones still on earth.

The goddess Maat was an ancient example of humankind's intimation that a supraconscience with emotional wisdom would judge individuals for their humanity. Since their lives on earth had proved the eternal value of their soul, they should be allowed to guide and guard the living who remain there. That would be a wise reward.

Let us consider the effect of theism on the evolution of the human psyche. As we have seen, religion in ancient Egypt oscillated between polytheism and monotheism. Moreover, with the successive visions of *Ptah* as Creator, of *Atum* who personified the sun and its powers, and *Thoth* who personified conscience, we can trace a conceptual evolution of the idea of God. In actuality, ancient psyche was becoming aware of its own increasing powers. This itself is evidence that psyche was evolving toward supraconscience.

Furthermore, though the Egyptian recognized and worshipped the power of distinct gods, their collection into one pantheon was clear evidence of the transformation taking place in the communal psyche. Psyche's capacity to coalesce knowledge and experience was evidence it was evolving a superior comprehension of self. Yet, many more centuries would pass before psyche would be able to realize its own remarkable potentials. That would require psyche to teach itself how to evolve. It would take later monotheistic religions to accelerate the unification of psyche's evolving powers. Eventually, that would enable psyche to integrate its mystical experience, secular knowledge, and emotional acumen into a truly evolved supraconscience.

Ancient Judaism

The two chapters that follow present a secular interpretation of the Old Testament. Consequently, the last section of the present chapter limits itself to examining the influence of early Judaism on the evolution of the psyche.

The ancient Hebrews shared the pessimism of other peoples in the Middle East. The Hebrew *Sheol* was the abode of the dead where everyone went, either good and wicked.

In the *Book of Ecclesiastes* (X, 21) Job in his despair spoke of "the country of gloom and death's shadow." Yet, as final wisdom he counseled man to "enjoy life with the woman he loved—for there is neither work, nor thought, nor science, nor art--among the dead where you are going."

The idea of God evolved out of belief in a glorious future for the Jews who awaited a Messiah to conquer a corrupt world. They believed in the End of the World, the Last Judgment, a New Age, and the Resurrection of the Dead. They also believed in resurrection of the flesh and a blessed life for the righteous.

To the Israelites, conscience meant keeping the Commandments, being just, and acting righteously. Human life was sustained by law, by worship of Yahweh (Jehovah), and charity to kindred believers. Belief in the Deity meant they believed that one universal law must govern their lives. Thus they established a unified religious ethic in which moral perfection had become the ideal.

In psychological terms, as the idea of God developed, they were inspired by the omniscient wisdom in the Old Testament and a lifetime study of it. Hence, many dedicated their lives to all forms of scholarly knowledge. Gradually, from their religious history, they learned life had a plan and their destiny, a messianic hope. Thus monotheism positively affected their mental habits and stimulated their intellectual powers. Ever since the eighth century B.C.E., the prophets proclaimed that God was perfect in knowledge and wisdom. In a very real sense, this faith accelerated the early evolution of their communal psyche.

In fact, monotheism brings a distinct benefit to the human psyche. When sacred law assures the people of divine guidance, it can effect a profound conversion in people. It can transform hapless fatalism into confidence and trust in life. Ultimately, monotheism brings with it a conversion to the insight that life does have meaning. To accept divine order and law as a reality can transfigure an individual's despair into an enlightened comprehension of life's significance.

It is interesting to note how Hebrew Scripture can embrace contradictory interpretations of spiritual reality. One prophet warns that the enemies of God will not be brought back to life. But Daniel prophesied (XX,2) that "those who sleep in the dust will reawake—some to their eternal shame, some to a glorious eternal life."

Clearly, prophecies stir us to heed the wisdom of the ancients, even when they disagreed among themselves. They have learned bitter lessons from living

Myth, Ritual, Cosmologies and Theism 71

the untrue life. They have witnessed the effects of the subconscience in paranoid suspicions and in humankind's destructive passions. The evolving Hebraic conscience warned the sinful against shameful thoughts, unclean acts, and self-debasing compulsiveness.

By contrast, Yahweh's Commandments and the patriarch's wisdom inspired the dedicated Jew to obey the voice of his higher conscience. In terms of the thesis of this work, that superior consciousness would be considered evidence of humankind's evolving supraconscience.

So, gradually, as belief in the omniscience of the Almighty became absorbed into the culture, the sense of a human supraconscience gained recognition. The fact that Judaism could acknowledge that their people could be misled by inferior, unjust and immoral motives showed, in their superior and moral passions, how they as a people had matured ethically. As the millennia passed, their ethnic supraconscience accrued a lasting wisdom by which they were able to live resourcefully, sanely and sagely.

As expressed in scripture, the Hebrew concept of justice gave a metaphysical meaning to human justice. The certainty of God's punishment, as contrasted to the hope of eternal reward, inspired a deeper appreciation of the moral life. The consequences of human actions mattered in this world and in the eyes of the Almighty.

Since the Jewish people had suffered ostracism and injustice throughout the course of history, they not only learned to obey the dictates of communal conscience as defined by the Ten Commandments, but they began to evolve intellectually and mystically, to create a humanized conscience superior to the strictures of ancient law.

This took place most markedly when Rabbis revised the understanding of the abode of the dead, *Sheol*. Instead of endless punishment, they declared that some dead could expiate their imperfections their version of purgatory. Thereafter, the truly worthy could be resurrected to eternal happiness.

In terms of psychic evolution, both the influence of the vengeful subconscience and the damnation characteristic of testamental judgment were commuted by a more humane, compassionate conscience. The ancient severity softened in so far as it came to comprehend the frailties of the guilty and sinful. Punishment was no longer eternal.

The 'condemned' underwent a period of expiation and purification during which they made fit retribution for past acts of immorality. Once cured, they were fit to be in the presence of God. They could then know everlasting happiness.

The maturing of humankind's conscience is clear evidence of our gradual humanization. As we acquire tolerance and understanding of other cultures, our knowledge of humankind's psyche becomes truer and wiser. This transmutation of practical sense into moral wisdom is an essential characteristic of humankind's evolving supraconscience.

Along with this ethical evolution, there is still one more significant benefit of theism. In general, it expresses belief in one God as the source of life, man and the world. In His omnipotence, He is immanent in the world yet transcends it.

Hence His creative power transfuses each of us. It is the thesis of this book that humanity's evolution has been guided by the idea that God is omnipresent in human life. Along with this guidance, theism has taught us the exponential effect of concentrating all our mental powers on a specific goal in pursuit of a worthy lifetime purpose. Such lifelong commitment makes possible the incarnation of an individual's supraconscience.

Notes

1. James, E.O., *The Ancient Gods*, p. 160.
2. Ibid.
3. James, p. 166.
4. Ibid.
5. James, p. 198.
6. Hadot, P., *La Fin du Paganism*, p. 87.
7. James, pp. 267-68.
8. James, p. 237.
9. Ibid.
10. James, pp. 211-12.
11. James, pp. 261-62.
12. James, p. 263.
13. Ch. 125.
14. James, p. 266.
15. James, p. 174.
16. James, p. 272.
17. James, p. 273.
18. James, p. 309.
19. James, p. 150.
20. James, p. 201.
21. James, p. 204.
22. James, p. 205, 261
23. James, p. 302
24. James, p. 109

Chapter Four

Four Archetypes of the Emerging Supraconscience

A Brief Introduction

Four archetypes prefigure the emergence of humanity's supraconscience. They have been effective throughout European cultural history.

Archetype One was bequeathed to modern man by ancient Greek tragedy. The ideal of *sōphrosynē* (moderation, temperance, inner harmony and balance) influenced European education for twenty-three centuries.[1]

Archetype Two is expressed by the metaphor the "great chain of being", which taught one hundred generations of philosophers, theologians and thoughtful individuals that three eternal conditions of nature explain the world of Being. The nineteenth century theory of evolution supplemented the three principles of Being by re-interpreting existence as a process of Becoming. Hence in actuality, archetype two embodies four principles which together epitomize the cohesion, vital energy, and measured transformation of life on earth.[2]

Archetype Three analyzes four levels of meaning that Scripture can teach us. These significant dimensions of Holy Writ encourage the individual to search his experiences for guidance in regard to his destiny. The Bible may be understood at four levels: 1) the literal or historical, 2) the allegorical or metaphorical, 3) the moral, and 4) the mystical. A person can live at any of these levels or all four simultaneously. This third archetype can educate each of us to seek the deeper significance of life.

Archetype Four focuses our feelings and beliefs about the Divinity. Historically, the concept has affected humankind's evolution; it still exerts a great influence on the modern psyche. Our human understanding of the Supreme Being has had an enduring effect on our self-image and the self-realizations we are capable of in a lifetime.

Indeed, a modern conception of God as the supraconscience of the universe urges us to transform and perfect our lives. That omniscient Being empowers each of us to pursue self-knowledge and self-integration in so far as we emulate the Omnipotent. Throughout human history, the archetype of the divinity has nurtured the finite supraconscience of our species as evinced in our creation of magnificent cultures and civilizations.

In sum, the four archetypes provide four world views that enable us to come to terms with the ultimate meaning of our experience. Knowledge of the true significance of each archetype can positively affect that outcome of an individual's destiny. Though the four archetypes came to be part of the human heritage in past centuries, they still have the power to teach us the wisdom of the ages.

Archetype One
Sōphrosynē

In ancient Greece, *sōphrosynē* referred to a sound-minded man who acted in accordance with his nature or basic character. In Homer's epic *Odyssey*, Odysseus and Penelope were used as examples of *sōphrosynē* in man and woman. Odysseus was the model Greek hero: resourceful, adventurous, courageous. His wife Penelope was faithful to him for almost two decades of their separation.

In the archaic age of Ancient Greece, *sōphrosynē* became part of the moral of Delphi: "Know thyself", "Nothing in excess", and "Think mortal thoughts."

Hybris versus *Sōphrosynē*

To the ancient Greek, the original term *hybris* (hubris) meant "excessive pride" or "insolence" in one's conduct. It inevitably called for retribution. Greek tragedy dwelt on the tragic consequences of inborn fault. An example of its power is Aeschylus' trilogy the *Oresteia* (458 B.C.E.). It is the gruesome story of a cursed family and a fatal sequence of acts of retribution carried out by descendents of the House of Atreus.

The blood feud began after a bitter quarrel between Atreus and his brother Thyestes. As an act of revenge, Atreus killed his brother's children and fed their flesh to him at a banquet. In turn, the son of Atreus, King Agamemnon was betrayed and murdered by his wife Queen Clytemnestra for having sacrificed their daughter Iphigenia to gain fair winds for the Greek fleet sailing to Troy. Urged on by his sister Electra, Orestes avenges his father by murdering his own mother Clytemnestra and her lover Aegisthus. Orestes is then hounded by the Furies for his matricide. Finally, the goddess Athena frees .him and ends the curse.

The story reveals how an original *hybris* infected the descendants of the House of Atreus and delineates its fatal consequences: crime for crime, body for body, thus demonstrating the awesome power of fate.

From this tragedy, we learn that *hybris* is an act of transgression against a moral law due to arrogance, extreme vanity or passion. Often it is accompanied by *hamartia*, blindness to the consequences of one's actions or blindness to one's effect on others.

Characteristic of tragedy over the millennia, *hybris* is often the mark of a superior person with a 'tragic flaw', some trait which involves him inextricably in a situation from which there is no escape. Despite his fatal predicament, the hero fights to free himself and refuses to submit to his fate. Faced with either moral disintegration or death, he achieves a moral victory by coming to terms with his own destiny.

The reader immediately recognizes the primeval source of the tragic hero's basic temperament. Primitive man often found himself trapped in situations that tested his ability to survive. His reaction called forth both heroic courage and the need to hero's basic temperament. Primitive man often found himself trapped in situations that tested his ability to survive. His reaction called forth both heroic courage and the need to control emotions while exploring his chances of escaping death. Often he was stalked by camouflaged predators or enemies who plotted against him. Any blindness to the true intentions of others or to the consequences of his own arrogance ensnared him in a self-made web of fatal delusions. In a sense, the tragic figure represents the primitive subconscience torn between paranoia as to whom to trust and blindly slaying anyone whom he suspects of disloyalty or deceit.

Of course, the ancient Greek of the seventh century B.C.E. was already evolved beyond our progenitors millennia earlier. Nevertheless, the human psyche was still at a stage when it easily lost control of its more reflective nature. After all, in the past, the life instinct and rush of emotions had often rescued it from death.

The tragedies of Sophocles (5th cent. B.C.E.) also dramatized the need to understand self and others in realistic terms. Heroes as Ajax, Antigone, Oedipus and Electra were blind to their innermost nature. His tragedies demonstrated that ignorance of self could prove lethal—fate ended life in ignominy. Such plays pitted the hero's emotional integrity against his emotional excesses. They show us high-born individuals unable to obey the dictates of traditional conscience, the innate principle which secured a measure of justice among humankind.

With the tragedies of Euripides (4th cent. B.C.E.), tragedy focused on the conflict between the rational and irrational. Even an excess of chastity must be controlled by moderation and all human actions needed to be tempered by wisdom.

So, ancient Greek tragedy illustrates how that culture had grown conscious of the danger of impulsive decisions and rash actions. They could bring about the destruction of the proud and eminent. Excessive emotions and conscious of the danger of impulsive decisions and rash actions. They could bring about the destruction of the proud and eminent. Excessive emotions and uncontrolled passions--erupting from humankind's primeval subconscience could become life-threatening and drive even the strongest psyche to a breaking point.

Thus, in essence, the lesson taught by tragedy was *sōphrosynē,* the avoidance of immoderate or unsound behavior.

The Greek philosopher Plato (428-348 B.C.E.) made *sōphrosynē* a central virtue in his thinking about morality. In his dialogues, he portrayed Socrates as a man of self-knowledge, self-control, and independence of thought. Plato himself believed virtue was illustrated by the orderly harmony of the soul's faculties. In *Republic,* Book IV, he defines these virtues as courage, temperance, justice and wisdom. They exerted a positive influence on moral education for the next two millennia. By achieving a balance among them, either the individual man or society as a whole could maintain equipoise and inner harmony.

By pledging ourselves to act in keeping with such virtues, we not only acknowledge the sentient truths of antiquity. We also affirm our faith in the capacity of humankind to evolve a sound and superior conscience.

In the 4th century B.C.E., Aristotle sought to define *sōphrosynē* with greater precision. To do so, he established the golden mean between the extremes of excess and defect. Similar to Plato's sense of the just measure required to reach moral decisions, Aristotle defined the concept as the capacity to avoid sensuous pleasures and sexual excesses. In his *Rhetoric*, he declared that *hybris* must be opposed by moderation and temperance.

The Epicureans of the Hellenistic period pursued hedonistic pleasures but also advocated self-restraint and emotional calm as the highest good. Hellenists pursued intellectual pleasures as they took them to be superior to short-lived sensualism. By contrast to this, the Stoics advocated near complete detachment from pleasure and intellectual pleasures as they took them to be superior to short-lived sensualism. By contrast to this, the Stoics advocated near complete detachment from pleasure and pain, thus teaching self-discipline and composure.

Of special interest is the Roman author Cicero, who believed that *sōphrosynē* was a human instinct for order, decorum, and reasonableness. He believed in the individual's worth, dignity, and potential for self-realization.

Hence, since Greco-Roman antiquity, humankind has nurtured not only a sober and sound psyche but also a superior conscience in its aptitude for defining viable truths about human nature. Thus the story of psyche turns out to be an Ariadne thread which runs through the labyrinth of humankind's moral history.

As Christian apologists came to define their own system of virtues--purity, chastity, sobriety, and self-denial, they became more tolerant of the wisdom inherent in paganism. The early Church Fathers came to understand that *sōphrosynē* aptly applied to the asceticism required in the struggle of good against evil.[3]

Proper development of conscience became a two-fold responsibility. First, it meant avoidance of evil because it brought self-destruction and damnation. Second, a good conscience made possible self-integration and the realization of the good life.

Thus, in sum, *sōphrosynē* taught the need for self-knowledge and self-mastery. From the general notions of balance, harmony and moderation, the ancients extracted the four leading virtues of pagan antiquity (courage, temperance, justice, and wisdom). In time these coalesced into the Pauline virtues (faith, hope and charity) to guide the moral evolution of Western humanity over the centuries.

Nevertheless, self-control and self-mastery were repeatedly challenged by the primeval instincts deep in the human psyche. In the Christian era, seven vices challenged the seven virtues for Nevertheless, self-control and self-mastery were repeatedly challenged by the primeval instincts deep in the human psyche. In the Christian era, seven vices challenged the seven virtues for dominance. In one's soul, the struggle between good and evil would decide one's destiny in eternity.

Archetype Two
The Great Chain of Being

Archetype two identifies the processes of animate nature which explain all life: Being and Becoming. These universal phenomena sustain and energize all existence. Moreover, three principles *plenitude, continuity* and *gradation* describe the substance and spirit of our world. In essence, their value is in their capacity to teach us how to live sensibly, creatively, and morally. These principles also make clear how the concepts of Being and Becoming epitomize humankind's understanding of our world as a living entity.

The Principle of Plenitude

The ancient Greek philosopher Plato saw the created world as self-sufficient but also able to initiate its own activities and processes. In addition to regarding it as self-sufficient and perfect, he perceived the universe as self-transcending. This latter process accounted for the multitude and variety of earth's life forms--each realizes its own potentiality for being. To Neo-Platonists, the world emanated from the Godhead; hence God's presence in the universe explained the self-transcending power of life itself.

The idea of plenitude underwent various interpretations in centuries subsequent to the time of Plotinus. Late Medieval Christian writers found that God's love consisted in the creative and generative rather than in promising deliverance from evil or intervening in human affairs. Moreover, Saint Thomas Aquinas believed the universe was its own reason for being and not "merely a means of man's salvation".

In other words, important Church figures intended that each individual discover his own reason for being. Moreover, each person is fully responsible for his or her own life. Each individual must confront the evil in the world by relying on his or her own strengths. Each discovers his own reason for being. Moreover, each person is fully responsible for his or her own life. Each
individual in his capacity must confront the evil in the world. Each should undertake to relieve humanity's suffering. These truths were taught to us by the powers of reason that God implanted in us.

Moslem and Jewish Medieval thinkers also espoused the idea of plenitude. God had not only created all life forms. His presence also assured that the principia of perfection and ultimate justice would eventually reign. These truths human reason also embraced.

The Principle of Continuity

Aristotle introduced the principle of continuity into natural history. His *De Anima* suggested a natural aristocracy--all living beings were to be understood as arranged on a natural scale according to their degree of perfection, their powers of soul. However, he surmised that some organisms have not yet realized their potential and others might already exist at superior levels of being.

Two millennia later, the 18th century philosopher, J.B. Robinet, recommended that this classification of creatures be supplanted because human reason itself failed to see life as a continuity. Indeed, he proposed that nature was manifestly "striving toward a particular goal via trial and error toward a consummation not clearly foreseen." Moreover, he averred that the fundamental reality of nature was not matter, but activity. Clearly he not only anticipated the 19th century theory of evolution (Darwin), but also 20th century quantum theory.

To be sure, implicit in visualizing nature and life as a continuity is the assumption that animate nature is teleological, where teleology is the conviction that natural processes are directed toward an end or shaped by a purpose.[4] If nature's designs display perfect adaptations to their environment, this must mean that life forms possess their own powers of self-transformation and self-realization.

How does this self-evident fact of nature apply to mankind? Granted that the biogenetic evolution of our species has made us capable of survival. We have clearly benefitted from nature's powers of powers of creativity and integration. However, in spite of the fact that we have created remarkable societies, cultures and civilizations, all too often "we lay waste our powers" (Wordsworth).

In other words, individual members of our race fail to develop themselves so as to gain greater control of their own lives. Seldom do we conscientiously develop skills to promote the realization of our own genuine talents and aptitudes. Rarely do we attempt to pursue an ultimate goal in life. And, when we neglect to create our own destiny, we fail the second principle of nature--continuity, i.e. self-fulfillment.

The Principle of Gradation

Aristotle introduced a third principle in nature. Contrary to the rational classification of creatures, he made clear that nature's fluidity was beyond distinct lines of demarcation. He also envisioned a hierarchical order of organisms starting with our rational nature and extending to levels of being superior to man. As zoologist, he had classified plants and animals, yet he also studied organisms for their ontogenetic differences, which, to him, seemed to imply a hierarchy of intelligence in nature.

Neo-Platonic cosmology conceived nature as self-transcending due to the power emanating from the divine mind. Thus it proposed that all animate beings were impelled by a life force, spirit or intelligence and this force accounted for the many transformations evident throughout nature. By the Renaissance, the principles of continuity and gradation in biology played a decisive role in understanding nature as evincing a state of Being with an eternal potential for Becoming.

But do these three principles have any psychological significance for modern man and woman? The first principle, *plenitude,* offers us a very basic type of wisdom. Above and beyond biological gratification, we should undertake to enjoy a range and variety of life experiences.

The second principle, *continuity*, advises us to discover what our experiences in life have meant. They should reveal our basic character as it transcended itself in successive stages in life. These traits foreshadow our potential for creating a future of our own.

And what experiences in life have meant. They should reveal our basic character as it transcended itself in successive stages of life. These traits foreshadow our potential for creating a future of our own.

And what does the principle of *gradation* teach us? If nature is both evolutionary and teleological, how are we to understand the various stages of life? Clearly our own life is a continual process of transformation as we grow up, mature, and, with luck, grow wise.

Up to a certain period, the greater the number of years with a sound mind and sound body, the longer the perspective in time and the clearer our focus. At this stage, we are aware of what we have become. We have pursued goals, endured conflicts, and experienced both successes and failures. Yet at midlife we may come to realize we have not yet found our purpose. It seems like it should be more important, nobler, more meaningful than anything we have done thus far. The approach of death— even though it may yet be distant—challenges us to come to terms with the meaning of our lives and of life itself.

In sum, what does 'the great chain of being' teach us? One interpretation of it might be that it shows us how knowledge is to be gained and life is to be lived. By integrating what we have learned and know, we can better integrate ourselves as human beings. If reality is ultimately one, the individual should undertake to unify his or her life through work with some significance. More broadly speaking, we should seek to link our lives more completely and perfectly with other members of humankind. After all, all humanity taken together makes up a greater chain of being.

The metaphor "great chain of being" has been interpreted in diverse ways over successive generations of thinkers. Some understand its metaphysical meaning whereas others see it as referring to the intricate bonds between humankind. Others considered it the way the mind relates theoretical knowledge and practical experience. Still others want a simple, concise dictionary definition.

But metaphors transcend dictionary definitions. In the end, history reveals that the 'great chain of being' has transformed our perception of reality. Indeed, the evolution of the human mind depends on our But metaphors transcend dictionary definitions. In the end, history reveals that the "great chain of being" has transformed our perception of reality. Indeed, the evolution of the human mind depends on our progressive perception of this world as it, too, is perpetually undergoing transformation. Being and Becoming describe our somatic and genetic evolution, our cerebral and spiritual transfiguration.

We all need to both be and to become. We need to unite our various life experiences and share our wisdom. In this new millennium, it would seem the future is calling humanity to become a new species.

Thus, archetype two urges us to find greater meaning in our personal life by studying the sum and substance of our cultures and civilizations. The metaphor encourages us to discover our purpose so as to better integrate ourselves. The archetype of Being and Becoming teaches each of us to choose a meaningful destiny of our own.

Archetype Three
The Bible: Four Levels of Significance

A conscientious reading of the Bible makes us aware that there are different levels on which it can be understood. Of course, we first attempt to grasp the literal and historical sense of it, particularly the *Book of Revelation*. At the very least, contemporary knowledge of the Old and New Testaments has provided us with the substantial evidence of what is historical fact.

Yet, the stories of the prophets and of holy figures are aglow with surreal accounts of their legendary and mystical lives. These personages express symbolic truths about ancient human experience. Some interpreters regard these figura as expressing allegorical verities greater than literal truth. It seems that the psyche of antiquity was confronted by experiences of greater spiritual intensity than those undergone by people in any previous time period.

To be sure, Biblical stories, events and preaching underscored moral lessons to be learned by common folk. The lessons reminded them that life offered wisdom, and scriptural accounts revealed God's real presence in human life.

Then again, implicit in events of this era were spiritual meanings beyond mundane reality, common understanding and down-to-earth reasoning. These sacred accounts of prophecy and visionary experiences seemed to open direct communion with ultimate reality, and so establish the immanence of God through heightened human intuition and deepened insight.

If studied with an open mind, scripture should awaken even the skeptic to the fact that life itself can be experienced on a deeper level–and thought about with a measure of awe. When it is interpreted as a source of lessons in life, scripture teaches us that our lives can be understood in either an *exoteric* or *esoteric* sense, or ultimately as a guide to realizing a plan for life. In brief, we can live life pragmatically and without imagination; we can live life creatively and reasonably; we can persistently seek out life's moral lessons; or, if we are so gifted and inclined, we can search for the mystical significance of existence. We begin to do so when we sense that our finite life has been created by some infinite, ineffable power in the universe.

In any event, it is the individual's decision whether to realize his destiny solely in realistic, down-to-earth ways, or to live a superficial, uncommitted life deriving pleasure entirely from social success. This would be the exoteric life exclusively given over to appearances.

However, most of us cannot escape our inner feelings and experiences. Our more private thoughts and secret musings tell us life has a deeper meaning, one that needs to find expression. With age and maturity, the mysteries and paradoxes of existence usually provoke in one the need to search for a personal, esoteric understanding of life's purpose. Hence, the need for a life plan. A person who makes such a commitment seeks greater maturity by reading scripture for its various levels of meaning. And, reading scripture at different stages of life may prepare the adept to comprehend how its spheres of significance reveal the supraconscience of humankind.

Actually, the Bible is to be read on four levels or spheres of significance:

At the literal or historical level, it gives an account of events in the Middle East that can, to an extent, be verified by documents, archeological research, and reliable accounts from credible witnesses. Obviously, if we were to review our own life as an autobiography, we would have to distinguish facts and real experiences from the gaps and distortions of memory. An honest assessment of what really happened would be the only way to write it.

However, unlike the journalist's notation of who, what, when, where, and how things happened, you realize that you have experienced other emotional dimensions usually undetected by those around you. Sometimes, you are a mystery to everyone but yourself. There are your private dreams, deeper feelings and hunger for recognition. This may be your psyche's way of living an adventurous or legendary life and where even the supernatural may have its place.

If one wishes to seek out moral lessons by turning inward, one might find in life's experiences analogical-allegorical truths that mock common sense or stolid reason. Though your mind knows perfectly well that you are fantasizing, it gives you great pleasure to indulge your imagination in this way. It is the child in all of us still hoping life is play. Or, metaphors may well up from archaic memory to enlighten you and guide you to a more meaningful destiny.

Then again, life may confront you with accidents or events that hurt or shock you by facing you with death. Your heart and mind may be plunged into the murky reality of the violence, viciousness, and senselessness that marks everyday life.

Harsh psychic experiences educate everyone to reality. They dramatize the ultimate truth: one day your own life will end. It is perhaps then that scripture's deeper levels of meaning impress upon us their ageless wisdom.

One comes to realize life should not be lived exclusively in the mundane, work-a-day world. There are profounder dimensions to life. Spiritual and symbolic truths haunt us. Indeed, one's biography might be summed up with a metaphor: as an adventure, a journey, a challenge, a revelation as to life's significance. For some, one's life is represented by an amulet or religious symbol worn around the neck as a sign of the zodiac, an ankh, a star of Solomon, or a Christian cross.

On the matter of symbols, let us consider for a moment the Torah, the Bible, and the Holy Qur'an. Each holy book requires the individual's commitment to a religion and a moral philosophy. Such dedication demands further self-education. If one is to plumb the exoteric and esoteric truths which these books have made accessible to mankind, one begins, in one's innermost being, a search for the sacred.

In sum, the three salvation religions teach that the books dedicated to Yahweh, God or Allah reveal how life is to be lived in all its dimensions. Through embracing the sapience of these religions, our kind became more fully human.

Whenever our ancestors and forebears lived a life committed to one of these faiths, their commitment aided them in integrating their lives and facing death with composure. Wherever secular man and woman open themselves to the sage judgments of venerable writings, they often discover dimensions of esoteric meaning long neglected by our pragmatic modern civilization, truths which can heal the anxiety and malaise of a life lived without wisdom.

The Exoteric versus Esoteric Dimensions of Scripture

The surface, *exoteric* meaning of Scripture is often at odds with its deeper, *esoteric* significance. The exoteric indicates the factual, literal and exterior sense, whereas the esoteric is the interior, figurative, spiritual truth.

The physical body may show us the appearance of a person, but the inner reality is a confluence of intuitions, emotions and passions. Scripture appears as words in a book which are part of the real, material world. But within that physical reality, the Word suggests multiple, momentous meanings.

To the devout, the Word intimates the invisible Presence of Yahweh, God or Allah. In every letter, word, metaphor, proverb, psalm and story, the Supreme Being makes Itself known. Through the pages of Biblical revelations and Koranic suras, there radiates an Infinite Reality, one which underlies the finite reality we take to be real.

A special communion develops between the reader and the text, between humankind today and the unforgotten men and women of thousands of years ago who sensed and witnessed the visible/invisible presence of the Supreme Being of the universe.

Let us not forget those astounding experiences were recorded by men and women of flesh and blood, individuals swept up by a power beyond ordinary, earth-bound imagination. It is important to bear in mind that our ancestors had impassioned natures as well as emotional intelligence. The scribes who recorded the events of the lives of their kinsmen and the fates of the prophets were the ancestors who emerged stronger and wiser from the tragedies they lived through. Thus they learned the deeper significance of human destiny from the direct experience of the divine.

In short, the esoteric dimension of meaning is vaster and deeper, more intimate and sacred than any literal or historically accurate reading could possibly be.

Despite the self-acclaimed superiority of fundamentalist, literal explanations of Holy Scripture, the intuitive, esoteric explanation of the hidden sense of a holy text is motivated by an equally sincere, but more humane wisdom.

When reading Scripture closely, if we are to fathom its concealed significance, to extract the sacred from the profane, we need to shed our conceit that we know how to read prose well. Rather, we need to uncover and to recover the emotional intuition and intelligence of our spiritual ancestors, to feel what they must have felt when they recorded the presence of the Omnipotent.

As modern skeptics, scientists and humanists grow in intuitive intelligence, the mystery and majesty of ancient texts can begin to reveal important Truths for our time. Accumulated human knowledge and contemporary science reveal that the Almighty actually is the *Supraconscience* that pervades the world. It is the inwardly attuned man and woman who are still searching for a higher meaning to human destiny who will discover that humankind possess a finite supraconscience that is able to commune with the infinite supraconscience of existence.

Often readers think of themselves as realists. They are eager to scoff at the suggestion that the esoteric meaning of things is of any practical, secular worth. However, a brief look at what modern man trusts the most, namely, numbers, may enlighten him as to their historical, cultural meanings. Perhaps this purview will disabuse some readers of the popular conviction that numbers deal solely with empirical reality. Generally, ever since Pythagoras (6th cent. B.C.E.), innovative thinkers have used numbers to surpass the confines of factual reality, rather than to limit themselves to it.

Throughout history, numerologists have sought out the connections between quantity and quality, between number and the numinous. Through such orientation, mystics studied how abstract knowledge, rooted in number and quantity, might relate to or conjoin with spiritual experience of the sacred. Mystics believed humankind **was** being guided toward an eschatological destiny. They undertook to transmute the cryptic in the Holy Writ into a deciphered eternal truth from God.

Though the modern reader may think such numerology is largely superstitious nonsense, let us briefly take account of numbers as used in everyday language in contrast to their use in religious explication.

Why do we speak of the four seasons in nature, four cardinal directions to the world, four corners of the earth, four celestial angles (sunrise, sunset, zenith, nadir), and four seasons of life? Biblically speaking, there were four rivers around Eden, four branches of the Cross, four great Old Testament prophets and four sacred figures (the angel, the bull, lion and eagle) associated with the four evangelists.

Furthermore, there are four parts to the New Testament: the Gospels, the Epistles, the Acts, and the Apocalypse and the four basic materials used in rituals--wine, oil, water and bread. As the reader now knows, the Bible itself is susceptible to four meanings: the historical or literal sense, 2) the allegorical, 3) the moral, and 4) the mystical/spiritual.

Then there are seven deadly sins (pride, envy or malice, wrath, lust, gluttony, avarice and sloth). There are also seven virtues, i.e., the four cardinal virtues from pagan antiquity (justice, temperance, courage and wisdom) plus the three Christian virtues (faith, hope and charity).

Christ spoke seven words on the Cross "My God, Why have You Forsaken Me?" There are seven holy sacraments (baptism, penance, the Eucharist, confirmation, ordination, matrimony, and extreme unction). In the Apocalypse, there were seven series of virtues. The angel spoke seven words to the Virgin; the gifts of the Holy Spirit are said to be seven. Jesus manifested the power of God by seven miraculous events. The number seven is the symbol of eternal life, and there are seven sacramental paths of initiation to that life.

Similarly, the number twelve has Judaic and Christian associations. There are twelve minor prophets subordinated to Isaiah, Jeremiah, Ezekiel, and Daniel. Twelve patriarchs are matched by twelve apostles in the New Testament. The Mass has twelve parts, etc. Hence it would seem that numbers have been used allegorically throughout the history of Western civilization.[5]

Though numbers obviously bring precision to secular knowledge (mathematics, engineering, science), religion has also used them to give Scriptural wisdom a superior logic and orderliness.[6]

In the guise of allegorical virtues and vices as well as theological ideals, numbers helped fix the meanings of truths considered sacred. Through them, seemingly irrational beliefs and states of ecstasy were given a semblance of rationality and order. Reason was needed to discover and conform one's life to the divine order of existence: If we, as mortals, wished to find eternal truths, numbers seemed to bring us closer to an understanding of eternity.

Though they were used for mystical purposes, numbers may simply seem evidence of human superstition, yet numbers represent real things and phenomena in the material world and are an important stage of man's developing skill in abstraction. Moreover, abstractions as ideas, ideals, theories and concepts are the basis of humankind's present day knowledge.

Much of the history of religion has been given over to offering rational arguments, developing theologies, and presenting philosophies to explain the ineffable. The ingenious use of numbers in the past has been supplanted by their universal use today as a means for claiming that all things human can be explained by surveys, charts, equations, patterns and progressions of all sorts. One wonders how long it will be till mathematicians learn to formulate a scientific theory describing the essence of the Supreme Being.

Consider what mathematics means today. It is, by definition, "a science of numbers and their operations, inter-relations, combinations, generalizations, and abstractions, and of space configurations and their structure, measurement, transformation and generalization."[7] Consider as well symbolic logic, a "science of developing and representing logical principles by means of a formalized system *consisting of primitive symbols*, combination of these symbols, axioms, and rules of inference.[8] It is noteworthy that the words number and numinous have a common linguistic origin.

It would seem the secular sciences have for centuries been preparing the psyche to visualize the Supreme Being not only as an abstraction in human form, but as a scientific reality.

How disrespectful would it be to humankind's self-image and to religious traditions to alter our anthropomorphic vision of God as our Father in heaven? (The idea of a paternal power was comforting to many in the past.)

However, we no longer refer to the earth as Mother Nature, as colorful and respectful as the metaphor is meant to be. Instead, today we speak of the planet's ecology and of the biosphere. Biology and evolutionary biology in particular have shown us that nature contains within it the powers of self-creation and integration; and in human nature these account in part for the evolution of our psyche/mind. So the sciences tend to demystify body and soul by revealing the structure of the innermost processes of our being and becoming. We are learning to discard appearances for inner realities; to unveil matter to be, in essence, atomic energy; to disclose the solid, eternal earth as a sphere of molten magma and shifting tectonic plates which cause continents to drift across the globe over billions of years. The inner reality of the physical world is not fixed and static as believed over the millennia. It is dynamic and self-evolving.

An intelligent interpretation of divinity would be intimately co-related to the human psyche as it evolved along with the cultures and civilizations it created. Human evolution demonstrates that we have, in effect, been aspiring to the omniscience we have historically attributed to God. Indeed, though mankind is inspired by the emotional intelligence at the heart of religion, man's secular nature has co-evolved with our religious intuition of the Deity. Consequently, the human psyche has transformed itself, inspired not only by the appeal of God's omniscience, but also by the creation of secular knowledge, science and wisdom.

Indeed, over the past twenty-five centuries, humankind has been evolving a *finite supraconscience*. We are at the threshold of a New Revelation. We are now able to envision the universe as empowered and evolving by the grace of a *cosmic supraconscience*.

Thus esoteric numbers, images and symbols not only retrace the evolution of our cognitive and emotional intelligence. They show how we have undertaken to fathom the supraconscience that created and integrated our physical universe.

But, practically speaking, at the most basic level, what does this identification of humankind with the *supraconscience* mean? Perhaps we are now beginning to sense the purpose behind our evolution. All along we have been learning to consolidate our instincts, intuitions, forms of reasoning and spiritual aspirations into a single vision of life. The psyche's purpose has come to be establish and integrate body and mind, personality and character, religion and philosophy.

The real aim of our cultures and civilizations has not been exclusively to survive, but to acquire knowledge and wisdom useful to the future of humanity. However, all that our species has thus far accomplished has been to enable the individual to realize the fulfillment of his or her personal supraconscience. By conscientiously developing one's talents, intelligence and noble ambitions, the human being can do this.

In the end, each individual defines who he or she is by achieving what was truly possible in a lifetime. Each age defines its own supraconscience by its works, by leaving behind evidence of its emotional intelligence, and by providing the future with some wisdom to live by.

So, archetype three demonstrates, how the exoteric and esoteric dimension of psyche and existence reveal, in the end, one reality and one eternal Truth. By perfecting one's finite supraconscience, we become worthy of communion with the Supraconscience that created us.

Archetype Four
The Divinity

The Divinity, the Symbol and its Signification by the French psychologist Paul Diel explains archetype four according to his *theory of motivation*. The Foreword of his work makes clear that Diel's discussion of the *superconscious* and the *subconscious* differs from Freud's use of these key terms. For Diel, superconscious refers to metaphysical images in myths, which symbolize the Divinity. He regards images and symbols as the means by which psyche functions.

For him, conscience is logical and conceptual. By contrast, the unconscious is instinctive and automatic because it derives from our animal nature. The subconscious expresses exalted imaginings which are beyond the scope of our real experiences in the material world.

Diel's conception of the superconscious is that, as a consequence of its evolution, it pursues one essential desire in life. It thereby stands in sharp contrast to the usual, senseless chase after multiple exalted desires. Because superconscious and subconscious are antithetical to each other, interaction between them occurs in symbolic terms. For Diel, the superconscious is realized when the essential desire effects inner harmony and when the superconscious is idealized by the symbol of the Divinity. Otherwise, these psychic functions are in conflict.

The metaphysical terror evoked by the mystery of life and death rouses the essential desire to give life a sensible direction. As creator and judge, the Divinity rewards and punishes mankind. In general, divinities represent the laws of life and teach us our authentic responsibility. However, God as Supreme Being is the ultimate law.

For Diel, also, whereas the subconscious victimizes the human psyche, the superconscious positively energizes and integrates intuitions, ideas, and moral values. Specifically, vanity is the mother of all vices since it leads to all psychological excesses. It can frustrate the influence of the superconscious by turning our lives into a banality. Hence through psychic self-integration, we can be victorious over vanity—and therein lies our salvation.

In the Biblical *Book of Genesis*, Diel avers that humanity sinned in not meeting God's expectation of total obedience to His will. Thus we often think, in symbolic terms, that God rewards and punishes us, but in reality, the psyche as superconscious rewards our obedience or punishes us for succumbing to the subconscious. Only when we learn to integrate these two aspects of our being can we overcome evil. If we succumb to it, we are punished for allowing our life to become a banality.

Diel believes Jesus' message of love for all humankind can overcome egocentricism. Jesus' resurrection made it possible for us to purge and purify ourselves from the senseless, vain and subhuman. In this way, salvation can be attained in this lifetime—thus the Gospel's message of joy.

In Diel's view, the devil as a symbol represents lies, false promises, and sexual perversions. Any attempt to destroy faith in any spiritual meaning to life is also the work of the devil. In Christ's temptation in the desert, the devil is the subconscious that tries to seduce the superconscience of an evolved, noble soul. Moreover, Diel sees the theological notions of Heaven-Earth-Hell as corresponding to the psyche's superconscious, conscious, and subconscious. Light and dark symbolize the psyche's superconscious and subconscious.

He believes a person can find salvation by devoting all his energy to the essential desire of his life. Such devotion can give conversion a new meaning in life. Rather than God providing salvation, it is our commitment to grasp and appreciate the full implications of human evolution that saves us from ourselves.

Unfortunately, the preceding paragraphs are just a brief sampling of the rich complexity of Diel's thought as worked out in *Divinity*. A good deal of his intricate reasoning has, of necessity, been omitted here for the sake of brevity. Nevertheless, this brief account attempts to demonstrate the depths of insight into the human predicament that is made possible by interpretation of the scriptures in light of cultural psychology. Semi-consciously, when we draw upon the wisdom of cultures, we accelerate the evolution of our humanization.

(We now pass beyond Diel's psychological interpretation of the Divinity. It should be noted that all of his references to superconscious, conscious, and subconscious are markedly different from the terms *supraconscience, conscience,* and *subconscience* used in this work.)

The *Supraconscience* interprets the Divinity not in anthropomorphic terms, but rather as an ideal which permeates psyche and guides mankind toward the acquisition of wisdom. In effect, as the Idea of the Supreme Being became better understood, humankind's anxieties and fears became transformed into greater mutual trust and compassion. If the supreme virtue of God is His infinite emotional intelligence, then we realize we can only break free from our human imperfections by emulating His Perfection. What we expect of Him, we should expect of ourselves. Humanity evolves as we grow in knowledge of the gifts He has bestowed on every human being. As our comprehension of the psyche becomes more thorough, the ultimate purpose of human intelligence will become clearer. In particular, there seems to be a direct correspondence between our increasing use of intuitive intelligence and the Almighty's future expectations of humanity.

If we are to attempt a scientific description of Divinity, we need first to explain It in the light of twentieth century microbiology and ecology. These new biological sciences are the basis for a re-interpretation of evolution. *The Creative Conscience as Human Destiny* undertakes to describe how nature's powers of creation and integration produce all forms of life and drive evolution itself. Indeed, on the basis of this enlightening evidence, we can define Nature as a creative conscience, the source of humanity's finite creative conscience.[9]

If the synergy between creativity and integration produced our creative conscience, humankind's innate originality is one reason we often question traditional mores and generally accepted modes of cognition. In the context of evolutionary biology, we are impelled to originate mental skills that surpass those of the past. In other words, the creative conscience of our species has been the driving force behind human evolution itself.

The mutual reciprocity between Nature's powers of generation and consolidation proves that these interdependent processes serve a joint purpose. Similarly, in the human being, when multiple psychic experiences consolidate, they become unified into meaning.

In turn, every experience that discloses the significance of life fosters the evolution of human intelligence. In this way, the creative conscience gave birth to cultures and civilizations, and by so doing, it effected the transformation of the human psyche as a whole.

In so far as we rely on our innate capacities to make sound life decisions, we learn how to promote human evolution. At the personal level, self-realization is central to any definition of life. We ourselves evolve by integrating the energies nature has so freely given us.

In the context of the history of human culture, the creative conscience is a power that endures and transcends the rise and fall of civilizations. In a biological sense, so long as life is stronger than death, nature's intelligence will succeed in guiding humanity through the world's worst disasters. As Nature's evolving intelligence has ruled the earth for billions of years, so will humankind's natural intelligence guide and succor us for millions of years to come.

The explanation of how humankind's psyche evolved out of nature's creative conscience was a necessary prelude to describing the Supreme Being as *Supraconscience*. It should be noted that this description is intended to supplement, but not supplant, the traditional conception of the Supreme Being. What follows is a cultural-scientific description of the *Supraconscience* of existence.

Human evolution was initiated when we originally became aware that the Supreme Being must be Omniscient. With the development of secular knowledge over the centuries, our early religious intuition seemed corroborated. The physical sciences (physics, chemistry, astronomy) made clearer the material nature of Existence. The human sciences (sociology, psychology, and anthropology) studied the variety and universality of humankind's ways of life. Mathematics taught psyche that there are myriad means of discovering and demonstrating the infinity of truths available to the human mind; ergo, its own form of omniscience. With humanistic studies (history, literature, the arts, and philosophy), secular wisdom added knowledge of the intimate, sentient nature of humankind. All of these became paths to knowledge of the cognitive and emotional intelligence of the Divinity as *Supraconscience*. All of these attempts to probe the intrinsic nature of the world and of humanity reveal a teleological purpose behind human evolution. And that purpose seems guided by an omnipresent Supraconscience.

This cumulative knowledge and these evolving mental skills suggest there are infinite ways of discovering the omniscience of the *Supraconscience*. The secular-scientific understanding of Divinity proposed here is intended to make clear how far the human psyche has evolved in the past three millennia. In fact, we have been evolving a finite supraconscience which reflects the reality of the Supreme Being as Supraconscience. This fact alone suggests that psyche has powers which can unfold exponentially—and these hold the promise that our species has an infinite future.

The Four Archetypes and the Emergence of the Supraconscience

From the etymological changes that *sōphrosynē* and the 'great chain of being' underwent in history, we learned how psyche used archetypal ideas with an intuitive, cognitive purpose. This trait marked the development of the history of knowledge as discovery and demonstration. Steadily, an idea accumulates significance in so far as the psyche strives for greater comprehension and precision of meaning. An archetypal idea may come to us through related languages and so become a sophisticated concept. Such clarification of the meaning of essential truths reveals itself where religion, philosophy, literature or science are earnestly studied.

Sōphrosynē

The lesson of ancient Greece was moderation, temperance, inner harmony and mental balance. The culture warned men and women of excessive pride, arrogance and blindness to the consequences of our rash acts against others. Thus the essence of ancient Greek philosophy was

The Great Chain of Being

The four major principles outlined here suggest that the human psyche evolved through four stages: three were concerned with Being and the fourth with Becoming. The ancient Greeks identified self-knowledge and self-mastery as the foremost wisdom. The succeeding two millennia till the Enlightenment envisioned existence as ruled by three interacting principles: 1) the created world evinced self-sufficiency and perfection; 2) the ultimate goal of life was self-fulfillment; and 3) a superior form of intelligence had manifested itself throughout nature and humankind. And, finally, 4) nineteenth century, evolutionary theory, concerned with Becoming, proved that all forms of life single-mindedly pursue the sole purpose of survival. This theory inadvertently implies that purpose governs the life of the psyche.

The archetype of the 'great chain of being' described the created world as self-sustaining and self-transcending. Nature's perfections were based on the self-perfection of each species. The theory of evolution showed us the significance of *becoming*. It reminded us that our lives were forever evolving toward some future. Such an understanding of one's life is fundamental to self- realization. Hence the reader has now been made aware that to become fully human, he or she is responsible for fostering his or her own superior nature.

The Lesson of Holy Scripture

The third archetype teaches us the benefit of learning to read Holy Scripture objectively. As we read and became aware of the consecutive meanings to sacred language, we came to understand that each level of interpretation suggests a distinct level of commitment to proper living. Taken together, they can help us realize that we can choose between living a very mundane existence; or, we can pursue intellectual and moral excellence, or we can explore the mystical meaning of life. In other words, scriptural study can stimulate various dimensions of imagination, moral commitment and devotion to the sacred.

All of these levels of learning help us realize more fully who we are and how life can be interpreted and lived. A well-rounded personality will want to fulfill life in all possible ways. Patience, self-education, and pursuit of an ideal can give your life its fullest meaning. Living by a self-chosen truth will lead to a rewarding destiny.

The Divinity

Humankind has understood God as the Supreme Being. That means the Deity is the apex of all existence. Since He originated creation, He must also have initiated the evolution of every form of life from the microscopic to all species that ever lived on earth. A religious understanding of earthly life can only mean that God is our reason-for-being. Hence in the religious context, to understand the Divinity is to give our lives an ultimate purpose.

God is seen as the perfection of creation. Since He created evolution, its purpose must be the gradual perfection of all species. He must have created us so that we perfect ourselves.

Evolution not only transformed our species' instincts into the intelligence of the human brain. It also developed the mind's capacity to comprehend the spheres of significance in existence. If we are to understand what we have yet to learn about human destiny, we must learn to heed the higher calling of the psyche.

When humankind first believed there must be a Divinity, that belief was the true origin of psyche's evolution to becoming *Homo sapiens*. Use of intelligence was also the beginning of man's finite supraconscience. Over time, our commitment to religious and secular knowledge awakened us to the superior powers of the intuitive psyche and the rational mind. Understanding God humanized us. We moved from being one more species on the planet to becoming humankind.

We have undertaken to describe some of psyche's archetypal experiences and reasoned that the progression of psyche's potentials through time has encouraged it to develop a supraconscience in emulation of the Divinity's omniscience. Our present day knowledge of the material cosmos and the discovery of the psyche's secret universe tempts us to identify humanity's infinitesimal superconscience with the Supraconscience of the Cosmos. It would appear they share an infinity of affinities.

Notes

1. This description of the Greek word *sōphrosynē* owes much to Prof. Helen North's "Temperance (*Sōphrosynē*) and the Canon of the Cardinal Virtues." *Dictionary of the History of Ideas*, Vol. IV, p. 365-78.
2. This explication is based on A.O. Lovejoy's *The Great Chain of Being*.
3. From Wiener, Philip P., Ed., Dictionary of the History of Ideas, Vol IV: "Temperance (*Sōphrosynē*) and the Canon of the Cardinal Virtues." Prof. Helen North, pp. 365-378.

"With the triumph of Christianity, the church fathers began to adapt the doctrines of pagan philosophy to Christina theology and morals." (pp. 370-371)

"Patristic innovations include the identification of biblical figures (Joseph, Susanna, Judith) as types of *sōphrosynē*; the interpretation of many scriptural texts (Matthew 5:28 and 9:12; Luke 12:35-38); the Sixth and Tenth Commandments; several of the beatitudes, as injunctions to the practice of virtue; the derivation of all virtues from love (rather than wisdom); and the recognition of the example of Christ as His Blessed Mother as the supreme justification of the practice of temperance." (p. 371)

4. Webster's Dictionary, 10th ed., p. 1207.
5. For a comprehensive study of the use of number, see Georges Polti, *L'Art d'Inventer les Personnages*. "Essai sur les nombres," pp. 112-23, Paris, France. Editions Montaigne. 1930.
6. For a detailed numerical ordering of the Bible and Jewish Scripture, *Merriam Webster's Collegiate Dictionary*, 10th Ed., p. 110.
7. Webster's Dict. 10th Ed., p. 715.
8. Webster's Dict, 10th Ed., p. 1190, my emphasis.
9. My book, *The Creative Conscience as Human Destiny* (2004), Ch. 2, "Being and Becoming," pp. 19-34, shows affinities to Lovejoy's work. The thesis of my book maintains that the bio-processes (generation and integration) are the driving forces which our psyche replicates. The book largely investigates how psyche functions via the in-tandem interactivity of human creativity and conscience derived from the same proto-activities of nature. Hence, the metaphor "creative conscience" applies both to evolving nature and the human mind itself.

Part Three

The Bible as Evidence of Humanity's Evolving Supraconscience

Chapter Five

The Old Testament:
The Law and Historical Books

A Secular Interpretation: Part One

The *Book of Genesis* is a record of the history of Israel from creation to the death of Joseph. In addition to describing the origin of the world and the great flood, the book narrates the lives of the patriarchs Abraham, Isaac and Jacob, ending with the story of Joseph in Egypt. It thus explains the origin and early stages of the Jewish religion. Its passionate recounting of the lives of these figures and its clear sense of purpose reveal the Hebrew commitment to the Supreme God, Yahweh or Jehovah.

The Old Testament offers historical evidence of the way religious faith can unite an entire people by drawing them toward a higher spiritual purpose. The biographies of the individual patriarchs reveal how they were absorbed in--and how their lives ennobled by--their earnest search for guidance from the Highest Being. The solidification of the people's faith resulted in the development of a cultural conscience. Eventually, belief in a Supreme Being led the community to interpret historical events in the light of their faith.

The sense of Hebrew unity had a profound influence on the Jewish people's sense of themselves as a chosen people. It not only enhanced their chances of survival, but also motivated the faithful to focus their spiritual energies. By committing themselves to fulfill the sacred law and by submitting their lives to God's eternal will, they were realizing their historical destiny. In this sense, Judaism was one of the earliest manifestations of humankind's emerging supra-conscience.

The Bible's version of mankind's primeval beginning states that God created the first man Adam and the first woman Eve. Placed in Eden, they were commanded by God not to eat from the tree of knowledge, but because they yielded to the temptation, the Almighty expelled them from the garden. This became known as "man's fall."

Of greater consequence to human history was the story of Cain and Abel. When God favored the offerings of Abel over those of Cain, jealousy drove Cain to murder his brother. According to Biblical interpreters, this was the true beginning of the evil inherited by mankind. A third son, innocent Seth, was born thereafter to Adam and Eve.

In the story of Noah, we learn that man's wickedness provoked God's rage, and He sent a Flood to cover the earth and drown humankind. Yet because Noah had "found grace in the eyes of the Lord", Yahweh forewarned Noah to build an ark for his family and also put aboard it pairs of male and female of all the other creatures on earth. (Chs. 6-8).

God's punishment of virtually all mankind for the wickedness of some made it clear that the fury of the divine was to be feared, and any future under God's protection required total obedience and purity. There was no questioning His Justice, for was He not the Creator?

Such punishment evoked fear and respect for the Infinite Power, but it did not awaken love. Yet, his severe Justice also revealed how deeply He cared for humankind. On the other hand, for those who understood Yahweh's conception of good and evil, there was the beginning not only of a collective conscience but also an awareness that man must develop a power *within* himself in order to be able to combat his own tendencies to excess, disorder, and evil. Since fear of God awakened this consciousness, for the Hebrews this was the origin of their embryonic supraconscience.

After the Flood "the whole earth was one language". In other words, as a result of this catastrophic event, people forgot their previous differences and contentiousness ceased. They gave one another mutual aid so that all could survive. Thereafter, their single language of gratitude ensured them renewed faith in a forgiving God.

However, in their competition to erect the tallest tower ever, i.e. the greatest religion, their old perversities, quarrels and belligerence arose once again. This time God's anger was aroused by what they had done with His gift of language to mankind. Originally, it was meant to bring about concord and keep peace among mankind. He had given them language so as to unite the races of man, to remind them they were all of one kind, one family.

So what is meant by the claim that the 'confusion of tongues' stopped the tower from reaching to heaven? Yahweh was angered by men's reversion to disputes, squabbles, and mutual contempt, and by the fact that they had forgotten the days when their unity enabled them to survive. God destroyed the tower, confounded their languages and scattered the people abroad in Babel (Genesis 11:1-9) in an effort to punish them for being blind to the true purpose of language.

Since that event, men have been using language at cross-purposes, self-righteously, egotistically, and arrogantly. Indeed, to this day we sometimes 'babble' unashamedly. Since then, thousands of different languages have been developed and still mankind understands one another so little. This Biblical story is a caveat for future mankind: We must once more seek out a common language of ideas, ideals, and moral principles that all races and peoples can use in their daily lives.

The Life of the Patriarchs
Abraham

Abraham (Genesis, 11:26-25:00) **was** a patriarch who fully obeyed God's will. Indeed his faith and character were tested many times. When God destroyed

Sodom and Gomorrah as punishment for the people's wickedness, He spared Abraham's nephew Lot and his two daughters. Thereafter, God promised to make Abraham the father of a "multitude of nations".

Abraham's wife Sarah gave birth to a child in her old age, and they named him Isaac. God approved of Abraham because he had undergone many trials and tests to prove his faith to the Almighty. He was even ready to sacrifice his own son, Isaac, to God, but at the last moment, God sent an angel to stay the dagger in Abraham's hand. God did not need such a sacrifice as proof. He needed the faith of those who obeyed their higher intuition. Abraham's own power came from his total commitment to God.

But what does modern man make of this Biblical episode? The intercession of an angel, whether real or experienced as an epiphany, seems to mark the emergence of an individual's superior self.

In chapters 27-36 of Genesis, Jacob becomes the central figure. His life is described as one which was subject to strong cross-currents of emotions. By stealing the birthright of his own brother, Esau, the first born, Jacob demonstrates how easy it is to succumb to the primeval subconscious. Yet, Jacob has some of his grandfather's spiritual faith as witnessed in his vision of a ladder on which angels ascend to the top toward God, where they renewed their covenant to aid humankind, and then descend to earth again.

What does 'Jacob's Ladder' mean to modern man? And the actions of the angels? The vision certainly reminds us of the Buddhist belief in transmigration of souls. Those who are endowed with pure '*bodhi*' consciousness, Jacob's angels seem akin to the *bodhisattvas* of Mahayana Buddhism, human beings who have achieved Nirvana and so are worshipped as deities. In Jacob's vision, the angels appeared so that they might ascend to God to renew their commitment to aiding mankind, and then return to earth to continue their work for another lifetime.

There is another story associated with Jacob. He is said to have wrestled all night with an angel, who once conquered, changed Jacob's name to Israel, meaning "contender with God." In general, one could say this episode indicates Jacob wrestled with his own conscience. However, because the power is pictured as an angel sent from God, in our modern understanding, we would say that he wrestled with his own evolving conscience. Or, his supraconscience wrestled with his subconscience, which had urged him to disenfranchise his brother Esau. After that night, he could once more meet Esau as his spiritual brother. Both of Jacob's experiences were epiphanies of his evolving psyche.

Chapters 37-50 of this book tell Joseph's story. Because Jacob loved Joseph more than all his other children, Joseph's older brothers threw him in a pit and left him there to die. However, a traveling merchant rescued him only to sell him as a slave in Egypt. There, when his master's wife falsely accused him of trying to seduce her, Joseph was put in prison.

There he came to be known as an interpreter of dreams. When he was unexpectedly called to interpret the Pharaoh's dreams, Joseph did so with remarkable insight. He took them to mean that there would be seven years of plenty followed by seven years of famine. He advised the Pharaoh to store enough food to assure sufficient provisions when the crops were poor. This plan saved the Egyptian people from starvation.

When Jacob's own brothers came to buy food, he forgave them and sent for his aging father. In its own right, this capacity to forgive a grave wrong and his thoughtfulness toward his old father showed Joseph's magnanimity of soul. Perhaps it was a sign to God of his gratitude for his extraordinary spiritual endowments.

In any case, the power to interpret the significance of a dream relating to future events is a most noteworthy gift. In science, the ability to predict future events is based solely on considerable, comprehensive knowledge of nature and the earth in its present condition. For instance, we know from the recurring patterns of natural disasters such as earthquakes and volcanic eruptions that they will happen again. But our knowledge is inadequate to predict exactly when these catastrophes will take place.

Moreover, we know from the study of volcanic rock and ancient strata of earth that earth-wide changes have occurred intermittently over geological time. Contemporary geology knows by the reversal of magnetite in solidified lava that the earth's North Pole has reversed over periods of 11,000,000 years and has done so a number of times. Indeed, at present, the magnetosphere of the earth is undergoing such a million-year shift. It is one reason for the climate changes and fitful cyclonic storms.

But scientific predictions are a quite different matter from a human being such as Joseph using his intuition to prophesy future events. In the Biblical story, he was able to perceive in the Pharaoh's dreams a forewarning of unexpected natural events taking place as a seven year cycle of nature. True, Joseph may already have had an uncanny knowledge of nature's alternating rhythm. But having the intuition to see the inherent connection between such widely separated dimensions of reality as psyche's use of imagination and the creative powers at work in nature is quite a different matter. Of course, modern man can dismiss the story as so much legend because it is incomprehensible in terms of common sense. Because we have written elsewhere on *divination*, let us for the moment put aside what makes a good story to examine other prophetic gifts.

We are all familiar with the phenomenon of *premonition* and when it turns out to be true, it makes us wonder what mental potential this implies. Some psychics or intuitives seem to have the ability to decipher vague signs and omens to predict with some accuracy a future event.

To students, teachers and scholars of the humanities (especially literature, philosophy and history), it is possible to develop a keen, penetrating intuition into the underlying design, pattern, theme or progression of a story, philosophy, or trend to history. For instance, in Chapter Two, Archetype Three, the psychic dimensions in Scripture were described. Thus prepared, an adept student devoted to discovering the deeper meanings in Holy Writ could find both enlightenment and personal guidance he or she might not otherwise come to.

Then again, individuals with special mystical or prophetic gifts have used astrology, numerology, Tarot cards, Kabbalah and the Bible to interpret events in history or to foresee what may yet transpire in our lives. Also, it is hard to completely discredit the prophecies of such men as Nostradamus or Edgar Cayce.

In any case, the ancient Hebrews believed certain individuals were richly endowed with the power of prophecy. The second book of the *Pentateuch* narrates how people were made conscious of their destiny through the intelligence of one man, Moses. He envisioned God as the source and guide for the future of the Hebrew people. Moses' vision unified the tribes of Israel and taught them the moral significance of their religion. And, what he taught them inspired the long chain of spiritual events in Israel's history.

Readers are acquainted with the story of Moses. Found abandoned by the Pharaoh's daughter, he was brought up in the Egyptian court. As a grown man, he one day witnessed a Jewish slave being beaten savagely by an Egyptian overseer. Moses' instinctive empathy for his people enraged him so, that he killed the Egyptian. As a consequence, he had to flee. When he was living among the Midianite people, he married a priest's daughter and spent years attending his father-in-law's flocks. One day, an angel appeared to him in a burning bush and the Lord spoke to him from the flames. Moses was told to go to the Pharaoh to seek the liberation of the Hebrews from slavery.

One need not dwell any further on the many details that make this a compelling story, but only note that modern man feels impelled to ask, "Are we to take this account literally, or understand it figuratively or symbolically?" Surely, we would hesitate to claim that the events were merely a case of hallucination, delusion or distorted perception without any basis in reality. We have heard an account of Moses' suffering from a disorder of the nervous system. If he ever had such a neurotic or neurological illness, the subsequent history of the Exodus from Egypt, his leadership in searching the wilderness for the Promised Land (Chs. 14-18), the revelation of the Ten Commandments (Ch. 20) and the *Book of the Covenant* (Chs. 21-23) would never have materialized or become integral to the teaching of the Old Testament. Even though he was not personally the author of these works, they nonetheless provided the foundation for Judaism and the moral backbone of Western Civilization.

Scholars have come to realize that the first books attributed to Moses were, in fact, written between 1000 and 300 B.C. Can modern Americans even begin to imagine holding to a common purpose or Holy Ideal for 700 years with the intention of completing and perfecting that Ideal? Future events in history will prove how durable our faith in democracy will be.

For argument's sake we might ask how this ancient account of Moses' receiving the Ten Commandments and the *Book of the Covenant* would compare to Albert Einstein's own enlightenment as to the true nature of the universe. Fortunately, for Einstein, mathematicians and scientists proved his seemingly unsound theory of relativity. For Moses' part, the events of human history seem to substantiate the psychological fact that the epiphany he experienced was as real as Einstein's vision of the ultimate-meaning of the speed of light throughout the cosmos. Both of them tapped into the evolving supraconscience of humanity.

Furthermore, Moses had plenty of empirical evidence as to how unjustly the Hebrew slaves were treated. Growing up in the Pharaoh's court exposed him to men of the best knowledge of the time. He must have had an 'insider's' education as concerns the Egyptian customs, traditions, beliefs and personalities of his time. Such an education made him an eminently suitable messenger when it came to pleading for the release of his people. Why had his life been spared when he was an infant? And, why had he been brought to the center of the very power that oppressed his people? In sum, his "worldly" knowledge, his strong emotional bond to his people, and the obviously high-level emotional intelligence he brought to bear in laying the foundation of Judaism reveal an essential truth: The fact that Moses believed he received direction and commandments from God Himself demonstrates that either God activated Moses' supraconscience, or Moses himself evolved it by total commitment to a life purpose, namely, to free the Jews and to lead them to the Promised Land. In ancient times, Moses represented a solid, sound-minded example of humankind's emerging supraconscience.

Let us speak still more broadly on this topic. In ancient times, original ideas were seen as gifts from heaven. By contrast, today we have no sound, scientific argument to account for human originality, except to generally attribute it to human intelligence. However, intelligence seems just another word for spirit, soul, angel, or some manifestation of God Himself. For all the medical and psychological studies of the human brain, which have endeavored to identify various areas of aptitude, talent, mood or feeling, they have not been able to explain ideation.

For that matter, science is unable to explain how the brain either creates or shapes ideas. It seems as though human intelligence has been created out of nothing and is fundamentally inexplicable by science. Indeed, the myriad of ideas, concepts, breakthroughs, insights and schemata developed to explain existence and human experience emerge from the brain. But just what is it? It derives from raw matter and is a biogenetic form of intelligence. It is a neurological nexus of sensations, sentiments, imagery and symbols all of seemingly equal import until it perceives a need, identifies a relationship, or hits upon a purpose.

Otherwise, how do we account for all the ideas (practical, sensible, and ideal) that flow out of the human being? Whose idea was it anyway that there should be a universe and a Divinity?

Actually, our early ancestors were probably overwhelmed by a sudden upsurge of ecstasy when a truly original idea occurred. Such ideas must have appeared to have been heaven sent, or to have the quality of a dream which portended future events. Modern man may doubt that our ancestors actually saw angels but, at the same time, he must acknowledge that they, in fact, had remarkable ideas. Such angelic messages were the intuitive expressions of our evolving supraconscience deeply motivated by the faith in the God. Today we would call this Deity the *Supraconscience*.

The Old Testament recounts the Hebrews' forty-year trek through the wilderness to Mount Sinai where God called Moses to ascend to its top. There He gave him the Ten Commandments and the *Book of the Covenant*. (Chs. 19-40).

Let us be realistic about this extraordinary event. Moses had received an excellent education in the Pharaoh's court. In all probability, he would have learned of the moral codes of neighboring peoples, such as the Code of Hammurabi and the laws of the Hittites and Assyrians. So the Decalogue was a skillful summary of codes from other nations as well as a statement of an appreciation for the earlier Egyptian worship of Maat.

In essence, the Ten Commandments sum up practical recommendations for maintaining law and order in any society. Their universality reveals immense knowledge of human nature. The Commandments made sense to all mature men and women, for they were easy to understand, if difficult, at times, to obey. (*Exodus*: 20:1-17) They list negative definitions of what is sinful and criminal in communal life.

In chapters 21-23, the *Book of the Covenant* prescribes specific laws that are to govern trespassing, borrowing, usury, theft; adultery and fornication; witchcraft and murder; treatment of widows, servants and strangers; and the strict observance of the Sabbath.

Though the comprehensive nature of the Covenant seems God-inspired, Moses did not create it in a cultural vacuum. Rather, it was probably a syncretic statement of the legal and moral truths which had proven viable in neighboring nations. Hence this compendium of laws is an admirable lesson in the value of cultural syncretism. The best of what had been thought and practiced by foreign cultures was creatively integrated into Hebrew life. As such, the Covenant is also clear manifestation of humankind's supraconscience in antiquity where wisdom was balanced with practical knowledge to foster the survival of the individual and of whole peoples.

In the *Book of Leviticus,* the ritual laws of the tribe of Levi are presented. Intended as an addendum to the laws in *Exodus*, it too is an integration of materials from diverse sources. Of special interest is the fact that the completed work was the result of the dedicated labors of a series of conscientious writers from 800 to 300 B.C.

Again, modern man is struck by this total devotion to the completion of a holy work that required some 500 years, i.e. twenty generations to complete and implement. Not only is this evidence of a collective conscience defining itself, but such a sustained effort on a single, sacred project, inspired by faith in God, is evidence of the historical transformation of the human conscience.

Noteworthy were the laws concerning clean and unclean beasts, personal hygiene, the (Yom Kippur), a day of fasting and prayer which called one to remember the need to atone for our offences against, and injuries to, others.

Here again in obedience to the will of God, Hebraic law reveals that man's maturing conscience had begun to establish moral order on earth by sensibly defining just relationships between men and women. Central to all such law was the absolute need for a more humane system of justice.

Some readers may be skeptical about the claim that God guides man to formulate logical laws. They would rather believe that man's sober, rational judgment created secular jurisprudence. Yet, clearly ancient religion did influence our understanding of justice. In any case, by creating more just laws, conscience became humanized.

Traditionally ascribed to Moses, *Deuteronomy* was thought to have originated around 650 B.C.E., but in its presently accepted form, we know it to have been compiled between 650 and 300 B.C.E.

Assuredly, the act of compiling a body of knowledge and practical wisdom is in itself the exercise of an evolved conscience. This leads us to conclude that any sustained concentration of effort which integrates experiences in a meaningful way should tend to foster the evolving powers of the human supraconscience.

As a summary of law, *Deuteronomy* emphasizes the unity, supremacy and ultimate justice of God. The fundamental teaching of God's will encouraged the regulation of Hebrew life in so far as it stressed loyalty to the Supreme Being. A collective sense of purpose not only organized religious worship, but also defined the essential activities of daily life.

In general, law is a collection of truths which have practical effects on human attitudes and actions. Since any issues that arise concerning these are directly defined and resolved in the context of our commitment to God, the Supraconscience of the Universe, we willingly surrender our lives to the higher, universal wisdom of the Almighty.

Psychologically, such constancy of purpose must have affected the development of the human psyche by organizing it into a hierarchy of powers and potentials very much like that effected by our own intrinsic, organic, system.

We know that individual cells have the capacity of self-transformation, a phenomenon which allows stem cells to specialize and to unite with other cells to form all the body's organs, ensure that it functions properly and build its life support systems.

Rather than the neurons of the brain acting singly or independently, they are integrated into a superconscious neurological system capable of carrying out superior functions and exponential numbers of variations on these functions. This probably accounts for the abundance of ideas, thoughts, perceptions and concepts that endlessly evinced themselves throughout human history in various cultures and civilizations.

In sum, *Deuteronomy* is a significant example of the supraconscience we have been evolving ever since we learned how to learn and to integrate experience, knowledge, and wisdom,

Chapters 14-18 of the *Book of Exodus* provide a synopsis of the forty-year long period of wandering through the wilderness in search of the promised land. They also record how God became impatient with the incredulity, resentment, skepticism and cynicism of the weary Israelis. He warned and exhorted them to obey Moses.

Of course, the harsh conditions of life in eastern North Africa between the 16th and 13th centuries B.C. were much like the severely trying times of survival experienced by our primeval ancestors. Had it not been for Moses' vision of the future, the people of Israel could have succumbed to the chaotic, internecine conflicts characteristic of the primeval subconscience of ages before.

Moses had directly experienced the presence and the power of God before his people escaped from Egypt. When the grueling trek through the desert was undertaken, his supraconscience alone held sway over the mass subconscience of the rabble, the hopeless, and the desperate among them.

So, the Biblical account of this intelligent tribe clearly illustrates what has often taken place in humankind's psyche or soul. Undoubtedly, this period of disbelief, rancor, and mutual antagonism, caused by the hardships and suffering of the Jewish people surely moved Moses to relieve their pain by creating the Ten Commandments and the *Book of the Covenant*. These works would re-establish law, justice, and moral integrity among a people who had stared across the bleak horizon at their near extinction. As often in times of crisis, the ancestral subconscience rose up to damn itself and destroy others. Still, if humankind's maturing supraconscience is strong and resourceful enough, over the longer term it will find ways and means of transforming that violent energy into justice and moral good.

With the fulfillment of Moses' prophecy and promise, there came renewed faith in the mind's powers to foresee the future. There was always the caveat that the people must learn to distinguish between true and false prophets, but there was also the renewed hope that God would send a prophet to succeed Moses. This expectation may have encouraged future men and women to cultivate their own psychic powers and use them with greater care.

In the context of our theory of psyche, modern man may come to have confidence that the supraconscience can be trusted to guide our future evolution—a process that can only unfold a stage at a time.

In Moses' *Farewell Speech* to his followers, he not only exhorted them to obey divine guidance, but perhaps most remarkably, taught them that God was not *only* in heaven, but in their own hearts.

In other words, he urged his people to listen to the voice of their higher nature. The heart understood God's guidance. Moses may have adopted this wisdom from the Egyptian *Book of the Dead*. In this ancient text, the deceased's heart was weighed against the actual life he had led. If it was judged impure by the immortal judges, his soul would be devoured by hideous monsters. If it had remained pure, it would know a glorious afterlife.

The Egyptian belief in godly Justice (Maat) and in the heart's knowing the ultimate truths about life seems proof that the ancient Egyptians were aware of the presence of a superior power in the human person.

In the *Book of Judges*, the Hebrew author makes clear the significance of historic events. After the death of Joshua, the Israelites "Forsook the God of their fathers" to embrace the gods of neighboring peoples. God's anger was so great that He delivered His people into the clutches of their enemies. (2:12-14)

Subsequently, once the Israelis abandoned belief in their God, the situation of the Jews grew chaotic. Pursuing a wanton, irresponsible life broke with their moral tradition, and their unclean practices shattered their lives. Their self-discipline and self-respect degenerated into the excesses of the subconscience of primeval mankind.

By contrast, one of the most memorable stories from the days of the judges was that of the Moabite woman Ruth, whose Hebrew husband had died. When her mother-in-law was to return to Bethlehem, where there no longer was famine, Ruth implored Naomi: "Do not ask me to leave you or not to follow you: your people shall be my people, and your God my God." (1:16) Naomi took Ruth with her to Bethlehem.

Later, Ruth married Boaz, a wealthy Israelite, and from their union David was born. Of course, this story presents an example of mutual tolerance and its unforeseeable rewards. As we will learn, mutual tolerance is an important stage in developing the supraconscience of the individual and the human race.

The great grandson of Ruth and Boaz was David, the future king of Israel. As a youth, the shepherd-boy fought the giant warrior Goliath and slew him. Eventually, he became king of Judah and later king of all Israel.

In the *Book of Kings* (I), which tells of King David's death and the division of the kingdom after Solomon's death, it is recorded that kings were no longer judged by their material achievements, but by their moral purpose "in the light of the Lord".

Such a pronouncement merits comment because it reveals the use of developed powers of judgment. The growing consciousness of the need to do what was right in the eyes of the Lord is a significant step in human evolution. Concentration of efforts aimed at fulfilling a noble purpose is evidence of humankind's evolving conscience. The endeavor to obey God obviously transcended all egotism and dishonesty. Eventually, it could lead to the true humanization of our kind.

Solomon's forty-year reign is remembered as one of peace and prosperity. The essence of the man's life is illustrated by a dream he had. The Lord came to him saying, "Ask what I shall give you." Solomon replied, "...an understanding heart, that I may discern between the good and the bad." The gift was granted. But God also gave Solomon what he had not asked for "...riches, honor and long days." (Chs. 3-4) Such a reward is possible when humankind educates and truly cultivates their superior nature.

Out of the Northern Kingdom came the most influential prophet, Elijah, who foresaw that monotheism could unity all mankind. His prophecy was strengthened in the moral monotheism of his followers, Isaac, Hosea, Amos and Micah.

Completed after 350 B.C., the *Book of Chronicles* (I) offers little psychological insight into the genealogies it recounts. The ancestries retraced are of limited value to understanding the moral stature of the individuals mentioned. While the genealogical line from Adam to King David remains vague when it comes to understanding the lives of individuals, the period of David himself offers more genuine insight into the man. In the main, it is sufficient to know that most of the historical figures were committed to religious ideals.

However, in the light of the modern day popularity retracing one's own family genealogy, let us take a moment to examine the secular value of such a study. Aside from pride, what is the value of a family genealogy? If, by foresight, someone had kept a record of family aptitudes, traits and talents, that would help the young to appreciate characteristics in family members. A proper genealogy might suggest how great-grandparents, grandparents and parents had lived their lives and why. Some may have pursued a lifetime goal. Others may have lived an original life according to some ideal, principle or philosophy. Others simply lived life for what it was worth, come what may.

Whatever influenced their decisions, success in life would largely have depended on individuals doing what they really wanted to do in life. On the other hand, the older and more mature members of a family would have encouraged the development of family talents or the need to be practical in meeting life's material needs. The older and wiser ones would advise the gifted to do what they really love to do or are best able to do. In any case, life was too short to spend it being miserable. In short, a genealogy can be used to prudently guide those in need of family wisdom to choose a path in life when they are ready to decide.

Thousands of years ago, King David gave parental advice that both religious and secular parents can still respect. During a famous speech before all the leaders of his country, David bade his son Solomon to build the sanctuary of the Temple. He also exhorted him: "Know thou the God of thy father and serve Him with a perfect heart and a willing mind; for the Lord searcheth all hearts, and understands all imaginings of thoughts; if thou seek him, he will be found by thee; but if thou forsake him, He will cast thee off forever." (28:9)

This is still wise parental advice. Each individual should examine his or her heart and mind for their integrity. To the devout, God searches all hearts for their honest, truth, and dedication to an ideal, "Seek and ye shall find."

In essence, be honest with yourself and dedicate yourself to achieving something worthwhile in your lifetime. If you are faithful to yourself, you will be faithful to your ideals. Otherwise stated, to be faithful to an Ideal means being faithful to your higher self.

In sum, to evolve a personal supraconscience is to obey the Supraconscience that created all existence. To cultivate your supraconscience is to show God you are deeply grateful he created you.

Perhaps the lesson of a family genealogy should be this. Find a life purpose, and your life's meaning will reveal itself to you.

Chapter Six

The Old Testament:
The Poetical and Prophetic Books

To understand the intriguing truths of the Old Testament, a brief introduction to the use of metaphor and irony in the poetical books is necessary. Both views of the world search beneath the literal or surface meaning of words to their inner or deeper implications.

Metaphor transcends common sense and either-or logic. It integrates images, ideas and insights which rationally appear fundamentally different. The use of metaphor in the poetical books of Holy Scripture unveils some of life's most profound and sublime experiences.

The ancients believed the visible veiled the invisible. (cf. the detection of camouflaged animals in nature) This intuition of the hidden is not only characteristic of age-old superstitions, but also defines the essence of religious faith and even of scientific research.

By contrast, irony is used to warn someone against accepting skillful deception as actual truth. If it is aptly understood, the true sense of irony reveals the danger of being blinded by appearances: Eventually reality forces us to acknowledge their chimerical nature.

A mature individual may use irony to show awareness of the enigma of human destiny or the holy/unholy paradox of human nature. Irony cautions us to beware of excesses of faith or of gullible ecstasy at what is reported as marvelous. Ultimately, the use of self-irony warns us to be aware of our blindness to our own ignorance.

In literary terms, irony is fable whereas metaphor is fairy tale. Irony is the bitter wisdom of the Old Testament, metaphor, the faith, hope and charity of the New Testament. Moses saw Hebrews as God's Chosen People, but realized they must be reminded of the immense, punitive power in the universe. The Ten Commandments taught fear and respect of that power. The aim of prophecy and teaching was to return the people to self-discipline.

On the other hand, Jesus of Nazareth saw through the weaknesses, selfishness, duplicity and intolerance of humankind. By using metaphor, parables and symbolic stories, he awakened the hope that his followers could overcome their fear of hunger, thirst, sickness and death. Jesus illuminated the truth that the human heart contains all the knowledge and wisdom needed to live a life worthy of God's respect.

The power of irony and metaphor is the means by which the human mind acknowledges the bitter realities of existence and the desperate needs of humble humanity. The Old Testament is basically ironic in purpose whereas the New Testament is metaphoric and hopeful in intent.

The reader unaccustomed to poetic language also needs a few further guidelines for understanding the imaginative uses of language. Between things believed to be distinct, metaphor helps us discover certain similarities in quality or essence. The illogic which underlies metaphoric language intensifies the reader's curiosity, puzzlement and desire to know what is meant. Hence metaphor is what it is by reason of the expectations or probable inferences it calls forth. It aims at arousing awe and wonder at hidden truth or mysterious meaning.

Since it involves enigma, metaphor prompts us to solve the mystery of the many associations it evokes in us. As with irony, metaphor widens the implications of things, but unlike irony, which detects the fact that an ugly reality often contradicts a pleasant or innocent appearance, metaphor sees a spiritual reality beneath the deceptively commonplace appearance of mundane things.[1]

Metaphor and irony characterize the two pervasive world views in the Old and New Testaments. In the context of our thesis, they have helped sharpen the mind by defining and giving expression to the deeper meanings of human life.

The *Book of Job*

Job is the first book of five poetical books followed by Psalms, Proverbs, Ecclesiastes and the Song of Solomon. The pleasure that poetry can bring greatly increases the heart-felt affect of the human truths revealed.

These books also impart the universal truth expressed by human emotions. In particular sacred moments, devout individuals unveil the passionate nature of their religious lives. Such mortals come to exemplify humanity's evolving supraconscience.

The story of Job questions the justice of God. It was probably written in the fourth century B.C., when the ancient Hebrews still believed outrageous misfortune and personal suffering fell upon a man for some sin committed in the past. Yet, at times, the righteous were also subject to great injustice, despite their pious and moral lives. This made it seem like God was insensible to human pain, disease and dying. And, if this apathy were true, then the Hebrew God would be just another myth.

Job was a man perfect and upright, God-fearing and righteous. He possessed great wealth in the number of his sheep, and oxen. His household was large as was his renown. (1:1, 3)

But, Satan asked God if Job were not so favored by the Almighty, would he not rebel and reject the Lord? Satan proposed that God withdraw His protection from Job to see how he would respond to his misfortune. Consequently, Job was stripped of all his possessions and two of his daughters were killed in a storm.

Job's humble acceptance of this catastrophe revealed that his losses had little meaning compared to his devotion to God. "The Lord giveth and the Lord taketh away." (1:21)

This unquestioning acceptance of God's injustice is more than extraordinary. Actually, Job is forgiving God, and he still trusts in the Almighty's ultimate understanding. This forgiveness is a sure sign that Job was endowed with the wisdom of humankind's evolving conscience. At the most basic level, Job accepts life for what it is. Rather than yielding to human fatalism, his faith shows him to be superior to others who egotistically believe that they, above all others, should be rewarded by God for their religious devotion. Job's heart and mind reached beyond self-centered human judgment. His sense of humility stems from knowing that man's ignorance and limited intelligence cannot begin to fathom the mysterious ways of the eternal Deity. At the same time, his steadfastness is the mark of a man who foresees that humankind has yet a long history to undergo till it can begin to understand God's infinite justice. Modesty and humility alone can open us to His Wisdom.

Though Job must have wondered why the Creator had misjudged him, he showed gratitude for all the good he had hitherto received. He does not see himself as doomed or fated. If Job had yielded to the fatalism of past generations, it would have shown that he believed more in fate than in God. But his faith proved stronger than fate itself.

In all the years he had enjoyed God's benevolence and munificence, Job's evolved conscience was guided by the Supraconscience of the universe. His gratitude was evidence of his superior conscience: "What? Shall we receive good at the hand of God and shall not receive evil?" Unfortunately, there is here the suggestion that God Himself might at will inflict evil on a good man, but the intent behind of Job's statement, in the language of Uz, was surely: "Are we to be free from all misfortune and evil in the world?" The implied answer forgives God for whatever Job has had to suffer.

When in physical and mental agony, Job sank down to sit among the ashes, this submissive act showed he was no more worth than the dust. Later, in despair, he cursed the day he was born. (3:3-4, 7)

Yet, he remained without a word of recrimination against God. Even when his three friends urged him to admit to a previous sin, Job replied, "Till I die I will not remove my integrity from me." (27; 5) In other words, he has been incorruptible--firm in his allegiance to his moral values. He is incapable of being disloyal to his God. He has been faithful and always fulfilled his responsibilities to Him.

Finally, a voice spoke to Job out of a whirlwind. It did not respond to his desire to meet the Almighty to make clear his innocence. Out of the windstorm, God simply asked, "Who am I?" "What are thou?" The Lord then brought before Job's eyes the majesty and magnificence of the earth and universe and his bitterness turned to wonder and awe.

Job finally realized that God can do everything. He hates himself for doubting His omnipotence, "I abhor myself and repent in dust and ashes." (42: 2, 5-6).

Thereafter, gradually God restored all Job had lost and much more. When he died, his life was fulfilled with the reward he deserved.

The story of Job's enduring faith gives evidence of his advanced human wisdom. His loss of everything he had so earnestly gathered together in a lifetime, the tragic loss of two daughters in a whirlwind, the natural disaster, his disease-ridden body, and afflicted heart and mind—all of these things remind us of the conditions of early man's survival. In that primeval age, humankind was possessed by a primitive subconscience.

What Job suffered could certainly have led him to revert to the earlier, more bestial state of mind. Satan's sustained effort to debase his faith in God was an attempt to defile the essence of human nature, namely, its evolving conscience. By contrast, due to the influence of the subconscience throughout history, our confrontations and conflicts have demeaned and damaged man's commitment to higher ideals. Warfare, caused by our surrender to that subconscience, has inflicted pain, suffering, and sorrow upon humankind. In such periods of mutual murder and annihilation, the subcconscience seized control of the humane conscience and savaged it.

In Job's case, Satan himself could not degrade Job's superior conscience, bred by his lifetime of devotion to the highest ideal that humankind had so far conceived and cultivated.

The lesson Job learned should be taught by parents to their young. As children, we seldom understand the wisdom of our parents and grandparents. As we mature and leave behind childhood innocence and adolescent ignorance, we gradually acknowledge their intelligence, intentions, and wisdom. To comprehend the Idea of God, we still need for many generations of intelligent human beings to dedicate their lives to a nobler purpose than the "survival of the fittest".

Perhaps at some point in the future, our finite conscience will have absorbed an iota of the infinite wisdom of the cosmic Supraconscience.

In the meantime, we can try to paraphrase Job's human wisdom: "Let us learn to replace our ignorance with thoughtful knowledge. In so doing, we may, over time, begin to comprehend the wisdom that created our universe.

The second of the poetical books, Psalms, made up a treasured collection of prayer, verses which give praise to God, and expressions of passionate reverence for the Lord. Of Jewish origin, the Psalms were used as hymns in the period before the Christ and also by Christians in the early centuries of the Common Era.

The dictionary defines a *psalm* as a sacred song or poem used during worship; the biblical hymns originated with the *Book of Psalms*.

In our study of the earlier portion of the Old Testament, we learned how much of it was concentrated on Law, Commandments and the Covenant between the Jewish people and Yahweh (Jehovah). With the Psalms we hear expressed the nobler emotions and higher passions of the ancient Hebrews. In general, the exalted form of expression of this book of the Bible transformed everyday con-

The Poetical and Prophetic Books   111

cerns and desires into an idiom superior to that of the strict ritual and Law demanded by authoritarian conscience. Otherwise stated, and in keeping with our thesis, the Psalms provide rich evidence of the emotional life of the ancient Hebrews.

In general, since prehistoric times, humankind had been evolving. When groups established communities for self-protection, cultures began to develop. At that stage, human beings began to develop the intelligence to express deeper feelings. Hence emotional responses to the world came to be nurtured and refined by mutual understanding. Slowly, humankind came to realize the universe was as much a mystery as the life within them. Such relations matured the psyche. With the intimation that there existed a Supreme Being who felt compassion for the good, the loyal and the humble, the emotional acumen of the Hebrews found expression in the Psalms.

We review here a few representative psalms, not with the intention of analyzing them in depth, but only with the aim of understanding how they reveal the nature of human intelligence. *Psalm 23* is well known to most readers and will serve our purpose.

> The Lord is my shepherd; I shall not want.
> He maketh me to lie down in green pastures; he leadeth me beside the still waters.
> He restoreth my soul: he leadeth me in the paths of righteousness for his name's sake.
> Yea, though I walk in the valley of shadows of death,
> I will fear no evil: for thou art with me; thy rod and thy staff they comfort me.
> Thou preparest a table before me in the presence of mine enemies: thou anointest my head with oil; my cup runneth over.
> Surely goodness and mercy shall follow me all the days of my life;
> and I will dwell in the house of the Lord forever.

Clearly, *Psalm 23* reveals the psalmist's total faith in the protection and guidance of the Lord. There is evidence of a new intimacy and trust between humanity and the paternal Almighty.

The closeness of the Lord reveals an identification between creature and Creator. This new emotional bond marks a transition in man's gratitude to the Father. A link has now been established between humankind's evolving emotional comprehension, between their finite superconscience and the infinite Supraconscience.

When the Psalmist writes, "Surely goodness and mercy shall follow me all the days of my life, and I shall dwell in the house of the Lord forever" we find a new level of intensity in spiritual love for God. The singer of the Psalm is experiencing the reward of total commitment to his ideal image of Yahweh.

There is an obvious lesson here for us. Committing oneself, one's intelligence and deepest emotions to an ennobling ideal opens the individual up to experience life as never before. When a person devotes him or herself in such a way, one's life overflows with a new sense of joy and abundance. This does not necessarily mean material rewards or success, but, rather, that one will experience the deepest gratification possible in this life. The pursuit of a truly noble purpose, fills one with rapture--and a deeper understanding of one's reason for being.

Psalm 51, on the other hand, is a confession of sin:

> Have mercy upon me, 0 God, according to thy loving kindness
> .... blot out my transgressions.
> Wash me thoroughly from mine iniquity, and cleanse me from my sin.
> For I acknowledge my transgressions: and my sin is ever before me.
> Against thee, thee only, have I sinned.

Clearly, this prayer begs the Lord's forgiveness and asks that his soul or psyche be cleansed. In a sense, the supplicant is asking God to purify his/baser nature, humankind's subconscience. Yet, at the same time, the psalmist desires to make a commitment to his higher self, inspired by the intuition that man possesses a higher conscience.

By appealing to the Almighty, the psalmist was in essence praying to the cosmic Supraconscience.

Psalm 100 is an expression of thanksgiving to the Lord for all He has given humankind.

> Make a joyful noise unto the Lord,
> all ye lands Serve the Lord with gladness....
> ... it is He that hath made us, and not we ourselves;
> be thankful onto him and his blessed name.
> For the Lord is good, his mercy is everlasting,
> and his truth endureth to all generations.

This Psalm would admonish all uncommitted Christians, Jews, and Muslims to treasure and take delight in their own heritage. Most need to relearn respect for their forefathers, commitment to a life purpose, consecration of life to a noble ideal. Today, there seem to be so many shallow men and women everywhere, people wandering like lost souls without any sense of gratitude for the potential they still have to live a meaningful life. The challenges of this time and place beckon them to a destiny worthy of their talents and intelligence.

The *Book of Proverbs*

Since it expresses enduring truths about life and death in an occult way, the proverb needs a special introduction.

A proverb may offer a familiar truth or practical piece of advice. In vivid and picturesque language, it presents a point of view or a philosophy of life. A proverb often captures the essence of human experience.

Beyond what our five senses tell us, proverb uses figurative language (metaphor and irony) to seek out the esoteric meanings of life. Such language originates from belief in the supernatural. This fact alone is an indication that men have always been aware that existence is governed by unique powers and energies, as mysterious as those that bring the individual to life, sustain him, and, at his death, withdraw from his body.

Figurative language is the manifestation of a higher intelligence at work. It urges us not to rest satisfied with the appearance of things, but to find the hidden, enduring reality. Proverbs are representative of mankind's archetypal search for truths that do not die.

Part of the Bible's wisdom literature, the *Book of Proverbs* is a collection of maxims and wise sayings, written, collected and organized from 500 to 150 B.C.E.

The Biblical accumulation of such truths gradually matured the human conscience. Proverbial verities broadened and deepened our understanding of who we are, what life is meant to be, and how we are responsible to our Creator. Proverbs became an integral part of the psyche's archetypal wisdom.

Thus, in our review, the world view of the Hebrews progressed from a legalistic, almost abject respect for Jehovah to a gentler, more grateful apprehension of God's concern for humankind. Yet, the Hebrews could never forget how severe His wrath could be in the face of disobedience and ingratitude.

At times, proverbs seem flashes of foresight into human destiny. Or, they discover universal and timeless truths. Since proverbs arise from the human imagination, at the service of emotional intelligence, they can express truths above and beyond those found in philosophy and law. In typical prophetic, i.e. figurative, language, the prophet says "For who so findeth me findeth life, and shall obtain favor of the Lord." (8:23-25, 30, 34-35). Similarly, "He who finds wisdom finds life"--whoever studies life to learn its meaning, that person shall find more than ephemeral truths. Enduring verities express the psyche's supernal comprehension of mankind's evolving destiny. As long as psyche emanates fresh insights, sound ideas, and visions of the future, it advances the evolution of humankind's supraconscience.

The *Proverbs of Solomon* (10:1-22:16) tend to stress down-to-earth, practical judgments. Solomon uses stark contrasts to make clear how our actions determine who we really are. What we do right and what we do wrong define each of us. He juxtaposes virtues and vices in an effort to show their consequences and to teach common sense morality; he also contrasts the man of knowledge to the fool, who is only skilled only in bringing about his own destruction. Lastly, Solomon juxtaposes the conduct of the upright who fear the Lord and the perverse who scorn Him.

We conclude our commentary on Solomon's proverbs by citing one last passage. "A wise man is strong; yea, a man of knowledge increaseth strength." (24:5)

The claim that knowledge is power is commonplace--and true. But, above and beyond that, the fact that it increases one's strength evokes a number of interpretations. Knowledge does give one a sense of greater mental capacity, and, in turn, that sense increases the feeling of well-being and abundant good health. Yet, psychologically speaking, knowledge opens us up to the universe, to the universality of human intelligence and, finally, to the psyche's natural sapience.

By contrast, ignorance generally leads to self-defeat and self-destruction. Awareness of one's ignorance can lead to a decisive conversion. With education, you can decide on--and direct--your own destiny. You can fulfill whatever aptitudes, capacities or talents you have been born with.

So, it is possible to live a life beyond fear and submissiveness or servitude to some unjust, cruel fate. By acquiring knowledge, we can glean its wisdom. Ultimately, we will know God as He actually is—all-knowing and all-wise.

The *Book of Ecclesiastes*

As if it had been written by a skeptic or a pessimistic philosopher, the author of this book of the Bible commends us to remember the Creator and keep his commandments.

It conveys the philosophy that all purely human wishes are vain. Instead of becoming attached to things of this world, we ought to "...search out wisdom concerning all things that are done under heaven...." In 2:12 he says, "I saw that wisdom excelleth folly, as far as the light excelleth darkness". Otherwise, "All things here below are vain...."

Such pessimism reveals itself to be a form of wisdom—it counsels you to restrain from the pursuit of vain pleasures or goals in life because such pursuits will eventually only prove to you how meaningless your life has been. Such a discovery would bring with it the realization that you have thrown away your life, a pathetic judgment on the worth of a lifetime.

On the one hand, pessimism is the expression of humankind's philosophical *subconscience*, which sees death as the ultimate truth; on the other hand, pessimism protects one from excesses, uncontrolled emotions, and vengeful passions because, in the end, we see everything is futile.

"Vanity of vanities, saith the Preacher, vanity of vanities, all is vanity." (1:2) That judgment seems to include any kind of human activity--building, planting, collecting possessions, accumulating wealth, and even seeking pleasure.

Yet, beyond this existential despair, the Preacher also offers wisdom: "To everything there is a season, and a time to every purpose under the heaven" (3:1-15). All of us may end in dust, but charity and benevolence bring their own rewards. "Cast thy bread upon the water: for thou shallt find it after many days." Such pessimism transcends self-pity.

Finally, the author advises," Rejoice in thy youth; walk in the ways of your heart", but remember that "for all these things God will bring thee into judgment." (Ch. 11)

In sum, *Ecclesiastes* teaches much wisdom about life from the perspective of old age. In addition, its despairing mode reveals the influence of the subconscience. Yet, in effect, it reflects the beginning of a wisdom that surpasses pessimism. Skepticism is the necessary prerequisite to the transcendental wisdom of the supraconscience, which sees through time--past, present and future.

The *Song of Solomon (Song of Songs)*

This is a poem of human love. Though the Jews undertook to sanitize its meaning by interpreting it allegorically as signifying the relationship between God and Israel, and the Christians undertook to recast its meaning once again in chaste terms as the love between Christ and the Church, the *Song* remains a poem of healthy, erotic love. It inspires man and woman to enjoy it for its sensuality and earthy truth. One line warns that jealousy is as cruel as the grave. Nevertheless, love itself can be as strong as death.

This poem requires a final comment, however. Though rare and fleeting, erotic love is the opposite of despair. Not only can sexual love be fulfilling; but it is, in itself, the promise of new life and reinforcement of the couple's commitment to create a meaningful life together.

The Prophets of Israel

Israel was renowned for its unforgettable prophets: Isaiah, Jeremiah, Ezekiel and Daniel.

Isaiah

Isaiah's call to prophecy is recorded in memorable language. Active between 738 and 700 B.C.E., his style is exalted and his language poetic. He regarded God as a friend to the Israelites, but on the condition Israel acted as His servant to teach His Word.

How remarkable it is that we remember--over centuries and indeed millennia--any individual such as Isaiah, a person who prophesied the truth as he envisioned it.

Today, by contrast, it is doubtful that any man or woman who endeavors to teach original wisdom will be remembered more than a decade. The present age is glutted with mediocre, fashionable publications that offer virtual reality and virtual truth, but rarely the real thing. The bottom line for publishers of such texts is almost always, "How much money will it make?" But, what price has humankind paid for ignoring Isaiah's priceless prophecies?

Characteristic of his sayings were the following. First, he urges us to 'wash ourselves clean of evil'. Then he adds, "Learn to do well; seek judgment; relieve the oppressed; judge the fatherless; plead for the widow."

There is also the impressive, "Let the wicked forsake his (way) and the unrighteous man his thought (of injustice). Let him return to the Lord, and He will have mercy upon, him; God will pardon him."

This is a remarkable historical and psychological turn-about. Whereas previously it was a matter of damnation for the wicked and the unrighteous, here we are told that Jehovah willingly forgives past immorality and crime--as long as the guilty cease doing ungodly acts.

If and when the meaning of the prophecy were understood, how would it affect mankind's subconscience? If it can abstain from violence and homicide, there would be reason for hope that an individual's subconscience could be healed by accepting and absorbing the sensible lessons and wisdom of the human supraconscience.

And, if humankind accepted its truth, that would mean that our primitive subconscience must acknowledge the fact there is much goodness in humankind. It would come to understand what humane justice, charity, fatherly patience and maternal compassion mean to living a life free from fear and anxiety-- and from dread of the unpredictable future.

Moreover, acknowledgment of the human supraconscience would mean that the individual had come to accept the fact that humankind's accumulated knowledge and wisdom reveal the superior nature of humanity. To survive in peace and enjoy mutual respect, we need to know that good is superior to the aberrations and mindless violence that the human race has experienced in various periods of history we now know have been evil.

By recognizing the subconscience for what it was in our age of primitive survival, and by acknowledging its continual influence on human history in the guise of cosmic, i.e. Satanic, evil, we can now understand what *conscience* has meant. For centuries, even millennia, it was infected with forms of primitive paranoia, masochism and sadism. Even though it could be strong some of the time, the sub-conscience relentlessly harassed, mocked, and inflicted wounds on the conscience of individuals, whole societies, and civilizations. Eventually, however, by our belief in one Supreme Being, humankind was inspired to fulfill its own potentials and hence to evolve a supraconscience.

Stimulated by our belief in the omniscience of the infinite Supraconscience, we accumulated secular knowledge, scientific laws, and pursued our quest to comprehend the purpose of human destiny.

It was Isaiah who taught us that our understanding of God could evolve. Modern knowledge has identified evolution as the inherent factor in humankind's metamorphosis from a subhuman state of being toward a supraconscience aware of our potential to reach a superior level of being human.

Jeremiah

For forty years, Jeremiah called for spiritual reform and few listened. About 598 B.C., he witnessed the Chaldean invasion of Judah and the capture of Jerusalem. He deplored his country's sinful ways and bewailed her coming doom. Indeed, his vision of chaos is unforgettable.

> I beheld the earth, and, lo, it was without form, and void; and the heavens,
>   and they had no light.
> I beheld the mountains, and, lo, they trembled, and all the hills moved
>   lightly.
> I beheld, and, lo, there was no man, and all the birds of the heavens were fled.
> I beheld, and, lo, the fruitful place was a wilderness, and all the cities
>   thereof were broken down at the presence of the Lord, and by his fierce
>   anger. (4:23-26)

Here we witness how easily an angry God could destroy mankind and all that he ever accomplished or created.

Jeremiah prophesied an invasion and conquest as punishment for Judah's sins. The Babylonians came, conquered and occupied the land. Yet, in the darkest period of this occupation, he prophesied that the people of Judah and Israel would regain their land.

It is interesting to note that his sharp criticism of his own people became modified and milder. He foresaw a time when they truly would know the Lord in their hearts. Indeed, he hears God say, "I will forgive their iniquity, and I will remember their sins no more." (31: 33-34) So, Jeremiah began to praise those who had remained faithful to God's guidance. It was then that the prophet predicted God would make a new covenant with Israel and Judah.

Since he observed this change of heart in his people, he foresaw a covenant that would enable humankind to become more understanding of one another and make their relationship to God more personal.

This change in the relationship between men and God appears to be akin to the new relationship between the finite supraconscience of evolved humankind and our conception of the infinite Supraconscience. There now existed an intellectual, emotional, and spiritual link that never before in history had been imagined. To be sure, we are no way equal to our supernal conception of the Supreme Being, but the human race has matured and become educated to the point we can better understand what the Deity expects of us. Perhaps now we are ready to be taught the wider significance of His infinite nature. Perhaps now we can sit before Him as fully awakened students who are spiritually prepared to listen to a true, master teacher.

Jeremiah's prophecy of a new covenant is worthy of further reflection. The idea of a modern day covenant opens up the possibility of a new form of psychic therapy. Is it possible that the supraconscience of modern man and woman could establish a covenant with our subconscience? As improbable as this sounds at first, the real question is this: Can we now come to terms with what we once believed to be evil, impelled by a cosmic force we called Satan?

Psychologically speaking, how might we establish a compact between the lower, instinctual energies of our subconscience and the higher, intuitive energies of the psyche's supraconscience? At least such therapy is theoretically possible. The supraconscience can learn to listen intently to the griefs, frustrations, and angers of the subconscience so as to therapeutically release the subconscience from its nameless terrors, guilt and rage. In exchange, the subconscience would learn from the supraconscience what humankind has learned over the past 5,000 years. Our inferior self could then come to realize what our superior self has accomplished in that time.

Perhaps this exchange could be presented in dialogue form between the inferior and superior nature of humankind–a kind of dialectic between the polar extremes of the psyche.

Ezekiel

As a talented prophet, priest and mystic, Ezekiel confronted the crisis of his time: the invasion and fall of Jerusalem followed by its eventual restoration. He vigorously rebuked his people when there was a need for it. He denounced false prophets, lying priests, and people for having given up just and righteous living. Yet, he himself came to know the limitations of self-righteous prophecy.

That he acquired a deeper insight into humanity is clear from the following: "...when the wicked man turneth away from his wickedness that he hath committed, and doeth that which is lawful and right, he shall save his soul." (18:27)--a rather startling suggestion since it asserts that salvation is possible for, and available to, all. In other words, we ourselves determine our chances of salvation in so far as we have an honest relationship with ourselves and God.

Another of his remarkable declarations was "...the son shall not bear the iniquity of the father, neither shall the father bear the iniquity of the son: the righteousness of the righteous shall be upon him; and the wickedness of the wicked shall be upon him." (18:20)

This prophecy shows a genius for justice. Not only are the sins of the father not the responsibility of the son, nor vice versa. Of course, this assumes the son has been properly educated in their religious tradition, and that the father has not himself become wayward, disreputable or immoral.

Most of all, this prophecy rejects the heritage which proclaims the sins of the fathers are visited upon all mankind till the end of time. In sum, each person becomes an individual solely by assuming full responsibility for the outcome of his or her own life. Hence everyone is responsible for what he does with his or her own life. In the context of our thesis: *decision determines destiny*, especially as regards our ability to choose the right and reject the wrong. The consequence to reaching a life–changing decision is its conversion of one's inferior self to the superior. Ezekiel's emphasis on individual responsibility and personal judgment is a decisive step in the development of the individual supraconscience.

Yet, Ezekiel's vision of Israel's revival after her defeat remains one of the most memorable prophecies in the entire Old Testament. He dreamed he found himself in a valley of human bones when a voice out of the stillness commanded him to speak the word of Jehovah to the bone-littered field. Ezekiel obeyed. The prophetic voice told him to tell the wind "Thus saith the Lord." He told the wind, "O breath, from the four winds, breathe upon these slain that they may live. And the skeletons stood upon their feet, a great army." (Ch. 37) Miraculously, every where the scattered bones collected into the complete skeletons of men and women.

To be sure, this vision calls up a number of possible interpretations applicable to our own lives today.

A skeleton reminds us that one day we will have become just *that*. Between now and then, there are decisions to be reached which will add up to fulfillment or frustration, fullness or emptiness, meaning or senselessness.

More obvious is the intended message of the prophecy: humankind should have faith that beyond the power of death there is a greater power. Beyond the matter-and-dust of existence, there is a life-creating energy able to irradiate what is dead and so bring it into life anew.

Sometimes archeologists sense this supernal power when they unearth an artifact that was buried millennia ago. A timeless presence seems to shine forth from it as if the light of day has brought it back to life.

Otherwise, realistically speaking, how is modern man to understand Ezekiel's remarkable vision? Aside from identifying it as an allegory, the prophecy startles us because it goes beyond anything humans had ever experienced before. Moreover, the resurrection of skeletons defies natural law, but, at the same time, the prophecy heralds a new truth about human fate: Death is a delusion.

Delusion

The prophecy declares that God's powers surpass and transcend all else. Its message for mortals is that, despite the defeat we experience in life and the despair we encounter, have faith. The individual who has faith in self and in the highest power in existence will experience personal rebirth and resurrection. Do not accept death as an irrefutable reality—it may be only an appearance.

Beyond this exhortation to spiritual trust, Ezekiel's vision embodies a great psychological truth. From the fact that the bones assembled into whole skeletons to become animated by the universal power of life, there must be a vital lesson to be learned. As scattered and disunited as the powers of our psyche may often seem, our determined and deliberate unification of them can enable us to review and redesign our entire life. Once we have chosen a purpose to live by, our aptitudes, talents and emotional needs can be integrated in such a way that we will have become matured human beings and focused on what is truly important in life. In unity of personality there is not only strength, but superhuman psychological strength. In the process, we can establish a more thoughtful identity, one which can become the true statement of who we were in life.

Because of its inherent creativity, the psyche's potential for self-mastery and self-transcendence can accelerate and further the evolution of the supraconscience. To realize our highest potential is to define the ultimate meaning of our lives.

The *Book of Daniel*

The *Book of Daniel* was written during a time of religious oppression (approx. 160 B.C.) when the Temple was desecrated. It is said that his visions were apocalyptic in nature. But, in point of fact, the term apocalypse refers to Jewish and Christian writing between 200 B.C. and 150 A.D. These books were written under pseudonyms to protect their authors from martyrdom. Using symbolic imagery, they predicted an immanent cosmic cataclysm at which time God would destroy all of the evil in the world and uplift the pious and righteous to life everlasting with Himself in heaven.

Hence the term *apocalypse* means prophecies which predict a universal disaster that will culminate in the revelation of the ultimate destiny of the world. Such doom awaits the wicked. The term *apocalypticism* refers to a doctrine describing "the immanent end of the world and ensuing general resurrection and final judgment" of God upon us. (10th, p. 54)

The reader should note the bond here between this religious fatalism and the fear, anxiety and paranoia which characterized humankind's primitive subconscience. It should also be observed how both these are echoed in the present-day doomsday talk of modern scientists who often seem to consider themselves prophets. The mathematical odds against many of their predictions ever coming true in the next millennium or two is infinitesimal.

As regards the life and death of the earth herself, let us be reminded of the two pervasive theories held by geologists. There are those who embrace the theory that the earth's crust has often been unpredictably changed by subterranean forces operating in ways that cannot yet be studied. Catastrophism lends weight to this theory and contributes to the widespread anxiety that earthquakes, volcanic eruptions, tsunamis, and life-threatening climate changes can happen any time.

By contrast, there is also a group of geologists who uphold the doctrine that the processes at work at present are the same as those in the past; hence they are sufficient to account for future geological transformations.

The point is that the earth sciences and astronomy are really just beginning to become reliable predictors of some events, but they are not yet sufficiently sophisticated to predict with confidence what is yet to happen to the earth, the sun, our solar system or the cosmos. Alarmist documentaries as to the fate of future mankind are therefore premature. Let us hope the apocalypicists in the scientific community stick to science and stop simulating the ancient prophets.

As regards Daniel's apocalyptic visions, he intentionally used esoteric language to mystify the profane; still, the faithful would understand him. His seemingly obscure utterances conveyed a deeper, truer spiritual meaning than did the *lingua franca* of the populace.

Briefly let us summarize Daniel's teachings. His central theme was that God's power was immense and overwhelming. Yet, to those who kept His Commandments, lived by His Covenant, and faithfully worshipped Him, the Almighty would be merciful. Furthermore, he believed angels were messengers from God, and, as certain passages of this book suggest, he also believed in life after death.

Also, his teaching no longer seemed to aim solely at the Israelites, but implied that God's kingdom was spiritual, therefore universal. All of humankind could seek admission to it. With this notion of the universality of the kingdom, Daniel's apparent intention is to put an end to the Jewish claim to exclusivity as God's chosen people. This had had the adverse affect of seeming to exclude the rest of mankind from God's protection and understanding.

Finally, some of Daniel's statements refer to the Son of Man, and Jesus himself referred to Daniel in Matthew (24:15)

Daniel's teachings seem to have influenced the prophetic *Book of Revelations* through his references to the Messiah. Hence he represents a spiritual link between the Old and New Testaments.

Stories Associated with Daniel's Life

The period of Daniel's prophecy was associated with a number of remarkable accounts of his life. They revealed his personal spiritual power and illustrated the fact that he seemed to always enjoy divine protection. Here we review only the stories of the Fiery Furnace, Nebuchadnezzar's Punishment, The Handwriting on the Wall, the Lion's Den, and the Restoration. These stories of remarkable imagination provide valuable spiritual insights to modern man.

The Fiery Furnace

Daniel had found favor in the eyes of King Nebuchadnezzar. When the king's astrologers, magicians and sorcerers were unable to explain dreams that deeply troubled him, he had them executed as frauds. The king then summoned Daniel to interpret them. Realizing their fate might befall him, he prayed for divine guidance and received a vision which foretold the rise and fall of kingdoms, culminating in God's eternal kingdom. He explained his vision to the king, and Nebuchadnezzar declared Daniel the wisest man in Babylon.

Later, however, Daniel and his three friends were commanded to bow down before a Babylonian idol, even though the religious convictions of the Jews did not allow this.

Infuriated by Daniel and his companions' refusal to co-operate, the king threatened to throw them into a fiery furnace. To the amazement and anger of the Babylonians, Daniel declared Jehovah would deliver them. The king took their religious defiance as a personal insult, and had them thrust into the blazing furnace. After the time allotted for their cremation, the king ordered the furnace reopened. Daniel and his three friends stepped out unharmed-- accompanied by a fourth figure radiant like the "Son of God". (Ch. 3)

Whether or not this story is factually accurate, it seems to point to an unforgettable spiritual truth, i.e. It reveals a universal fact about the human psyche: Whosoever has absolute faith in the power of the Omnipotent to ensure eventual justice and reward will be able to survive any fate. A further implication seems to be that, if they had been cast in hell itself by some demonic injustice, their faith in God would save them from harm and everlasting death. In sum, the story teaches us that true faith can itself become a supernatural power, one which we would, even today, call miraculous.

A King's Punishment

In the story of King Nebuchadnezzar's punishment, Daniel is again asked to interpret another dream. He predicted the king would be punished with a period of insanity—and this happened. When his period of madness ended, the king repented and praised the God of Israel. (4:3)

It is interesting to note how arrogance is viewed as a form of insanity, one which is transient and curable. The story makes clear that any individual who assumes god-like condescension toward the sincere, sane faith of others will be punished. He will be ostracized or castigated by those who wreak vengeance upon him for his disdain and arrogance. On the other hand, in the context of human evolution, this story may actually refer to the insanity inflicted upon us by our primitive subconscience. In reviewing the history of humanity, we must wonder about those times when whole populations were plunged into a state of mental suffering or even madness. In such moments, was the anguished subconscience rebelling against the growing strength of the Judeo-Christian conscience?

The Handwriting on the Wall

There is also the story of the handwriting on the wall. The successor of Nebuchadnezzar, Belshazzar flaunted the faith of the Jews by using wine cups pillaged from the Temple of Jerusalem. This impious act brought forth a supernatural event. Human fingers were seen to write a message on the wall, striking fear in the hearts of all who were present. Daniel was sent for. Bluntly, he interpreted the omen to mean the end of the kingdom was near. "Thou are weighed in the balance, and art found wanting." That night Belshazzar was assassinated, and Darius, the king of Persia, overtook the kingdom. (Ch.5)

This story is a clear warning against showing contempt for the beliefs of others. Through haughtiness and scorn for the defeated and downtrodden, one can expect swift and deadly retaliation by those hungering for justice and revenge.

We often hear today the expression "the handwriting on the wall" when we have an overpowering premonition of oncoming danger or disaster. It not only teaches us to seek out the possible meaning of portents and forewarnings but also to sensibly foresee the consequences of our own thoughtless actions and disregard for others.

The Lion's Den

Still another unforgettable story is about Daniel in the lion's den. When Darius became king, he honored the prophet with a respectable position. This appointment led envious court officials to conspire against Daniel.

By royal statute, the king had established that no petition could be made during a thirty-day period, except to Darius himself. However, Daniel's daily prayers to God were interpreted by his enemies as an appeal to the Almighty, hence he had defied the royal command. They pointed out Daniel's disobedience and convinced the reluctant king to have him seized and thrown into a den of unfed lions.

Once inside the den, the lions approached him, but suddenly a glowing angel appeared. With a wordless command, the angel subdued and calmed the hunger-maddened beasts. The door was then opened, and when the king saw Daniel had not been harmed or attacked by the quiet lions, he released him "because Daniel believed in his God." (Ch. 6)

The psychological truth this story tells us is that unswerving faith in higher ideals and in some supreme purpose in life will protect us from the doubts and fears that could otherwise **destroy** us.

In sum, all of the above are memorable stories. Their sense of poetic and ethereal justice remains with us. The faith in this justice is such that we would not challenge it. Perhaps they embody an otherworldly lesson for humanity: unearthly truths may ultimately prove truer and more real than earthly reality.

Daniel's Final Vision

In Daniel's interpretation of Nebuchadnezzar's dream of the four kingdoms visualized as four beasts, he interpreted the fourth one as the kingdom which "shall devour the whole earth, tread it down, and break it to pieces." (7:23) Thereafter, an everlasting kingdom will be forever ruled by the most High.

Following this interpretation, Daniel had a final vision. After a period of mourning and fasting, he saw the end of the world as he knew it. He alluded to a war between north (Syria) and south (Egypt). Under the victorious Syrians, the people of Israel were oppressed and experienced a great deal of suffering. But, at last, miraculously, the angel Michael appeared to deliver them. He declared that many "that sleep in the dust of the earth shall awake, some to everlasting life, and some to shame and everlasting contempt. And they that be wise shall shine as the brightness of the firmament, and they that turn many to righteousness as the stars forever and ever." (12:2-3) In modern terms, what does this prophecy tell us?

At the time of the final judgment of mankind, the earth will cease to exist. We will have turned to dust. The good souls will be reawakened to live a life everlasting with God in heaven, and the wicked will exist in shame in some oblivion, damned for all eternity. Special rewards will be reserved for the wise and those who taught humankind to act in accord with divine and moral law. These souls shall brighten the night sky as sparkling stars in the far reaches of God's universe.

Hence Daniel foresaw the end of the earth, of humanity, and of time. All that will remain of life on earth will be the resurrected souls in heaven and in God's firmament. If this prophecy is true, as so many of Daniel's proved to be, then there still is time for every human being to judge his or her contribution to the destiny of humanity and to determine what his or her moral worth will be at the end of time.

The Secular Understanding

To appreciate the substance and ultimate sense of the stories associated with Daniel, we need to consider in a general way the nature of prophets as it is evidenced in Isaiah, Jeremiah, Ezekiel and Daniel

Where does a prophet's fervor and conviction come from? Evidently, he is empowered from within. Certainly prophecy amounts to more than self-righteous satisfaction at seeing one's enemies undone, more than judging evil and predicting final retribution. Indeed, it contains an important message. The prophet seeks to use his ability to foresee danger and disaster so as to help others avoid impending pain and suffering. The prophet's knowledge of humankind enables him to see what others cannot. His fervor arises from a kind of fatherly instinct to protect the blind, ignorant and innocent from the life-threatening evil in this world.

On the other hand, most prophets have witnessed the oppression and enslavement of their people at the hands of the powerful and victorious. When this happens, a prophet's world has been inverted, its moral values have come to be despised, despoiled and even extinguished. In such circumstances, he feels powerless, yet still keenly aware of what is just, righteous and sane.

The prophet's vision of a ruined world is reminiscent of the anxiety, anger and fatalism of primitive humankind in the earliest age of our primate survival. However, there is a marked difference between the two. In place of the paranoia and rage that prehistoric man must have experienced at times, the prophet of antiquity reveals that he has become a transformed human being. One might say that his raw emotions have become transfigured—and, in turn, these spiritualized passions suggest that the psyche of humankind may become uniquely empowered during recurrent periods of crisis.

Over the various stages of successful survival, humankind has learned to measure its emotional responses to crises. The experiences that have threatened our survival have caused us to effectively develop a new mental capacity, namely, emotional intelligence. And, gradually, by the consistently wise and astute use of his emotional acumen, the prophet accumulated wisdom.

Otherwise stated, Daniel's intuitive knowledge of humanity helped him measure the meaning of the events he foresaw. By continuous evaluation of the validity of this foresight, the prophet slowly but surely developed his power of prophecy to a high degree. This practice evolved his supraconscience. And, generally speaking, the prophetic aptitude in humankind has nurtured our supraconscience.

Isaiah, Jeremiah, Ezekiel, and Daniel—what did these prophets undertake to do for mankind? They labored to awaken kindred souls who had become wayward or lost their sense of purpose in life due to the destruction of their homes and villages. The Jewish people may have been conquered and enslaved to 'soulless' barbarian neighboring tribes. Or, feeling they were trapped in a time and place where there seemed no future other than servitude, their past beliefs and traditions had become empty and meaningless. Whatever the reasons, when the prophets spoke of their people's weaknesses, failings or faithlessness, it was ultimately for the purpose of recalling to them the omnipresence of God--even when He seemed to have abandoned them. By reminding them of who they once were because of their beliefs, accomplishments and achievements, the prophet himself empowered his own supraconscience. It told him to speak the words of God to his people and to future humanity.

It may not be unreasonable to think of prophetic intuition as a manifestation of humankind's supraconscience given that it is directly inspired by the awareness of the presence of God. In other words, the prophecies and spiritual teachings which resound through the Old Testament seem to have been spoken by the Supraconscience itself.

Let us review the evidence for a human supraconscience, as it was recorded in the real world of recorded history. The secular record reaches back some five millennia. It demonstrates the fact that all of the races on earth have created and accumulated knowledge.

Every culture has developed skills in survival, and in separate regions of the world, viable civilizations have not only sustained themselves but also evolved systems for educating the intelligence of their people. Are we to believe that human accomplishments were restricted to practical skills and instruction in morality, either from a religious or from common sense perspective? Rather, exceptional individuals everywhere taught themselves to hone their talents and aptitudes to a superior comprehension of their world. Moreover, through developing mutual trust and cooperation, men and women educated one another's powers of emotional discernment.

In so far as they aided one another, they were able to achieve advances in civilization far beyond what our primitive beginnings could ever have foreseen. So, men and women in the real world can, together, attain to levels of excellence and perfection that previous ages would have thought to be superhuman. What humankind has achieved thus far in taming nature and converting raw reality into sophisticated civilizations is itself superabundant evidence of humanity's supraconscience.

If the supraconscience was initially inspired by religious faith, the purposeful accomplishments of our secular intelligence revealed our species' superior pragmatic abilities and cultural endowments. Collectively, we have become conscious of humanity's intelligence and sensitive to the spiritual bond among humankind. Together humanity manifests a finite version of the divine Supraconscience in this infinite universe.

Yet, the study of prophets and prophecy leads us back to still more humble realizations: The spiritual travail of the prophet remains a mystery. What, if anything, does a prophet do to encourage the visionary experience? Daniel spoke of angels who were direct messengers of God. That may be, but prophecy may simply be a poetic way of describing original thought, spiritual breakthroughs, or basic truths that a prophet calls wisdom.

We do know something about what it takes for an individual to become a prophet: Solitude and openness to the powers of one's imagination. But these are also requirement for developing a supraconscience whether it be religious or secular in nature. Actually, original ideas or prophetic visions come through as images which have a powerful emotional impact. Since they are associated with supernal experience, it is easy to believe they are messages delivered by an angelic power directly from God. And, in a society which is imbued with a sense of the mystery of existence, the belief that angelic powers animate the mind is understandable.

Then again, in any society where religion is an important element in the life of the people, there are educated individuals who bear in their memories the wisdom of the past. Though the populace may have forgotten their ancestors or become indifferent to everything except what is happening in the present, there will still be those who cherish knowledge and wisdom. In the third millennium (C.E.), such rare individuals are likely to be involved in contributing to the further evolution of humanity. And, individuals who possess the gift of prophetic intuition might sense that, from the beginning, the evolution of humankind seems to have been guided by an infinite Supraconscience.

But what about most of humanity today? The fact is that they work in order to live. The greater part of humanity is overwhelmingly occupied with the responsibilities of parenthood, with learning new skills, with fulfilling vocational responsibilities, and generally with everyday survival. They are intent upon building and securing a global community. For these reasons, it might be more appropriate to call modern man *Homo hablis*: pragmatic man, one who survives through resourcefulness, skills and realism.

The fact remains that only a small percentage of humankind has the money, security, time or freedom to live as *Homo sapiens*. (i.e. as wise and intelligent man). *Homo sapiens* are supposed to be even-tempered, well-informed, experienced in life's ups and downs, thoughtful of others, and wise in the ways of the real world. In this day and age, not many human beings meet all of these criteria.

Yet, quite remarkably, the ancient prophets would have done so by reason of their fervent interest in educating people to higher order truths and showing them the transformative powers of these truths. So, it would not be an exaggeration to aver that the Old Testament prophets were some of the world's first identifiable *Homo sapiens*.

In the secular world of the ancient Greeks, historians, writers of the great tragedies and philosophers would also represent this level of human intellectual and spiritual development. Of course, non-Western civilizations also created moral codes, systems of education, and laws which ensured humane treatment for all. *Homo sapiens* had this wisdom at his disposal to guide his own evolution.

There have always been individuals dedicated to study, speculation, contemplation, musing, imagining, ideation, the conceptualization of higher truths, and the religious cerebration of life.

In essence, the world's poets, patriarchs, prophets, and philosophers all fit into this category—they were and are all striving to understand human life. Any man or and woman who thinks creatively, holistically, logically, and systematically is doing just this, particularly in attempting to consolidate or systematize human experience into some form of knowledge or wisdom.

Moreover, such men and women may well exceed the basic definition of 'sapiens', *i.e. someone who knows or is in the act of knowing*, by the fact that they have already discerned that there is at work--in either their conscious thought processes or their moments of spontaneous, spiritual inspiration--a level of intuition that may transcend the definition of knowledge which their particular society, race, or culture recognizes. Indeed, given our present-day understanding of the goal of human evolution, such people may now recognize in themselves the intrinsic power of our evolving supraconscience

Let us return to the prophet Daniel and his renowned ability to interpret dreams. Beyond his apparent contact with the Supreme Being, we need to consider realistically what his gift of interpretation means to the modern individual.

Most of us are familiar with general human psychology or theories about the human psyche. For instance, psychotherapists interpret the significance of private dreams to explain how the *unconscious* (Freud's use of the term) conveys the meanings of particular experiences in an individual's life. Also, dreams may well up from what Jung terms our "collective unconscious."

Yet, as with Daniel, it is quite another matter to interpret dreams as messages delivered by Angelic powers from God Himself. The sound-minded, realistic interpreter would surely balk at asserting he or she is blessed to have a direct hot-line to the Almighty.

However, there is another, very real possibility that such dreams or even prophetic visions may be grounded firmly in our biological nature. It would be quite a different matter to understand that one's dreams might be psychic intuitions pointing to one's future evolution. That is, dreams could be prophecies of what we might accomplish in a lifetime. They can become reality if one nurtures and develops a distinct form of intelligence. They may become psyche's self-fulfilling prophecy of a destiny that will prove to be true.

In the sciences, it is expected that experiments achieve predictable outcomes and results. For the evolving human psyche, a similar guideline may be applicable. Hence, by way of a positive interpretation of the human powers of prophecy, the individual psyche can have faith in the fact that what he or she is shown in his visions may be born out in reality.

Of course, some realists will mention the fact that there is another, down-to-earth source of such special insight. In the twenty-first century, we are now able to make realistic forecasts concerning the conditions of future life on earth based on a common sense assessment of social, political and geo-cultural conditions, and a given suite of historical events.

Nevertheless, there is a lesson to be learned from our discussion of Old Testament wisdom literature and from our review of the prophetic powers of Isaiah, Jeremiah, Ezekiel and Daniel. It is that we ought to place ourselves in intimate contact with our own developing supraconscience. Be guided by what it positively prophesies you can be or become; then do your utmost to fulfill that prophecy by making a lifelong commitment to it.

Notes

1. Strauch, *A Philosophy of Literary Criticism*, 1974, pp. 120-21.

Chapter Seven
The New Testament

Introduction

So much of Christ's life is known from the Four Gospels of the New Testament that it is not necessary to belabor the details here. Moreover, since several respectful and sensitive versions of his life have recently appeared in movies and the media, there seems little advantage in simply abstracting from the accounts of the Gospels according to Matthew, Mark, Luke and John.

It is more pertinent to concentrate on memorable insights which illustrate the presence of the human supraconscience. In other words, our aim is to present the sense and substance of Christ's life.

The common ground of understanding that exists between the traditional religious and secular interpretation can help identify meaningful similarities. Some readers are already familiar with the fact that Christ's use of sacred terms differs from the terminology used in the Old Testament. This is especially true when Jesus speaks of God's omnipresence in nature and in our lives.

Let the reader bear this in mind: He announced that his role was to make clearer the laws and prophecies of the Old Testament. Yet, he found it necessary to reinterpret the traditional understanding of the Father. Consequently, Christ came to teach the people of his time a new way of thinking about God. He taught Christians a more intimate way of conceiving the Almighty and of comprehending God's guidance of human destiny.

The Christian's patience is therefore requested as regards what follows below. Some references and passages are so familiar as not to call for commentary; still, the reader may feel that the twenty-first century calls for a secular review of Christ's message.

The *Gospel of Matthew*

The first three Gospels are those of Matthew, Mark, and Luke. They present the established biography of Christ, His teachings, crucifixion and resurrection. The fourth Gospel, that of John, is based on oral tradition and written testimonies.

The impact of Christ's life on mankind is most perceptible where our conception of time is concerned. The abbreviation B.C. alludes to all events in antiquity prior to his appearance on earth. Generally, this earlier period of time is referred to as 'pagan'. When first used, this term meant the time of the polytheistic religions of ancient Greece and Rome. In the eyes of later Christians, it meant any hedonistic or irreligious person. On the other hand, the Church used the expression *Anno Domini* to describe the beginning of the Age of Christianity. It meant, in essence, "the year our Lord was born".

However, secular historians in the twentieth century undertook to establish a more objective historical time by introducing the abbreviation B.C.E. (Before the Common, i.e. Christian, Era) and C.E. (The Common, i.e. Christian, Era). In sum, the conception of time was transformed radically. Christ's life gave it an entirely new meaning.

In Pre-Christian times, people often subscribed to a fatalistic philosophy of life--pagans believed in the 'science' of astrology. One's fate was determined by the alignment of the stars at the time of one's birth.

By contrast, Christians could no longer believe the stars decided their destinies because the Savior had promised the faithful an afterlife with God. The Christian was to become responsible for his own life through personal decision. Time was given a teleological meaning. Life was to be lived for a purpose. This could be the secular insight of our time as to the message of Christ's life.

Christ's decision to pursue his earthly destiny changed the world for billions of people in the ensuing centuries. In the face of death, He taught the sacredness of love, forgiveness, courage and resoluteness. His decision to take up the cross ennobled and humanized humankind.

Matthew believed that Jewish history could find new hope by proving Christ was the Jews' long awaited Messiah.

According to theological genealogy, Jesus descended from Abraham and David. Indeed, the birth of Christ is purportedly the fulfillment of Isaiah's prophecy, "a virgin shall be with child, and shall bring forth a son." (7:14) An angel guided Joseph to Bethlehem where Jesus was born.

An actual genealogy of this is unlikely, but, if we speak of Jesus as a great figure in religious history, that is another matter. His teachings alone are remembered across twenty centuries. They exemplify wisdom and humaneness and will remain with us as long as there is at least one Christian remaining on the planet.

Yet, let us consider the possibility that Ezekiel's prophecy of the birth of the Savior could be substantiated by secular reasoning.

Studies in evolutionary biology reveal that humankind went through successive stages of physical and mental evolution. Over time, we developed the skills of manual dexterity, creative versatility, and resourcefulness. Today, we could easily identify them as human beings.

As with the evolution of all species, sudden mutations can occur. In a single evolutionary step, a marked progression in an animal form can emerge. In the case of human evolution, superior intelligence has successively appeared over the millennia.

Certain conditions and circumstances precede the birth of an exceptional human being. Though his life may initially appear unexceptional, in times of cultural crisis, such charismatic individuals can transform their time. To that extent, the Old Testament anticipation of the arrival of a Messiah could explain how Christ became the realization of an ancient prophecy.

Prophecy itself is built on expectation and the need for hope in the future. At the time Christ was born, the Jews themselves were at a turning point in their history, ready for momentous fulfillment in their lives.

In Bethlehem, an angel told Joseph the child "shall save his people from their sins."(1:21) Beyond the literal sense, what else could this have meant? In the context of Jesus' impact on history, it meant that the Savior could save human beings from leading lives without true meaning. Life itself became meaningful only by proving that one was worthy of God's love.

Perhaps most noteworthy is Matthew's narrative of the savior's work in Galilee (4:12-25). It reports that Jesus taught in synagogues, preached the gospel and healed the sick.

Let us speak realistically about healing the body and the mind. Today many sicknesses are known to be psychosomatic. Often physical sicknesses are revealed in neurotic behavior or as the affect of emotional crises. In this day and age, psychosomatic medicine is a medical specialization.

In ancient times, the Greek physician Hippocrates (ca.460--377 B.C.), the father of medicine, developed the art of body-mind healing. In the time of Christ, when people's lives were largely governed by superstitions and fear of demons, it is likely that many people suffered psychosomatic sicknesses.

Consider the impact of Jesus' teaching on those who had faith in him. Individuals believed the promise of the kingdom of God. They welcomed the hope that Christ's Father in Heaven would relieve their suffering and revive them, after death, to life everlasting. Moreover, Jesus persuaded the humblest individuals to take control of their lives by believing faith could cure all sickness.

To a degree, the truth of this gospel is confirmed today. As Jeanne Achterberg's work, *Imagery in Healing. Shaminism and Modern Medicine* (1989) so well demonstrates, when an individual has faith in the body's capacity to cure itself, life-giving imagery can uplift and inspire the psyche to actually heal the body and restore its natural equilibrium.

Of course, it has been known for millennia that certain herbs have medicinal and curative properties. It is entirely possible that Jesus possessed such knowledge. Coupled with spiritual persuasion, He could indeed effect cures that must have appeared miraculous to the meek and uneducated, to those who were not knowledgeable of human biology and spiritual psychology.

When Jesus healed in the name of faith in God, those who were possessed--and generally all onlookers--believed he had superhuman powers. By his words and the persuasion, he spoke for God. Jesus was able to cleanse people's souls of the fiends that had seized them. And, when people accepted that he was acting on behalf of God, he brought about deep psychological changes in them, releasing them from the physical diseases caused by their subconscience.

The meaning of Jesus' acts of healing resides in the faith that ultimately one can cure oneself. The power of the subconscience over the vulnerable conscious mind will persist until mankind undergoes a conversion to the faith that life itself has some ultimate purpose and meaning. When modern man and woman gain superior insight through faith in God, their lives can be transformed. Individuals who conscientiously develop personal inner power will create a meaningful life of their own.

By nurturing an ideal, an individual can be healed and transformed. Individuals who conscientiously develop personal strength will create a meaningful life of their own. Indeed, faith in man's superior nature can be turned into an effective therapy that can bring about the remission of diseases and the restoration of a sound mind in a sound body.

The comments above concerning Jesus' probable knowledge of medicinal herbs are intended to prove how intimately he felt God's blessing in the good earth. Moreover, his superior soul was revealed in the Sermon on the Mount, the Lord's Prayer, and countless sayings which expressed his superhuman intelligence. Whatever he said strikes us with a Truth beyond common sense or even the astute reasoning of deeply educated Pharisees and Sadducees. It was Supernal Truth.

Matthew recalls a statement only the Messiah would have made. Christ stated He would return to earth with "all the angels with him". Are we to take this literally or figuratively? From a respectful, secular point of view, it could have a quite realistic meaning. In the future, when an enlightened humanity finally understands his teachings, we will be spiritually prepared for His return–but only then. When mankind truly *lives* the message of His life, the prophecy could come true. Only then would He actually be among us again.

In our contemporary secular terms, humankind must first learn to confront their savage past and the primeval subconscience before any significant collective enlightenment can be reached. They need to devote a part of their lives to fostering humanity's superior nature. Later, we will examine in closer detail how this can be done.

For now, let us realize that we have caused evil in the past and deserved some form of damnation. Yet today, we have the means to be our own salvation. Faith in a Supreme Being is ultimately faith in the future of humanity. Our evolving supraconscience has much to teach us about ourselves, including the purpose of human evolution.

During Jesus' time, Palestine was occupied by the Roman army, and deep resentment smoldered in the hearts of the Jewish people at the severity of Roman justice. The extensive use of crucifixion to execute criminals was used to instill fear in the masses and so to control them. This kept the populace under constant stress and justified the secret hatred of their oppressors.

Moreover, though the populace of Jesus' time no longer remembered their ancestors' struggle for survival, the Roman conquest re-opened old wounds and goaded their primitive subconscience. Its instinct of survival at any cost ruled the mind. Its readiness to betray and entrap, the ease with which the subconscience bore false witness against others marked its coarse mentality. The tendency to rage, violence and murder ruled their mental world. This was the world gentle Jesus was born into.

The Jews had been impatiently awaiting a militant Messiah who could lead them in a revolt against the Romans. Hence when their envious priests declared

Jesus to be a charlatan and false Messiah, the mob turned on him. It was under these strained political conditions that Christ was crucified. But, in fact, it was man's savage subconscience that slaughtered Christ—whose appearance in the world was the clearest, early sign of mankind's evolving supraconscience.

Evidence of Christ's superior nature is found in many parables that ended with a moral or universal truth. In Matthew's gospel, one sermon, the Beatitudes, described the blessed. "Blessed are the poor in spirit for theirs is the kingdom of heaven. Blessed are they that mourn, for they shall be comforted." (Matthew 5:3-12) He also taught the people how to pray. "Our father who are in heaven." (Matthew 6: 9-15)

His spiritual truths were spoken to help Christians live without fear of tomorrow. He taught them how to live their futures. "Lay not for yourselves treasures upon earth. But lay up for yourselves treasures in heaven." (Matthew 6:24) Learn the truths of the heart, mind and soul, for that is the proper way to worship God in heaven.

The *Gospel of Mark*

During the reign of Emperor Nero (54-68 A.D.), the early Christians were persecuted and many were senselessly put to death for their faith. So, the conditions of life during this period also bore marked similarities to what prehistoric man and woman had undergone. The life of early humankind and of the early Christians was continually threatened by death. The menace of predators and the threat of martyrdom must have benumbed or emotionally damaged the survivors, and constantly tested their sanity. Anxiety, fear and recurrent experiences of bloody incidents in which people were put to death surely infected mind and body of most people. Such mental confusion and unrelieved psychic pain was endured by the early Christians.

The *Gospel of Mark* was written about 70 A.D., shortly after Nero's reign ended. Its paramount purpose was to uphold the faith of those whose lives were endangered daily.

Mark narrates John's baptism of Jesus, which he notes was pleasing to the Holy Ghost. (1:5) This ritual has a specific psychological effect on the individual who was baptized. When baptism is undergone by an adult, it is said to cleanse body, mind and soul. Its significance is evident from the influence it exerts on one's decision to live a clean life. This message is clearly implied in the story of Jesus' life after he was baptized.

He went into the wilderness for forty days to meditate upon his life and ultimate destiny. There he encountered his own demon—Satan himself. The devil offered Jesus various temptations unworthy of Christ's earthly mission, but "angels were there to minister to his needs". (1: 12-13)

What is meant by this? The connection between his baptism and his decision to reject what was unworthy of him leaves a message for us. By fasting and purifying his body, mind and soul, he could face any enticement which would defile, corrupt or debase his divine purpose in life. In terms of our thesis, he faced his own primitive subconscience as a man and came to terms with it.

As the Christ, He was able not only to transform his inherited human weaknesses, irresolution and indecision as to the purpose of his life. He also transfigured his resolution by deciding his ultimate human destiny. This single moment in religious history teaches the true Christian to reach a final commitment to live a life of purpose and meaning. So, the Christian of Mark's time should commit himself anew to faith in Jesus Christ.

Jesus taught the parable of the lost sheep to reassure each individual was precious in the eyes of God. He reminded parents of their sacred trust in rearing the young. "Suffer the little children to come to me, and forbid them not: for such is the kingdom of God." (10:14)

Clearly, children are in need of attention, protection and love. Beyond that, Christ insists that we must be aware of the child's future. In fact, its future will help decide that of humanity. Proper parental guidance is needed for the child to realize his or her goals and live a worthy life

But how is this to become a reality in the light of tragic human history? Modern man has the advantage of historical hindsight. What is needed in the third millennium is a deeper faith in a positive and self-fulfilling prophecy for humankind.

Modern man has the advantage of perceiving the meaning of humanity's evolution from primate to *homo sapiens*. For example, we are now better able to interpret Christ's allusions to his Father's kingdom in broad cultural terms. Human history has made it self-evident that our highest level of evolution has been due to the cultivation of the psyche's aptitudes and talents. These innate gifts have actually guided us to teach ourselves all we know and to reassure us of what we are truly capable of achieving. The belief that God created us inspired our own god-like creativity.

In essence, what Christ has urged upon us in plain words should also be a prophecy of humankind's future. We have evolved superior foresight by incorporating hindsight through becoming cognizant of the cultural history of humanity. Thus our responsibility to our children, and to ensuing generations, is clear. We must nurture and educate their ever maturing intelligence in every way we can. Surely, this includes teaching them how to teach themselves how to live a meaningful, fulfilling life.

Of course, to be competent enough to be the guides of our own children, we ourselves must first educate ourselves well. This means cultivating our intuitive intelligence as far as possible.

Christ was not always the Christ. In the beginning of his life mission, he was a carpenter's son. Who taught him what he knew? Surely Jewish Law and moral tradition provided him with the basic knowledge of Judaism. But the wisdom he is known for came from what he taught himself about the world, about humanity and about the miraculous powers at work in nature.

Hence education should take in to account the immense importance of the psyche's evolution and the significance of the supraconscience to our future survival.

Mark quotes Jesus as saying "Heaven and earth shall pass away, but my words shall not pass away." (13:31)

Thus, for Jesus, everyday reality revealed eternal truths. By his example, he taught humankind to see through reality at the mundane level and contemplate it at the level of the angelic and the divine. Humanity was to find sacred meaning of the most finite forms of life. Why? Because everything revealed the infinite presence of God. Even in the infinitesimally small, startling universal truths were to be found.

Moreover, humanity still had much to learn: to see beyond the trials and tragedies of this world, beyond human suffering and sorrow, and beyond our fear of fate. Death itself was but a finite, final moment. The transient nature of life was the measure of its meaning. In the end, what did any individual life mean?

However, Christ was also a realist. He was fully aware of the power of primitive human nature. He knew that what defiles a man "comes out of a man. From within come evil thoughts, fornication, theft, murder, adultery, wickedness, deceit, licentiousness, envy, slander, pride, foolishness. All such evil things defile a man." (Rev.,7:20-23)

Here, Christ matter-of-factly describes the effect of the primeval subconscience on humankind—which challenges even the Ten Commandments and the Covenant with God. Indeed, human history has made abundantly clear that our prehistoric subconscience could defile the most self-assured and spiritually oriented conscience.

Christ's insight into the baser elements in human nature also led him to offer an unforgettable challenge to the conscience of every man and woman ever born: "What shall it profit a man, if he shall gain the whole world, and lose his own soul?" (8;34-36)

Clearly, he admonishes us to get our priorities right. What should our purpose in life be? It should *not* be to accumulate wealth and possessions at the cost of our own true worth. In other words, we should not forsake our ideals. Jesus' every word and act became the realization of a higher destiny. And, if humankind is to evolve further, people must empower themselves by actively seeking to realize the purpose of life itself. Christ's teachings expressed an imperishable truth: Let us treasure life itself for the immortal wisdom it can teach each of us.

Chapters 14-16 of the *Gospel of Mark* center on Christ's Passion and Resurrection. Instead of dwelling on Christ's life-embracing message, Mark stressed the ignorance of those who condemned him to die. They knew not who he was. At his trial, Jesus uttered no word in his defense because his life's work already spoke for him. Below the tribunal, the rabble had been provoked to fury by the Jewish fundamentalists and zealots. When Pilate asked, "What evil has he done?", the mob roared "Crucify him!" So, as Roman procurator of Judea, Pilate ordered the crucifixion. And, as is well known, Jesus' last words on the cross were "My God, my God, why have you forsaken me?"

Biblical scholars explain that this desperate outcry is an allusion to Psalm 22, which begins with the same words and ends with the assurance of salvation. This certainly establishes a spiritual continuity between the Old and New Testaments, but there is, perhaps, also a secular lesson in it for the twenty-first century.

If we consider Christ's lifetime mission in the context of human evolution, we realize that it reveals the emergence of the evolved supraconscience. Confronted by the irrational sadism of the rabble's subconscience, he experienced the fate of history's unforgettable martyrs, saints and heretics.

These holy individuals were often hated for living life as if it had some sacred meaning. Despite their disastrous fates, the appearance of exceptional human beings suggests that humankind is destined to evolve a higher species.

Each of the Stations of the Cross shows Christ abused, humiliated, and eventually tortured to death, all sadistic acts which characterize the primitive subconscience. Yet, he accepted such suffering because, in those hours when he was on the cross, he believed that his Father would make known to the world that Jesus was his Son.

Christ's ordeal was akin to Job's mistreatment at Satan's will. The reason for Jesus' physical death was so that he learn what it meant for human beings to die without hope.

Similarly, there was a purpose to Christ's entombment in a dank, dark cave before his Resurrection. Three days in utter silence and darkness taught him the ultimate meaning of the physical decomposition that the individual undergoes after death. By experiencing this corruption himself, Christ would gain the fullest understanding of human fate, of lives lived without faith in some ultimate significance to life.

The *Gospel of Luke*

Written between A.D. 80-90, Luke's Gospel portrays God as the sovereign of heaven, naming Him the Divine Father. Luke also foresaw Christ's Second Coming. He spoke of God's kingdom as ubiquitous and the Lord's sympathy with universal humanity. The poor and humble would be welcome in the kingdom. All in all, his Greek is full of beauty and grace, and reflects a sense of compassion for mankind. Luke was an educated man who emphasized repentance and faith in order to receive forgiveness and merit salvation.

Characteristically, he provides the details of Jesus' birth, baptism, and the Temptation in the wilderness. He also retraces the Galilean Ministry (4:14-9:50) thereby illustrating Christ's healing of the broken-hearted and the recovery of those who were blind and ill.

Luke repeated the *Sermon on the Mount*, which names those who are blessed--the poor, the hungry, and those who suffer injustice. All shall receive their reward in heaven. Jesus concluded the Sermon with the unforgettable words:

> Be you therefore merciful, as your Father also is merciful. Judge not, and you shall not be judged: condemn not, and you shall not be condemned: forgive, and you shall be forgiven." (6:20-30, 36-37)

The New Testament 137

Jesus also taught open-heartedness to those who seek him:

> Ask, and it shall be given you; seek and you shall find; knock, and it shall be opened to you." (11:9-10)

This Gospel concludes with the stories of the trial, passion, persecution and ascension of Christ. (Chapters 22-24).

Luke's version of Christ's life inspires many, yet the realist, the skeptic and even the cynic find his crucifixion to be reason for despair. Has the world really changed because of his sacrifice? History seems to be an endless series of tragedies. Outside the boundaries of our brightly lit civilization, there seems a dark chaos swirling about us like the vast black holes, vortexing in outer space and slowly devouring the light of the universe. Faceless terrorists have recently vowed to incinerate the civilized world, so that there is today much reason for fear and despair, and little hope for everlasting light and life.

To some, Christ's dying for the sake of humankind seems an act of utter futility. Assuredly, his unblemished example inspired Christians to be more compassionate, but those who still practice the virtues and demonstrate a sense of human decency grow terrified by the fanaticism and insanity of the subhuman killers who are now at large in the world. The faithful's awe and veneration of Christ's unforgettable life often gives way to the fear that they soon will be victimized by the rabid hordes who have no other purpose in life than to exterminate those whose beliefs differ from theirs.

The *Gospel of John*

The *Gospel of John* was creatively planned and written by a man with intimate and deep knowledge of Jewish culture. Purportedly, he himself witnessed many of the events of fifty years earlier. His gospel is dated at about 85-95 A.D. The historic details it contains suggests that he personally knew the private thoughts of both the Apostles and Jesus himself.

This gospel is presented as evidence that Christ actually was the Son of God. So, his purpose was to persuade the skeptics that Christ did indeed rise from the dead. He assured them that, if their faith were true and abiding, they too would be resurrected. He himself witnessed Christ performing miracles before the multitudes. What makes John's work original is his ingenuity and the depth of his spiritual insight into Christ's use of symbols as: the bread and wine of the Last Supper, the Incarnation, and God's Word creating all things.

Let us consider any word as both a verbal reality and as a religious symbol. Among our primitive ancestors, the discovery of speech by the first individual to use a word must have been a remarkable moment. When others repeated the word, it came to have a shared meaning. This conscious understanding created the beginning of human intellectual exchange. Over time, we learned to substitute hundreds and thousands of words and recognize their common meanings. Language became the common bond of humanity.

Moreover, something unusual also took place in the individual when this happened. When a word expressed a shy or deeper feeling, that moment was like the exploration of the recesses of one's inner being. Words discovered something that humankind came to call 'soul'.

John undertook to explain Jesus' symbolic use of common words which today make up an idiom of special, sacramental significance. Jesus transformed the literal meaning of bread and wine, the Last Supper, the cross and crucifixion into a sacred language, one that is now used by more than a billion Christians worldwide. In our daily lives, we witness the miraculous power that words have to unite humankind.

In his Prologue (1:1-18), John wrote "In the beginning was the Word, and the Word was with God, and the Word was God."

Let us try for a moment to imagine the first primate-human to utter an appeal to the Great Spirit above. That first prayer linked his or her inner being to the Supreme Being. Such utterances, such attempts to reach out to that infinite power would have left a lasting imprint on mankind's collective memory.

But where did language come from originally? That remains a timeless mystery. Whatever its origin, it made us human.

John's Prologue also contains words revered by Christians. "And the Word was made flesh, and dwellt among us."

The obvious reference is to the Son of God, Christ. Yet, the imagery may conceal yet another interpretation, i.e. it could mean that God gave us language so that we could share feelings, good will and intelligence. If so, the emergence of language would be proof that God has given us the ability to establish peace among peoples, races and religions.

To be sure, a skeptic or cynic would not fail to point out that, over the millennia, we have misused and abused that gift. Indeed, it would seem our primitive subconscience has used language to provoke misunderstanding and enmity among mankind. And, their objection would be justified on the basis of historical and empirical evidence.

Yet, when used interpersonally, language helps us express our anguish and suffering. It also makes us more able to show compassion for others' sorrow. Charitable words allay fears and mitigate despair: Language enables us to give and receive love.

On the other hand, etymologies and the history of a language enable us to retrace the various stages of humanity's mental evolution. In addition, language empowers us to build majestic edifices of secular and religious knowledge: the natural and human sciences, the humanities and comparative religion. All reveal realms of the psyche's universal experience. The history of language itself gives expression to humankind's evolving supraconscience. Language makes possible contact and communion with what we believe to be the Supraconscience of Existence.

John's Gospel also makes mention of the marriage feast of Cana. This event, too, seems to point to a secular explanation of its sacred significance. John reports that, when the hosts had no more wine to serve the guests, Jesus turned jars of water into wine. Skeptics smile and declare that this was just a magician's trick, but John insists that it was evidence of Christ's otherworldly powers. His insistence on the verity of the story requires us to grapple with what it meant to John.

Obviously, changing the water into wine was meant to enhance the guests' enjoyment of the marriage celebration of the man and woman. In the ecclesiastical sense, this act on Christ's part foreshadows the trans-substantiation of the bread and wine in the Christian ceremony of the Eucharist. But at Cana, it is the union of man and woman that symbolizes the joy of natural love, which produces the miracle of children. The couple becomes a father and a mother, and, from this day forward, in their role as parents they are born anew.

In essence, Christ taught both the wedding guests and the couple an earthly lesson. Love itself is the true miracle of existence because it forever creates new life. What is needed is for two to have enduring faith in each other. In marriage, we celebrate the holy power of life.

The *Book of Revelation* and its Teachings

The *Book of Revelation,* the last book of the Bible, is the only prophetic book in the New Testament. It centers on a series of astonishing visions, all of which have mysterious meanings. It also brings together prophecies of the Messiah and those of Ezekiel and Daniel.

John writes in apocalyptic terms of the coming of a new heaven and earth under Christ. The *Apocalypse* describes the anxiety before an imminent cosmic cataclysm. God will annihilate evil on earth, but will rescue the righteous in order that they may live in a renewed world. At Christ's Second Coming, mankind will be saved and redeemed. And, He declared firmly, "I shall come quickly."

Unfortunately, so far Christ has not re-appeared in two thousand years of human history. Perhaps the Divinity measures time differently from humankind. In the third millennium after Christ's crucifixion and resurrection, Christians have come to believe the prophesied cataclysm is upon us with our world terrorized by homicidal fanatics and the genocide of entire populations. Perhaps He will yet return with infinite power to judge what man has learned from history and from his own evolution. Or perhaps He will not return at all.

At present, there seems to be many once-faithful Christians who are disappointed, disillusioned and in despair. When will the Last Judgment take place? Perhaps the series of astonishing visions in the *Book of Revelation* will eventually reveal to us humanity's fate in terms the lay person can understand.

Remarkably, John's understanding of the Old Testament prophecies of Christ's return in glory seems to replicate what has taken place in the evolution of the human psyche ever since the first human being sought to conceive the Supreme Being.

In previous chapters of this work, we traced the stages of the evolution of the human supraconscience from the accumulation of real world, practical knowledge and the gathering of life experiences to understand their definitive meanings. We now propose that the ultimate purpose of human evolution may be not only to discover the significance of sacred truths, but also to treasure the secular wisdom we have acquired.

Otherwise stated, if we are to judiciously interpret the angelic visions of *Revelation*, secular knowledge and some degree of cultural sophistication are required to probe and illumine the deeper meanings of John's mystical insights.

What do these visions announce? Does *Revelation* clarify the purpose of human evolution? Will man's acquired knowledge, his ingenuity, his maturing emotional acumen decide his destiny?

In the Prologue (1:1-19), the author tells us he received these revelations while on the Greek island of Patmos. He heard a great voice, as if sounded by a trumpet."I am the Alpha and the Omega, the first and the last...." John was to record his visions of "the things which are and the things which will be" (1:10-11, 19).

With such a pronouncement, we expect the voice to speak of the beginning and end of every life and of human history itself. And, as both the Old and New Testaments illustrate, the message will include the accumulated knowledge and wisdom of mankind's previous cultures.

John's visions are cited in (4:1-22:5). He writes not only of perpetual processes in world history, which, to us, also describe the processes inherent in the cultural evolution of the human psyche. When the struggle between forces of evil and good is described in figurative terms, the language of the text actually points to the struggle between our inferior and superior nature, that is, it reveals our evolution from a prehistoric subconscience to our present-day supraconscience.

After the vision of the throne of God and the adoration of the Lamb, we are presented with the *Book of the Seven Seals*, each of which miraculously reveals yet another vision (6:1-8:6).

Based on modern man's encyclopedic knowledge, we may interpret this book as follows. Consider the history of science. Once science developed a universal method for investigating the physical and natural world, that method was used to explore unfamiliar areas of knowledge. This created foci of specialization. Each new field of study derived from a previous proto-science, and each specialty, in turn, opened up further insights into reality understood in macroscopic terms. Thus the original logical assumptions behind scientific inquiry continued to proliferate specialized studies of the physical, chemical and astronomical world.

The life sciences also illustrate the spiritual lesson which the seven seals teach. Derived from biology, such specializations as botany, ecology, zoology, evolutionary biology, and microbiology generated further specific studies. For instance, microbiology led to the study of micro-organisms and micro-cultures, micro-fossils and micro-flora, micro-environments, micro-morphology, and micro-evolution.

Consider the human sciences: anthropology, ethnology, sociology and psychology. Each of them has original theories and corresponding areas of specialization.

The New Testament

In sum, the vision of the *Book of the Seven Seals* is such that, when it is unsealed and read, one discovers another new seal. Each one opens onto a further prophetic vision. Indeed, this Book alone prophesies the future of ever-evolving knowledge. The sciences themselves substantiate the insight that humankind's supraconscience is consummating its own form of omniscience. Thus as each Book prophesies the discovery of a new form of intelligence, each seal may, in fact, be revealing another phase of human evolution.

In *Revelation* (chapters 8-11), John describes seven trumpets, each of which announces another vision. These trumpets seem to allude to humankind's need to express their emotions, passions, hopes and joyous faith.

The study of the humanities reveals how human beings express themselves in art, poetry, music, literature and philosophy. These multiple modes of self-expression fulfill an emotional need of the more sensitive, sensible representatives of our race. Impressionists seek to effectively evoke subtle moods and delicate feelings. Surrealists seek to recall the mysterious atmosphere of dreams and nightmares through fantastic, irrational imagery. Expressionists express subjective emotions, by using distortions of reality to convey existential pain, anxiety and despair.

Through ever-developing means of discovering nuances of reality in pencil drawings, ink sketches, etchings, water colors and oil paintings, the arts evolve of their own accord.

In stone and marble, the sculptor can create a figure of a man or woman that endures for centuries. Majestic figures of the Christian patriarchs have long stood in the porticos of the great cathedrals of Europe. The sculptures of Michelangelo, Donatello, Bernini and Rodin remind us of psyche's own evolved grace and power. Architecture finds expression in doors and windows that bring in the light; in angular roofs reflecting sunlight; in graceful, spiraling staircases; in elegant columns and towers; in magnificent arches, arcades and domes. All of these designs express the genius and evolving intelligence of architects through various periods of history: Greek, Roman, Christian, Byzantine, Romanesque, Gothic, Renaissance, Baroque, Neo-Classical, Islamic.

Music also developed a multitude of ways to produce distinct sounds, voices, tempos and rhythms--all of which entice and move both the musicians and their listeners.

Poetry can express all forms of feeling. It can be lyric, heroic, nostalgic, remorseful, despairing, ecstatic.

Through fable and fairy tale, comedy and tragedy, tale and story, literature records every feeling and passion, witticism and wisdom ever expressed by our kind.

Philosophy undertook to guide humanity in secular terms. In keeping with climate, genius and belief, it taught that sound thinking is the goal of life--the greatest achievement possible is mastery of the mind.

Thus, the vision of the Seven Seals seems to prophesy the ways the human psyche will accelerate its own evolution. It suggests that knowledge will become universalized by the proto-sciences when they evolve ever-superior methods of perception and conception.

On the other hand, the *Vision of the Seven Trumpets* seems to spell out how the creative self-expression of the humanities will lead to ever-superior revelations of human thought, emotion and insight. Alternatively, one might say that the skills evolved in the practice of art, music, literature and philosophy will eventually lead humankind to a superior level of sophistication in interpreting life. Universal truths, in so far as they are accessible to man, teach us that there is both an intellectual and an emotional basis for all of humanity's knowledge. Ultimately, creativity accelerates the humanization of our species.

In sum, the vision of the seven seals and the seven trumpets prophesy phases of future human evolution. As the generations come to new knowledge and invent new skills in self-expression, slowly but surely they will find the universal Omega of human destiny.

The providential visions above offer us auspicious insights into the nature of reality. By contrast, Chapters 12-13 of *Revelation* contain dire warnings of a coming catastrophe. Specifically, there are visions of woman judged by the 'seven deadly beasts.' Such an indictment of womankind offers, however, little promise for our further humanization.

This image implies that at the Last Judgment womankind will be seized by creatures from Hell. She seems fated to be damned for all eternity on the basis of some 'evil' in her nature. It is possible such judgment reflected the paranoia in antiquity aroused by the dread of venereal diseases. Or, it may be based on the story of Adam and Eve's 'sin' in Eden. It is irrational to malign woman for Eve's sexual complicity with Adam, which supposedly introduced evil into God's pristine world. Or, possibly, John felt the need to reiterate the Old Testament warning against submitting to evil in any form at all--even that of a beautiful woman.

However, to judge from John's obvious education, we are called upon to offer an enlightened secular re-interpretation of this ancient damnation of womankind. In fact, he may be showing woman to be unjustly accused and villified by coarse, malicious zealots. The abuse and villification of her clearly recall the taunting, revilement and torment inflicted upon Jesus on Calvary. Hence, John may be warning men that insulting, harming, or thrashing women will lead Christ to judge their tormenters as no more than beasts from Hell--deserving eternal punishment.

Hence the image of woman threatened by subhuman forces would make clear John's level-headed, compassionate understanding of her traditional fate. Throughout history, women have been ill-treated, raped, injured and oppressed in cultures which are marked by absolute male dominance. In today's ultra- traditional societies, it is not uncommon for women to be judged by their own fathers, uncles and brothers and to be harshly punished by them. Surely, such unsound judgment and victimization of women is evidence that the prehistoric subconscience is still alive in our world and is still virulent in the world.

Chapters 15-16 of *Revelation* envision seven vials of wrath, each sufficient to produce a plague. Though the word *plague* literally means pestilence or epidemic, figuratively speaking the vision is even more foreboding. With regard to man's prehistoric nature, the vision may be interpreted by our barbaric past. In that case, "vials of wrath" could represent violence, vengeance and murderous acts. Vengeful rage leads to revenge. In turn, retaliation leads to reprisal--and eye for an eye, measure for measure--until everything is destroyed and everyone is annihilated. The history of humankind has largely been governed by such vicious cycles; hence this vision is not actually a prophecy, but a warning: Unless we can change by educating the human mind and the psyche to their higher nature, the savagery of our past may be our future.

Chapter 17 (1-22;5) ends *Revelation* with a vision of God's forces emerging triumphant. We are promised that "there shall be no more death, neither sorrow, nor crying; neither shall there be any more pain; for former things are passed away." (21:1-4)

Our argument thus far has suggested that much of the world's evil was originally provoked by the unremitting mental pain our ancestors endured in prehistoric times. The daily struggle to stay alive in a predatory existence inflicted continual fear and anxiety and infected people's minds with mental disorders such as paranoia, masochism, sadism and an unpredictable killer instinct.

To interpret the final vision of *Revelation*, we must revisit the overall argument of our book: The description of God's final triumph over evil seems to prophesy the eventual victory of humanity's supraconscience over the subhuman past dominated by our subconscience.

Altogether, Revelation presents three reassuring visions which demonstrate God's mastery over evil. Chapter 4-5 show God enthroned in heaven where Christ, the Lamb, is adored. Chapter 14 reveals the Lamb enthroned with angels of judgment at His side. The third and last vision establishes God's complete omnipotence.

The three visions of Christ and God in heaven, culminating in the affirmation of the supremacy of the Almighty, is John's final prophecy. In terms of our analysis of human evolution, this would suggest that the plenary power of mankind's supraconscience will be consummated and used for the good of all humanity.

Thus, the *Book of Revelation* has been interpreted here in terms of ideas that modern man and woman can understand and appreciate. Ultimately, the hope is that the evolving supraconscience will continue to educate our conscience and humanize our subconscience. Let us have faith that our evolving human nature will eventually enable the members of our species to judge one another with justice and charity.

Part Four

The Supraconscience: Historical and Modern

Chapter Eight

Mystics and Mysticism

To understand mysticism in the modern age, we need at least an acquaintance with a few mystic figures of the past.

Our first example of mysticism comes from the Middle Ages in France. The story is associated with the famous French philosopher and theologian, Peter Abelard (1079-1144). An open-minded thinker in an intolerant age, Abelard's writings showed a courageous tolerance toward different religions and preached the ideal that ideas should be freely exchanged.

His most memorable work was *Sic et Non*, i.e., *Yes, But Also No*. To the consternation of ecclesiastical authorities, he compared and contrasted some 1800 passages from Scripture and the Church Fathers, who contradicted one another in answering basic questions of faith. By demonstrating this, he taught the reader to come to his own sound decisions independently. Abelard's dialectical method, which is reminiscent of Socrates' method of systematic doubt and pursuit of truth, challenged Church authority. [1]

Though his procedure left its imprint on the scholastic method used to write massive summas, the history of mysticism remembers him more as a man with red blood in his veins. When he tutored the seventeen year old Heloise, they found that their hearts and minds were meant for one another. Once family discovered their secret, an outraged uncle arranged to have Abelard castrated. The lovers were separated. She was sent to a convent to spend the rest of her life there. The two exchanged letters, and Heloise remained true to their love till he died. She sent for his body and had it buried near the convent. When she died, she had herself buried next to him. Her love remained sacred and everlasting.[2]

Through this tragic love story, we learn an eternal truth from the secular world. The intimacy of man and woman can transform itself into a sacred love, however the world judges them. By self-surrender and the purity of their passion, lovers can know the ecstasy of the great mystics.

Yet, for all our admiration of male mystics pursuing their spiritual search, their commitment is not greater than womankind's. What the sensitive, educated, love-centered woman experiences also fulfills the heart and uplifts the soul. For some women, love is salvation from a life marred by with lack of understanding on the part of the sex-centered male. Such a love is her reward for the lifetime responsibility of motherhood, for protecting her children and educating them to the realities of life.

For certain women, without such love, life offers only the consolation that giving birth can bring. But in her heart of hearts, she would be willing to give anything to once know this kind of holy love.

Young Heloise was a heretic in so far as she defied the mores of the Church. Her society was basically indifferent to the real right of woman--to be respected for her mind and character and adored for her soul. The mystic in woman deserves the love she secretly holds sacred.

Another figure of the Middles Ages was Joachim of Flores (1145-1202), founder of the Brethren of the Free Spirit. His visionary conception of Judeo-Christian history moved him to describe the Old Testament as the age of the Father and the New Testament as the age of the Son. The age of the Holy Ghost would take place when God Himself would teach mankind. This radical revision of history obviously reduced the final authority of the Church. Beyond this, the Brethren recast the doctrine of the Holy Trinity and questioned the value of the sacraments. Heaven and hell were mere symbols not actualities. Moreover, where there was love, there was no sin.[3]

The main concern of the Brethren was to transcend human imperfection and to strive for perfection. Their thought has an affinity with the thesis of *The Supraconscience of Humanity*. Today, we know that humankind has undergone successive stages of physiological mutation through the ages—changes which were activated to adapt to worldwide environmental conditions. If we apply that paradigm of long-term evolution to the transformation an individual undergoes in his or her life, it could explain the urge to strive lifelong for greater self-reliance and personal perfection. So, the Brethren's decision to overcome the challenges at different stages of life by achieving moral wholeness is a sound philosophy. Modern man can sympathize with the reinterpretation of his religious tradition. Gradually, a person shifts from naiveté to maturity, and the self-reliant individual undertakes to reach ever higher degrees of self-perfection.

On the other hand, the Brethren believed that anyone who seeks God can never be defeated, but will ultimately be rewarded in life—a view that still has validity in the twenty-first century. Any individual who has a higher purpose to fulfill in life senses the presence of God. Unlike those Christians who seek God only when they feel pain, anguish or remorse, the Brethren experienced joy in working to transform and ennoble humanity. Their commitment to freedom enabled them to liberate themselves from the fatalism of belief in the power of evil. They did not allow themselves to become obsessed with demons, delusions, or phantoms. They were committed to making the here and now sacred.[4]

They had unearthed an important psychological truth. If one is preoccupied with the good, one is basically protected from sin because of its relative banality. The same seems to be true when one lives for a worthwhile purpose and has faith in human goodness. Dedication to the good in humankind turns one's sin into a mere misdeed, not some ever-lasting reason for shame.

With their emphasis on the joy to be found in this life, the Brethren avoided the widespread despair of medieval Christians whose tendency was to renounce this evil world. In good conscience, the Brethren could enjoy the life they had.

This they demonstrated by embracing the spiritual joy in the act of love. Men and women met as equals. They believed God had sanctified love ever since creating Adam and Eve.[5]

How is this an example of mysticism? Contrary to the dishonesty, deceit and dishonor they witnessed, in the world, the Brethren embraced the faith that God would reward the honest Christian who dared to think for him or herself.

Meister Eckhart (c. 1260-1328) is also one of the great Christian mystics. Though his age was predominantly influenced by scholasticism and all of the logic that it entails, his mystical fervor transcended it. In other words, his emotional acumen proved more powerful than his learned, rational intelligence. While preaching, he is known to have felt completely detached from himself and the real world around him.[6]

This is a common experience to those deeply concentrated on work of any significance. As long as one is immersed in the process, there is no self, no consciousness, only movement toward fulfillment of a purpose. One seems to be a spirit searching for the meaning of the moment or of a self-chosen task. Sometimes one does not foresee how the work will end.

Eckhart was much concerned with the nobility of the soul. As noted, in terms of our thesis, we believe that, throughout human history, the soul referred to actually is humankind's evolving supraconscience. Since man identified God as the Supreme Being, theologians and secular thinkers alike have undertaken to define the metaphysical significance of the Divinity. Today, because we are enriched by new knowledge from the natural sciences, the humanities and the human sciences, we may come to see God as the Supraconscience of the Universe.

What lessons are we to learn from Eckhart's experience while preaching? What of our own 'absence of mind' when fully concentrated on a line of thought or completing a project? There seems a connection between the mystic's deep intuitive commitment to his salvation and his relation to the paranormal and what we ordinary mortals experience. By devotion to an ideal and by self-education, certain individuals come to the knowledge needed to gain mastery over their destinies. Such dedication can become the means of accelerating the evolution of one's own superior nature. In any case, mental concentration expedites the completion of goals. It also brings with it the knowledge that you can carry out any noble task that has been seriously undertaken. Trust in your purpose in life may enable you to realize a unique destiny.

Meister Eckhart did not believe evil existed nor that the devil's temptations kept one from reaching for God. Instead, he thought it was important to detach oneself from the mundane and the banal. Moreover, Eckhart believed that God made it possible for the individual to perfect the self through a series of mental and emotional rebirths.[7]

This commitment to self-perfection bears a striking resemblance to the modern view of human history. Eckhart's vision of the process that the Christian should go through in a lifetime reminds us of the stage-by-stage evolution of humankind.

In other words in retrospect we have evolved by increasing our knowledge of the world and cognizance of our own mental capacities. Man has actually proceeded through millennia of self-education and surpassing the past. Conditions of survival necessitated such self- evolution.

In a way, the whole process of human spiritual evolution has been a cyclical confrontation of past experience and present knowledge. By this instinctive/intuitive dialectic between the inferior and superior in us, we have raised ourselves above our primitive nature to such a level that we are now endowed with rational and emotional understanding.

We may have Meister Eckhart to thank for the intuition that the Christian's destiny should parallel the achievements of human evolution.

Mystical Numbers

Before proceeding further it is important to introduce the reader to the unusual way mystics have historically used numbers.

From the eighteenth century to the present, thinkers have been cynical as to the value of studying mysticism per se. During that period, science accepted only empirical evidence as pointing to truth; philosophy accepted only sound arguments as valid sources of knowledge. However, since mysticism dealt with the ineffable, how could it provide any reasonable interpretation of everyday experience?

The author hopes that such evaluations will be reconsidered in the light of what we have learned about infallible judgments, be they religious or secular. If nothing else, the evolution of the human psyche is evidence that truth itself evolves. So a measure of tolerance toward religious and secular mystics is necessary.

As early as the sixth century B.C., the Pythagoreans held the belief that numbers held some mystical message. Pythagoras himself believed in the eternal recurrence of nature, in the harmony of the spheres, and in metempsychosis (the passing of the soul at death into another body, human or animal).

Similarly, the medieval and modern system of Jewish mysticism developed a cipher method of interpreting scripture. The cultivation of an awareness of esoteric meanings camouflaged in exoteric passages was characteristic of this method. Indeed, the study of scripture revealed strange and remarkable coincidences. When the Hebrew alphabet was translated into numbers, as in the Kabbalah, miraculous messages appeared before the cabbalist's eyes. Such exercises in ingenuity pointed to a different understanding of reality and suggested that reasoning itself had dimensions beyond those assumed in the physical sciences or practiced in the procedures characteristic of arithmetic and mathematics.

A deeper perception of reality seemed to emerge from the reassurance that numbers created order out of chaos, helped us make sense of the circumstantial. They replace disorder with some kind of superior order. However, unlike their practical use in arithmetic and mathematics, in the Kabbalah, numbers go beyond being integers to become symbols of religious meanings. It is as if they somehow sum up the significance of life and existence.

Thus, even if the conclusions of Pythagoreans, cabbalists, and numerologists remain questionable, these thinkers nevertheless seem to have intuitively come to understand something important. The numerologist seeks out the hidden connections between quantity and quality, between number and the numinous. Through such orientation mystics study how abstract knowledge, rooted in number and quantity, might relate to experiences of the sacred. They believe mankind has an eschatological destiny and seek to grasp the final meaning of existence by transmuting the cryptic into a deciphered message from God.

Mystical Metaphors and Symbols

Let us now consider briefly the use of metaphor and symbol in poetry and religion.

As a figure of speech, a metaphor can compare a truth about life and a thing: When in bloom, love is a vibrant rose, but when it withers, its beauty is turned to dust. A symbol can stand for an idea, a truth or even a destiny. Often it is a visible sign of an invisible, eternal verity.

Let us make this point still clearer. How does a metaphor become a symbol? To answer this, a glance at Christian symbolism may serve our purpose. In the medieval period when illiteracy dominated the western world, the Church sought to instruct the people through a vast encyclopedia of symbols. Everything recalled or conjured up the most important event in the history of man--the descent of God upon the earth, his assuming flesh and bone, his terrible suffering as a human being, his death, Resurrection and final Ascension. This story provides the context for nearly all of the religious symbols employed in the age.

To mention only the most familiar, Christian symbolism included: *animals* (donkey, ox, dragon, fish, lamb, and dove); *plants* (the apple, tree, palm, rose, lily, and thorns); *colors* (blue, red, gold, green, purple, and white); *people* (the Christ child, Christ on the Cross, the four evangelists, fishermen) as well as *objects* (bread, fountains, books, demons, garden, hand, crib, nails, sword, staff, left and right, and numbers).

If we arbitrarily choose a few to search for a clue to the transformation they represent, we find the fish is the symbol of Christ because the Greek word *ichthys* (fish) represented the early password "Jesous Christos Theou Soter." The dove represents the Holy Ghost in its associations with flight, gentle presence, and the angelic. The apple reminds us of the sins of Adam and Eve and God's law; also, in paintings where the Christ child reaches for the apple, it is the symbol of His readiness to take upon Himself the sins of the world. The crown of thorns worn by Christ represents the human sins for which he must offer expiation. A lily symbolizes the Virgin's immaculate conception. The red garment Mary wears in medieval paintings symbolizes the blood of the sacrifice of her son, and the blue one, air, truth, the breath of life and the Savior Himself. Sheaves of wheat depict the bread of life, the Eucharistic bread or Christ's body. Hence for the faithful, every symbol re-evoked the event of Christ's death and resurrection, and deepened his or her feelings for Christ, and all the memories they recalled.[8]

What energizes these animals, plants, colors, people, objects and concepts to become true symbols? What empowers an image to transform into a symbol so as to always call forth a certain meaning in a given context?

The change from image through metaphor to symbol occurs when an image becomes the sign of an unforgettable event. It becomes memorable when it illuminates the meaning of a life. It often reminds us of the power of death in our lives. Hence mystical symbol urges the individual to pursue a lifetime purpose which will guide one to true salvation.

The above discussion of numbers, metaphors and symbols was intended as background to understanding the mysticism of Dante Alighieri (1265- 1321).

Dante wrote *Vita Nuova (The New Life)* at the age of twenty-seven. Two years earlier, his beloved Beatrice had died, and his grief led him to love her beautiful spirit as only a mystic can. Throughout the remainder of his life, his love for her transformed him from an early master of lyric poetry into Italy's greatest poet with his completion of *The Divine Comedy* just prior to his death in 1321. This masterpiece describes Dante's progress from personal grief and the horror of damnation in hell to bliss for heaven's pardon of earthly failings. His works are, in essence, magnificent translations of the mentality of Medieval Europe.

The *Vita Nuova* describes young Dante's search for the direction and meaning of his existence. This quest required him to face life's ultimate riddle: death. In so far as he contrasted present and past in this work, Dante's working out of *Vita Nuova* led him to discover his deepest self; this discovery, in turn, prepared him to pursue his life's purpose.

Already as a youth, he recognized in existing things the enigmas of matter, form and reason. As a Christian, he understood man's being as an earthly trinity of vital, animal and natural spirits emanating from the Holy Trinity--God. Thus, his work is evidence of the fact that number mysticism seemed to hold the key to explaining the mysteries of human destiny.

Moreover, to him, love appeared to be the center of a circle. It extended outward to the circumference of the entire universe. Love itself was a universal truth. In fact, since ancient times, such a circle had been a symbol of the Deity. For Christians, the love irradiating through the universe came from Christ the Savior. Similarly, Beatrice had become the very center of Dante's life.

Her death matured his understanding of the meaning of love. When he viewed her dead body, he visualized her soul ascending to heaven. There she received the gift of Divine Love. This vision led him to comprehend the transsubstantiating power of love. For him, the miracle of her transfiguration resolved the riddle of death in life. In mystical terms, the death of the poet's beloved was his own resurrection. Her life and death initiated his quest to solve the riddles of existence.

Dante understood that the patterns of the universe influence our lives on earth. He discovered symbolic consonance and concord between personal experiences and his beckoning salvation, between his earthly life and his eternal destiny. In short, he aspired to Holy Grace.

In his dreams, ancient myths taught him the need for personal atonement, and they confirmed his faith in a personal immortality. In Mithraism and Gnosticism, he found further confirmation of his belief in the doctrine of redemption through a personal savior--Beatrice and Christ. These past religions taught him wisdom. He learned that life's experiences and mystical intimations were guiding his quest for meaning. Indeed, they inspired him to strive for greater spiritual and moral perfection.

In the years following the production of *Vita Nuova*, the poet became a mystic by seeking to understand human destiny in symbolic terms. Through his devotion and dedication to one woman, he created for himself a new destiny.

Dante's *Divine Comedy* is based on a theo-centric concept of existence with the HolyTrinity as its essence. The work visualizes the earth with Jerusalem at the middle. Hell is depicted as having nine circles proportioned according to the seven deadly sins. Purgatory had nine ledges on which repenting souls purified and prepared themselves to merit entrance into Paradise. In Heaven, the motionless Empyrean sphere enclosed nine concentric circles at the center of which were enthroned Christ and the Holy Virgin.

Besides Dante's autobiography, which describes his earthly and artistic development, the poet's experience became a mystical quest. The *Commedia* recounts the faithful's attempt to find their way through this and the transcendental world. Dante's life became a mystical journey through space and time aimed at realizing the ultimate meaning of human existence.

Pascal

Known for his work in mathematics and physics, Blaise Pascal (1623-1663) invented a mechanical, calculating machine, worked out a first principle of hydraulics, and developed a statistical probability theory, which dealt with the relationship between possible and probable outcomes in a given circumstance. In the 19th century, his theory was formalized into the mathematical discipline of probability and statistics.

Of special interest is the fact that he divided reason into two modes: the *l'esprit géomètrique* (the *spirit of geometry)*, or the work of analytical judgment, and *l'esprit de la finesse* (the *spirit of finesse)*, or perception of the world through intuition.

Because his was a mathematical and scientific mind, Pascal is of particular interest to us. At the age of 31, he underwent a mystical experience which influenced the rest of his life. While in a darkened room for two hours, he was blinded by a radiant light. It overwhelmed him as if God were present and utterly real. He then wrote a testimony to this epiphany on a small parchment and secretly wore it around his neck till the day he died. It was only then that his servant discovered it.[9]

Pascal testified that God had filled his soul with a luminescent vision of reality which completely transfigured his perception of this world. He withdrew from society to the seclusion of Port Royal to purify himself of sin and save his soul. There he became a defender of Jansenism, which opposed the Church's opulence, Jesuit rationalism and Augustine's doctrine of predestination, i.e. the claim that God's foreknowledge of events infallibly guides those destined for grace and salvation. Instead, Pascal believed in pious asceticism and held that the dispensation of grace depended on man's will.[10]

Pascal's religious and philosophical reflections are found in his *Pensées* or *Thoughts on Religion and Other Topics,* published after his death in 1670.

Central to this work is his appreciation of the vastness of space and the infinity of time before we are born and after we die: The only certainty mankind knows is uncertainty. Though he is but a frail reed in nature, he is a thinking being. Nature and natural things are unaware of their own existence, but man is superior because he is acutely aware of the fact that he exists and thinks about the significance of his life.

Based on his probability theory, Pascal proposed to use a wager to determine whether or not God exists. Humans cannot avoid speculating either on God's existence or against it. If He does exist, to believe in Him is to know eternal life, but to deny Him means that nothing is lost. Thus, "if the wise gambler chooses to accept the reality of God, to win the wager is to win all, but to lose it is to lose nothing at all."

Pascal was one of the great mathematical minds influenced by Europe's reawakening to the intellectual beauty and value of classical Greek and Roman literature, art and architecture. His work also foreshadowed the Enlightenment's respect for secular, human knowledge and its distrust of authority. He would have appreciated Diderot's *Encyclopedia*, a compendium of human knowledge and especially of contemporary, i.e. 18th century, knowledge.

Yet, even given all of his achievements, Pascal deserves our deepest respect for his mysticism. Despite his firm faith in man's rational powers, he was able to trust the reality of his epiphany even more so. That single hour converted his doubting spirit into a life of mystical devotion to the reality of God in his life.

The depth of the feelings he expresses in his *Pensées* reveals the wisdom underlying his passion. His unforgettable words are those of a philosophical mystic.

Lessing

The German author, Gottfried Ephraim Lessing (1729-1781), illustrates the spirit of the Enlightenment as well. His remarkable play, *Nathan the Wise,* is set in Jerusalem during the third crusade (1189-1192). The drama contrasts three main characters: Nathan (a Jew), the Sultan (a Muslim) and a young Knight Templar.

Using a trick to extort money from Nathan, the Sultan demands that Nathan decide whether Islam, Judaism or Christianity is the true religion. Well experienced in the ways of the world, Nathan offers a parable of three rings. No one can tell them apart, yet one of them is thought to be able to confer the grace of God on whomever believes in its supernatural power. Nathan shrewdly and poetically states that the only way one can tell the true ring is the conduct of the wearer. He or she is proof of its genuineness.

It is often remarked that this drama is a plea for religious tolerance, but it is far more than that. The wisdom Nathan expresses through the parable urges us to give up self-righteousness, prejudice, and unfair judgments. The parable shows us that we should value each person for his conduct before mankind and God.

Nathan's self-effacing wisdom is worthy of Solomon. Each of us who wears the ring assumes a trust and responsibility and pledges him or herself to the humane principles of religion. As the individual opens heart and mind to the rest of humankind, he or she moves toward awareness of a higher truth, albeit sometimes unaware of this fact. The purpose of true religion is to overcome cultural discord. Mystical vision transcends meanness of spirit and heals old wounds.

Blake

Among poets of the 18th and 19th centuries, William Blake (1752-1827) was both an artist and a mystic. His drawings and paintings portray mythical and supernatural beings with a mastery that can only have as its source mystical inspiration. His early poem, *The Divine Image,* uses language which is marked by childlike simplicity, but which also becomes transfigured with a mystical sense of God's immanence in humanity.

> To Mercy, Pity, Peace and Love
> All pray in their distress;
> And to these virtues of delight
> Return their thankfulness.
>
> For Mercy, Pity, Peace and Love
> Is God, our father dear.
> And Mercy, Pity, Peace and Love
> Is Man, his child and care.
>
> For Mercy has a human heart,
> Pity has a human face,
> And Love, the human form divine,
> And Peace, the human dress.
> Then every man, of every clime,
> That prays in his distress,
> Prays to the human form divine,
> Love, Mercy, Pity and Peace,
>
> And all love the human form,
> In heathen, turk or jew,
> Where Mercy, Love and Pity dwell
> There God is dwelling too.

The first two stanzas tell us that Mercy, Pity, Peace and Love are God. When man embraces the virtues named, he is in truth the child of God.

The metaphors in stanza three reveal that Mercy has a human heart, Pity a human face, and Love the human form divine.

The last two stanzas declare that in every clime, every man prays to the divine form. So, all must love the human form in heathen, Turk or Jew. Where Mercy, Love and Pity are, there does God reside.

Wordsworth

Nineteenth century English romantic literature also manifests the ethereal. The poet laureate William Wordsworth (1770-1850) felt a mysterious bond to the ruins of a country church. His poem *Tintern Abbey* (1798) describes how, in his hours of weariness, he long remembers the beauteous forms of nature. When they were distilled out by his higher mind, such forms motivated his "little, nameless, unremembered acts of kindness and love." The presence behind these forms of nature was God.

In nature, he learned to hear the "still, sad music of humanity", a presence that brought him joy, one "whose dwelling was the light of setting suns" and "in the mind of man". That feeling and spirit impels "all thinking things" and "rolls through all things." He completes his thought by saying that nature is "the anchor of my heart and soul, of all my moral being." The poem reflects the transcendental in nature--for him, life is suffused with God's mystical immanence.

Hugo

The French poet, novelist and dramatist, Victor Hugo (1802-1885), provides a clue to the influence of the theory of evolution on the century. His magnificent *Legend of the Centuries* (1859-83) poetically narrates "the flowering of the human race" as it scaled the ages from darkness to the ideal. His faith in human intelligence envisions fable, religion, history, philosophy and science as mysterious and miraculous guides to humanity's higher destiny. Here a transcendental perception of time and history begins to emerge in modern man.

Whitman

The American poet Walt Whitman (1819-1892) is renowned for his *Leaves of Grass*, his declaration of faith in life. He gives voice to the energy and idealism of life in a new world. His impassioned style is full of feeling for humanity, his breadth of knowledge, religious and scientific, is impressive. The poet has understood the meaning of mankind's cultural past. Yet, his poetry shows that his life was centered on the vital present to express a mystic's faith in the future.

It is, therefore, important to grasp the hidden meanings in *Song of Myself* (1881-82). Sometimes, the "I" or "myself" does refer to Whitman himself, but he also alludes to kindred creatures in the animal kingdom. Most often, he identifies himself with mankind. In sublime moments he feels his self touched by some cosmic power.

Early in the poem he states his belief that there are millions of universes like ours, and beyond it, millions of new lives to live. Man's hope should be as infinite as the cosmos itself. In this vision, where science and mysticism meet and enrich each other, spheres of spiritual significance seem to prophesy an ultimate, universal meaning.,

Walt's credo is the inverse to the "Vanity of vanities" theme of *Ecclesiastes*. He declares there never will be more inception than now, and never will there be any more perfection than there is now, nor any more heaven or hell. Thus, he places his faith in the perfection, harmony, balance and ever-fresh beginning of the *now*. The present is the focus of all the creativity irradiating through the cosmos--now.

He feels the spirit of God as brother to his own. To him, one is as lucky to die as to be born. After death, perhaps our soul migrates to other worlds to take up a new existence there.

The seasons pursue one another so that cycles of time enable us to sow and reap. A moment comes when he knows his purpose is to solve the mystery of existence:

> To me the converging objects of the universe
>   perpetually flow,
> All are written to me, and I must get what the writing means
>   I know I am deathless.

Whitman feels the amplitude of time. He is content to come into his own today, in ten thousand or in ten million years. A force is working through eons of time to bring about the purpose of the cosmos, and his deathless soul will learn its secret in due time.

Again,

> The minute that comes to me over the past
>   decillions,
> There is no better than it or now.
> What behaved well in the past or behaves
>   well today is not such a wonder,
>
> The wonder is always and always how there
>   can be a mean man or an infidel.
> *This* minute is all there is.

The proof of providence yesterday and today makes it unfathomable how anyone can lack faith in the power of the good. Time is the bringer of possibilities and yet the good in this moment reveals a mystical power in the present. Time alone is without flaw, it alone rounds out and completes everything.

Whitman himself is a *kosmos,* a microcosm within a macrocosm. Through him, many voices of the past find expression. The past finds a voice in the present, and all things culminate in the ever-actual *now*.

Whitman visualizes the gods of the past (Kronos, Zeus, Osiris, Isis, Brahma, Buddha). They were once alive and did the work of their days. They provided him with "deific sketches" to better fill himself out. These deities are evidence of man's early efforts at groping toward a superior form of life, one which time will allow us to realize. Yet, they do not humble him, for, as a human being, he finds himself

> ... waiting my time to be one of the supremes.
> The day getting ready for me when I shall do
> as much good as the best,
> and be as prodigious.

To this point, he has identified himself with all humankind, from the dregs to the exalted. All are promised fulfillment. Indeed, he makes clear the meaning of that promise when he declares that all human beings will duplicate what he himself has experienced. A grand destiny also awaits them. To reassure them, he asks "for what were the saints and sages in history—but for yourself?"

Finally, he visualizes death as a birth, an *accouchement*, and he is ready for the future. He pictures his life after death as if he would become part of the grass over his grave. The grass of the earth unites his soul, self and God into one Being. In the here and now of the after world, the poet is waiting for us to join him.

Mysticism and Modern Man

To understand mysticism in the contemporary world, we need to be cognizant of the way humanism and science have adjusted our perception of reality. Though our traditions and emotions are still strongly influenced by the faith and hope of Judaism, Christianity and Islam, the secular interpretation of existence is pervasive among the educated of the world.

Archetypally and historically, reality has been perceived as either static or dynamic. The static view looks at the geological earth and the stars and in the unchanging aspect of things, forces and generally the solid presence of the universe. For the religious individual, however, these things seem to be proof of God, His Eternity, and the likelihood of truths that last forever. As such, they console man for his frailty and for his passing away as an individual.

This faith we associate with transcendental time. It is the central vision of the salvation religions. Over time, it came to be associated with mystical experiences, those which gave us access to a world beyond our senses.

The transcendental element in things points to the omnipresence of God in the universe and His immanence in human life. This intimation encouraged humankind's expectation that life itself held the promise of a higher, spiritual meaning. Whoever felt that immanence felt a oneness with God, humanity and the universe. In this mystical realm, religion taught us to value intuition over reason. Moreover, the ethereal *c*ould be felt in prayer and by the commitment of life to a higher purpose.

Aristotle

By contrast to the mystical worldview, the ancient Greek philosopher Aristotle (384-322 B.C.) provided posterity with a view of time which inspired humankind to live by laws mightier than the individual. Aristotle saw reality as continually evolving and maintained that all living things *realize* a distinct form over time. Based on his botanical and zoological studies, he conceived *entelechy* as the actualization of all animate form. This concept led him to a vital realization. Like the potency in a seed, each human being has within him-or herself the potential for self-realization, for directing life from within so as to attain the definitive form one's life could take. Implicit in Aristotle's concepts of potentiality and actuality is the theory of evolution and, perhaps, even the protean power of the atomic realm which offers mankind endless nuclear energy.

In sum, from antiquity we inherited two conceptions of time, the *transcendental* related to the eternity of existence created by a Supreme Being, and the *entelechial* related to metamorphosis, transformation, and the evolution of earth's life forms.

Lucretius

Remarkably, the ancient Roman poet and philosopher Lucretius (ca. 96-55 B.C.) encompasses that understanding and knowledge in his didactic poem *On the Nature of Things*. His purpose was to free men from fear of the gods by pointing to the ancient legends to show how religion led to crimes committed by the men and women of great Greek families.

Lucretius sought to aid men in overcoming fear of death. Basing his argument on the durability of the atom, he reasoned that we continue 'in afterlife' as atoms. Man had to learn to live by such laws of nature and therein find solace.

He points out how nature compels all to transform and recounts the changes in mankind from our savage beginnings to the start of civilization. He gives a new definition of man when he says piety does not lie in worshipping capricious gods, "But rather this: to look on all things with a master eye."

Men puzzle about how the world came about and marvel that such wonders can glide on through measureless ages. Yet, says Lucretius, the rolling ages change all things. What we have that is good is destroyed by something better, and little by little, time draws forward each and every thing. Hence man's inborn powers of reason have given us speech and civilization. Lucretius' poem is asking man to discover his true potential and realize his natural destiny.

In it, he first emphasized the laws of nature. In *Proem*, Book III, he relates the effect of entelechial time. He describes the formation of the world by the primal germs or atoms. As Nature compels everything to transformation (ll. 726-731), he says the earth no longer bears what she bore of old. (e.g., the great reptiles) In contemporary terms, he is speaking of evolution across geological ages.

However, when he wonders at how the world came about and marvels that the world can stand the strain of constant motion (ll. 952-961), when he wonders how they glide through measureless ages, he has entered into transcendental time.

He pictures the ages which change things so that success and glory pass. Furthermore, a force draws forward each and every thing to endow reason with energy to uplift man to shores of light. The universe shows man that things take place after a plan and in a fixed order. (ll.1106-11).

On the Nature of Things, seems a two thousand year old prophecy of the humanistic, scientific, and philosophical mentality of our contemporary world. Not only do we respect the critical spirit of classical philosophy and believe life should be governed by human values. Not only do the physical sciences (physics, chemistry, and astronomy) prevail in our understanding of the universe, but we now see life on earth as the outcome of evolutionary biology. All living creatures evolved over time. So, too, did hominids become humankind and eventually human beings. In the twentieth century, atomic science taught us that the matter that makes up the universe is charged with infinite particles of atomic energy. The doctrine of atomism even suggests that our minds replicate the atomic processes of the universe.

Does his poem make Lucretius a scientific prophet and mystic? Whether or not this is the case, he has prepared us to consider how mysticism might express itself in the twenty-first century A.D.

Third Millennium Mysticism

With the Third Millennium barely begun, the reader must wonder how it is possible to describe what has not yet happened. But, we can undertake to foreshadow the future by understanding the psyche's powers as they affect the present, by knowing well what has happened to the secular mind of man in the last three centuries, and finally, by having retraced the evolution of the psyche over the past three millennia.

We have spoken of the peoples of the ancient Mediterranean and of the Near Eastern religions which enriched Judeo-Christianity. By an almost universal tendency to syncretism inherent in humankind, different peoples are attracted to one another. The ultimate reason? To learn from and teach each other.

Today, we realize the Idea of God has contributed significantly to the evolution of humankind. It has stimulated psyche to mature by enabling us to understand knowledge and wisdom of many peoples. With maturity came communion of emotions which has the power to draw humankind together and generate communal wisdom. In a way, this perception of our mutual ingenuity, common sense and astute judgment opened our minds to universal intelligence. Consequently, the Idea of God, shared by people worldwide, transcended orthodox religions and found ultimate expression in mysticism across the millennia.

In a turbulent world of religious and sectarian conflict, mysticism turned out to be a comforting constant for all races and religions.

Most likely, it evolved in tandem with the psyche. From primitive beginnings, it transformed itself from ecstatic experience into organized religions. As mankind accumulated various forms of knowledge, the psyche exponentially expanded its thinking skills, developed keener perceptions and evolved more universal conceptions.

So, we can surmise that the Third Millennium will reflect these knowns and at the same time probe what has been ignored or remained unknown in previous centuries.

In addition, a modern mystic would need sound knowledge of the age he or she lives in. The mystic would not be ignorant of the realities of this world. The individual's experiences would not remain concerned solely with one's own view of life. Our century possesses extraordinary insights into the essence of human nature, which has revealed itself through much of human history. This means the endowed man or woman of our millennium should be aware that the human psyche now represents the emotional wisdom of our race. Humankind's religious and secular evolution has made this possible.

Thus, the third millennium mystic would not only respect mankind's past but also sense the infinite potentials in the present. If truly gifted, the mystic may have an uncanny, prophetic intimation of humankind's future. Indeed, for millennia, we have been evolving a finite supraconscience inspired by faith in God's Omniscience. Moreover, the intuition of the Third Millennium mystic would be the conclusion that humankind's evolution was probably initiated by and guided all along by the Supreme Being.

Well and good, but where would an initiate mystic start? If you decide to follow that spiritual path, where would you begin? The undertaking could begin by retracing the stages of your mental growth, by meditating on your own evolution, re-examining the various stages of self-education. Doing this would help you recall meaningful moments of self-realization and understand what was valuable in the whole stream of life experiences you have.

What event, passage or saying from a Holy Book remains unforgettable? What did it teach you? Or, the subjects studied in school--in the humanities, human sciences, or natural sciences? What truth or philosophy of life did they reveal? In sum, by reminiscing about what you have learned, you find out who you could become in a lifetime. By so doing, you begin to understand the life of the mystic who is seeking to find his or her way in the world.

Let us now consider what might prove to be insights characteristic of third millennium mysticism.

Introduction to the Essay
Insights

The reader should bear in mind that what follows is not a discourse, exposition or treatise on mysticism, but a collection of chance insights without plan or conscious purpose. Though they emerged unexpectedly at different times of the night or day, in retrospect, they seem to have clustered around incandescent ideas of significance. These were: the Self, Religion, Evolution, and the Supraconscience. This spontaneity leads us to believe there was some kind of subliminal psychic progression from the finite to the infinite, from the infinitesimal psyche itself toward a mystic's idea of the supernal mystery of the cosmos.

The Self
Feeling Alive

At times we feel kinship with the people and things in the world around us. We sense this when we stroll through a woods. We feel "at home" in it when we see the beauty, majesty and uncountable forms of perfection in every niche of the world. All gives us a feeling of friendliness and adventure in life.

But, what does it mean exactly to feel at one with nature? Together we are evidence of the mystery of life and we understand that the soul of nature is also our soul. A communion exists between us and the mystery that created life.

Moreover, in solitude, the individual sometimes senses another presence. This entity is concerned that you are alive and glad that you appreciate life. It is a religious feeling, an intuition that life is the miracle of the cosmos. You are privileged to feel it with every breath you take and every grateful thought shows you worship life.

Mysticism and Emotional Intelligence

Among mystics, it is well known that abstention from the appetites is necessary to arrive at greater self-realization. Self-control is characteristic of mysticism, which combines calm and contemplation in an effort to achieve psychic equilibrium. This well known practice needs further qualification.

Whereas self-discipline and self-control derive from a venerable conception of conscience, mysticism itself is a manifestation of emotional intelligence. Mysticism intuitively reaches beyond knowledge and cultural ethos to exceed the limitations of the conscience of the past.

In so far as mysticism contemplates what lies beneath common, visible reality, it seeks the invisible verity within existence. Mysticism transcends the five senses, common sense, and complacent realism. It undertakes to uncover the purpose and meaning of our perceptions, our empirical experiences--all that disguises the spiritual verity of reality.

In an important sense, mysticism reveals to us our ignorance. That revelation challenges us to ascend above all that we thought we knew. To achieve this, we need to learn to observe life more keenly and methodically than is done in the sciences. We must learn to speculate creatively on the improbable or impossible, to wonder at the paradoxes and enigmas of the world. We need to acquire new knowledge which can lead to new insights as to the meaning of our own life. Much of our common, everyday life is spent in blindness as to who we really are.

Mysticism is the mother of humane understanding and compassion.

Mysticism is the passionate spirit in us seeking to be worthy of the superior being which we sense is yet to be born in and through us.

A Visualization of the Soul

A third millennium mystic might envision the soul as a "seed of light" passed on from parents to child. As complementary polarities of psyche, men and women represent a dialectic which is conveyed to the child in the form of a synthesis. Of course, each parent was a synthesis of the grandparents' dominant and recessive genes or characteristics as well. However, the soul of each individual is even more intrinsic to a person than genes.

It is also deeper than C.G. Jung's conception of the animus and anima, where the masculine animus may be part of the female soul and the female anima, part of the male soul. Certainly your soul is more profound than your persona, the role the individual plays in life. The soul is your potential to create and decide a destiny.

Yet, it transcends the processes of being and becoming encompassed by a single lifetime because it is guided by the power of evolution itself. The significance of soul as a "seed of light" is that it has the potency to bring about its own rebirth in whatever body it finds itself. In this way, it travels and transforms itself across eons of time

The soul can take a single lifetime to grow, become perfected or more complete. Over hundreds of generations of human evolution, it can proceed through many, many lives. In this way, it evolves over eons.

Let us explain the soul on a more intimate, family level. The primeval souls of the first man and woman (cf. the myth of Adam and Eve) would have experienced together the earliest epiphany when they recognized the power of love between them. That first intimate ecstasy made them conscious not of original sin, but of something sacred between them: Guilt did not exist before religion explained how sinful we allegedly were by being *natural.* That first fusion of healthy, young bodies awakened a mutual recognition that making love, when two are truly in love, is one of the wonders of eternal nature.

Moreover, with maturity, that first couple bore witness to the beauty and innocence of their newborn. The parents had transmitted the unnamable essence of their selves into their child. Indeed, their love made it possible for their soul-seeds to transmit to their offspring everlasting faith in life itself as the one true religion.

Surely they must have felt gratitude for God's gift to them, making it possible to join together and love each other at will. What more powerful, irrefutable proof can there be of soul and God's presence? Love fulfilled, a child radiant with life and a new soul. The three together know the moment is blessed by communion with the creator.

Moreover, their sacred bond is itself evidence of an eternal truth: Wherever there is true parental love, there humankind communes with the eternal. As long as there is undying parental love on earth, God will forever protect humanity.

In one sense, mothers are closer to God because they nurture in their womb a new soul, the embyro of God's supraconscience in humankind.

Love is sacred. Sex between those truly in love is holy. The sacred seed is implanted in the beloved to ensure ever more love in the world.

Religion
On Religious Belief

Given the crises that contemporary civilization confronts and the increasing number of incidents of violence everywhere, what justifies religious beliefs?

This depends in part on how reasonable they are, and, also, on our understanding of nature's major events, especially those that are beyond the individual's control or responsibility, such as natural disasters. You may pray for them not to happen or "to go away", but they will take place because they are obeying laws set in motion before life appeared on earth. In other words, many natural phenomena such as droughts, floods, earthquakes, tornadoes, hurricanes and typhoons occur without our being able to avert them. Religious faith has no effect whatsoever on the outcome of unpredictable "acts of Nature".

On the other hand, the human being has a measure of control over what happens in his or her lifetime. If the individual demonstrates responsibility and decency toward others, if one lives life trying to achieve self-realization and self-mastery, if a person lives in the faith life has a meaning, then that person will shape his or her own destiny—in so far as this is humanly possible. But, would such behavior and commitment assure life-after-death?

It may be naive to assume moral conduct and devotion to a religion guarantees such a reward, but it is a virtual certainty that other rewards will be forthcoming in this life. Moreover, by living an exemplary life, you may set an example for your descendants and theirs. To be remembered by generations to come would already be a measure of immortality.

Otherwise, the truest evaluation of the life you pursued will come with recognition of what you have done. As you mature, you will learn to go beyond self-centered and self-engrossed activities. Finally, you may undertake to fathom the wisdom of religion.

As you educate yourself to become a wiser human being, you are, in fact, evolving your own supraconscience. One day you may sense the infinite significance of God's Supraconscience. At that point, you will have arrived at the edge of eternity.

Monotheism: Orthodox Religion

Herein lies the arcane truth of monotheism. It asserts that all in nature and in the universe is under the control of one power. Although the agency of that power may be endlessly disputed, nevertheless, it awakens in humankind the faith and hope there is only one ultimate form of knowledge and one eschatological wisdom governs all.

All of the different views of knowledge might be seen as so many schisms asserting their own 'absolute' truth, and we see in the sciences and philosophies that each asserts its own supposed superiority by its focus on particular phenomena or argues that its world view is the one Truth. So, the factionalism of the philosophers, theologians, and scientists seems in one way to simply carry forward the sectarian, dissident, schismatic, separatist, heretical traditions of the world's religions.

Worldly belief in dualism and the promulgation of antinomies seems to be an equally non-comformist, unorthodox, single-minded mode of thinking--a heritage of strong-willed, self-righteous, self-serving 'servants' of 'knowledge' and 'wisdom'.

Monotheism has given us three, related religions--Judaism, Christianity, and Islam, all of which have a distinct advantage over polytheisms, namely, that the three passed on the faith that knowledge and wisdom were one. This perspective, in turn, tended to lead to the hope that, after all, humankind is one. Such a hope could unite at least a portion of mankind in mutual tolerance and reciprocal aid.

Of course, it would be ridiculous to exclude the rest of humankind from the monotheistic club. On the other hand, polytheists who believe in sundry gods (Hinduism, for example) or in great men (Buddha, Confucius, et al) are not benighted or lost souls. Indeed, polytheists find gods in all of the sacred places where supernatural events have occurred; similarly, animists find conscious life in objects and in both the most minute and the most vast of natural phenomena. These views should teach the rest of humankind to study our world with greater curiosity and care and to try to come to terms with the deeper meanings of such worldviews. They can awaken us to a more universal understanding of human nature, to the mutual search for evidence of God.

Moreover, monotheism provides a religious ideal. Humankind should endeavor to live harmoniously as one race, pursuing mutual goals, undertaking to better the conditions of all. But, just as importantly, monotheism provides a model of supraconscience in keeping with which the individual can integrate personality, character, intelligence, mind and heart into one identity. It should inspire all to seek out the most meaningful destiny possible for one's culture and time.

In this way, men and women can unify, consolidate, and integrate their lives in emulation of their fundamental faith in the integrity of their one God. This would be the truest way to approach God and worship His presence in the universe.

Salvation and Conversion

William James states that when we reach "our own upper limit and live in our own highest centre of energy, we may call ourselves saved..." These "forms of regenerative change--have only a psychological significance." [11]

A realistic interpretation of this might be the following: Actually, an individual can 'save' his or her own soul by becoming immersed in any serious study or activity which motivates mind and psyche to pursue excellence. Any person seeking to perfect his mind as far as intellectual passion or emotional intelligence can carry him probably has 'the right stuff.' Decision and determination convert personality and character from ignorance into knowledge by steadfastly pursuing any study as a lifetime goal.

James also says that "Sudden conversion is connected with the possession of an active subliminal self." [12]

Stated somewhat differently, the individual must periodically surrender his rationality or purpose-filled life to the spontaneous urgings of the psyche. In such periods, one gives free reign to intuition and passional intelligence. Through such surrender of conscious identity, more evolved modes of perception and conception may displace the classical logic or scientific induction which modern man habitually uses. Such self-surrender may be a form of trans-mental meditation that taps into our evolving supraconscience. This could become a means of discovering the strength, direction and wisdom of one's own finite supraconscience.

However, a caveat is in order here. History has revealed how often someone aspiring to sainthood can easily fall prey to delusions or some form of madness. While the experience of the subliminal may be thrilling and spiritually vitalizing, one must be wary of delusions of sainthood and of self-deification.

If one consciously sets out to become a saint, there is a very real danger of failure. One cannot *will* such a state or status. Moreover, failure can lead to endless self-reproach, chastisement, and mortification because one finds oneself unworthy of God. Better to aspire to sanity--the middle road—neither too pure, nor too impure. That way a person can remain human and humanly happy.

A sensible caveat. Moreover, sensations more overwhelming than usual can arise from our primeval subconscience, calling forth awesome passions which can mesmerize us to commit destructive or homicidal acts. By contrast, our supraconscience is recognized by the fact that it prompts us to do creative and charitable things to aid humankind.

Moreover, individuals who experience ecstasy (not induced by drugs) might easily believe the experience is a sign of God's approval. That ecstatic feeling might involve any of a number of psychic events. It might manifest itself in a sudden transformation from our savage subconscience or tortured conscience to an accelerated healing of psyche by the supraconscience. Ecstasy could come from total enlightenment, i.e., a supraconscience insight into the individual's psychic destiny. Rapture could be a miraculous 'saltation' (a major species mutation) the likes of which are rarely detected in evolutionary biology.

But there is another caveat to be heeded in this. If you experience a real, spiritual conversion, do not expect others to rejoice for you. Rather, expect many to be utterly incredulous, jealous, and envious. (How could it possibly happen to *you?*) People will mock you behind your back.

The world has not changed because of your conversion. To the contrary, humankind's insidious subconscience will not accept anyone's spiritual victory. The subconscience is primitive precisely because it finds its greatest gratification in maligning others and denying that men and. women can live by faith in themselves. It cannot fathom the fact that there are individuals who possess a beautiful soul because they fervently believe in the sublime significance of existence.

Religion's Influence on the Evolution of the Supraconscience

Ancient myths gave way to more evolved religions when thinkers undertook to explain existence and the purpose of human life on earth. As consolation for death, the salvation religions offered hope for survival of the individual in an afterlife.

For this reason, Judaism, Christianity and Islam were superior to pagan myths and earlier religions. Each prescribed a moral code and developed a system of rituals which enabled the committed individual to demonstrate loyalty to God in the Temple, Church and Mosque. The constancy of the faithful could be rewarded with a worthy, otherworldly destiny.

As recorded history teaches us, 'sacred events' bore witness to the veracity of the scriptures on which the original salvation religions were based. Each religion became centered on some form of redemption and personal salvation. Each in its own right encouraged the development of a more advanced stage of consciousness and conscience. And, all of them drew on some sort of testament to their beliefs. Personal epiphanies were proof that the religion had come to possess eternal, verifiable truths. True believers could live with the mysteries of existence because they would be saved in the end.

Nevertheless, the ensuing millennia brought with them questions which required answers. They motivated doubters and heretics to better understand the meaning of life in its brevity. The idea of eternity made life paradoxical, seemingly senseless, because each of us is born only to die, to disappear in the oblivion of eternity. Such troubling realizations and heretical insights were to plague rabbi, priest and imam through the centuries.

The record of mythology and religion reveals millennia-long progressions, advances in the level of human understanding of this problem. The ancient myths about feckless, erratic behavior of the gods could satisfy only the confused and passionate natures of superstitious humankind.

Eventually, humankind wanted gods who represented an explanation of the forces at work in nature and the universe.

Two religions influenced Judaism and early Christianity. Zoroastrianism (10th century B.C.E.) envisioned existence as a cosmic struggle between the good god Ahura Mazda of the universe, and the evil one, Ahriman. Mazda needed man's good deeds in order to defeat Ahriman. Similarly, Manichaean dualism (3rd cent. A.D.) saw existence as the struggle of the human spirit to free itself from evil matter.

The dualistic vision of these religions reverberated through Judaism and Christianity and markedly shaped the world view of our evolving psyche. Man's soul came to be viewed as the burning focal point of clashing cosmic forces.

In cultural-psychic terms, since that ancient time, psyche has undergone a series of changes, successive stages of sensing and feeling as a result of which it discovered viable truths to live by. As men and women tried to come to terms with the good and evil in the world and in themselves, they had to confront the basic fear that they were fated by a demonic power that they believed had created the world and humankind. Over time, this, ominous apprehension of the human condition shaped the psyche into dualistic conscience.

Eventually, practical reasoning came to provide men and women with confidence that these invisible powers could be placated; their anger could be averted and they could be appealed to for protection.

When salvation religions arose, they undertook, by means of ritual and sacrament, to interact with the benign powers in the world so as to ward off the malignant ones. They believed it possible to establish communion with the Supreme God through various rites. The growth of conscience meant the overcoming of schizophrenic dualism. It required unquestioning and total acceptance of the one and only God.

The ecclesiastical certitude that there was one and only God, a deity with whom one could communicate, led to the exclusion--and even excommunication--of the nonconformist, the dissident, and the apostate. Such judgments were a means of condemning weak and heretical souls to eternal damnation. However, religious absolutism also led to opposition, fratricide and the widespread homicide that is termed war.

Individual religions were capable of integrating their own beliefs and ritual practices so as to avoid social conflict and live in harmony with fellow believers. Yet, at times, members of one religion displayed disdain for another. Those who found their faith insulted became enraged and responded in kind. Eventually, intolerance, mistrust, and mutual hatred reached such a peak of passion that it led to mutual murder. The combatants failed to see the irony that, though each side taught God's love and wisdom, by turning vehemently against one another, both made a mockery of their own sacred teachings.

Sadly, once this mutual enmity had been aroused, many religions were prepared to malign the faith of others, to claim that they were unworthy to worship the true God. If there is any emotional intelligence left in people of religious faith, let them pause long enough to realize what inhumane things they do in the name of God.

By contrast, a true salvation religion would be prepared to learn and teach the moral message of other religions. For each in its own way nurtures humankind's supraconscience. Throughout religious history, humanity has sensed the omnipresence of a Supreme Being in the universe. Our intuition tells us that that Creator guided our perfection as a thinking species and our humanization as emotionally moral beings. Gradually, the truly devout psyche realizes it is developing its own superior nature when it acknowledges the immanence of a Supraconscience, a presence which is to be discovered wherever we are and wherever we look.

Religion and the Supraconscience

In the famous Pléiade edition of *L'Histoire des Religions*, a chapter on *L'Eglise Orthodoxe* presents a map of the Orthodox Church locations across the globe. Clearly, that religion is very widespread. Regions as East Africa, South

America, Middle East, Russia, East Europe, India, Australia, the U.S.A. and the tip of Alaska all exhibit concentrations of Orthodox faithful.

This branch of Christianity is constituted mainly of the Eastern Orthodox Church of Russia, Middle East and Eastern Europe. It is astonishingly diverse and well distributed around the world. The Orthodox diaspora manifests two characteristics witnessed in nature: 1) the phenomenon of *divergence* as illustrated by the dispersal of waterborne and windblown seed and the migration of birds and animals across different continents; 2) the phenomenon of *convergence* of groups of orthodox faithful from all across the world--not unlike the groupings of eco-niches of plants and animal species.

Such divergence has the effect of causing beliefs and religious practices to converge around centers of worship. Otherwise stated, these patterns demonstrate how centers of faith form. Indeed, as evidence of religious intelligence, it points to the conclusion that man's supraconscience itself is disseminated worldwide.

This migratory experience displays humankind's need to be free to worship at will. It expresses their desire to worship collectively in safe places far from the sub-humans among us. They are free to believe what they want to believe.

Moreover, the universality of religion the world over manifests what seems an omnipresent Spirit. Man's spiritual passion justifies speaking of the supraconscience in humankind, a species which supersedes all others in its mental powers. Throughout history, virtually all branches of the human race have recorded in oral, sculptural or written form a deeply felt need for the worship of a Supreme Being.

That deep need may mean that a psychic vitality exists in humankind and that it is responsible for the acceleration of our mental evolution. This endowment may be the result of an integration of subconscious animal energy, religious devotion, and the self-transcending presence which is self-evident in human evolution itself. Hitherto unrecognized and unacknowledged as a reality, the emerging supraconscience of humankind may be guiding the humanization of our species.

The history of religion is the history of variable definitions of the Supreme Being. Any definition soon generates a number of variations and takes on diverse connotations favored by a given religion or sect, by this mystic or that heretic. Nonetheless, mankind's cultures and civilizations continue to define and redefine what the Divinity means to them. Otherwise, an anthropological study of religion would reveal one enduring fact: as human intelligence acquires sounder knowledge and more humane wisdom, our religion co-evolves with our moral maturity. In essence, such co-evolution means that monotheism itself must continue to evolve as must our Third Millennium comprehension of God.

Correspondingly, our maturing ideas of God lead us to a superior comprehension of psyche's stage-by-stage journey through time. Nurtured by nature and by our psyche's intuition of the Cosmic Supraconscience, our own finite supraconscience represents an evolved, pure power capable of subduing the excesses of our primeval subconscience and converting our judgmental religious mindset into mutual understanding between humankind.

If we acknowledge that all humankind possesses the potential to develop a supraconscience and that all humanity is of the same skin, flesh and bone, how can we continue to allow the murder of what is most sacred to our kind—life itself? This no Third Millennium mystic would understand.

Religion and Mystical Experience

As earlier comments have made clear, orthodox religion established and maintained its ultimate authority in all matters of dogma, doctrine and the exoteric interpretation of Scripture and Gospel. This was true of Judaism, Christianity, and Islam.

Great Judaic and Christian philosophers appeared on the scene as did Islamic *Falsafahs;* the latter reinterpreted their theological tradition in the light of ancient the Greek philosophers Plato and Aristotle and also drew on Neo-Platonism to refine their cosmology. Attempts at more rational explanations of the Holy Writ satisfied the human noetic nature, yet they left humankind's deeper psychic nature largely neglected and impoverished. In plain terms, man's instincts, intuitions, sentiments and emotions needed to be expressed. And, such expression was stimulated by his contemplation of the majesty of the universe, the mystery of life, and the enigmatic meaning of human destiny.

The reason orthodox religion has sought to establish norms, codes of conduct and moral guidance was to ensure continuity in life. This it did through ritual and sacrament. For the devout individual, religious rites provided a degree of emotional reassurance. In itself, religion guided the faithful to integrate their lives through obedience to God's will and commandments.

Despite these reassuring practices, many worshippers evidently concluded that the approved path of the church, the synagogue or the mosque was not enough. Emulating the ecstatic experiences of the patriarchs, mystics and prophets as Moses, Jesus, Saint Paul, Plotinus and Mohammed, these doubters seek more definitive explanations of ultimate reality and so feel a deep need to undergo an inner conversion, to discover the higher self. He or she longs for a truer identity through numinous union with the power radiating from the center of the universe to the innermost recesses of the self.

Secular literature records how gifted, thoughtful individuals have had their own mystical experiences. Such was the case with Dante, Pascal, Spinoza, William Blake, William Wordsworth, Walt Whitman, Emerson, Tennyson, and Thoreau.

But, if religious sacraments provide the framework for experiences whereby profound feelings may be gratified, often they only sharpen a keener longing for the fulfillment which seems to beckon from the distant future. The seeker who has purity of heart and total submission may experience a gentle flash of lightening illuminating the darkness within.

Some mystics have reported that such an experience wipes away all tears, doubts and questions. It also sweeps away all hesitation and indecision about the future.

When the mystical experience occurs, the graced person realizes life has a purpose and a magnificent meaning. By integrating our lives into a destiny that we alone can decide, we vanquish all fear of the meaninglessness of death. The presence and power that radiates light and life throughout the endless cosmos assures us that no darkness will ever be final. Such experience teaches us that our own conception and birth, in and of themselves, ensure that the light of life will continue as long as humankind love and believe in the future.

Evolution
A Mystical View

The psyche of early humankind awakened when people began to imagine there were invisible powers in nature. Everywhere, vegetation moved and undulated as if it were inhabited by invisible spirits and souls. The movement of the wind intermingled with sunlight and shadow to reveal mysterious and intriguing powers in nature. Throughout the mountains, forests and trees, nymphs could be heard, but not seen. The murmur of streams and rivers and the lapping along the shores of lakes seemed like the gentle voices of watery naiads.

Vast, grassy plains, rolling hills, and magical mountains seemed to whisper of wanderers who had already passed there before early man came on the scene. Had those roamers gone on their way to distant lands, leaving behind memories of a now forgotten time? Though their footprints vanished, their departed spirits still live on in the dust of time.

Though the mysteries of nature seemed to overshadow man's life, humankind understood that otherworldly powers had to be propitiated if we were to know what they expected of us. Slowly, we learned to mark mother nature's rhythms and to tame the wilder spirits of the land. Thus agriculture developed and man became domesticated.

We learned that practical intelligence brought rewards, and we also learned how to demonstrate to the gods our obedience. Pragmatism must have been our species' first sensible philosophy of life. Being practical meant teaching ourselves how to improve our chances of survival. This instinct also made humankind more purpose-oriented. And, over time, this orientation led us to foresee that life might have a purpose beyond staying alive.

Closer observation of nature brought the discovery of the tinier life forms (ants, spiders, fireflies, butterflies, etc.). They all possessed a beauty and design of their own and knew how to survive. The world around us showed us that all of the plants, trees and forests had their own place and space, and they all co-existed in such a way as to ensure their mutual survival. The forests, with their thousands of trees, insects, birds, and animals, seemed to live in silent poise, rhythm and balance like the stars, constellations and galaxies. Gradually, it occurred to us that the limitless Supreme Being had created this vast existence. The earth with its countless mysteries reflected those lights in the dark universe.

Between the infinitely small and the infinitely large, a Supreme Being had to control everything that humans could detect.

Over hundreds of generations, we came to mimic the supernatural figures we created in our myths and epics. Exceptional men and women in every race appeared as heroes and heroines of their cultures. Geniuses came forth to express their creativity and know-how, to share with the world their knowledge and wisdom.

In time, it became clear to humankind that a God must exist. Indeed, when humanity conceived the idea of God, we consciously began more earnestly to develop religions, world literatures, philosophies and sciences. In short, these purposeful activities instinctively accelerated our own evolution. By the modern age, it had become evident that humankind was evolving a superior intelligence. Gradually, we identified with the omniscience apparent in the infinite order of the universe. Eventually, there came the intuition that some superior power in eternal time had initiated human evolution. Today, humankind intuitively knows that a Divinity is immanent in our world as well as throughout space and time.

Realistically speaking, is there reason to believe that humanity's psyche has evolved? And, does the psyche's millennia-long evolution have any real meaning in the life of the individual?

It is obvious that existence offers us a lesson as to how to live life. Everything in nature fits together seamlessly and every creature has a purpose of its own.

All of nature's creatures seem to have a sure instinct as to how to live. Yet beyond the trials of daily survival, humankind do not usually know their purpose in life. They know only that certain experiences bring satisfaction. As modest as one's aptitudes and intelligence may be, they seem to provide an answer to what to do with life. Eventually, one comes to understand that by pursuing any talent or dream, an individual can create a meaningful life. By the pursuit of a personal purpose, each can realize a true lifetime ideal.

In mystical terms, spiritual self-knowledge, self-reliance, self-education, and self-realization are the surest way to prove you value life.

A Heretical View of the Evolution of Religion

Anthropologists who study the evolution of early mankind believe humankind passed through periods in which the meaning of religion became clearer.

In the beginning, our ancestors sensed the phenomena in nature had a life of their own, that even rocks, trees, rivers and mountains emitted mysterious powers. Of course, the growth of plants and all types of creatures revealed that each had an indwelling spirit. Early man realized that, in death, the spirit departed from the living. So, animism was an expression of our earliest awareness that everything that was alive was the incarnation of an invisible vitality.

In turn, that vitalist vision came to believe natural phenomena represented supernatural powers. People and cults came to petition them for favors; or, they believed that protection could be gained by barter or bribery. The supplicant offered a thing of value to please the invisible god. If gratified, the power granted the prayer or request.

If the expected dispensation or reward was not forthcoming, the worshipper took the spirit to be impotent or mean. In that case, the person might appeal to another of the many gods in nature. If still no relief or reply were given, then, perhaps, the supplicant might admit that he himself was not worthy to be favored. At that point, the moral instinct was awakened. Primitive pantheism became polytheism.

In time, to hedge their bets that a nature god would listen and grant what was in its power, our ancestors learned to pray to one deity after another. As the ancient Greeks eventually learned, many gods proved fickle, unreliable, or false. This led to the hope that one Superior Being might listen to those who believed in Him.

Today, a heretical anthropologist might suggest that *all* monotheistic religions should be practiced to assure all supplicants a proper judicial hearing as to the eternal justice deserved. In time, it is possible that the Divinity of every religion on earth will be prayed to *in turn*, or for efficiency's sake, all Gods prayed to simultaneously. Of course, in the end, the worshipped would realize his or her prayers could be heard only when the heart was truthful, contrite and sincere.

In sum, perhaps religious worship did begin as a form of bartering with or bribing the gods. This practice continued over time until the truly devout came to realize the following: Not all prayers were worthy of an answer, nor were all gods. When the actual truth became self-evident, humanity stopped placing its bets on imagined deities. The credulous could no longer believe the fictions of imaginary events lost in the mists of time.

Throughout human history, heralds and harbingers of monstrous events all too often turned out to be what they really were: imposters or counterfeiters. All they actually offered was fiat faith, a currency doomed in time by its worthlessness when it came to gaining entrance to heaven or God's respect. Their scam insurance policy could guarantee no afterlife. The policies the gullible bought and paid for would only ensure that they would turn to dust and experience final oblivion.

The Actual World and God

Throughout the world a plentitude of myths have developed, all with their imaginative stories as to how life and existence came to be. The faithful of the three salvation religions know that God created the entire world in seven days. Though today we know that the earth is some five billion years old and the cosmos has been in existence perhaps some fifteen billion years, these estimates are largely educated guesses or scientific speculations. In any case, primitive and modern man, confronted by the mystery under our feet and extending outward to all infinity, would agree that a cosmic power or event must have created all that we perceive.

Since the time of primeval man and woman, there has been a hominid evolution. Anthropologists have identified *Australopithecus africanus*, a type of pre-human who lived about two or three million years ago in Africa. Later came *Homo erectus*, who lived 500,000 to 100,000 years ago. There were *Neanderthals*

125,000 years ago who apparently went extinct 50,000 to 15,000 years ago. *Cro-Magnon* man, also called Stone Age man, is aptly characterized by his use of stone tools. Finally, we, the supposedly wise hominid called *Homo sapiens* emerged. This anthropic history of human evolution raises interesting questions.

When we use the word 'creation', we usually refer to the order and unity of the earth's biosphere as well as the apparent regularity of the movements and cycles of the sun, moon and other celestial bodies. As understood in antiquity, it meant the permanence, stability and eternity of the earth and heavens. To our species living as best it could in an age of predation and struggling to survive, the earth itself provided shelter and protection.

It was home. Its very durability and solidity led us to believe that creation was unchangeable, permanent and forever.

In the Old Testament, the work of creation was completed in seven days. This meant that the forms of all creatures, great and small, were eternally fixed, complete and perfect as species. It was a perfect world because God had created it. So, humankind's original perception of the stability and fixity of the earth led them to believe in things immutable and eternal as God and the human soul itself.

But, with Darwin's 19th century theory of evolution, we began to perceive that mutability and impermanence were the condition of the earth's species. Then geology described how the earth itself perpetually changes--sometimes over billions of years, sometimes abruptly in earthquakes, tsunamis, and other natural disasters. Paleontology also provides evidence of universal change in species over hundreds of millions of years.

With the 20th century understanding of the nuclear essence of matter as atoms, electromagnetic energy, force fields and the like, we came to understand that matter itself was potentially dynamic and self-transforming. Despite both the outward appearance of sameness and inner stability, all now seemed to be subject to an intricate, universal, dialectical process.

In the light of our present scientific knowledge of life on earth and the nature of micro and macro-matter, we are ineluctably led to revise our sense of the destiny of humankind, the universe and our idea of God.

Since all is dynamic and dialectical in its innermost nature, we need to come to terms with such metaphysical concepts as God and the human soul. Evidently, if God is immanent in His universe and that universe is actually perpetual polar activity, then it follows, as the day does the night, that God Itself must be an eternal process, one which sustains, maintains, transforms and evolves Itself through endless time.

Moreover, on earth our species has evolved over time. We now understand that the individual life undergoes continual change through stages of physical and mental immaturity and maturity. It, therefore, follows that life is a process from birth to death. What is crucial to understand is how our psyche transforms with maturation and age through our interaction with past, present and future.

Beyond a simplistic understanding of our situation vis-à-vis time, we have to define the meaning of these temporal terms more concisely.

Usually, the past is thought to refer to one's personal life. But formal education is a part of that past. Education involves learning the sentiments, feelings, and understandings of people of bygone years and centuries. It means acquiring their thought processes and skills. It means recapitulating what was learned, thought, created and invented in the past: mathematics, science, history, literature, the arts. It means developing skills in writing, thinking, defining, and expressing one's own thoughts.

Education means we are absorbing the mentalities, insights, knowledge and some of the wisdom accrued in past centuries and millennia. It means we have absorbed the collective consciousness of our culture and civilization. This is one definition of maturity, namely, that humanistic education becomes an undeniable, indelible part of your psyche.

Of course, each individual hopefully acquires self-knowledge largely by passing through the various stages of maturation. At each new stage, one sees one's previous immaturity; at the same time, one is inspired to be a wiser, emotionally more cognizant person in the future. In other words, our own life experience should complement what our culture has taught us.

So, the psyche is a dialectic between past/present and present/future. In a loose sense, the past is the cause of our present state of knowledge and education, whereas the future is our motivation, the purpose of our life yet-to-be.

In addition to this is, there is the psychological fact that family, friends, and one's own feelings nurture our emotional intelligence. To be sure, religion and the humanities have also influenced the quality, depth, and universality of our comprehension of self and our level of empathy for other human beings. It is important to realize that emotional discernment has probably a great deal more influence on how you will live your private life than will your formal education. The same may not be true of your self-education which is guided by your ideals. These will direct your emotional judgment in deciding your future.

Scientific breakthroughs in the past three centuries require that, in the twenty-first century, we re-evaluate what we have held to be true and sacred for two thousand years. The earth's history reveals that uniform processes and catastrophes account for major geological changes. Modern biology has substantial evidence that all living species have evolved. Nuclear physics has demonstrated that atomic activity explains that matter on earth can be transformed into the energy of the sun and the stars. Certain astronomers as Eric Chaisson argue that the cosmos itself is evolving. Hence, we can, with some certainty, scientifically conclude that existence itself is continually subject to transformation. Judging by life on earth, All things are evolving.

This accumulation of evidence calls for a new vision of our idea of God and of human destiny. God may be evolving. Psyche is evolving, as are human perception, conceptual powers and even truth itself. The evidence cited here does not prove the relativity of all things in heaven and earth. Rather, it shows the value of what was, is, and will be.

For the human being, the ultimate value is life itself. Thus it is important that we synchronize our lives with the dialectical rhythm of life on earth and in the perceivable universe. As stated in scripture, there is a season for all things. As a species, we now comprehend that a life means living in all the religious, scientific and secular dimensions which the psyche incarnates.

We must learn to relive the past as intelligently as we can, live the present with all the education and self-knowledge we can acquire, and live the future by creating a destiny worthy of humankind's finite omniscience and matured emotional wisdom.

The Idea of God and the Evolution of the Psyche

At the end of paganism in ancient Greece and Rome, the gods lost all credibility by their childish, contemptible and immoral excesses. The educated could no longer believe in them.

In the Common Era, a similar decline in belief has taken place because the contentiousness between Catholics and Protestants has aroused mutual antagonism. Eventually, intolerance between the two religions, both of which believe in Jesus Christ as God, grew as their different rituals, versions and interpretations of scripture came to the fore. Each group believed that they alone offered *the* true understanding of God.

The splintering of Protestantism into many sects further exacerbated the decline in faith. Heretics from both branches of Christianity sought deeper verities than those offered by the dogmata and doctrines of organized religion. In our day agnosticism, skepticism, and cynicism characterize most non-believers.

This tendency to judge other beliefs unfairly or harshly seems to be the common fate of theologies, philosophies and world views. Hence today's technologies, sciences, religions, and depth psychology interpretations of psyche will probably suffer a similar fate in the future.

However, a psychological theory built on an explanation of the evolution of humankind's creative conscience is already a major advance toward a better understanding of the psyche. But beyond the pervasive influence of nature and evolution, we need to bear in mind the influence of religion on human development. Over the millennia, the God-idea has been nurtured in one form or another. As compensation for the tragedies humankind suffered in its struggle to survive, that idea offered comfort and consolation. It lessened and relieved the omnipresent fear of death. It promised that there was some meaning for all that humanity had endured.

What effect might this idea have had on the evolution of the psyche? Because faith sustained humankind, it may well have stimulated and promoted the growth, intricacy and efficiency of the brain's neurological connections.

If true, the power of the God-idea was such that it galvanized psychic energies to coalesce and consolidate along bio-electrical/ syntactic lines of force into a new integrated nexus. In other words, this electrifying emotion-energy gradually concentrated experience into the essence we call psyche. And, this experience produced a superior mentality: Emotional wisdom gave rise to our humane supraconscience and, over time, co-evolved with our creative intelligence.

Hence through our evolving perception of God, psyche further matured its humanity by creating ever greater spheres of knowledge. Thus humankind's supraconscience evolved when our idea of God matured. In the context of our new knowledge of psyche's evolution, God appears to us now as the Supraconscience of the universe.

The Influence of Conversion on Psychic Evolution

R.M. Bucke's *Cosmic Consciousness. A Study of the Evolution of the Human Mind* (1977) provides a number of excellent examples of the religious conversion of eminent historical figures (e.g., St. Paul, St. Augustine). Such conversions illustrate the human psychic capacity to experience feelings of exaltation that open one to the sense that life has a higher purpose. Similarly, William James' *Varieties of Religious Experience* (1902) investigated and described the character changes and emotional excitement that created new centers of personal energy in highly intelligent individuals. They underwent a remarkable process of moral maturation as a consequence of their conversion. Hence both the psychologist Bucke and the philosopher James discover in this religious experience a remarkable truth about the power inherent in the human psyche. Indeed, the instinct to surrender to the power of higher passions, which may reveal the deepest truths about life, reveals that the human being is able to become aware of a superior power in himself or herself.

While these analyses may give great comfort to those who take such ecstasy to be a sure sign of God's grace, others of a more scientific disposition find a psychological truth about humankind may also account for our evolution.

It is not unusual for those who undergo conversion to attribute it to the presence of a deity. Yet, the experience of the nobler passions may actually be the way we apperceive a reality superior to that of the physical world. It may be that such individuals have actually experienced the birth of their own supraconscience.

Prior to conversion, individuals are often in a depressed state of mind or immersed in a deep sense of hopelessness. Sometimes there is anger that there is no higher truth in existence than our biological death. At such times, life seems not worth living--and certainly not worth enduring sickness, poverty, sorrow, injustice or continual suffering. Or, sometimes the individual has exhausted all hedonistic pleasures and finally found both them and his life senseless. Also, a preoccupation with material possessions can leave one in a state of utter boredom.

In any event, what follows a conversion is something like a miracle. Beyond being a mental metamorphosis or transformation of temperament, an authentic conversion reveals a deeper truth about the nature of human evolution. In fact, over the millennia of recorded history, religious conversions have left their indelible imprint on human memory.

For men and women who have experienced this, it seems to illustrate the point that such individuals possess the power of self-regeneration or self-transformation. Put another way, certain individuals have the power of self-transmutation--a kind of self-resurrection.

If so, this potential of the psyche divulges a direct connection to human evolution. In the light of such experiences, we must ask: "Is it unscientific or irrational to wonder if conversion has a lasting effect on our mental evolution?" Is it disloyal to convert from outworn conceptions and sentiments to new beliefs and convictions? This psychic phenomenon seems analogous to what evolutionary biologists call a 'saltation', i.e. the origin of a new species through a single evolutionary mutation due to an unknown cause.

A conversion might be the sequel to an epiphany, the experience one would feel in the immediate presence of God. Or, for the solitary thinker, it might take place at the moment when one perceives a superior truth about his life.

Such transcendent experiences evoke powerful emotions in gifted individuals, but also persuade more common folk that some supernatural power is involved in their destiny as well. In other words, while emotional judgment plays an undeniable role in the evolution of the individual psyche, the idea and direct experience of God may actually be the motivating power behind the accelerated evolution of humankind. Hence, the emergence of the supraconscience would largely be due to our ardent attachment to the ideal of God guiding our lives.

The Meaning of Mystical Experience

For the true mystic, a sphere of light or the sense of an immense presence seems to encircle the individual. He or she feels enfolded by a kindness and caring comparable only to the intimate protection and closeness of one's mother soon after one's birth. In the beginning of life, a baby cannot see or focus; neither can it see the guardian present, yet the infant feels the mother's warmth and tender love.

Birth is an awakening to a new world. The infant hears the soft sounds and smells the sweet breath of mother for the first time. It is its first mystical experience in life. Later, if grace is granted to the soul, the grown person again feels enfolded. It is the loving embrace of an angel or the caress of a messenger from afar, sent to reassure one that all will be well. Grace emerges out of the mysterious womb of the universe.

That moment teaches us there is a future life beyond anything we could possibly foresee or imagine. Then as unexpectedly as it happened, the moment is gone, leaving the human being alone once again, yet somehow more ready to contend with life. Our journey through time is still ahead of us. Later, when the destined moment has come, the individual will reenter the infinite womb of life. The journey will be completed, at least for this lifetime.

If we ask ourselves why anyone may experience such an extraordinary event in a lifetime, if we consider the possible, evolutionary meaning of such a supernatural occurrence, what sensible conclusion are we to come to? The ecstasy we experience as contact with the numinous may actually be a direct experience of our evolving human supraconscience, which has been in the process of transformation over thousands of generations. If we had never freed ourselves from our primeval subconscience or our simian primitiveness, we would probably never have become open to the ecstasy of the eternal.

On the other hand, despite the vast span of time during which we evolved from hominid to humanoid to human, our primeval subconscience has continued to control our animal body. Since it controls and governs in large part our survival instincts--survival at any cost--any situation or threat perceived as dangerous will provoke a "kill or be killed" response.

At the level of survival, present day man still exhibits extremes of emotion as we react to the threats from the world around us. We have gone through hundreds of millennia during which the human mind and form have evolved. If we have learned anything, time has taught us it is time to decide at which stage of evolution we are going to live out our lives. Thus far we have retraced the steps in the struggle between the savage subconscience and our humanized supraconscience. The future of humanity will be determined by either human indecision or decision.

But, human evolution is not based solely on our biological development through successive anthropoid stages. Though our mutations are self-evident through the transformations of our skull, there is other evidence which is not attributable to evolutionary biology, ecology, or anthropology. Our kind has steadily demonstrated an exponential increase in manual and
mental dexterity. Our developed ability to create what has never before appeared in the world is astounding.

We have accumulated insights to explain all manner of natural phenomena, organized immense libraries to encompass all existing knowledge. We have systematized everything ever discovered or learned in universal dictionaries and established schools, colleges and renowned universities to make sure that all that is known can be taught at varying levels from the basic to the acme of specialization in every academic discipline and science presently known to mankind.

What is most striking about the evolution of our" knowledge is that the human race educated itself, designed its own methods of learning, materialized the means of advancing humankind beyond anything imagined or accomplished in the past. It is we who have readied ourselves for the future and made the achievements of the future into a reality. It is we who have established entire civilizations spanning continents and now the entire planet. All these accomplishments not only set off *Homo sapiens* as a species onto itself. So far as we know, we are the most evolved intelligence in the universe.

In sum, what we identify as human evolution has been, in fact, the consequence of humankind's self-education, self-cultivation, self-surpassing, and self-stimulated evolution. We have learned as much as possible about existence. We have developed an almost infinite variety of creative capacities and range of rational systems for discovering greater knowledge. But our transcendental intuition of God becomes immanent and real when we pursue with a passion the evolution of our finite supraconscience.

Inspired at first by the power we perceive in the celestial universe, our evolving mystical intuition led us to believe a Supreme Being had blessed our decision and validated our determination not only to survive as a species but also to make possible a worthy destiny for all human beings.

That power has been guiding us to master the world, urging us to use our resources wisely, and to perfect human nature. By our devotion to the labor of comprehending the awesome reality we live in, by envisioning the Creator of the human race, we have a clear purpose before us. We are destined to continue our evolution till, in some future time, we will prove we have deserved the faith the Supraconscience has placed in us from the very beginning of human time.

In the end, humankind's mystical intuition has been the primary cause of inspiration to humanity to evolve the loftiest form of incarnate intelligence yet to emerge in this universe. Though our finite supraconscience remains infinitesimal, our commitment to know God's world and to dedicate ourselves to just and humane wisdom is modern man's testament to the Supraconscience of the universe that future humanity will prove worthy of the Creator's trust and patience, His protection and compassion.

Supraconscience
Supraconscience as Mysticism and Heresy

This brief addendum focuses on the universal dialectic that governs and guides all evolution. Not only is this process evident in the creativity cum integration omnipresent in animate nature, but the human psyche co-evolves with the cultures and civilizations it creates.

William James' *Varieties of Religious Experience* provides abundant evidence of the spiritual orientation of humankind's supraconscience via mystics, saints and mystical experiences.

By contrast to this, Walter Nigg's *The Heretics. Heresy through the Ages* offers ample historical evidence of humankind's heretical supraconscience in memorable examples of the lives, works and martyrdom of renowned heretics.

These two distinct lines of thought and emotional conviction seem to be in total opposition. Yet, their co-existence in time clearly demonstrates they have actually worked in tandem. Through their interaction, they have fostered the evolution of two sides of psyche throughout history. Each explored realms of psyche beyond the mundane and the imaginative, the orthodox and the unorthodox. This interplay has been psyche's way of evolving its intellectual and emotional powers, yet remaining governed by common sense and maintaining its sanity.

Psyche's Supraconscience as Reality

Over the past four millennia, religions have taught humankind that the Almighty rules over human history. Venerable ancient scriptures have characterized God as all-knowing and omnipotent. The ideal of such a Supreme Being has not only had universal appeal, but it likely encouraged the evolution of the human psyche. Its soul-uplifting affect was one reason why sensitive, intuitive individuals sought to embrace mystical experience.

How could an idea influence a bio-psychological evolution? Over the millennia in which we have been conscious, is it possible the God ideal has acted on the human brain? Perhaps transformed its synaptic intricacy? Generations of humankind have felt protected and blessed by a Divinity. This sense of being blessed could have stimulated greater neurological integration and also increased our passion for knowledge of God's Wisdom.

An analogy may be appropriate here. Bio-electrical stimulation of the brain over time could be likened to the effect of waves against a shore, the pattern of which slowly changes its contours and evolves the distinct forms of life that inhabit it. Such would be the effect of recurrent stimuli effecting changes in brain and psyche. Though the mind advanced by microscopic mutations between cells and electrified synapses, over time prayer seemed to confirm the presence of the divine in our lives and justified a lifetime of devotion. Slowly but surely, the ideal became the real. The commitment proved salutary, healed despair, and turned worship into a form of protection against fear, anxiety and tragedy: Faith transfigured the human psyche.

There is solid evidence for such conjecture. What psychological effect would belief in God's omniscience have? In the earliest cultures, it would have motivated people to improve their survival skills. Over time, such skills created monuments of engineering and architecture. Furthermore, once humankind had established its various cultures, people's insatiable curiosity turned to learning and then to seeking wisdom hidden in knowledge itself. In following their mystical urge, they had begun to probe the secrets of the mind itself. In the process, the human psyche evolved.

These preoccupations led to a new appreciation of proverbs, maxims, folk tales and expressions of human wisdom which taught humankind a more empathic understanding of the best in human nature. Later, memorable literature--stories, dreams and poetry--enriched heart and mind by teaching lessons in compassion. With knowledge and wisdom came a greater comprehension of what the Almighty must know about us. A similar psychic progression occurred when theologians and philosophers undertook to explain the universal mind of God.

Hence, the mystical intuition is deeper than any rationalized religion can explain. It reveals how our life instinct has become religious in nature. And, that inveterate instinct tells us that all life mysteries and realities conceal and reveal one ultimate reality.

Thus the mystical experience reveals the secret of life–how to live and how to die. To learn from experience is to discover your own truths about life. You alone can decide what meaning you want to glean from life. You will need to concentrate and integrate all your inborn gifts in order to realize your destiny. Your purpose must be self-chosen. Use your intelligence to educate yourself and your life energy to become fulfilled emotionally. In this way you can achieve your most cherished dreams.

Perhaps by so doing, you can contribute to the supraconscience of humanity. The realization of a lifetime work may convince you that the Supraconscience and the cosmos are as real as you and your finite creation.

The Effect of Mysticism on our Supraconscience

Across history, individuals have had mystical experiences. Preceding such experiences, the person may have felt adrift and then as if he were being pulled down by a powerful undertow.

Without meaning, life seems to be drawing to an end. Then, one day, a sudden illumination can envelope the most lonely man or woman. Its radiation seems to pour from a center within. It is like the light from a candle filling a pitch dark room. It pushes back the darkness to where it came from. Where there is a sphere of light, there is no reason to fear.

The mystical experience comes to the solitary soul. The individual wonders where this inner radiance comes from. Perhaps the presence of an angel or even of God, but no one really knows. It happens to people of all races, religions and cultures. Though its ultimate source remains unknown, the person experiencing it is renewed in body and mind. Energy surges forth as he or she searches for new meaning to life. A sudden maturation of mind has taken place, but why?

A religious explanation would provide comfort here, but non-believers are bound to wonder why anyone would be chosen for such an extraordinary experience. Many of us are rational of mind, skeptical, and unreligious. Many are not inclined to seek emotional answers for the empirically unexplainable. Yet, clearly the strange joy experienced by the mystic brings the chosen one a sense that life has some greater meaning than hitherto suspected.

Perhaps an objective and scientific explanation can bring a little more clarity.

Sometimes the person affected begins to perceive reality as a unified, spiritual whole. He or she becomes aware of an inner principle that energizes everything. The experience brings with it a pristine feeling within, a kind of inner springtime. There is a new apperception that the past is past because it has been surpassed. Something in us is being made into a new identity.

We do know that the mystical experience takes place when an individual becomes aware of the beauty and majesty of the earth itself. Or the person may know rapture at the infinity of the cosmos. Such ecstasies express our humility and awe before the omnipotence felt in all creation.

But other instances occur when the isolated soul believes that some power intimately cares about him or her. Is that power *out there* or *in here*? Is it particular to one lonely individual, or is it universal to all humankind?

Over countless generations, our species has sensed some power growing within it. A driving principle of nature seems to shape human intelligence and enable it to perceive the world as never before. In turn, that principle appears to be consolidating a centre of passionate spiritual energy. This is the creative power of evolution as it is concentrated in humankind. Mankind's evolving supraconscience is the new identity that will explain the realities and mysteries of human destiny.

Born of our worship of the Divinity, humanity's emotional wisdom has nurtured the faith that the infinite Supraconscience of God brought forth the earth, the universe, and the creation of life itself.

As brief a review as this is, the cardinal directions of humankind's exploration of knowledge and wisdom point to a self-evident probability. Throughout much of history, humans have believed in the omniscience of the Deity. (He could even read our hearts and conscience and inspire us with sacred truth.) As a consequence, we have gradually come to realize that God has always wanted us to comprehend the world He created. Thus learning would be the ultimate form of worship. If this is true, then by pursuing knowledge, we have an even greater destiny to fulfill than to merely ensure the survival of our species.

Hence in an age where secular intelligence must be given its due, we demonstrate our enlightened faith in the Creator by identifying Him, rationally and scientifically, as the Supraconscience of our Universe. To educate ourselves is to foster our personal supraconscience. To learn is to believe that life has a sacred meaning.

In so far as we understand the mystical significance of human evolution, we come closer to learning the ultimate purpose of God's guidance. The Supraconscience has brought us into the world to create our own destiny.

Notes

1. W. Nigg, *The Heretics. Heresy Through the Ages*, p. 166-67. All references in Chs. Eight and Nine of this work are paraphrases from Nigg's work.
2. Nigg, p. 163.
3. Nigg, p. 228.
4. Nigg, p. 233.
5. Nigg, p. 235.
6. Nigg, p. 239-40.
7. Nigg, p. 242.
8. See Strauch's *Beyond Literary Theory as the Search for the Meaning of Human Destiny*. Lanham, MD. University Press of America. 2001.
9. Nigg, p. 362.
10. Nigg, p. 366.
11. James, W., *Varieties of Religious Experience*, p. 212.
12. James, W. p. 213.

Chapter Nine
A Twenty-First Century Version of Heresy

History's judgment of heretics is based almost entirely on the verdicts of the established Church. Any Christian who questioned its competence or integrity as far as interpretation of the Gospels was concerned was declared a heretic. Those thus condemned were either excommunicated or put to death. The ecclesiastical authorities were both prosecutor and judge. No one dared defend those damned for heresy.

Almost all heretics were judged to be wicked, seditious, or initiates of the devil. Indeed, heresy was declared to have been instigated by Satan. However, most educated heretics were concerned that the Church no longer lived by the truths of Christ's life. Some felt that it was missing the deeper meaning of the Gospels and had interpreted the Eternal Truth mainly in terms of dogmata and doctrines. This discord led to the historical split between Western Christianity and the Eastern Orthodox Church, and later between Catholicism and Protestantism.

In spite of the Church's condemnation of individual heretics, a closer study of the intellectual character of the most renowned among them reveals they had much in common with Old Testament prophets and even with saints later canonized by the Church. All were impassioned to live life by a sacred truth and to die for that truth, if necessary. They were convinced they perceived the original meaning of God's Word. Such opposing views inevitably led to the development of hermeneutics (methodical principles of Biblical interpretation).

As we saw in Chapter Four, *Four Emerging Archetypes* (of the supraconscience), the Old and New Testaments themselves suggest four strata of significance: 1) literal or historical, 2) allegorical, 3) moral, and 4) anagogical or mystical. It took the martyrdom of generations of heretics for ecclesiastical authority to acknowledge the deeper meanings encoded in Scripture.

For almost two millennia, heretics challenged the Church's infallible judgment as to the fixed and final meanings of Holy Writ. The emotional intuition of some heretics called for creative insights into Scripture; it was as if they imitated Jesus' own 'heretical' ways of reinterpreting the Old Law. Unlike saints who submitted in blind faith to the teachings of the Church, heretics were persuaded that they perceived in them a more sophisticated truth than the literal account of Biblical events. They delved deeper for sacred truths than was typically done in interpreting the holy laws in unassailable doctrines: The heretic listened to the voice of his conscience rather than to authoritarian pronouncements. Unfortunately, such stalwart opinions most often led to damnation and martyrdom.

Among the noteworthy thinkers outlawed for their original approach to the intent of Holy writ was Origen (185-254), a Christian writer, teacher and mystic. He examined the writings of earlier poets and philosophers for the purpose of discovering their wisdom. His passion for truth and knowledge led him to suggest that the apostles had not actually been able to interpret the greater truth of Christ's teachings. Origen himself proposed a procedure by which to attain the mystical and moral meaning of the Holy Writ. His stage-by-stage method of uncovering the truth inherent in Scripture aimed at teaching the devout Christian to seek out the whole truth.

Origen's open-mindedness enabled him to study the writings and declarations of the heretics in order to learn from them. At times, he found himself in sympathy with their dangerous lines of thought. Based on his study of Judaic and Christian sects, he found himself a wiser Christian. Thus in contemplating others' arguments, he could detect their errors and false modes of reasoning, which gave his own declarations greater certainty. The third and last stage of his self-education came when he developed an appreciation of the pursuit of secret knowledge in ancient gnosticism.[1]

In sum, with scholarship to reinforce his intuitive faith, Origen urged Christians to imbibe all forms of genuine learning and devotion to fortify and invigorate their own faith. To him, God the Teacher encouraged us to decide our own destiny.[2]

However, Origen was horrified with the threat of hell and its eternal fire as described in Mark 42-47. Here God appeared unforgiving and vindictive. Origen could not believe that God's mercy did not reach into Hell itself. As a consequence, the theologians condemned Origen for arguing that even the damned should have hope. Incensed by this claim, the Church condemned him not only for casting aside Church doctrine but also for putting too much faith in his own conscience.[3] Though he remained condemned for centuries, he bequeathed to Christianity an unforgettable model for spiritual self-education.

The second-century heretic, Marcion, was much influenced by the gnostics of his time. He saw God's world as imperfect and nature as evil. How could God have created such a world as ours? Hence he could not accept the God of the Old Testament or the teachings of its prophets.

In the Old Law, God was cruel, merciless, fanatical and His justice was arbitrary. Even the Commandments were morally questionable. The severity of His Justice did not match Christ's all-embracing love and mercy. The profound difference between the Old and New Testament he attributed to a conspiracy among scribes who had falsified the facts. For this, the Church condemned Marcion as a heretic.[4]

The Fathers judged Marcion to personify evil. Though they thought him a genius, they rejected his unflinching application of logic. Nevertheless, for this heretic, the tremendous mystery of the Gospels filled him with ecstasy. In them, he found the Divinity radiating infinite mercy and love. In short, Marcion judged love to be a greater power than justice.

By the second century A.D., heresy had emerged as a counter-force to Christianity. Irenaeus, Bishop of Lyon, became the principal antagonist of heretics. He recognized Gnosticism as the predominant philosophy of his time, yet generously thought of the heretics as human beings, but bad interpreters of the Bible. However, instead of rejecting their arguments outright, he undertook to suggest that there was a superior truth to be found in Christ's teachings. He argued that Christ was the essence of the moral evolution of mankind in so far as he ensured man's salvation through His own Resurrection.[5]

Irenaeus himself believed salvation to be possible only through adherence to Church dogma. When his impatience with the heretics became intolerance, he began to misquote them, treat their arguments unfairly, and reject their ideas as outlandish. Finally, he found no real significance or worth in Gnostic theology.

However, the Church's inflexibility in rejecting alternate interpretations of Scripture led to increasing defection from single-minded adherence to dogmata. The result was widespread abandonment of the laity's loyalty to the Church or straight out rejection of the faith. All such individuals were persecuted as apostates.

In the late second century, the Montanist movement stressed apocalypticism and strict ascetic discipline; they also practiced the art of prophecy. Montanus declared himself to be the Paraclete (the Holy Ghost) and so the fulfillment of the prediction of St. John's Gospel. As such, he offered a Revelation which supplanted that of the Old Testament. He insisted that revealed truth was not limited to the past, but could appear in any age, present or future.[6]

As shocking and objectionable as this assertion may be to Jew and Christian alike, the belief that all revelation was expressed only once in the past defies common sense and controverts modern man's knowledge of evolution. Why would God give the ancients His Divine Truth only once when His concern would be for all succeeding generations of humankind as well? Why would God not emanate revelations to every age till the end of human time? Are we today less deserving or less worthy of this than our ancestors? If so, how? And, why?

If nature is an example of God's sending forth new forms of life as evinced in evolution, why would He not reveal new forms of His Truth across human time? Even as hominids evolved through different evolutionary stages—Neanderthal, Cro-Magnon, Homo erectus, Homo sapiens--God would have sent us intuitions, intimations and revelations suited to our evolved capacity to understand.

Moreover, as humankind created cultures and civilizations, we accelerated our own intellectual evolution through increased secular knowledge and wisdom. It seems logical that God would send ever-new revelations to guide mankind as human intelligence evolved. Furthermore, as humankind became better able to grasp the universal wisdom of these Divine Truths, we would better understand God and the essence of human nature.

Would prehistoric man have been able to understand our twenty-first century knowledge of the cosmos? Would not God guide us through successive revelations, revelations which corresponded to the various stages of evolution?

Hence Montanus' insistence on recurrent revelation makes sense. Yet, he also prophesied the imminent end of the world. To be worthy to survive, the Christian had to practice self-discipline. One must prepare for the New Jerusalem, become as pure as the Apostles were. Sensuous pleasures were to be shunned, and sexual purity became the ideal. Fasting and forms of self-mastery were rigorously practiced. His followers had to be prepared for martyrdom, to withstand the test of their integrity and demonstrate the purity of their cause. [7]

To most normal people, the idea of seeking martyrdom appears to be not only an act of fanaticism but also a sign of insanity. To the educated individual, any form of suicide demeans the soundest lesson of human evolution, which teaches us not only to survive for the sake of our descendents but to respect life--that of others and our own.

The Church responded to the Montanist movement with an edict of excommunication. The Montanists were considered to be under the spell of the devil. They were accused of unchaste conduct, apostasy, and murder. They were deemed guilty of having renounced the teachings of the Church.

Another case of heresy arose from Donatism practiced in the fourth century. Inspired by the Bishop of Carthage, Donatus, this Christian sect in North Africa spoke out against the moral laxity of the priesthood. The laity were offended at the mortal sins of the priests because those responsible to administer the holy sacraments should be sinless. When the Emperor Constantine (306-337 A.D.) was notified of the sect's indignation and criticism of the clergy, he ordered them to obey and submit to religious authority. In response, the Donatists revolted. They became convinced that the powers of the Church should be separated from those of the state.[8] (Today this sensible judgment is the very foundation of law and order in the modern state.) Though they were suppressed through ruthless measures, the idealism of these early Christian heretics left an imprint on secular history.

Such religious idealism relates directly to our conception of what might become a modern religious ethic. Modern man acknowledges the fact that religious upbringing motivates much of what we do in life. Despite the skepticism and cynicism displayed daily in the media, it remains a moral fact that religion urges every individual to overcome weakness, sickness and suffering by inner fortitude. In so far as possible, we should master our failings.

On the other hand, in a world of temptations where reward or punishment in an afterlife seems unreal and unprovable, living a sinless life seems impossible.

Yet, we should encourage a form of 'sinlessness' that few think about. In the main, you should not sin against those who trust and love you. But there is a deeper sin: to fail yourself, to fail to develop your natural talents or pursue an ideal in life. To reach an advanced age only to realize you wasted your life must be the most sorrowful judgment you can make about yourself. A wasted life, one thrown away as if it had no value.

When the British monk Pelagius (350-418 A.D.) arrived in Rome, he was affronted by the corruption he found in the Church. As a theologian, Pelagius had already rejected the idea that newborn children were infected with sin. Consequently, Adam and Eve had not passed on their "sin" to all humanity. Sin was not inborn, but was the result of acts committed in life. What he found in Rome amply confirmed this truth.[9]

Of course, Pelagius' rejection of original sin stood in stark contrast to Saint Augustine, who maintained sin was transmitted by our inherent sexual lust. "Through the sin of Adam, man's freedom will have been entirely lost. Given his present corruptness, man can only desire evil."[10] Moreover, he held that God only favored a few with grace and the rest were born damned.

Though belief in original sin was probably inspired by man's prehistoric subconscious, the modern, educated person finds condemnation for one's ancestors' sins unacceptable. Nevertheless, today an individual may commit an 'original' sin by intentionally and wantonly harming another, causing that other human being pain, anxiety and humiliation.

Let it also be made clear that our ancestors have not passed their "sinfulness" on to us via "evil genes". Actual iniquity takes place when someone torments or dehumanizes another. If such wrongdoing fails to awaken a sense of guilt, but gives sadistic satisfaction, an individual has truly sinned. Or, if one feels barbaric satisfaction at repaying some "insult", this in itself is a sort of 'original' sin in so far as it can only provoke further injustice and inhumanity. Inevitably, a vengeful person will meet his nemesis. Justice metes out punishment equal to the pain inflicted. Such "sin" is inevitably punished in this lifetime.

The monk Pelagius believed in man's freedom to reach his own decisions. The Creator had endowed every person with a conscience to decide between good and evil. Christians were to know their responsibility to God.[11]

Modern man would agree with this view. God does not want us to be marionettes or sycophants. Nor did He manufacture humans to be androids. Assuredly, He did not create humankind to be obedient, mindless, docile animals. Rather, as is abundantly evident from human ingenuity, devotion to ideals, and conscientious work, He created highly intelligent beings who are passionate about accomplishing what needs to be done. He wanted strong men and women able to learn what it took to survive in the world, what the world was made of, and how it worked. He wanted men and women to create families and societies where mutual understanding helped shape the future. The purpose of humankind's collective soul is to make human evolution a realizable reality for all humanity.

Contrary to St. Augustine's belief that only a select few were predestined to receive God's grace, Pelagius questioned why God would want to predetermine anything. Thus, he championed faith in man's free will.[12]

If we accept human evolution as a reality and acknowledge that, along with the evolution of our psyche, truth itself has evolved through time, how can we accept the belief that only certain individuals are absolutely predetermined for salvation and others not?

The progress from the beginning of life on earth through the consequent evolution of ever-new forms of life points to the conclusion that God Himself must be behind the continual creation of new life forms. True, each creature is influenced by biochemical and environmental conditions. Yet, to survive, all forms of life have to continuously develop new strategies of survival. They need to form ever more efficient life-support systems, not only to stay alive but also to ensure the survival of their progeny.

If it is true that God's creativity brought forth Creation, then all its creatures must be born with certain intrinsic powers. They all have inherited the power of self-creation, innovation, mutation and evolution. Also innate is the power of consolidation, self-healing and self-integration. Hence the world God created is pervasively empowered by His creative conscience.

Ultimately, since all advanced forms of life must be organically and neurologically conscious of being alive, such processes cannot simply be biochemical, involuntary, mechanical or automatic. Moreover, since evolution provides abundant evidence that evolutionary change is initiated from within a given entity, self-determination must play a predominant role in the overall process. Otherwise stated, human evolution itself has been significantly guided by *decision*. Today, we perceive that the evolution of our finite supraconscience either is due to our commitment to the Idea of God or is a direct consequence of guidance by a Supreme Being.

Another figure from the history of heresy was the medieval monk Gottschalk. As a youth, he was deprived of his rightful property by monastic authorities. He was kept more or less a prisoner in the monastery till adulthood, and, at maturity, claimed restitution and freedom. He was freed but his property was retained. This injustice led him to initially accept his fate as predestined by God.[13]

Modern man would question the logic and soundness of the doctrine of predestination. If God already foresees who will lead wicked or good lives, free will and decision are a delusion because predestination makes it a matter of moral indifference how anyone lives his life. No matter how they live, the elect are favored by God whereas the rest of humanity struggling to give moral meaning to their lives may be damned eternally anyway. But, God cannot be such a tyrant. If he arbitrarily affixed certain fates to individual lives, He would be more like Satan than God. Such an interpretation of the Divinity's actions is unworthy of our idea of God. Today, it is quite impossible to accept predestination as the eternal will of God. So much for eternal truths.

For all Gottschalk's courage and intelligence in his arguments against the injustice that befell him, his words fell on deaf ears. He was placed in solitary confinement for twenty years. He died in prison a heretic to the end. The Swiss historian, Walter Nigg, praised Gottschalk for his determination, his freedom of thought, and for his earnest search for a truth deeper and truer than blind belief in dogma.

Yet, another heretic was Erigena, also known as John the Scot, a Faustian figure with respect to his scholarly learning. His book on nature is said to have foreshadowed Hegel's 19th century philosophy. Erigena believed God created the world to reveal His Nature to humankind. The Scot found no evil in nature and declared evil was the product of unsound imagining. He also considered the doctrine of predestination to be a form of logical madness. He took belief in heaven and hell to be states of mind, nothing else.[14] Clearly Erigena had an intuition that hell arose out of our primitive subconscience, and the idea of heaven came from a superior intimation inspired by God. As with other heretics, he suffered for obeying his own conscience and intelligently working out original conceptions of theology. Because he questioned the validity of the Church's dogmata, Erigena faced a heretic's fate.

As one of the most unforgettable heretics of the Middle Ages, the French philosopher Peter Abelard, is known to us as the author of *Sic et Non*. In general, his writings reveal a remarkable tolerance toward different religions. He believed ideas should be freely exchanged. Since he was ahead of the mentality of the Church of his time, his open-mindedness and unorthodox conclusions came under the intolerant scrutiny of ecclesiastical authority.[15]

As we know, Abelard's dialectical method questioned the 'eternal truths' of Christian theology and thus served to undermine its authority. His chief opponent, Bernard of Clairvaux (1090-1158), found his reasoning both vain and heretical. Bernard, was, however, aware of how the contradictions evident among the teachings of the Church Fathers cast serious doubt on the absolute authority of religious truth. The foundation of the Faith was now open to question.[16]

Abelard had confronted the Church with its own internal disagreements. Yet, his method became indispensable to posterity. His juxtaposition of antinomies (contradictions between equally valid principles) revealed the necessity of freeing reason from self-contradiction. He aimed at a more objective form of reasoning based on verifiable inferences, one which pointed to more sound conclusions. Centuries later the inductive mode of inquiry implicit in Abelard's works became the core of scientific reasoning. Thus his writings raised the threshold of human consciousness and moved it toward the higher level of skill characteristic of contemporary cognitive processes.

By contrast, Bernard skillfully used sacred metaphor and symbol to achieve a mode of argumentation superior to the purely rational. In essence, he used his emotional acumen to counter abstract reasoning typical of Abelard. Though Abelard was condemned as a heretic, the confrontation between these two figures showed that the psyche was capable of both loftier forms of reasoning and that it possessed the power of adroit, emotional persuasion.

In the early centuries of the second millennium (1000 A.D. and after), Catharism arose in southern France. A Cathar was a member of an ascetic and dualistic Christian sect which taught that matter is evil. The Cathars professed faith in an angelic Christ who did not really undergo human birth and death.

Catharists held many of the dualistic beliefs of the early Manicheans, who found the world to be a place of evil. Members of the Catharistic sect saw evil as the greatest threat to one's soul, for, to them, the world had been created by a god of darkness. The Cathars also believed in a good God of light, who had created the noble and pure illumination of the universe. Thus for them, good and evil were supernatural forces which tested their ascetic resolve to live only a chaste life, inviolate and unprofaned. Sexual activity between man and woman was the worst sin. Such fanatical abstinence seems unnatural and undesirable to us, yet the

Cathar endeavor to lead a life of perfection and chastity was the view of many a mystic.[17]

The Cathar belief that the world was inherently evil expressed the age-old fear of our prehistoric subconscience as it held in thrall the conscience of medieval man and woman. However pure their purpose and noble their ideas, this shadow side of their faith showed how they distrusted human desire. They even mistook it to be inspired by Satan. Centered in the psyche, this mortal conflict between the god of darkness (the subconscience) and the god of light (the Christian conscience) was a bitter burden for the devout to bear.

A final medieval 'heretic' was Waldus, who, in 12th century southern France, established a community known as the Waldensians. He felt 'called' to preach the words of Christ and to live the life of a pilgrim. He attracted the illiterate who needed to hear him profess his faith. When the Pope banned his preaching, he faced a crisis of conscience whether to obey the Church or the command of Jesus to preach to the poor. He obeyed God rather than men and was condemned.[18]

The threat of excommunication proved ineffective against the Waldensians because they chose to obey the Law of Christ, i.e. the words of Christ Himself, rather than merely accept the dogmata and doctrines of the Church. In their total commitment to purity, they rejected the doctrine of purgatory which allowed sinners to purify themselves and so be redeemed. The Church began to persecute the Waldensians mercilessly and exterminated as many of them as they could find. Finally, however, the martyrdom of these simple, devout pilgrims enraged many against Rome.[19]

This instance in history makes evident how difficult it is to assume full responsibility when one decides to lead a life dedicated to integrity. Only the individual conscience can decide what one's life will be. Often the choice is between what one holds to be profane and what sacred. For the Christian, that meant adopting the conscience of Christ as a guide to one's destiny on earth. For others the 'call to conscience' may mean a decision to consummate some lifetime ideal known only to one's evolving psyche.

The Inquisition

The Inquisition is defined as: a) a former Roman Catholic tribunal for the discovery and punishment of heresy; b) an investigation conducted with little regard for individual rights; c) a severe questioning.[20] Behind these concise, dry, impassive definitions is concealed one of the blackest periods in human history.

The Inquisition is a 400-year story of human injustice, cruelty and mass murder. What follows is a brief, secular account of the genocide that hundreds of thousands of innocents underwent as they were judged heretics.

A preliminary comment is called for here. Let us situate ourselves in the time. If your family originated in Western Europe, it is highly probable that you had forebears who either were persecuted and put to death for heresy or who were among the Inquisitors, torturers or murderers of the innocent. It is likely that many of your ancestors faced the Inquisition as victims or victimizers. Today, this fact should teach us how our species' barbaric subconscience was able to dehumanize us and still can in the present.

In early Christianity, those who doubted or questioned Church doctrines or practices were treated tolerantly because they still were considered brothers and sisters. However, the ensuing centuries were marked by increasing intolerance of, and exasperation with, 'heretics'.

For a time, the more serious offenders were excommunicated, which censure deprived a Christian of the rights of Church membership. However, as educated and defiant heretics questioned the authority of the Church and proposed alternate interpretations of Holy Writ, tolerance turned to public denunciation. Some denied the explanation of the Holy Trinity (the unity of Father, Son and Holy Ghost as three persons in one Godhead). Others denied that Christ could possibly have been resurrected. Still others argued that the Apocryphal writings were of dubious origin and authority. Such denials and assertions were crimes in the eyes of the Church and self-declared heretics of this sort were put to death.

Despite increasing protests against the execution of fellow Christians, the Church continued to approve of such punishments. The reaction was the spread of heresy among the populace. To counter this uprising, the Church claimed that thousands were possessed by the devil. To 'save their souls', the authorities condoned the crudest measures, namely, violence. And, faithful Christians understood that such aggressive tactics belied the holiest teachings of the Gospels.

It is a fact that the Inquisitors found passages in the Old Testament which could be used to justify the most inhuman punishment against those deemed to have violated God's trust and laws. Though the secular segment of the local government carried out the torture and executions at the behest of the Church, many local priests were surely horrified and shamed upon witnessing the death of innocents from their parishes.

Educated inquisitors used guile, duplicity, and casuistry to entrap the little-educated and bewildered innocent into confessing to mortal sins they had not committed. Ingenious forms of physical torture and psychological torment were used to break down the terrified victim, all of which reminds us of the 'game' a predator plays with helpless prey before eating it alive.

Perhaps some of the inquisitors pursued their task with zeal in the blind faith they were doing their sacred duty to cleanse Christianity of those possessed by the devil. Yet, today one wonders if it were not all a stratagem of the prehistoric subconscience to give free rein to its own predatory instinct. Or, maybe that residual subconscience believed it had become God's weapon in a ferocious struggle with Satan? Wherever in human history we meet the killer instinct, we have reason to believe it arises from the primeval subconscience reliving its struggle for survival.

The ostensible purpose of the inquisitorial procedure was to prove the accused guilty. Only proof of guilt was accepted as an outcome, and no counter-evidence, i.e. no arguments for innocence, were admitted. Under such circumstances, no clear-headed individual dared rise to the defense of the accused for fear of being accused of a comparable heretical act and hence incriminated.

To be sure, the unrelenting practices of the Inquisitors evoked the population's horror of the Church. A growing nihilism and atheism was the consequence. In place of keeping to Christ's message of compassion, the people saw the Church as Satanic; it seemed to worship death and destruction. Finally, Christians asked how God could have permitted such evil to persist for so long.

Particularly odious was the witchcraft craze based on a pseudo-scholarly work by two monks who were motivated by a pathological hatred of women. They claimed witches prostituted themselves to Satan and were capable of every sexual perversion. Hence witches were shown no mercy and were often burned at the stake.

Clearly, the witchcraft hysteria stimulated the subhuman and inhuman element in the human psyche. The relentless persecution of women revealed the ever-present danger that psyche's primeval subconscience could lash out against any perceived threat. Surrender to mindless passion led to the slaughter of thousands upon thousands of innocents. Individuals were tortured until they confessed they were witches. Those who protested against the mass madness were themselves often seized and burned.

It is an historical fact that both Catholicism and Protestant-Christianity engaged in the practice of burning women alive. The Salem witchcraft trials in early America are further evidence of such male hysteria. In modern Islamic countries, we have stark evidence of women's martyrdom at the hands of fanatical male Muslims as well.

Hence the Inquisition serves as an indelible reminder of our past. Succeeding periods of history witnessed how the subconscious of our species exerted a dehumanizing effect on all of us. Today, it remains a very real danger. We must all be wary of emotionalism, intolerance and judgments based on heresay, superstition and ignorance. Knowledge alone guarantees our sanity.

In contrast to our history of intolerance and violence, there always was present the quiet strength of women and the wisdom of mothers. Indeed, the protective nature of women nurtured and safeguarded human evolution. Mothers humanized mankind across the ages. From their teaching came expressions of concern and acts of compassion, and these, in turn, became instinctive humane behavior.

Fortunately, men of sound mind came to defend women against inquisitorial madness. By the time of the 18th century Enlightenment, the emerging humanitarian conscience put an end to such practices. When a young monk went to Frederick the Great of Prussia to describe the decimation of the population due to the Inquisition, the monarch forbade the practice in his kingdom. Before long, the rest of Europe followed and executions ceased.

Centuries before the Reformation and the establishment of Protestant churches, John Wycliffe (1330-1384) had attacked the Church openly. He saw the papacy as the Anti-Christ and repudiated the very foundations of the Church when he denied the doctrine of trans-substantiation.[21] (This sacrament expresses the Christian faith that bread and wine are indeed Eucharistic evidence of the body and blood of Christ.) Though he was damned as a heretic, secular history honored him for his forthright courage.

Martin Luther (1483-1546), German Reformation leader, struggled for years against the devil in the flesh and a relentless fear he was fated for hell. But, one day, while rereading the Epistles of Paul, he came to realize Christ was not a punitive but a merciful God.[22]

Luther understood that it was possible to be mistaken in endeavoring to prove one's soul worthy of God's grace. A man could practice asceticism and display spirituality, yet God would remain indifferent to him. Why? Egotism in the pursuit of personal salvation would not merit His approval.

How then does one deserve the grace of God? Is not ostentatious dedication to Him a subtle form of ingratiation or bribery? If so, millions have little hope of God's grace by persuasion or any guarantee of life after death.

Sincere, honest people realize that God cannot be bribed. Then what does He want from us? When and why should God reward man? The answer may be found in the reverse of what common sense would commend us to do. First, God does not reward opportunists or importunists, nor egotists who seek to ensure their own spiritual advantage or salvation. He certainly does not bend to the strong-minded or the willful; nor does he yield to cajolery, insinuation or attempts at ingratiation.

On the other hand, God would take notice of the individual who is not self-serving or aspiring to spiritual recognition or moral admiration. He begins to observe a person more closely when he or she is not preoccupied with rewards, pay-offs, or kickbacks for doing good deeds, but does things quietly, humbly, even 'invisibly'. But just what does 'invisibility' mean?

It takes place when an individual performs a spontaneous act of kindness, speaks a thoughtful word to help someone find his or her way, or provides material help but that remains unacknowledged. Such individuals live their lives--not in quiet desperation, but, conversely, in quiet dedication to those in any kind of need. They give not the slightest thought to God's grace, nor do they muse about any vague reward in an eternal life, or strive to be on someone's list of saints.

In fact, practical recompense is not really an issue for such a person. The individual knows instinctively, intuitively, even metaphysically that such actions are expected in life. We are supposed to love our brothers and sisters in humanity unobtrusively and helpfully. Why?

Because we all descend from a father and mother who loved us selflessly so that we could live free, worthy, decent, meaningful lives. This teaches us that we all have love to give for as long as we ourselves live.

In rebelling against the Church, Luther contributed to human history a fresh understanding of Christianity. For him, rebellion had become a necessity; it replaced the effetist conscience of the clergy He was incensed at their sale of indulgences. (Indulgences were sold to any sinner who could pay money to have sin remitted.)

Luther also turned against priestly celibacy as unnatural because it denied bodily needs. Most importantly, his study of the Catholic history of heresy had revealed to him how many thousands of guiltless persons had been martyred. To him, the Inquisitors had ever re-crucified the innocent Christ. Thus Luther accused them of perverting the Gospel and betraying Christ Himself.

The widening revulsion at and revolt against the excesses of the clergy and the unconscionable decisions of Church authorities led to the Reformation. This 16th century religious movement rejected certain Roman Catholic doctrines and modified numerous practices so as to establish a new orthodoxy, namely, that of the Protestant Church. Regrettably, it did not take long before the Protestants were punishing their own heretics with self-righteous zeal. Only those who sought amelioration of social conditions in the spirit of the Gospel seemed to listen to the new, emerging conscience. A later Christian thinker, Sebastianus Castelli, concluded "those whom we call heretics are simply those who disagree with us." [23]

This realization could have led not only to mutual tolerance between the Churches, Old and New, but also it could have contributed to a more universal understanding of the mind of evolving humanity. Unfortunately, each new religion or sect tends to dismiss the others as inferior because they want to claim that only the true Christian has found the superior path to God. Such claims prove to be as delusional as assuming there is only one way to worship the Supreme Being.

The Italian poet-philosopher, Giordano Bruno (1548-1600), was declared a heretic because he would not accept the central teaching of the Church: God as a Holy Trinity. However, Bruno's intellect went far beyond dogmata and doctrines. He had read and understood the implications of the universal vision of the Polish astronomer, Nicolaus Copernicus (1473-1543). Inspired by the sidereal view of the universe, the poet envisioned an infinite number of worlds. ("There are countless worlds similar to the earth.")[24]

This declaration was, of course, a direct refutation of the Church's Ptolemaic description of one world with the earth at its center: The sun, moon and planets revolved around us, hence the universe was held together by the power and majesty of our God.

Bruno's exponential expansion of consciousness led him to understand that God permeated all Nature. Specifically, his philosophy opened the mind of future man to the infinity of space and the cosmic reality of God's nature.

For this heresy, he was imprisoned, but he resisted all attempts to get him to recant. When threatened with an auto-da-fé (burning as a heretic), he formed a firm, silent resolution. When he would be burned at the stake, he would die without showing his pain. With the flames surrounding him, when his executioners held up the crucifix to him the last moment of his life, he turned his head away from the cross in contempt. [25]

The Historical Effect of Heresy

Let us consider the final effect of heresy on the development of the modern psyche. What began as a rebellion against the dogmatism of *orthodox* religion affected Judaism, Christianity and Islam. In other words, the various 'heretical' movements were *unorthodox* in intent and philosophy.

Generally, the term *orthodox* refers to the doctrines, sacraments, rituals and established readings of Scripture. These come to represent the conscience of religion.

In contradistinction to the orthodox, the term *unorthodox* is used to express reservations, dissidence, and the need for a new investigation of Holy Writ in order to discover heretofore hidden truths. Often, the unorthodox individual unearths deeper, recondite verities. Cautiously, he or she challenges accepted canon and authoritarian interpretations of 'revealed truth' thus questioning legalistic, administrative and official views of the Church, Synagogue, and Mosque. But, in fact, the unorthodox individual is seeking to know the parameters of a larger conscience in order to grasp more universal dimensions of meaning.

Sometimes, he or she proposes that there is a need for more scholarly sophistication in the interpretation of Biblical passages and commandments. This approach stands in relatively stark contrast to doctrine and dogmata, which seem 'closed', fixed, and out-of-touch with the real world. The unorthodox want to learn the ultimate meaning of God's message to mankind. It is noteworthy that the Occident's scientific beginnings were often condemned as unorthodox in so far as they sought universally significant truths about the world.

Thus, historically conceived, Church doctrines may be considered a stage in the evolution of a religious supraconscience. Doctrines tend to satisfy our rational nature, our need for law and order. They also gratify our need to obey moral principles and to experience communion, the sacraments and communal prayer. Such practices bring orderliness to the lives of billions of people. The positive effect of rule and regulation, ritual and righteousness is that, when these become habitual, they reassure us and give the private life a spiritual purpose.

However, at times such repetition and regularity can become soporific or addictive since constant prayer, churchgoing, and unrelenting religious talk can turn compulsive and virtually meaningless. It is against such mindless behavior that heretics rebel. They need more from the orthodox than vacuous reassurances of salvation and forgiveness.

Dedicated heretics trusted their personal experience of God more than the predications of priests, rabbis, or madrasa teachers. They trust the admonitions and outpourings of the prophets to a greater degree than they do the judgments, pronouncements and politics of the Synagogue, Church or Mosque.

Otherwise stated, the tendency of the heretic to seek out unorthodox understandings of God has left its imprint on secular history. Though the fearful would have shunned them as eccentric or even mentally ill, others secretly admired the courage of their convictions. Still others wondered if their heroic commitment enabled them to foresee what commonplace minds were unable to conceive.

In any event, in the face of the dehumanization and brutalization of the defenseless and innocent by the dominant religions throughout history, heresy eventually inspired silent respect and admiration. Moreover, it set in motion the trend toward independent thought and belief. Gradually, there began a search for answers in secular terms. Slowly, this reorientation caused more and more individuals to undertake to educate themselves. This led to the development of their inborn intelligence and honest questioning of what they thought they knew. Out of the confines of obsolescent orthodoxy and blind faith, the psyche-mind undertook to transcend the tragedies of history. By seeking to create and accumulate universal knowledge, secular men and women today are attempting to give new meaning to the future of humankind.

Tentative Conclusions

Our review of Walter Nigg's *The Heretics. Heresy Through the Ages* has led us to unexpected conclusions. In contrast to the traditional view of heretics as dissenters and deviants from religious truth, Dr. Nigg presents a thorough, substantiated understanding of heresy per se. In addition, his book demonstrates how heretics have contributed to the modern understanding of today's secular psyche.

Heretics often insisted on a deeper devotion to the principles of their religion. They insisted on the need to organize one's life according to noble ideas, on being dedicated to a Christ-like life. These heretics were *figurae* of men and women of today and tomorrow, ready to accept the fact that humankind is endowed with a superior nature as a result of the evolution and humanization of our species.

Over thousands of generations, human evolution resulted in our becoming the quintessence of nature's creative conscience. When humankind became sufficiently evolved to grasp the idea that the world must have had a Creator, who called into being all forms of life, then we began to experience the need to dedicate our lives to a higher purpose than just survival. The idea of a supreme God helped establish in mankind the faith that life must have an ultimate meaning.

Thus, beyond early man's supernatural superstitions which explained nature's patterns and cycles in terms of gods and goddesses, the emergence of monotheistic religions transformed our comprehension of existence. Monotheism provided the original idea that the individual should pursue a purpose in life. By integrating one's talents and guiding one's personal conduct in morally acceptable ways, the individual could hope for salvation from a world full of danger, mystery and evil. Succinctly stated, the salvation religions had the power to save us from living meaningless lives.

However, over time, the growing literacy of the laity and man's increasing knowledge of the real world led to doubt and incredulity. The mythical account of creation and the story of how Adam and Eve introduced evil into human history were simply not believable. As a consequence, dogmata came to be questioned. Eventually when heretics began to distrust the clergy and express doubt about the integrity of the religious institution itself, there were cruel and vicious reprisals. But to generations of heretics, ecclesiastical authority had come to believe itself to be as infallible as God Himself.

Yet, heretics were rebels with a cause. They revolted against subjugation to authority which seemed to expect the obedience of serfs in their followers. Literacy, education and the resulting evolution of human intelligence made it increasingly impossible for the educated not to see the ignorance and mediocrity of many of these 'servants of God', who not only did not practice what they preached, but, in effect, did not even truly understand it.

Hence heretics seemed destined to challenge the teachings of the Church. Their revolt widened and continued unabated over the centuries that followed the Inquisition. The survivors of the Inquisition had little religious loyalty left in their hearts. By the eighteenth century Enlightenment, the educated had become skeptical of religion and cynical that it could offer any salvation from mankind's inhumanity to man.

By the end of the twentieth century, with its bitter lesson of two world wars, the emotionally adept in the human race began to search for something which would restore their faith in human nature. Could the history of heresy provide us with any possible guidance? What precisely did the heretics teach us? If anything, belief in God today would necessarily be different from that of the past. The individual would need to look beyond personal disillusionment, beyond self-pity or surrender to fatalism, and undertake some form of self-education.

What could offer hope of a profound renewal of faith in man? In terms of human evolution, man's new brain, i.e. the neo-cortex is a sort of index and itself neurological evidence that psyche is prepared to evolve further, possibly to another superior stage.

We have already argued that man's creative conscience emerged from nature. Moreover, our intuition of a Supreme Being seems to have provided the stimulus for the accelerated evolution of our psyche. Recent centuries dedicated to secular knowledge have especially advanced our cognitive powers. This realization of our inborn capacity to educate ourselves urges every sound-minded individual to develop one's creative and emotional intelligence to the utmost capacity.

In the pursuit of a destiny, we begin to perceive the purpose of human evolution. Beyond our prehistoric subconscience and past the guilt-ridden conscience of our religions, we discover humankind is evolving superior forms of intelligence. Indeed, our microcosmic psyche seems to incarnate a finite supraconscience.

The Effect of Modern Mysticism and Heresy on the Modern Psyche

Let it be said that both mysticism and heresy have had their salutary effect on the development of psyche.

In the mystical experience, devotion to religious practices and to God not only brings comfort and serenity. It also is a form of emotional education. The intensification of feeling that comes with prayer and devotions enriches the person's sense of the sacred in our lives. If one dedicates hours and years to the hope of having an ecstatic experience or epiphany, the steadfast concentration of psychic powers is bound to effect a gradual and sometimes startling transformation of the individual's existential or spiritual understanding. In effect, the person's emotional intelligence can acquire a universal compassion for all humanity. Or by communing with the most sublime idea ever conceived by humankind, the psyche can be metamorphosed into a superior state of conscious being we can call the human supraconscience.

In the heretical experience, one undertakes to cast off all inferior stages of conscience—the idea of God has the power to produce this effect in an individual. The heretic distrusts disquisitions that declare the absolute and final verity of life has been found, fixed, and enshrined by some cult, religion, or establishment. He scorns professionals who claim omniscience about all topics whatever and disbelieves the claim that there is no further truth to be found because the ancestors got there first.

His conscience tells him he must find out for himself whatever truths are revealed by human existence. He feels intuitively that some inborn power is urging him to look forward in time to discover yet undreamed of truths about human destiny.

To the heretic, truth is ever-unfolding; it has been so throughout his life from childhood, adolescence, adulthood, middle age and beyond. What he has learned of history makes clear that each epoch was a stage of human intellectual or emotional development. Moreover, the modern heretic can scan the geological ages for the evolution of life forms to learn that forms of conscience have been evolving as long as life has existed on earth. The heretic of yesteryear has become secular man and woman today.

So, in effect, both mysticism and heresy led the individual thinker to put greater trust in the capacity of one's own psyche to find the answers to life's enigmas or to discover the secular truths needed to renew faith in mankind's ability to decide its own destiny.

The Secular Sciences

The reader will recall our discussion of the *Book of Revelation* in the New Testament. That discussion was a secular interpretation of the book of seven seals, each of which, when opened, revealed another vision. A sketch was made to show how the Revelation seemed to prophesy new forms of knowledge and to foresee the fields of modern science. Was it therefore anticipating the secular sciences?

These sciences have already been discussed here briefly; however, the following descriptions serve to make clear how extensive our knowledge has now become through the sciences. Let us consider what they have taught mankind over the past three centuries.

Geology studies the history of the earth and its forms of life. Geological history is recorded worldwide in rock and rock formations, so the geologist has amassed abundant evidence of the actual age of the earth. Previously, churchmen and theologians had estimated it to be about 10,000 years, based on their knowledge of ancient civilizations in the Near East. By contrast, twentieth century geologists have empirical evidence that it was formed some four and a half billion years ago.

This scientific estimate is corroborated by the findings of a specialized science called *paleontology* which examines fossils from past geological ages.

Paleontologists have identified successive eras based on the earliest appearance of life forms in the sea and on the land. One basis for the theory of evolution is the existence of skeletons and remains. During the Paleozoic era (570-245 million years ago) the earliest forms of life appeared: fish, corals, land plants insects, vascular plants (ferns and mosses), winged insects and reptiles.

The Mesozoic era (245-65 million years ago) was the age of dinosaurs. It produced the earliest birds and mammals, flowering plants and the dinosaurs.

The present era, the Cenozoic (the last 65 million years), has produced the earliest large mammals, grasses and hominids. The earliest humans emerged about two million years ago. Our relatively recent arrival as a species is humbling. Yet, the history of human evolution is awesome as evidenced by our worldwide cultures and civilizations.

Astronomy observes and studies planets in our solar system, stars and galaxies in far outer space. Not only do astronomers study celestial objects for physical and chemical properties. They theorize that the entire cosmos came into being about fifteen billion years ago. Though such vast eras of time must bewilder us, they do expand our capacity to imagine infinity itself. Astronomical time must be humbling to anyone who still believes we are the center of the cosmos.

Nineteenth century *biology* has become the most influential science of the modern age. It studies living organisms and their vital processes, including plant and animal life from every environment and region in the world. Of special interest is *evolutionary biology*, researched extensively and conceived by Charles Darwin. His theory maintains that various species of plants and animals originated from pre-existing types. Over evolutionary time, successive generations adapted and evolved in response to geological and climatic changes. The theory of evolution includes evidence that some five million years ago, humankind descended from simians. Further evidence from zoology and anthropology demonstrates that hominids underwent physiological changes in the succeeding stages of human evolution.

It is interesting to note that one twentieth century astronomer Eric Chaisson, offers evidence that the universe itself seems to be a progression of interrelated phenomena much as described in the evolutionary theory.

Twentieth century *ecology* studies the interconnections between organisms and their environment. *Microbiology* deals with microscopic forms of life. The microscopic world contains an endless multitude of bacteria, viruses, hormones, enzymes, cells, and microbes. The entire earth itself is now visualized as a self-sustaining biosphere.

The study of humanity itself is the focus of the *human sciences*: anthropology, sociology, and psychology. Of special interest is the fact that these secular sciences question the dualistic heritage which taught us that human existence illustrates a cosmic conflict between powers of good and evil, God and Satan. This belief is no longer credible in a universe studied by the objective sciences. Yet, this world view is still intrinsic to Judaism, Christianity, and Islam.

Among these human sciences, *anthropology* is the study of human beings, their physical appearance, classification, origin and distribution in various environments, societies and cultures. It is interesting to note that some theologians have updated their knowledge of humankind by studying anthropology.

On the other hand, *sociology* has made the study of societies its central focus of investigation. In addition to the study of social relationships, it systematically examines the collective behavior of organized groups and carefully analyzes social institutions. There are even sociological studies of the world's religions.

Psychology is the science dedicated to the study of the mind and human behavior. It studies individuals and groups in their characteristic activities. Popular knowledge of Freudian psychoanalysis and of Jungian analytical psychology indicates how fascinated educated men and women are with the human psyche, its illnesses and potentials.

Hence, in these three human sciences alone--anthropology, sociology, and psychology--we have further evidence of the exponential growth in knowledge that the modern student is exposed to. By understanding the significance of this new knowledge for the moral education of the human being, we realize how these sciences can further humanize our species, make us aware of our common humanity. "They are much like us, and we are much like them." (Strauch) At the very least, we are all genetic cousins.

At this juncture, we have finished our review of modern secular sciences as a possible interpretation of John's vision of the seven sealed books. In the next prophecy, he envisioned seven trumpets, each of which, when sounded, revealed another vision. Our puzzlement deepens when we try to decipher its meaning.

Trumpets have special significance in the Bible. In Joshua's battle at Jericho, they were sounded by the priests and the people who shouted while circling the besieged city. A miracle took place. The mighty walls collapsed. This miraculous victory allowed the Israelites to enter the city to slaughter the vanquished. (Conquest of Canaan, Ch. 1-12 (10:12-13)).

Hence the trumpets in the Old Testament were used to carry out vengeance and bloody retribution. By contrast, John's vision in the last book of the New Testament, is markedly different. There the trumpet announces the Second Coming of Christ, a new heaven, and a new earth.

But, what could bring about such a marvelous transformation of humankind? Clearly, it is the humane message of Christ which teaches that all human beings deserve care, understanding and compassion. The Christian trumpets announce that the time will come when all humanity will be united as one family. In contrast to the vehemence and revenge so loudly expressed in Chapters 1-12 in the Old Testament, John's vision prophesies the triumph of the love that radiates throughout the New Testament.

But what is the meaning of the vision of seven trumpets, each of which, when sounded, reveals another vision? As the vision was interpreted in Chapter Seven above, John's trumpets seem to prophesy the unfolding of the humanities as creative expression of humankind's ingenuity and humanity's emotional wisdom.

The reader knows that the generic term *humanities* encompasses the study of languages, literature, arts, music, history and philosophy. To be sure, it also implies the development of all the skills needed to express the simplicity, intensity, and sophistication of our feelings, desires, and passions. In other words, the humanities give free us rein to develop our emotional intelligence, acumen and wisdom. By the study or practice of any of them, the participant is freed from banality, frustration, isolation and loneliness. Not only does each form of creativity let others know who we are, but we finally come to recognize who others are and what makes them human. Moreover, each distinct branch of the humanities enables the individual to discover the amazing number of creative potentials we all have.

That discovery not only brings us joy but also opens mind and heart to all the different peoples of the earth. We perceive the special grace of those who create beauty, truth, and meaning and possess wisdom.

So, seven trumpets multiplied by seven reveal how the expression of man's superior nature will bring forth a new heaven on earth. Humanity will teach itself to fully engage its own creative genius.

Closely akin to the wonder and pleasure of self-expression is the historical development of *humanism* and the *humanistic tradition*. Humanism is a devotion to the humanities: literary culture, the study of the classics, the revival of the spirit of intelligent criticism--all characteristics of the Renaissance. Life is centered on human interests and values. Humanistic studies stress the worth and dignity of the individual and underscore the human capacity for self-realization through study and the expression of one's passion for life.

Today, we seem to be undergoing a form of syncretism, something that we have already witnessed at certain times in human history. The gradual yielding of polytheism to monotheism, the idea of one Supreme God, seems to be taking hold of the intellectual and emotionally intelligent members of our species. There seems a growing psychological and philosophical need to unite and integrate the natural and human sciences, the humanities and the humanistic tradition into one coherent, all-encompassing body of knowledge. The modern psyche's openness to both the religious and secular knowledge seems to imply that humankind is evolving toward some superior stage of universal apperception.

It is time to consider the effect of the Inquisition and heresy on human history. As we already know, it eventually aroused resentment, skepticism and cynicism toward the Church and toward religion itself. Though Protestantism tried to avoid the excesses of the Catholic Church, it too alienated those who disagreed with the modifications and corrections of the old teachings and ritual practices. Inevitably, criticism of the old, orthodox version of Christianity led beyond heretical thinking to give birth to secular education.

Furthermore, the alienation of intellectuals, thinkers and creative individuals gradually turned them away from religion altogether. Instead, they discovered faith in the secular sciences based on tested facts and knowledge founded on unequivocal truths.

These would establish solid knowledge, guide superior reasoning and enable mankind to reach sound decisions in moral matters. Hence, secular philosophy burgeoned and the ancient Greek trust in the *logos* was restored.

Yet, the new, emerging world had learned from both mysticism and heresy. Let it be remembered that the patient study of the Bible had taught literate generations to examine in detail words, images, numbers, symbols and their sacred meanings. Moreover, all were examined in the context of a mighty, if complex, theology.

Undoubtedly, this habit of patiently seeking out the masked meanings of Biblical passages gradually disciplined men and women to study nature for her secrets. What may have begun as innocent curiosity devoid of any hint of sin led, over time, to the foundation of the natural sciences. Of particular value were the discoveries of herbs and medicines that could heal and cure. Moreover, let us not forget the value and influence of the scholarly studies of all of the world's holy Scriptures.

These mental exercises went beyond the development of literacy or respect for the Holy Word. The patience and adroitness required in distinguishing between literal and figurative language meant exploring multiple, hidden meanings. The skill carried over into the study of natural phenomena to discover their implications and inferences. Thus psyche was trained to perceive and apperceive.

Hence, the mysticism motivating medieval scholarly study not only taught students to probe for deeper meanings which could reveal sacred, eternal truths. It oriented the student of nature to search for signs of universal, secular laws therein.

On the other hand, by the seventeenth century, philosophers doubted everything but the fact that they could think, (e.g., Déscartes). Even such a fine mathematical mind as Pascal's was skeptical and doubtful until he experienced a private epiphany. By then, history had disciplined thinkers to doubt everything they themselves could not directly experience.

Thus, the history of heresy had taught men to query, question, and seek beyond common knowledge and ready-made answers. History had revealed that authority was not infallible and its reportage may be colored by self-deception, primitive superstitions, and cultural delusions. By contrast to this, heresy taught men to be fearless in seeking the true and the real.

Many heretics objected to Church doctrine based on the theology of the Old Testament. The claim that Scripture represented absolute, eternal truth may have comforted the faithful in the early centuries of the Church, but as time went on, doubts arose among the laity who daily faced common sense reality.

As educated heretics emerged, perceptive individuals began to juxtapose and contrast the teachings of the Old and New Testaments. It became evident that what had been true at one time might no longer be so. This meant that absolute truth might be a *static truth*. God perceived as Yahweh or Jehovah was not the same God seen as Jesus Christ. Truth had evolved. For some heretics, Christianity was a *dynamic truth*. This perception seems especially true if and when we understand the prophetic vision of the *Book of Revelation* as foretelling the future of secular knowledge and science.

In sum, the juxtaposition of the Old and New Testaments led heretics to realize that truth grows and proliferates other truths into vital ideas. So, too, with the ideal of God.

Thus, by fostering both a static and a dynamic understanding of God, the history of religion inadvertently led secular man, first, to seek out the constants of the material universe, and, second, to try to understand the dynamic universals animating life on earth.

On the other hand, the history of heresy will not let us forget the consequences of emotionalism and the fanaticism of the Inquisition. That period of savagery reminds us clearly of the heritage of humankind's subconscience throughout our history. Fortunately, with the healing effects of time, heretics and heresy gave rise to scientists and sciences committed to verifiable truth, sensible logic, and to freeing humankind from subconscience supersitions and irrationality.

However, in contrast to the reasoning of religion where Holy Writ is supposed to embody absolute, eternal Truth, the secular sciences discard all thought and argument centered on religious concerns and concepts. They do so with the expressed intention of studying the Creation empirically--as it actually is. Science is always discovering the hidden. As a consequence, empirical evidence determines the conclusions of modern science.

Some sciences became committed to the study of matter, energy, their interrelationships and transformations (physics, chemistry, geology, astronomy). Others specialized in confronting the problems threatening our survival. The life sciences (biology, botany, medicine), came to be focused on curing sicknesses and relieving human suffering. In human sciences such as anthropology and sociology, the scientific method was applied in the study of human nature in every stratum of society and in every culture; and, psychology probed both the sick and the sane, the creative and the sage psyche.

Correlatively, humanities as literature, art, music, history and philosophy provided sense and substance to better understanding human potentials. These methods of educating our emotional capacities became the secular means of humanizing humankind.

Yet, in retrospect, heresy did not displace mysticism. The two were intimately intertwined. Both sought universal truth; both inspired emotions, intellect and intuition.

And, both undertook to differentiate appearance from reality. For the mystic, the pain, suffering and sorrow in the world would disappear in eternity. By contrast, the heretic would not accept the mystic's illusion that all life's pain and injustice would be absolved. He could not accept that the afterlife would resolve all enigmas, right all injustice, salve life's wounds, and ensure that poetic justice would be done.

Parenthetically, it is interesting to note how mystic faith and heretic realism found expression in folktales.

Folk literature has always dealt with the question of appearance versus reality. Like religion, the fairy tale promises hope, reward and poetic justice will triumph in the end, i.e., evil will be punished and good will be rewarded. It also believes in good fairies and angels from heaven hovering around to protect us from harm. Fairy tales also claim the good is everywhere if we but look for it. Its faith is that a deeper, higher truth will guide us through life to a safe haven and lifetime happiness.

On the other hand, the fable has always been based on humankind's ingrained hunger for authentic truth. However grim or harsh they may be, fables undertake to warn us against the hidden dangers of illusion and untruth. Like irony, they caution against being blind to the primitive and predatory aspects of human nature.

What conclusions can we draw from the dialectic between the mystic and heretic, both of whom are convinced their truth is what mankind needs?

Contrary to the honest heretic's claim that we must live *by* empirical truth and that pain, suffering and death are ever-present realities in human life, the educated mystic would counter that, despite death, the perpetual generation of new life on earth is undeniable proof that life itself is eternal and has a reason for being what it is. The heretical scientist who believes religiously in empirical truth is himself a secular mystic. Our concept of God has guided humankind to have faith that one day man will be able to integrate all knowledge and undertake to consummate his evolution through superior, universal wisdom. The mystic would have faith that human life has a purpose--to realize the meaning of our destiny on earth.

In sum, mysticism inspired humankind to form, evolve and perfect their *religious supraconscience*, which, over the millennia, has educated us with respect to emotional wisdom by teaching us the need for justice and the meaning of compassion.

On the other hand, the various heretical movements may have set in motion the dispassionate search of the natural and human sciences for secular truths, truths by which we could decide our own destiny and guide the future of our species. These sciences, along with the self-expression and self-realization taught by the humanities, sublimate the baser passions of our prehistoric nature and impel us toward the evolution of the *secular supraconscience* of humanity.

Today, by the education and cultivation of noble ideals, creativity, and superior intelligence, the human psyche may be able to fully realize the awesome potential of our evolving supraconscience.

Notes

1. Nigg, *The Heretics*, p.50. All references in Chs. 8 & 9 of this work are paraphrases from Nigg's work.
2. Nigg, p. 52.
3. Nigg, p. 56.
4. Nigg, p. 63.
5. Nigg, pp. 75-76.
6. Nigg, pp. 103-04.

7. Nigg, p. 105.
8. Nigg, p. 114.
9. Nigg, p. 133.
10. Nigg, p. 135.
11. Nigg, p. 133.
12. Nigg, p. 139.
13. Nigg, pp. 145-46.
14. Nigg, pp. 154-55.
15. Nigg, p. 164.
16. Nigg, p. 166-67.
17. Nigg, pp. 184-85.
18. Nigg, p. 198.
19. Nigg, p. 204.
20. Webster's 10th, p. 602.
21. Nigg, p. 264-65.
22. Nigg, p. 292.
23. Nigg, p. 347-49.
24. Bruno, cited in Nigg, pp. 347-48.
25. Nigg, p. 346.

Part Five

The Inferior versus Superior Destiny of Humankind

Introduction

The essays that follow were written as completely independent ideas and insights without any thought they might be connected. Only when they were randomly gathered together, did it occur to the author to see if they by chance revealed patterns or progressions of thought. To his surprise, they did. Somehow psyche had collated them into holistic truths.

In other words, the essays were not written with a purpose to develop a scholarly argument or present a scientific explanation. They showed that the creative exploration of ideas often produced an integrated series of condensed insights or axioms. What could we infer from the way psyche came to conclusions? Does such writing perhaps divulge a pattern of psychic development? Perhaps the essays rested on a form of cognition entirely natural to psyche.

In the process of collating them, an unexpected realization surfaced: There might be a connection between the way psyche made discoveries or created ideas and its evolution. Since evolution has proceeded by the reciprocal coalescence of nature's powers of creation and integration, was it not likely that our psyche replicated this process?

A preliminary look at the essays showed that they psychologically grouped themselves into spheres of significance. Finite insights seemed to converge into universal meanings.

Chapter Ten develops two primary topics: (1) the conflict between our inferior and superior nature, and (2) the evolution of the human psyche. In other words, the first set of essays explores the conflict between subconscience and supraconscience, and the second discusses our early evolution, the effect of religious and secular conversion, and the idea that God initiated actual human evolution.

Chapter Eleven explores corresponding themes: (3) the co-evolution of our inferior and superior nature and (4) the actualization of human evolution. In other words, as our species evolved, so did our psyche. In addition, by the creation of cultures and civilizations, we accelerated our own evolution. This realization that the human psyche evolved through its own powers of creation and integration calls for closer attention to its natural processes of perception and apperception.

We need to re-examine the very foundations of Western civilization, especially as regards our age-old belief in cosmic powers of good and evil, God versus Satan, soul versus body.

In essence, we are talking about the superstitious belief that dualism is the predominant principle of existence. It has had a marked effect on human history. Our mental evolution can be seen in the antinomies we have inherited; they lie at the very base of human knowledge. This heritage has never allowed us to resolve the self-evident contradictions between apparently equally valid principles. So, ironically, nearly all of Western man's perceptions and conceptions find expression in terms of antonyms. Our knowledge appears to be a vast collection of self-contradictions.

Dualism tends to lead opponents to believe they alone are right because their principles are as valid as all others. This points to the conclusion that the history of the world will always be centered on conflict. Moreover, the human psyche seems fated to develop along the lines of much the same biography of inner conflicts.

Yet, the discussion of psyche's evolution holds promise of its graduating from ignorance to knowledge. Its self-evolution not only reveals its inherent resourcefulness, but also demonstrates that dualism is a figment of ancient humankind's imagination.

Today, we need to come to the sensible understanding that mankind is not doomed to mutual extermination in some final apocalyptic struggle between nations or continents. Instead of continuing to accept the dualism inherited from religious superstition, it is time that we began to make some attempt to understand the significance of psyche's evolution.

Knowledge of the power of our subconscience and supraconscience should help us realize they can co-evolve as psychic poles; they can learn through time to co-operate and benefit each other.

Moreover, religious and scientific, secular and humanistic developments have revealed themselves to be the primary powers behind the acceleration of human evolution. Together, they have fostered humankind's supraconscience. It has not only surpassed the subconscience, but also superseded our rational mind and superstitious conscience. The development of the brain's neo-cortex seems clear evidence of our psyche's biological evolution.

The essays that follow therefore inquire into the way psyche records impressions, creates ideas and integrates insights to express itself ever anew. Throughout human history, its intuition has been searching for its reason for *being,* and it has done this by *becoming.*

Instead of judging psyche to be in eternal opposition with itself (right versus wrong, good versus evil), we have endeavored to demonstrate that it has evolved *through* the confrontation between our inferior and superior stages of knowledge. Though at times our species may succumb to the power of the superstitious past, we can, at any time, also break through the present to humanity's future.

Thus, endowed by evolution with exponential powers of self- development, the psyche can actualize its own evolution by creating and integrating ever-.new spheres of knowledge and meaning.

In sum, these essays demonstrate the self-organizing and self-integrating capacity of the mind and so its ability to apperceive universal truths. Left to its own devices, the evolving psyche will learn to utilize the positive powers of both subconscience and supraconscience. That will take place as the supraconscience discovers what is positive and useful in our primal psyche. By working in tandem with the everlasting power of evolution, it will be able to transform the subconscience so that it embraces healthful, life-affirming goals. By its superior wisdom, humanity's supraconscience will enable all humankind to realize a fortunate destiny here on earth.

Chapter Ten

The Conflict Between the Inferior and Superior Human Nature

The Conflict
Psyche's Innermost Being
In prehistoric times, our primeval subconscience held psyche in thrall, made it a slave to fear, anxiety and hatred. Yet, the constantly alert subconscience was watchful for ever-present dangers and predators. It also trained us to stalk, ensnare and kill prey, small and large. The survival instinct of the subconscience kept us alive.

Through the growing awareness on the part of man and woman of their parental responsibilities, our earliest forms of conscience developed to assure the security of the family and safety of the children. The maturing psyche also began to take control of our impulsive, animal instincts. Successive forms of early conscience sought to becalm our excesses and wilder emotions. Hence the prehistoric psyche slowly evolved elementary forms of conscience, both natural and supernatural. Yet, these were repeatedly challenged by the moody, unpredictable subconscience.

Despite our developing forms of early conscience. The subconscience long maintained its power over our inferior self. But when the first signs of our supraconscience appeared, the subconscience reacted as if it were itself a predator trapped by a more powerful being.

Thus, an inner polarity was established that set in motion the evolution of our psyche. Human history revealed that psyche possessed opposing propensities--toward the destructive and the creative, toward denial and affirmation. It came to be a 'nay-sayer' and a 'yea-sayer'. Today, we would identify these as the realist and the idealist. Over time, we came to realize psyche oscillates between temerity and courage, slavish obedience and independence, between submitting to one's fate and determination to decide one's own destiny. Time has revealed psyche's internal struggle to be between our inferior and superior self.

To be free is to liberate oneself from limitations and preoccupations that arise from both our subconscience and conscience. Throughout history, conscience has never known a total victory over our primitive subconscience. Moreover, conscience itself has weaknesses and strengths. On one side, religious conscience can reduce us to guilt-ridden creatures fearing eternal damnation. On the other side, conscience nurtures our sense of responsibility toward life, one's parents, one's own family and friends.

Conscience can extend to an abstract ideal of country, race and religion--all of which still are basically primitive, tribal loyalties. However, note what happens when conscience awakens to the supraconscience, when it learns to believe in self and undertakes to help others. A quantum leap in self-understanding takes place when one realizes one's purpose in life and when empathy for the rights of others becomes fundamental to our superior nature.

Another manifestation of our evolving psyche may have been the scientific discovery of the true nature of our solar system by Copernicus, Kepler, Galileo, and Newton. It revealed the essential unity of our universe and so may illustrate a comparable discovery about psyche. These scientists taught us that the planets orbit in tandem around the sun in perfect equilibrium and mutual harmony. Is it possible the supraconscience manifests a similar purpose, namely, to integrate the interacting powers of the psyche into a unified, dynamic system of intellectual and spiritual powers? In simpler terms, perhaps the role of supraconscience seems to be to transform and convert the discord and dissonances of the past into the accord and consonance of the future.

If our emotions, feelings and thoughts could find their center of gravity, that psychic centre could organize the whole life of the mind. Perhaps humanity's supraconscience is the gravitational power that draws together all our knowledge into a system which has purpose and meaning.

Another manifestation of our supraconscience takes place when people seek to communicate with the Supreme Being through prayer. In our age, the secular person may wonder if prayer tunes the devout into some ethereal frequency coming from the stars. Or does it establish communion with a superior power within? A Jungian analytical psychologist might observe that prayers open up the psyche's memories of one's racial, collective conscience. A contemporary psychologist might suggest that prayer synchronizes the body's biorhythms to effect a communion between soma and psyche. Anyway, to the faithful, prayer is used by the psyche to intimately open ourselves to what we hope is the omniscience at the center of our universe.

In practical terms, what would it mean to nurture one's supraconscience? It would mean that the individual would assume responsibility to teach him- or herself what one most wants to learn--to educate self to the utmost of one's ability. Self-knowledge would strengthen one's resolve to decide one's own destiny.

The supraconscience becomes a reality through self-understanding and faith in the future. Over one hundred generations of humankind, the supraconscience has become the repository of whatever wisdom humanity possesses today.

The central commendation of supraconscience would be to nurture physical and mental health over a lifetime. But, beyond that, we should undertake to evolve not only beyond our ancestors' limitations, but beyond the violent history of mankind. That commendation means we have a future to create for ourselves and our descendents.

It might be postulated that, where knowledge, intuition and creativity meld with noble ideals, our personal purpose should be to learn the wisdom of our species. Such an effort will allow the supraconscience to more readily manifest itself in all of humanity.

Subconscience versus Supraconscience

How has the subconscience revealed itself in civilization?

In Thomson's *The History of Sin*, we learned that the human race periodically appears to be addicted to moral turpitude, aggression, violence, and to inflicting pain in those whom we have at a disadvantage. Today, there seems a tendency to accept virulent crimes, family homicide, serial killings, murder, and endless war as 'just the way things are'--'They've always been that way.'

As to what others suffer, apathy often prevails. Indifference dominates when we or loved ones are not threatened. We are detached from the reality of the execution of hundreds of thousands. We withdraw from responsibility for the annihilation of millions of human beings in continent-wide genocides. Such withdrawal, detachment and indifference are supposedly a sign of stoic strength, or possibly, it is a way of asserting our own will to survive.

Of course, it might be numbness at the relentless upsurging of atrocities and events too gruesome to believe. It may be that we have learned to steel ourselves against such subhuman realities, as way of shutting out what hourly, daily insults our souls and shreds our sense of moral rightness and civilized justice.

Whatever one's reasons for such defensive postures and for blocking out heinous reality, the human psyche itself IS responsible. Such atrocious events are symptomatic of the present power of our prehistoric subconscience. As such, it exerts a strong counterforce to our humane intention to build a world ruled by justice for all humankind.

In other words, the still active subconscience is probably responsible for racial degeneration and the ageless recurrence of acts of murder. No type of devil, not even Satan himself is accountable for the delirious intoxication experienced when we mutually destroy one another. We alone are the nemesis of humanity. Such acts are the havoc wreaked on us by the subconscience.

In light of recorded history, our evolution is neither assured nor warranted. It is up to each responsible individual to examine with care his greed, baseness, and self-centered indifference to the fate of others, There seems a time to examine one's conscience to identify lies and malingering, unseemly habits, and covert hatred of others, races, and religions. It is up to each individual to be just in his or her judgments. Our sense of humanity should enable us to be generous toward those we have difficulty understanding.

Any time we give in to a tendency to lie about others, or cheat them of what is rightfully theirs; or any time we belittle or ridicule those different from us for whatever their defects may be--weaknesses, lack of beauty or intelligence, etc.--we are plainly allowing our barbarian past to reassert itself and thereby to also secretly approve of the malingerers in our midst.

In so far as we yield to the temptation to hurt, scorn, humiliate or assassinate another's character, we are still behaving as brutish beings governed by the power of our primitive subconscience. In so yielding to it, we personally express our hatred for our own kind and contribute to the crucifixion of humanity.

Indifference to one's religious conscience is no justification for neglecting to control our subconscious meanness of spirit. One's behavior is one's own. The individual alone is responsible to come to terms with his subhuman attitudes and actions.

In one's defense, one may ask what can be done about the viciousness that seems to prevail everywhere in the modern world. The answer is not hard to find: Honesty, understanding, decency, sincerity and friendliness are free for all to give. Reaching out to those too humble or too proud to ask for help is an act of charity we can all afford.

Inadvertently, giving of self may actually help the giver evolve as a human being. Each humane act is an expression of faith in the superior nature of humanity.

If the Subconscience Triumphs

We become aware of the subconscience when we witness the impulsive, out-of-control psyche of a neurotic or psychotic individual. Often the subconscience manifests itself as a chaotic state of mind. The individual is victimized by his or her own anxieties, fears, and anguish. Sometimes there are signs and symptoms of insanity which others can confirm.

Furthermore, the subconscience is seen to emerge when someone develops attitudes or acts on homicidal or suicidal tendencies. Such a person may believe that diabolic or demoniac powers are lurking everywhere--in the house, the backyard, the neighborhood.

Indeed, from anthropological accounts, we know that both religions of antiquity and traditional peoples of today speak of ghostly places haunted by malicious spirits. In modern countries, many believe that evil lurks in darkened areas of alleyways, poorly lighted streets, in no longer used prisons and insane asylums, on historic battlefields, and among the ruins of cities strangled by massive re-growth of the jungle In fact, all three salvation religions--Judaism, Christianity, and Islam—contain elements of dark superstition. All believe in evil incarnate.

In this context, it is easy to understand how certain sensitive men and women can be made mentally ill by fears and anxieties. Based on our knowledge of the subconscience, we can readily understand how such an individual may lash out in either self-defense or righteous vengeance. Ironically, by his preemptive attack he commits the very crime that he feels threatens his life.

The subconscience can, therefore, develop a perverted sense of justice. It can incite a person to punish others severely even when there is no clear evidence of guilt or offence. The punishment itself may turn barbaric. Unfortunately, revenge is sometimes exacted even for imagined disloyalty or treachery, e.g.,Othello's murder of his innocent wife, Desdemona. The poetic imagery of Shakespeare's tragedy admirably dramatizes the destruction of Othello's noble spirit through his suspicion that she is sexually involved with his lieutenant.

On a broader, cultural plane, paranoia can take hold of a church, a religion, or even a whole population. When the subconscience seizes a people's psyche, it becomes self-evident in their acts of brutality, torture and wholesale slaughter of innocents who happen to be on the wrong side of a given debate and are taken to be worshippers of Satan.

In secular civilizations, the subconscience is manifest whenever we traumatically interpret accidents, sicknesses or natural catastrophes as 'caused' by forces of evil or demonic beings of some sort. Similarly, in totalitarian states which give rise to power-crazed dictators, murder may be perpetuated on a vast social, national or international scale, e.g., Nazi Germany and Stalin's Soviet Union.

Thus, entire nations and regions of the world can become overwhelmed by the blind vengeance of a sadistic subconscience. The eradication of ethnic groups or guiltless masses of defenseless people takes place because the victimizers believe they themselves are morally pure or superior—instances of official, collective insanity.

One noteworthy fact about the subconscience is how often it aims at mocking humanity's evolved supraconscience, which came into being by humanitarian identification with those stricken by natural disasters or acts of genocide. The subconscience is indifferent to the needs of miserable humanity and ridicules the compassion which is a mark of our higher nature, a compassion which feels responsible to aid the helpless and to feed the hungry.

Secular men and women believe that we are all one humanity, that humankind are all blood relatives, that all of the races are genetically one and make up a single family. Therefore, to kill anyone is to sin against one's own kin and cousins.

On the other hand, secular man sometimes believes the subconscience is a scientific reality. It reveals itself whenever our impulses, fears and anxieties turn into acts of hatred. At times, it impels us to villify, brutalize, mutilate and slay one another. Such acts carry out the savage will of our inferior self. Hence, the subconscience provokes the emotional chaos of an age through acts of injustice, vindictiveness, vengeance, violence and sadistic murder.

The subconscience represents humankind at its worst, whereas the supraconscience reveals us at our best. But, they inhabit the same body and mind. Humankind is capable of the terrible and the wonderful. Obviously, our future will depend as much on our ignorant misunderstanding of others as on our conscientiously seeking out mutual understanding. Alas, it is entirely possible that humanity will degenerate into something subhuman. Individuals, societies, cultures and civilizations can and do deteriorate and even disintegrate.

The future is not guaranteed. If we degrade ourselves, ignore the value of our cultures, scorn our religions, deny our ideals, the supraconscience will weaken, falter, sicken and perhaps even die. In nature, all living things flourish for a while, then wither and die. So, too, with civilizations: One day we may look upon the

The Struggle between Good and Evil

The terms *good* and *evil* are real only as allegorical abstractions. They were born of our primeval imagination. The superstitious belief in their reality arose in the earliest time of our prehistoric existence when our progenitors came to believe predators were evil forces in the world. When they witnessed homicidal acts of their own kind, they came to believe they, too, were possessed of evil.

At the turn of our age, from B.C. to A.D., various fatalistic gnosticisms and Middle Eastern religions accepted good and evil as fateful realities. Such superstitions were hallucinatory imaginings inherited from our primeval subconscience.

In actuality, imagining celestial forces 'in conflict' throughout the universe--where powers of light were pitted against powers of darkness—was one way of explaining the archetypal discord between our earliest subconscience and our evolving supraconscience. This visualization of our universe was inspired by natural phenomena. The alternation from day to night **and vice-versa** seemed evidence of some eternal struggle in the heavens. On earth, there were times of rain and flood followed by periods of blazing sunlight and drought.

In the longer term, seasonal changes also made us think that opposing forces were at work in nature. The greenery and growth of spring and summer were succeeded by the fall and winter when vegetation turned brown, withered and seemed to die forever. Human life itself transformed from pristine birth to the bloom of youth only to shrivel to old age and the decomposition of death.

Directly or indirectly, nature's cycles must have left an imprint on the human psyche. Even our daily energy level seemed to rise and fall with the ocean tides. And, the ebb and flow of our life energies influence the psyche. As nature itself, the human mind recycles life's memories, explores the experiences of the present, and seeks to shape the future. From the beginning, it semi-consciously adapted itself to the tempo, respiration, and cyclical rhythm of our living planet.

Hence, at one level of its maturity, psyche imagined supernatural powers in conflict, but, in time, a deeper insight beckoned man to discover the universal laws of nature. Psyche came to perceive life as a dialectic of life energies which increased, subsided, then revived.

Eventually, we realized that nature was more than a relentless conflict between life and death. Life itself was more than an eternal struggle between good and evil. One universal law transcended and transformed the meaning of good and evil. It was revealed in the everlasting cycle of nature: that of being born, *living* a life, and creating new life. That was the natural law for humankind to obey: to pass on the miracle of life. By so doing, we confirm our faith in the future of humanity.

Healing Humankind's Subconscience

What do stings of conscience mean? Our religions command and commend that we live our lives in certain obedient and orthodox ways. When we fail to live up to these commandments and commendments, we feel guilt at our failings, or we are aroused to rebellion against religion's insensibility to the basic needs of flesh and heart. Unlike individuals who are able to commit their entire lives to a religious calling or to adherence to a doctrine, the average man and woman have the need to blot out the world of work, family responsibilities and social obligations and enjoy bodily gratification. One needs time for love and loving. One needs simply to be human.

Of course, at times, all of us are haunted by things done or left undone. But, beyond these reasons for regret or rebellion, many modern individuals are beset by depression, irritability, agitation, fatigue, nervous prostration, and even nervous breakdown. Modern psychology has a multitude of theories about neuroses, psychoses, and dementias.

However, when it comes to psychopathic personalities finding gratification in criminal acts, drug addiction, or sexual perversion, psychologists are confronted with a different order of mental disease. There are also examples of psychosis in individuals who have lost contact with reality. Today, psychologists largely contend that these illnesses are caused by the demands, stresses and strains of surviving in modern society. Purportedly, such aberrations well up from the *subconscious*.

It is probable that few modern psychologists give due consideration to humankind's history of mutual distrust, violence, homicide and genocide. Such manifestations are not simply evidence of individual neuroses, phobias or psychoses. The world's endless confrontations, territorial incursions, and wars surely have more ancient roots in our earliest, hominid experience struggling to survive alongside other species.

Perhaps tomorrow psychologists and psychoanalysts will take into account human evolution and culture. Religion did educate our moral conscience, which strongly influenced us for some 2500 years, but millennia before that, humankind had formed a *subconscience*. This primeval psychic state came about during the age of survival when human-like creatures came out alive and made it through tens of thousands of years as prey among predators and as predator among prey. Thus, that subconcience enabled us to survive with brutal and savage characteristics as well as with human courage, altruism and the parental love needed to give us the determination to have our young survive.

In any case, there seems abundant evidence in the contemporary world of psychosomatic dysfunction on a vast human scale. If such trans-historical and universal mental aberrations can be identified as arising from that subconscience, then psychological research should investigate this. Perhaps future research on the human brain and psyche will reveal how our neurological system is affected bio-chemically and electro-biologically by prolonged, life-threatening conditions and situations.

Possibly, the pattern of evolutionary stages of growth and integration can be detected in the brain in so far as it has neurologically progressed from the traumas of the subconscience to the creativity of our conscience and the serene wisdom of the supraconscience. Beyond providing an analogy for this pattern, such scientific probes may originate modes or methods by which to render the contents of the subconscience benign. By understanding and accepting its extremes and excesses, we may enable psyche to sublimate them into new self-understanding, equanimity, composure and even sangfroid.

This project is not so futuristic as skeptics might think. In Chapter Three, we described the archetype *sōphrosynē* (temperance or moderation). It is an enduring lesson from ancient Greece. The writers of tragedy--Aeschylus, Sophocles, and Euripides--ingeniously demonstrated the consequences of arrogance and violence, paranoia and irrationality. The Greeks not only had legends of families fated by terrible tragic flaws. For centuries, they had experienced the emotional excesses brought on by contact with Near Eastern religious rituals and their own blood thirsty Dionysiac rites. In short, these impassioned states were symptomatic of humankind's primal subconscience.

If this is true, then how can psychologists come to terms with such a deeply rooted affliction—such a scourge on humanity?

In our earlier discussion of ancient Greek tragedy, the reader learned the meaning of *catharsis*. In Aristotle's *Poetics,* he describes the emotional impact of tragedy on an audience. There the term meant the purgation or purification of their concealed passion through pity for the hero and fear of a fate like his. The effect of such purification is to release pent-up tensions and to bring about spiritual renewal.

An objective psychologist today would realize that such catharsis could cure a psychic dysfunction. The appropriate use of it could effect the elimination of such a complex by dramatically bringing it to consciousness, and thereby enabling it to sensibly express the meaning of repressed desires and memories.

In the event that future psychologists should benefit from this ancient insight, they could develop a scientifically sound method of meeting our residual subconscience on its own terms to try to heal it of its afflictions. Not only could the subconscience be taught forethought as to the consequences of its actions, but perhaps it could also learn trust in humanity.

However, we do not have to wait for the future to undertake the transformation and cure of ourselves of the hold which primeval subconscience has on us. Through secular knowledge and wisdom, humankind can begin to trust the secular supraconscience to interact sentiently, sensitively and sensibly with its ancestral psyche.

But practically speaking, can one achieve self-healing?

At the intimate level, everyone is subject to secret emotions, anger, and frustrations. Sometimes we learn to develop sensible responses to our own excesses. These private victories bring us more self-assurance than sedatives or tranquilizers. They give us a measure of confidence and detachment from childish emo tionalism or adolescent temperament. We all have lapses into moments of immaturity and self-indulgent pity.

Yet, there is more to 'coming to terms with' and 'fighting back' the irrationality of the personal subconscious or the prehistoric subconscience. In these little self-conquests, a much larger issue may be at hand. These seemingly insignificant gains mean that the mature you will not accept being defeated or humiliated by the immature you. As adults, when we confront our frustrations, self-doubts and outbursts, we do not simply want to tame them; we want to understand them. By so doing, a new level of self-knowledge emerges aimed at developing common sense, wisdom and a measure of self-mastery.

Though such presence of mind may seem a somewhat grandiose ambition, the instinct is sound and true to the heroic history of human survival. Throughout human evolution, man has not only showed his creativity but also his determination to integrate his innermost self. In the process, he has transformed mind and psyche into a superior power of perception of self and the world.

So, the tiny steps we take toward self-control and self-mastery are not only important privately. Self-guidance and self-education are actually modest expressions of an instinct which aims to prepare one for the future.

In retrospect, humankind has become more aware of the mind's potentials. Not only has it revealed its power to systematize knowledge and to use logic to rationally explain existence. Psyche also reveals its sentient nature through the sophisticated expression of religious and secular wisdom.

Hence by small, modest steps, by deciding for ourselves what direction our life should take, we actually replicate the decision making power that drives human evolution itself.

For beyond the electro-biochemistry that characterizes the cellular nature of living organisms, all evolved creatures have decided to evade death and to continue to live. Virtually all decisions made at the survival level make abundantly clear that decision making has been essential to the evolution of species. At some point, we must act to live, or else we will die. We fight to live and only succumb to a force greater than ourselves. The decision to live is clearly fundamental to the realization of the promise of human evolution.

The quintessence of this decisiveness is focused in the finite supraconscience humankind has evolved. It is perhaps the lesson implicit in our understanding of the Supreme Being as omniscient Supraconscience.

With this recognition of the purpose of man's evolved, higher nature, we discover the means by which we and psychologists may, in fact, affect the catharsis needed to cleanse the subconscience of its mental illness, psychic wounds and fatalism. The supraconscience knows the meaning of sound health and human creativity. It knows every individual is heir to exceptional powers, if he or she can learn to tap into humanity's own vast potential for new knowledge.

Perhaps our evolved supraconscience can purge the subconscience of its debilitating addiction to paranoia and homicidal violence. The irony of yielding to fury and foul play is that such excesses provoke pain, suffering and revenge in kind. It is then too late for regret. As in classical tragedy, the hero's rash actions undo him. He learns too late that he himself has caused his tragic downfall and death. Perhaps the supraconscience can teach the subconscience the deep wisdom of calm judgment and humane action.

The Dialectic That Will Decide Human Destiny

The subconscience of man represents rebellion and revolt against social mores, moral codes and obedience to any form of authority, including God. It has afflicted religions with insanity and brought mental disorder to civilization. Wherever moral evolution has once been established, the subconscience tends to destroy law and integrity, disgrace human honor, and ridicule all idealism.

The subconscience also manifests itself in the excesses of conscience, human intolerance, brutality and sadism. At its worst, it burned heretics alive and committed atrocities against religious dissidents and members of other faiths. The primitive subconscience intentionally undertakes to entrap human beings so as to return them to a primitive level of savagery. It tries to pervert the superior power which acts to heal humankind's pain and wash away the horror and despair endured throughout history.

By contrast, the supraconscience characterizes human achievement and creativity in the humanities, in academic fields, and in the sciences. In humane religions, the supraconscience sustains the hope of all humankind, especially the defeated, the rejected, the downtrodden, the misunderstood and the unjustly judged. Such religions express the kindness, charity, clemency and grace of a truly Supreme Being.

Evolution of the human supraconscience is confirmed by the growth of mutual tolerance and understanding. For instance, such mutualism describes the early relations between Taoism, Buddhism and Confucianism. In the early centuries of Islam, there was the hospitable relationship with Christians and, conversely, Muslims were welcomed at monasteries and hospices. At times, a similar brotherly acceptance prevailed between Jews and Christians. Such fraternal respect and generosity marked the evolution of a supraconscience. Moral principles were guided by sympathy and respect for a humankind dedicated to a common ideal.

Contrast this reciprocal understanding and mutual acceptance to the effect which dualism has had on human history. When Judaism, Christianity and Islam accepted the mythical theology of Zoroastrianism and Manichaeanism, existence was interpreted as an eternal war between good and evil. The human consequence of this was that any differences in interpretation of the Almighty became maliciously magnified by the subconscience and so distorted that the beliefs of others were judged evil. Thus one segment of humanity came to be pitted against another. Those who believed as we do were good; those who did not were suspect, untrustworthy, or outright evil. In fact, neither self-righteous interpretation is justified. It divides humankind against itself and creates a world of enemies.

Dualism is often used as a primitive, tribal, racial way of passing unfair judgments on other human beings: The judges are always right, the judged, always wrong. Our religion is noble, just and superior, theirs, ignoble, unjust and inferior. God is with us, Satan is with them. Of course, a more infantile ethic can hardly be imagined, yet it seems to govern the subconscience judgments of masses of mankind.

Religious, racial and moral dualism represent a mortal danger to human survival. In this new millennium, the fanaticism and fear, provoked by subconscience misjudgment, can unleash viral, chemical and nuclear weapons which can destroy all life on earth. (It is reported that a single US Trident submarine could destroyed 288 cities in one attack. The 'enemy' has comparable means of destruction.) So, the time has come to establish worldwide respect for all humanity.

It is time to recognize and acknowledge that in each of us there co-exist an inferior and superior stage of human evolution. History has shown how the subconscience has influenced our baser nature and how our knowledge, sciences and humanities generally promote the education of our higher nature and the evolution of humanity's supraconscience. History has actually been a dialectic between ourselves at our worst and at our best. It is between our primitive instinct for self-preservation and our intuition that humankind can perfect itself and wisely decide its destiny.

II. The Evolution of the Psyche
The Evolution of the Psyche and its Effect

Historically, the psyche has proceeded through the various stages of evolution by an increasing polarity between our inferior and emerging superior nature. At the same time, the interaction of these had the effect of developing a psyche which was increasingly intuitive, intricate and creative.

In the beginning, our subconscience asserted its dominance. It instinctively resisted and rebelled against any control by the group. After all, by courage, shrewdness and resourcefulness, it had assured its own survival and that of its kin. In short, paranoia and predation had kept the subconscience itself alive through the seemingly endless age of survival.

Gradually, its victim-victimizer mentality began to be calmed by the feminine imagination and worship of goddesses in nature. They were seen as powers protecting the new-born and young, so the goddess of fertility and of motherhood softened the male's aggressive instincts and educated his paternal, protective inclinations. Thus, both the male and female nature influenced the modification of the primitive subconscience.

As we know from earlier chapters, our species could imagine many spirits in nature, both malignant and benign, and because life persisted in spite of the continual threats of death, it was reasonable to believe that goddesses had superior powers to defend women against the subhuman. Eventually, these imagined gods and goddesses were drawn together into a coherent form of worship and such syncretism increased their strength and influence. In terms of psyche, it was discovering and creating intuitions, insights and even axioms by which to appeal to the higher powers in nature and in itself.

Overall, this slow transformation indicated a continual evolution from an inferior to a superior stage of psyche when the female finally gained recognition for her negotiating and nursing skills as well as her maternal wisdom. This metamorphosis from primitive survival instincts to superior, humane intuitions was, in effect, the true beginning of humankind's emotional intelligence.

The development of nature religions and the worship of female deities gradually freed mankind from mutual distrust and unprovoked aggression. Slowly, the next stage on the path towards our being fully human began to dawn: Our ancestors learned to trust moral emotions and positive passions. Within the relative safety of groups, mutual respect and compassion emerged.

Secular Conversion: Freeing Oneself From Fate

In this essay, we use the expression "secular conversion" because we are primarily concerned with worldly or temporal decisions. More specifically, since our discussion thus far has been centered on the evolution of the human psyche, our use of the term *conversion* here is concerned with the perpetual struggle between humankind's subconscience and our evolving supraconscience. The historical conflict energized the evolution of the supraconscience itself.

Our tragic past has led the superstitious among us to fear that modern man and woman are doomed. Often, this fatalistic world view is preached by fanatical fundamentalists. Their lurid interpretation of human history is that we are becoming victims of our own evil. This appeal to the subconscience is hardly harmless since it instills paranoia in those who feel themselves to be defenselessly caught in the claws of fate.

In part, the intent of the present book on humankind's supraconscience has been to wake the fearful from the nightmarish world of superstition and fatalism.

Today, an individual's subconscience may torment him in all sorts of insidious ways. It may taunt him with memories of childhood abuse. Family hatred may have inflicted him with unhealed wounds. Perhaps an older brother belittled his hobbies or dreams. Perhaps schoolmates thought him not worthy of their friendship. Perhaps he did poorly in school because his parents fought all the time. When he stayed away from home as much as possible, he was beaten for doing something wrong—something that he never did. So, he had become sure of only one thing: he would be a failure. His childhood and teen years seemed a prophecy of a senseless life. There seemed nowhere for him to go to escape his fate.

If you were that person, is there anything you could do?

No one could keep you from going to a library to educate yourself. Libraries are cozy, silent places where you can belong. Librarians are there to help and guide you. Just being among other learners should make you feel a quiet communion with other people who are also seeking what they want out of life. In a way, a library is a place to escape loneliness and to be accepted for who you are.

Moreover, all those books are friends just waiting for you to start a private conversation with them. A book can teach you what you never knew before.

Books from many countries and past centuries can become true friends. Along the way, you will be teaching yourself what is the most important lesson in life: to learn is to live well.

Of course, if an individual commits him or herself to years of learning, he or she will eventually learn to concentrate on one subject at a time. Knowledge in any chosen field will bring a slow-but-sure conversion, a shift away from ignorance and self-doubt toward a new confidence in life.

One will learn the meaning of ideas such as *religion, science* and the humanities and discover there are diverse beliefs in God. The special sciences about mankind, the earth and the universe will reveal themselves to the learner as will the many forms of creativity that express human feelings, insights, passions and simple wisdom.

Mature, sustained study leads the individual to understand what humanity has learned over the millennia as translated into sense and wisdom. In fact, the knowledge man has acquired becomes the supraconscience of our species. Perhaps today's imperfect, fragmentary and incomplete understanding of psyche will advance further when we more fully grasp the significance of past cultures. What is needed is a holistic comprehension of the process of psychic evolution. It would most probably make clear that all humanity incarnates our species' supraconscience.

In a large library with hundreds of thousands of books, an adult can experience a modern form of 'conversion'. As you scan the endless shelves, you begin to recognize the vastness of human knowledge. You feel a sense of awe at what humankind has learned about nature and the human mind itself. Eventually, when your powers of insight mature, they show you that, as religion taught us, God is omniscient. And, now we perceive that the human psyche has evolved numerous creative powers.

Thus psyche has transformed a species into the enlightened man and woman of this millennium.

This insight transcends all superstitious fatalism about human nature. It is a bio- psychological fact that we have been evolving some form of supraconscience. The change from child to adult is a form of conversion intrinsic to life itself. Our mutation from primates to hominids to humankind was, in essence, a bio-conversion. On the other hand, the transmutation of psyche's subconscience to conscience and then to supraconscience appears to be something on the order of a spiritual transfiguration. Parallel to the evolving perfection of the various life forms in nature, human evolution appears to have pursued a teleological purpose of its own.

What effect does such a conversion have on a person's private life? Conversion follows a recognizable path. A person may be in utter despair, unable to resolve the fear that life is senseless. As in the Ecclesiastes, the individual may come to consider all human effort "vanity of vanities". Such fatalism emerges when one feels overcome by the riddle of death. Anxiety may be compounded by believing in fate rather than in the self.

The reader will recall the despair of Blaise Pascal before he experienced a life-changing epiphany. He described our life on earth as follows. "We are crushed between the infinite of greatness and smallness, of life before we were born and after we die."

True, life limits the days of our lives. Yet, within those limits we have the opportunity to learn why we are here. To be sure, certain days bring sickness, sadness and perhaps tragedy. Nevertheless, human events are not fated. Seldom are we utterly helpless. Our species' survival has taught us courage, common sense and decision which enable us to endure grief and the loss of loved ones.

Now we believe a wounded mind can be healed. We ourselves can transform the anxieties, fears and sicknesses of psyche by pursuing interests, nurturing talents and seeking new knowledge. By developing a skill special to our intelligence, we can renew faith in ourselves. By probing our own psyche as to what we want out of life, we can discover who we really are and what we can be. By welcoming into our hearts the great human beings who lived before us, we can learn the ultimate meaning of beauty, truth and wisdom. Knowledge of their ideas, ideals and noble passions will help us decide what our own lives can eventually mean.

Over time, sorrow and suffering can be soothed and healed through sane, healthy, creative activities. Commitment to simple, homespun truths can guide heart and mind to the Intelligence immanent in life. With patient thought, we learn that our emotions are shared by all humanity because all have underdone what we have. The human heart shares the same pains, knowledge and experience. Instead of self-pity, compassion for others effects a conversion from helplessness to hope and renewed love of life.

On the other hand, if your life is engulfed by unhappiness, you have a right to rebel and free yourself in any decent way you can. You may have concentrated all your hopes for happiness on one person or on one place on earth. If this is your case, you have the right to unshackle yourself. Leave your self-imposed imprisonment to go where life can have a new beginning among the many possibilities it offers the freed soul. Be master or mistress of your own days. Your new-found freedom will lead you to create the person you were always meant to be.

In sum, the day you reach the decision to deal with all life's adversities and to come to terms with its tragedies, your new wisdom will heal your heart and mind. Converted to a new way of life, your decisiveness will result in a self-fulfilling destiny. Freeing yourself initiated your conversion to life.

The Ultimate Source of Human Evolution

Over the past five millennia, a force has emerged in the psyche as it focused its power on creating human cultures. This concentration of our mental and spiritual powers explains the accelerated evolution of our species.

It may have been the belief in a Supreme Being. What could have happened to the human brain when mankind first sensed the presence of God in the universe?

Today, we know that the brain is composed of neurons. These not only can discharge electrical impulses in an instant, but a micro-second later, they can recharge themselves. These self-perpetuating neurons maintain the intricate communication of the vertebrate central nervous system. They form the organ of thought and neural coordination intrinsic to the brain.

Any clear insight or universal idea seems to electrify the whole brain's network of neurons. In fact, typical neurological transmission of energy, images and ideas is ubiquitous throughout the brain. Not only does it keep the body alive, but it is probably the ultimate source of the accelerated evolution of humankind.

Moreover, as the brain seriously confronts opposing thoughts, feelings and intuitions, mental processes are sped up as if meeting a life-and-death emergency. Such a state of alertness takes place when a confrontation occurs between the hope that God exists and the abject despair of atheistic .fatalism. The threat arouses fear, calls forth courage, and inspirits the psyche to create a superior response.

When ancient man faced suffering, sorrow or death, a strong yearning welled up in him to counter the overwhelming helplessness he felt before fate. He was unable to escape the reality of death itself, but his life instinct, nevertheless, fought against his hopelessness: Somewhere there must be a deeper understanding of human destiny.

With the birth of the idea of a Supreme Divinity, man could fight back any omen of doom. He came to realize that his deeper despair was born of his own ignorance. He could not allow himself to yield to the anxiety and despair of his ancestors. From the moment he sensed the omnipresence of the Omniscient, he realized that a Supreme Being explained both creation and the mystery of life and death. That insight gave man a reason to live. If a deity had brought existence into being, he had created man and woman so that they might learn from His Infinite Wisdom.

Though man developed cultures, religions and civilizations, he always faced the same existential problem--was his life fated by 'the stars ' or did he deserve a destiny he himself could create? This enigma preoccupied him over the millennia. The contrast between his hope and the merciless reality of life continually challenged his faith that there must be a reason-for-being besides satisfying one's biological needs.

The unanswered questions at the core of his life sometimes led him back to prehistoric despair. How did he really know there existed a God in the universe? Of course, the physical reality of the sun, the moon and the stars seemed undeniable evidence but where did the idea of God come from? Where did <u>all</u> ideas come from? Moreover, why were there ideas at all?

The more he thought quietly and patiently, the more his mind gained pleasure from wondering and thinking. Though his old fears and anxieties still oppressed him, he found that hope re-energized his mind. Then he perceived old experiences and events in a calmer, wiser way.

This simple recognition of the power of ideas and the refreshment of spirit that came with them brought him a startling insight. Not only did his ideas occur more spontaneously, but his self-understanding was maturing more rapidly. Was that what knowledge of one's own culture did for the mind–multiply the number of exciting ideas and accelerate the realization of their meaning? Then he understood that his idea of God was nourishing the growth of his mind and the spirit of his people. Undertaking to visualize the Supreme Being initiated a magical mental transformation.

If God was omniscient, we had to learn all we could about His Creation and about ourselves--His creatures. If God was omnipotent, we must try to discover what our own powers were--those of reason, our emotional perception, our spiritual insight, our purpose in life.

Only much later we realized that the very opposition between hope and despair, courage and fear, idealism and cynicism activated the imagination. In effect, their dialectical confrontation energized and roused our need for greater knowledge and wisdom. This intense interaction of ideals and realities was the source of psyche's evolution.

Today we understand that the dialectical tension between psyche's potencies helped create and integrate our cultures and civilizations.

We also now perceive that prehistoric man's fatalistic subconscience was largely determined by our ancestors' struggle for survival. By contrast, we eventually comprehended that the universe was created and integrated by a Supreme Being. We now know that what we once called the Deity can be scientifically understood as the Supraconscience of the cosmos.

This must mean that human evolution effected the transformation of a part of psyche into the superior intelligence we now identify as humankind's supraconscience. There must be a reason for this evolutionary attainment. As the most highly developed species on our planet, our evolution has prepared us to finally to apprehend the significance of the infinite Supraconscience of the cosmos.

Thus we are here by reason of Him, and He is our reason for being. Man's purpose is no longer an enigma. Like God Himself, our evolved species has an endless future-before us--here on earth and perhaps somewhere out in His Cosmos.

Is God Guiding Human Evolution?

As the conflict between the subconscience and the supraconscience makes evident, human evolution has taken place on a rough journey from our primeval origins to our more evolved state of mind today. In the beginning, our subconscience was barbarous and savage. It took some 500 millennia to work out reliable survival skills. In the past 50 millennia, our species has undergone a remarkable process of mental and emotional evolution. In view of this, it would be preposterous to maintain that human evolution has been a matter of chance or serendipity.

Indeed, from the perspective of scientific induction and that of the deductive reasoning of the philosopher, the pace of our evolution has been so amazing as to be judged unbelievable. It has exceeded the predictability of science and the credibility of philosophy. In other words, the objectivity of science and the rationality of philosophy would hold that human evolution should not have taken place at all.

Yet, over the past fifty centuries, humankind has created countless ideas and inventions, introduced innumerable innovations, organized uncounted methods of learning, and developed and discovered manifold spheres of knowledge. Worldwide, we have established a multitude of cultures and civilizations. Nevertheless, according to the laws of physics or even the classical theory of evolution, humankind could never have evolved a moral conscience, let alone a supraconscience. The very notion would appear incredible to practitioners of these disciplines.

Nevertheless, there is a natural, justifiable explanation for mankind's remarkable evolution in the context of what we know about nature today. Intrinsic to our body and brain is nature's power of creativity (morphogenesis) and of integration (symbiosis). Together, these produced nature's creative conscience as is evident in the organization of our cells, chromosomes, genes and life-support systems. It is manifest in the body's capacity to grow and mature in a single lifetime. Moreover, the self-same powers of creation and integration seem to have driven the evolution of our species over millions of years. That creative conscience developed us into the exceptional creatures we have become.

A single living cell in our body maintains its inner balance and integrity by homeostasis, yet, that same cell can initiate growth and combine with other cells to produce every organ and life-support system of the entire human body. In the same way, the creative conscience in our species inherited the potential to initiate the transformation of human nature.

Are we to assume that the biosphere earth and the presence of innumerable, self-evolving forms of life is a matter of happenstance or a throw of the dice?

Many creatures on earth have based their survival on *mutualism*, the mutually beneficial association between different kinds of organisms. The term tends to disguise the dialectical essence of our being and becoming as survivors.

In view of this omnipresent process in nature, is it possible that the Supreme Being we call God is Itself dialectical in character–and evolving throughout eternity? If that were so, Its dialectical process would have some ultimate purpose. In other words, did God have a purpose in creating life and initiating evolution? If he had made a perfect creation, what particular sense could that possibly have for mankind? On the other hand, He would have created a world in which something worthwhile was to be achieved beyond surviving, some task to be accomplished, some great adventure to be undertaken by humankind.

Is it possible God first created us as primitive beings to test our capacity to evolve, to become observant, intelligent, compassionate? It does seem that the evolution of man and woman had some purpose beyond species survival. Together they humanized one another.

To survive, we also had to develop common sense, emotional sensitivity, and instinctive wisdom. Our inborn intelligence and perception grew keener and our thought processes became more skillful. Disaster and catastrophe taught us to detect the greater order in nature and the heavens. That order made us think about the Omnipotence of the Supreme Being who had called the earth and heavens into existence. That Almighty must have created everything alive with an inborn power to seek out its own future. Purpose is everywhere in nature. As humankind began to develop a finite superconscience, and as they became aware that all life has some ultimate purpose, they came to realize a Supraconscience was behind it all. If so, then every man, woman and child had a reason for being.

Gradually, through the interaction between subconscience and supraconscience, humanity began to evolve of its own accord. Our supraconscience discovered that its purpose was to transform, heal and cure the subconscience: The supraconscience converted our species into human beings.

By now, we begin to perceive the reason for God having created our species was to learn to evolve on our own. Once friendship and mutual trust have been established among humankind, the next stage of our evolution will be to integrate all human knowledge and wisdom into the essential supraconscience of humanity. Ultimately, the purpose of our future evolution will be to explore space-and-time for the essential nature of the Cosmic Supraconscience.

Chapter Eleven

Psyche's Journey Through Time

III. The Co-Evolution of our Inferior and Superior Nature
The Polarity of the Psyche

For millennia, our salvation religions have interpreted existence in terms of a duality which they took to be inherent in the cosmos. This mistaken, metaphysical belief saw the world as an arena of conflict between good and evil. Supposedly, that was the 'eternal nature' of things.

This meant human life was a perpetual struggle between virtues and vices, piety and transgressions, the godly and the ungodly. Existence amounted to imprisonment in a world where one spent life's best energies in defending the soul against self-degradation and mortal sin.

This superstition was advanced as a metaphysical philosophy to guide the future of humanity. It taught our ancestors to understand life as a struggle against extremes of body and mind. Our forefathers taught us to subdue and shun passions, immoral inclinations and shameful acts. In effect, these religions feared the devil lurking in the shadows of the mind. Thus superstition had discovered our primordial subconscience.

Consequently, religion undertook to educate psyche by the inculcation of moral maxims, by noble stories of prophets and saints, and by the examples of ecclesiastics and preachers. In other words, through ethical teaching and the practice of ritual, religion sought to spiritually educate the laity. Its purpose was to expel the subhuman in man and to paternally discipline the human being.

There is no gainsaying the worthiness of religious intent. Unfortunately, it believed evil had infected humankind by the irredeemable sin of the first man and woman. Today, a skeptic would argue that this myth was used as a ploy by Judaism, Christianity and Islam to hold mankind perpetually guilty of sin so that ecclesiastical power over the masses could be maintained forever.

Over time, the secular system of education gradually guides individuals to sublimate natural passions through activities of self-discovery and creativity. In other words, secular education undertakes to teach the value of common sense and realistic ethics. The natural sciences prepare the young to come to terms with the actual world and the physical universe. The human sciences (sociology, anthropology, history) introduce tolerance for the mores, customs and traditions of world cultures. The humanities (art, music, literature and philosophy) initiate the student to the beauty, truth, sensibilities and wisdom of the past and present.

Through secular studies, men and women develop greater self-discipline. By learning to pursue a personal purpose, they transform themselves into guides and mentors for their own families. Moreover, the human sciences and humanities humanize us by teaching greater respect for all mankind. Ultimately, when individuals assume responsibility for their self-education, they further the evolution of their own supraconscience.

If modern individuals are to merit the title of *Homo sapiens* (the wise species), they need to understand that the lessons of the past should not be lost, i.e., the consequences of failure and success, wrongness and rightness, superstitious fatalism and mature faith. These lessons have made clear to us the polar nature of our self-questioning psyche. They have tutored us in the need for balance, harmony, and cultural syncretism.

There have been dogmatic explanations of Scripture as opposed to the 'heretical' ones. In scriptural explication, texts have a literal and a spiritual meaning. There are early accounts of the unequivocal Word of God and later exegeses based on more exact knowledge of ancient languages and greater verification of actual historical events.

Finally, there also exists factual, everyday knowledge as opposed to the wisdom of plain folks—knowledge of what is true for all humanity.

This thumbnail sketch of psyche's dialogue between its lower and higher powers often takes place between the failings of the subconscience, our common sense conscience, and the maturing wisdom of our religious and secular supraconscience.

The Bipolarity of Human Nature

In 2004, *The Creative Conscience as Human Destiny* demonstrated how evolution proceeded by a dialectic within and between cells, genes, organs and life-support systems. In addition, physiological changes effected the adaptation of species to their environments. Furthermore, it is known that successful biological adaptation helps guarantee the survival of a species. Hence their evolution was largely the result of microbiological experimentation aimed at creating ever more perfect life forms.

Human evolution proceeded by a dialectic between humankind's evolving intelligence and the cultures and civilizations man created. From these facts, it follows that mankind's supraconscience developed a dialectic between his creative intelligence, his reasoning, and his concept of God as the perfect Being.

Biology also teaches us how nature is bipolar in the sense that a life form establishes inner stability by self-integration (e.g. the homeostasis of a living cell) and, also, in the sense that to increase its potential for survival, it can initiate growth and mutation and thus transform itself into a more viable form of life.

This bipolarity manifests itself in mankind's cultures and civilizations wherever they establish law and order in an effort to contain lawlessness and disorder. Yet, often societies and cultures seem to provoke acts of aggression against one another as if civilized conscience had become too much to bear for restless populations still struggling to survive.

Time and again we witness the fact that very highly developed nations and civilizations 'break down' or undergo outright revolution against secular or religious authority. Given this fact, it is possible to understand how historical change and transformation come about—they appear to undergo cyclical oscillations from one pole of influence to its direct opposite.

Religion can present the argument that humankind's conception of a Supreme Being was the origin of mankind's emotional evolution. The concept of an omniscient Being provided an explanation for creation and for human nature itself. Eventually through devotion to religious practices, cultures also evolved a measure of moral understanding.

As explained previously, the salvation religions visualized existence as a drama of evil versus good, but, actually, that struggle was between humankind's primitive subconscience and our evolving supraconscience.

Spiritually evolved men such as Moses, Christ and Mohammed were most certainly endowed with a highly developed supraconscience. Unfortunately, in the centuries that followed them, whenever religious leaders wielded power they yielded to the instincts of our sub-conscience. Thus, otherwise eminent, sane leaders temporarily surrendered their sanity and slaughtered other peoples or their own faithful in order to purge the world and their souls of evil. Sadly, crazed zealots perverted the core teaching of their original, noble religions. Hence, over the centuries, the prehistoric subconscience made religion itself a victim of imaginary evil.

When mankind was again awakened by the revitalizing power of faith in a Supreme Being, he experienced a renewed appreciation of life. A more mature understanding of the Almighty brought about an advance in human evolution. Humans once again undertook to propitiate this Being in so far as they could understand It. Eventually, when God came to be seen as the incarnation of charity, love and compassion, they yearned to be like Him.

Thus, over the history of Western religion, humankind's superconscience found itself engaged in combat with our primate subconscience. Rather than a struggle for survival involving cosmic forces, the conflict revealed itself to be a matter of assault and resistance between our inferior and superior natures. Having witnessed the pain, rage, and savagery of the irrational subconscience, the supraconscience became aware of its own evolutionary power, its resourcefulness, and its ultimate role in mentoring the advancement of humanity.

So, our superior self engaged the inferior one with the purpose of humanizing it. What was needed was a conversion from arrogance to discernment and from blindness to foresight. Rage has to come to wisdom, it must develop a sense of caution and thoughtfulness. In time, the age-old vices of discord, dishonor and disorder would be converted into the virtues of accord, honor and moral order.

Through this struggle, the supraconscience came to understand its purpose as guide to humankind. That purpose was not only to please the Supreme Being, but to prepare humanity for its future evolution.

Subconscience versus Supraconscience
Exorcism

In the modern world, some people still .believe that 'evil spirits' can seize a person, body and soul. This ancient form of neurosis has manifested itself for at least two thousand years. In the Judaic-Christian culture, possession by 'demonic powers' is thought to be a sort of paranoid/predatory foreshadowing of the Apocalypse when God brings forth a cosmic cataclysm to destroy the power of evil. At Armageddon, the final and conclusive battle between the forces of good and evil is to take place.

So, the salvation religions, including Islam, teach that evil is real and roves the world like some prehistoric raptor or hunts for easy prey as man-eating reptiles did.

A sensitive individual who believes in the omnipresence of demons from hell may readily succumb to his fears. By hiding from one's own 'guilt', the person can easily become a victim in his own real-life nightmare.

And, seizure by demons calls for exorcism, a religious act which supposedly expels an evil spirit from a human being. The victim shows various signs of physical and mental agony, often convulsing, screaming, clutching for help. Unlike being infected with a virulent disease which exhausts the body and silently seems to tear the person apart from within, the possessed individual may thrash about, injuring himself to the point of almost committing suicide in order that the inner torment cease.

Possession dramatizes the terrified psychic state our ancestors must have felt when trapped by a predator. Such near-death experiences must have occurred frequently during humankind's struggle for survival.

In the twenty-first century, there is no verifiable, scientific evidence for devils nor is there evidence of a physically existing Satan. We view the belief as a superstition or wild imagining. Demonology describes submission to demons as an affliction which temporarily overwhelms our sanity. At such times, the victim seems to relive the terror of the prehistoric past: The subconscience has not forgotten.

Eventually at some point, this sick superstition is seen for what it is. A sound-minded, thoughtful individual would ask why angelic powers could not dwell within human beings instead. Of course, persons of good will, charity and brotherly/sisterly love exemplify a solid religious upbringing, but, beyond such praiseworthy practice, is it unthinkable that some men and women are endowed with a kind of angelic intelligence? Why not believe that humankind have always been blessed with angelic mental powers? They may have been saints, sometimes geniuses, sometimes heretics, sometimes wise-fools.

At a more mundane level, what motivates a hero to act? One endangers oneself to save another's life. Religion does not teach us to do that. Rather, humans have a natural instinct which reaches deeply into the root of our being. Contrary to the assumption that humankind is evil, we know that individuals are more likely to save a stranger from harm or rescue another's family from danger. Most human beings would harm another with the greatest reluctance and then only in self-defense, or to protect fellow human beings from injury.

Such selfless actions are not necessarily the mark of a good Jew, Christian or Muslim. If anything, they show the angel in man or women as if we were in the presence of a warrior of God or one of his vigilant angels. In the light of our history of mutual aid to ensure collective survival, belief in angels is more plausible than belief in demons surging out of hell to traduce our souls and devour our dead bodies. Such perverted apocalyptic interpretation of the hopeful lesson of religion arises from the primeval subconscience residual in Homo sapiens.

On the other hand, all of the noble acts which are intended to save another arise from our evolving emotional wisdom, which over the centuries has sought to humanize us. When we instinctively act to save another human being, it is angelic nobility that takes charge of the fears and anxieties emanating from our primitive sub-conscience. In disregarding our own safety, we transform ourselves into something nobler than we have ever been before. For that moment we become superhuman. We acted as our own guardian angel would have acted. This itself is evidence of humankind's supraconscience.

The Subconscience in the Media and the Global Economy

In general, the media do a spectacular job of dramatizing the traumatic effect of the subconscience on the public. They seem to be driven by a morbid fascination with the savage rape and murder of young women, abducted children and the defenseless elderly.

This phenomenon is symptomatic of epidemic mass mental illness. Man's subconscience is indulged and pandered to in daily television programs. There is wide public fascination with movie versions of werewolves, vampires, the living dead, diabolical drug dealers, insane criminals and the devil incarnate. Apparently, the most educated and civilized individual can reveal a Mr. Hyde and Dr. Jekyll personality by his lust for crime and murder.

Obviously, the conscience of religion and 'civilized' society is presently incapable of converting the subhuman from its fascination with barbaric acts to a saner vision of life. Women, especially, experience anxiety because they have become the target of so much male hatred. Child slave labor exists in most poor countries, and prostitution is necessary for survival in much of the globe. And, the 'civilized' world conveniently turns a blind eye to these abominations.

A sound minded citizen must wonder at the acceptance of such subhuman conditions around the world and the emergence of so much evidence of the savage subconscience in modern life. In the wealthier nations, how closely does freedom approximate anarchy? How far is the vicious exploitation of the helpless from insanity and inhumanity?

Today, the collective subhuman state of mind that predominates seems to be reliving the dangers, horrors, and near-death existence of primeval man and woman. Unfortunately, all subhuman acts confirm the predatory power of the subconscience in our world.

The Apocalypse on Television

From today's widespread anxiety among Christians, swayed by fear of the impending Apocalypse, it is obvious that tens of millions suffer a growing terror at the real possibility of the end of the world. Bestsellers are making fortunes from this message of immanent destruction.

If there is any beast (i.e. Satan) threatening mankind, it has its source in our primeval subconscience. Figuratively speaking, a great, final battle (Armageddon) between good and evil may take place, but our actual 'struggle for survival' will be between our prehistoric subconscience and our evolving supraconscience. Judaism, Christianity and Islam have taught us to understand our destiny, but it is the steady evolution of our supraconscience that will decide our future.

If the power of the Supreme Being created the earth, It must also have initiated a dialectic between the reciprocal powers which generate and maintain all life, between nature's creation and integration of new forms of life. Over the eons, eras and epochs of geological time, these two self-perpetuating powers have proved themselves capable of prevailing over the ultimate adversary--Death.

If we accept the claim that God is responsible for Creation, we must also accept the fact that He initiated evolution. However, humanity has furthered its own evolution through innovation, invention, and creativity of all kinds. Our capacity for integration is seen in our monotheistic religions, our systems of secular knowledge, our sciences, and our methodologies which discover and verify the integrity of new knowledge.

Though the Creator has brought forth millions of perfectly designed plants and animals, and though they are truly wondrous and marvelous to behold, our idea of God has fostered in us a superiority of intelligence, intuition and comprehension far beyond the primitive creatures we once were in prehistoric times.

Hence *The Supraconscience of Humanity* challenges all these fatalistic television versions of the world's coming to an end. Against all odds, our species has survived for more than three million years. That fact would seem to indicate that we have the creative and emotional acumen to continue evolving for tens of thousands of years to come.

We must learn to accept responsibility for what we think, believe and do. If there is 'evil' in the world. There are no phantasmagoric four horsemen bringing disaster, plague, wars and death on us. We cause it! (The future may well regard the four figures of doom as pumpkin goblins glaring out of darkened windows on Halloween nights.)

The earth's surface is also changing, and we must learn to evolve with it as we did in the past. We ourselves are responsible for both the outbreak of war and the development of mutual understanding. We create the conditions that allow plagues to overwhelm us. Hygiene, healthful personal habits, and sanitary public places can do much to prevent diseases from becoming scourges. Though death is inevitable for all of us, we can live well, decently, and morally and die with dignity. By so doing, we prove our gratitude to our Maker.

We must not let ourselves be victimized by our primeval fears, paranoia and predatory instincts. We must prove to ourselves and God that we are worthy to survive as a species, and to continue to be allowed to evolve into a better, more humane and worthy race.

The Journey from Subconscious to Supraconscience

The subconscience has its deepest roots in our paleontological and biological past. Over the various geological ages, species emerged and disappeared. Yet, genes mutated and the deeper forces that propel the evolution of species continued to prolong and transform life in all its forms.

In the twenty-first century, we see evolution as impelled by innovation, experimentation, and transmutation as well as by consolidation, unification and integration. These reciprocal processes created and formed all species, with the teleological purpose of individual and species survival.

Though all species submitted to the same primary life processes, mammals breast-fed their newborn and looked after their young till maturity. By contrast, fish and reptiles who lay eggs abandoned them before or shortly after they hatch, thereby forcing them to fend for themselves. For instance, sea turtles, who lay their eggs in warm sand, return to the sea as soon as they have deposited them. They leave their hatchlings to find their way back to the sea on their **own.**

As early mammals, we could not leave our helpless young unattended, for they were at risk of being eaten by watchful predators. The male and female of our species were required to guard the young and feed them because, for years after their birth, they were basically defenseless. In the case of humans, we were required to keep mates and children close by so as to be ready to defend them and to ensure their survival. As one child followed another, male and female developed life-time relationships, and this, in turn, gave birth to rudimentary morality.

Yet, in primeval times, merciless predators were ever-present in our ancestors' dreams. In nightmares, they were stalked by monsters. Although this was stimulated by real life experiences, eventually they developed a terror of invisible spirits whose presence they sensed. Especially at night, these fiends seemed to invade both body and mind.

Over time, nightmares became the source of myths and legends. Shadows became demons. The whole earth seemed to conceal powers of evil. Over generations, such phantoms came to occupy an intimate dimension of the human imagination. Ultimately, primal memories influenced our patterns of perception, our world views, our metaphysical speculation. They reappeared as recurrent mythologies, superstitions, and religions.

Hence murderous images, metaphors and symbols intersected with the actual life experiences of early humankind. They provided a heritage in which the hateful, horrible and inhuman seemed the ultimate reality of a dark world. Man's primeval subconscious became our primitive subconscience.

Thus through the study of human history, we see how human decision making and action came to be infected by the darkness of our ancestral past. Throughout the ages, we have evidence of human barbarism and savagery. The all too numerous facts and events of this are recorded, e.g. ancient cults, salvation religions and their sects tortured, burned and exterminated heretics and apostates. Wherever religious fanaticism overwhelmed human faith, individuals suspected of evil were persecuted in the name of the god the fanatics worshipped. Clearly, such incidents illustrate the power of the subconscience to subvert the noblest dreams and highest ideals of any religion.

Indeed, today we perceive how the nihilism of the prehistoric subconscience came to pervert the accomplishments and achievements of civilized societies, how the subrational can undermine the rational, and undo the idealistic and moral attainments of advanced culture. As we have witnessed in the twentieth century, the rabid subconscience of religious fanatics aims to dehumanize our race through the spread of worldwide terror.

The Supraconscience

Correlative to the evolution of the subconscience has been the emergence and development of humankind's supraconscience.

Even in the remotest times, humans banded together for mutual protection and aid. Whether they were sedentary or itinerant, human groups learned to co-operate in order to survive. True, they often seemed to copy the hierarchical order of the animals with one individual as leader. Others highly skilled in various activities helped the group survive. Recognition of their importance also helped establish social order and a hierarchy of practical values.

Some sort of family, clan or tribal ethic evolved out of the necessity to arrive at compromises; so, too, a rudimentary notion of justice acknowledged that all individuals had certain rights. But the central, magnetic force holding the group together was the fact that they were all mammals, and so required to protect the females and assure the survival of the young. Progress in human morality came through the mutual education of man and woman who shared family rights and duties.

By humanizing us, this intimate co-operation enabled us to grow beyond of our primitive nature and begin to cultivate humanity's future supraconscience.

The study of religion in antiquity teaches us that male and female gods were worthy of worship. If male deities were depicted as warriors, adventurers and virile lovers in their youth, old, venerable gods possessed wisdom in addition to power. On the other hand, in the Mediterranean Basin, goddesses associated with conception, birth and the protection of children played a dominant role in everyday life in so far as they symbolized the life-giving powers of nature.

Once traditional religion identified the Supreme Being as omniscient, the ensuing centuries became occupied with accumulating secular knowledge and wisdom in 'the image of God' as omniscience. In this sense, our mental endowment came from identification with God as the Supraconscience of the cosmos.

Once humankind understands that we now possess a finite supraconscience, evolved through dedication to the cerebral and emotional gifts inherent in humanity, we are prepared to accept on faith the fact that the infinite Supraconscience is guiding our destiny.

With the metaphysical realization that we live in the super-reality of a cosmos guided by a Supraconscience, we can believe in the further humanization of our species. Continued evolution is possible if we accept human nature for what it is and can become. We need to acknowledge that our subconscience was formed in a savage age when there was a real possibility of our extinction. We also need to affirm we were not born evil. Nor are we to be damned for the subhuman acts that our subconscience committed centuries and millennia ago.

Nevertheless, the regional atrocities and the murderous world wars of the twentieth century teach us something. It is time to come to terms with our deeper psychological wounds. We need to understand how the psyche influences our decisions and actions. Humankind's evolved supraconscience needs to learn to understand the irrationality, excesses and homicidal outbursts of psyche's primate subconscience, and, if possible, to heal and cure it. Conscience has failed to understand its nature, frustrations, hatreds and shame.

It is time to understand that the human psyche has evolved. Both subconscience and supraconscience have made it possible to give new meaning to human destiny.

Since antiquity, we have learned to use our cognitive and emotional intelligence to create durable cultures and civilizations, each of which reflects its own kind of supraconscience. Today, we realize that our finite supraconscience is endowed with a teleological purpose. Our destiny lies in a future in which we are one with ourselves, one another, and the Supraconscience as it is omnipresent in existence.

The Actualization of Human Evolution
Time Lag and Its Consequences for Human Evolution

In the past century, humankind has acquired a 360 degree vision of the world's cultures. Most evident among them is the phenomenon of *time lag*.

Often, we hear the expression, "He is behind the times." Usually, that means an individual has failed to keep up with the latest knowledge in his chosen field of specialization or that the rate of technical advance is such that older citizens are more or less unable to cope. This is not necessarily a sign of lack of intelligence or failing acuity. Rather, for some, trying, to keep pace with the changing world just does not seem worth the effort.

Another example of time lag seems be when explorers discover tribes of people living at earlier stages of civilization. Such groups are of special interest to anthropologists and ethnologists. As if they were gods from another planet, they study the mores, customs, and beliefs of traditional peoples for whatever knowledge can be gained as to their humanization and capacity to survive.

Then again, within any given society, there may be time lags between the levels of knowledge available to the self-educated and to the lesser educated respectively. The unfortunate thing is that, in the health arena alone, adequate knowledge might alleviate much of the pain, suffering and hopelessness of people whose ignorance of certain vital health information exposes them to deficiency diseases and illnesses. Then again, either shame or pride may prevent them from accepting the help of those who sincerely want to educate them for their own good.

A glaring example in this century is ignorance of how to take proper care of one's own body and mind. In America, this phenomenon is demonstrated by the fact that every year many million people are crippled or die from quite preventable heart disease, cancer, diabetes, life-threatening obesity, degenerative bone disease, etc. Hence, within any given society, there is a time lag of one sort or another in so far as people fail to keep up with the-latest literature on nutrition and on health habits. Moreover, ignoring public warnings puts the person at risk of contracting, diseases. Unfortunately, the impoverished and uneducated often die early.

Another serious incidence of time lag manifests itself in educational systems. There is often the failure to link together the knowledge and skills which are to be developed from primary and secondary levels to the university. It takes time for new knowledge, discovered and created in the universities, to 'trickle down' to the lower levels.

Also, misconceptions as to the purpose of education emerge and take hold at all levels of education. Since the aggressive introduction of audio-visual aids and computers into the educational milieu, there seems widespread a false conviction that technical skills remove the need for creative, experienced teachers who are able to think holistically. Moreover, the young need to be taught the responsibility and gratification associated with educating themselves beyond the formal education to be had in school.

Another time lag occurs in the field of medicine and medical treatment. Few medical schools teach basic nutrition or the importance of vitamins, minerals, and herbs. Virtually no physician or specialist ever bothers to question a patient as to their eating habits or the nutritional plan they are following. Yet, it is responsibly estimated that half of all deficiency diseases are due to dangerous health habits and irresponsible consumption of food additives--sicknesses which can cause death. Doctors are focused almost exclusively on prescribing medication. Unfortunately, in recent years the drugs which doctors recommend have been killing a startling number of patients. That fact has been augmented by nationwide reports on the high percentage of inaccurate diagnoses of patients' illnesses.

Time lag also takes place where religious influence tends to gainsay sound scientific knowledge of evolutionary biology, genetics, and the psychosomatic causes of bodily sicknesses. Some sects absolutely deny the benefit of appropriate medical treatment or surgery, and depend instead entirely on sectarian faith to cure them. When a religion rejects secular knowledge out of hand, it or its leaders are suffering a clear case of time lag.

Time lag can occur also in an individual. A student specializing in a certain field can take a host of required courses, but he may exclude others that seem remote from his practical needs. Often the result is a very smart specialist, but a very dull, narrow-minded human being. In a sense he is culturally behind the times because he is ignorant of worthwhile individuals from the past who helped make us human. Though they may have lived centuries ago, their thoughts and ideals still are valued because they provide us with apt guidance and wisdom.

Hence, a specialist can suffer from time lag by ignoring the lessons of the good minds of the past. A part of him remains ignorant of what it means to be human in a cultured sense. His life will be lacking in experiences that would otherwise enrich him and possibly bring him a wisdom that goes beyond his professionalism.

However, intentional neglect of what lies beyond one's own ken can also characterize conservative, religious groups because of their commitment to certain principles. In short, they prefer to live in their own sphere of meaning. The Amish sect of Mennonites, followers of Amman who settled in America in the 18th century, are such a noble sect. Originating in Switzerland, the devout have kept to their Christian ethic, mores, customs, and traditions. Dedicated to righteousness, compassion and forgiveness and still dressed in 18th century attire and driving horse drawn carts, they live out-of-sync with the rest of America. This decision is based on a need to preserve their religious ideals. In the midst of much amoral and immoral behavior in modern American society, they seek to uphold the pure message of Christianity.

In stark contrast to this, there are other religious groups of zealots, bigots, and fanatics who are out of touch with contemporary life and with reality in general. Often, they keep to a severe, merciless interpretation of the Almighty's law, and so also represent another form of time lag.

They denounce the sciences for presenting secular accounts of Creation. Yet, the natural sciences teach modern man much about the material and physical world, its geological transformation over billions of years, and the astronomy of the timeless universe. Because they are based on verifiable, empirical evidence and on extensive research into natural phenomena, they may be said to approximate an understanding of the holistic complexity and intricacy of God's world.

There is also the traditionalist's insistence that the scriptural origin of man and the mythical notion of 'original sin' explain the fact of evil in mankind. Such ancient 'truths' run counter to and so dismiss the knowledge of the human sciences (anthropology, sociology, psychology). Yet, the intent of these same sciences is to study humankind without prejudice or passing judgment on them from our own cultural point of view. They undertake the study of mankind's cultural evolution, the reasons for social injustice, and the variety of racial cultures. Their intent is to enable us to appreciate humanity for what it is. This charitable spirit is the very essence of that scripture which is intended to unite in peace all races of humankind. So, such judgmental sects live in their own self-imposed time lag.

So long as monotheism does not end in monomania, it should have a positive effect on human moral development. Yet, the intentional exclusion of areas of knowledge unrelated to one's faith is bound to limit the world view of the faithful. Moreover, such exclusiveness warps their mental development because, in effect, they exclude the real world and the rest of humanity. The danger of such sectarian isolationism is that people will sentence themselves to live in a time capsule forever.

Like solitary confinement, life in a time capsule can seriously limit the rational powers and damage the sanity of whoever remains in it. The theory of biological evolution has shown us that all species that have been unable to evolve were surpassed by competitors and doomed to extinction. Those that lagged behind in time were almost always overcome by other, more aggressive individuals determined to survive.

What would have happened to our species if we had remained trapped at an earlier stage of evolution? We still might be ape-men doing acrobatics in the trees. At that stage, we would not have understood that there could be a future or that there was danger in lagging behind. But from the point to which we have ascended in our evolution, we can look back over the various evolutionary stages of hominids and observe that the laggards suffered and disappeared from the scene.

Is it possible that our moral conscience has not yet caught up with other aspects of the accelerated evolution of our species? In contrast to other mammals, we have undergone astonishing physical changes. Our paws became hands able to develop unusual manual dexterity. The eyes originally positioned at the side of our skulls (as with horses) gradually merged into binocular vision. When we learned to walk erect, our eyes gained perspective to see far ahead. Our jaws, mouth and larynx developed to enable us to produce speech. Our cranium enlarged and our mammalian brain became convoluted and intricately integrated. Thus, as it evolved, we gained ever greater capacity to reason resourcefully, skillfully and creatively.

We have undergone such an extraordinary process of evolution that our newly developed capacities must have given emerging humankind an intuition that some superior power was guiding us.

With the eventual encounter between primogenitors, at times there must have been recognition that one group was more advanced, clever, and skilled and the other less capable or mentally keen. The group that was better organized, integrated and intelligent must have realized some inner power had favored them--not only over the animals, but also over others of their own kind. A case in point would be the encounter between Cro-Magnon and Neanderthal.

Over the centuries, when traditional peoples encountered humans from more 'advanced' civilizations, they must have experienced bewilderment, humiliation, and anger at feeling inferior.

Here was another example of time lag from the vantage point of the more technically advanced civilization. However, the mistreatment and exploitation of aboriginal and native peoples was due to a time lapse in the conquerors: Their supposedly 'advanced' level of moral development actually lagged far behind their innovative and technological skills. For instance, it took centuries for Judeo-Christian morality to have an effect on mankind as a whole. What permitted the developed nations to ignore their religious conscience was their primeval subconscience. It overwhelmed the sense of justice and humanity they had come to in their own societies. Since more 'advanced' or 'enlightened' peoples and races have historically assaulted others and viewed them as subhuman, it is reasonable to conclude that they generally acted not out of any real condition of moral superiority, but were, in fact, impelled by their own barbaric subconscience.

So, in essence, time lag does not solely indicate that one is behind the times, or has failed to develop practical skills or to follow a given moral code. Ultimately, it is the failure to provide justice for all or to promote humane understanding in human relations. All levels of society need to be educated to respect the human rights of self and others. We must endeavor ecumenically to come together as one race to live in one time zone, and not remain separated by distinct views of ethics. We must not allow the backward among us to undermine the meaning of human evolution.

Even in our enlightened age, in some of the world's societies, fundamentalism and fanaticism still rule in lieu of justice and compassion. Entire populations still live by an archaic moral code spawned originally by the primitive subconscience of humankind. In such groups, human time has never really evolved.

If we are to know a future, we must all live in the same world of ethical equality so that each human being can make a life for him- or herself. Let us hope that, in the foreseeable future, humankind's further evolution will produce a finite supraconscience which emulates the Supraconscience.

Civilization and its Discontents

Today many are aware that there is something deeply wrong with our civilization. If we stop to really look at it, it becomes clear that it consists of a thin veneer of commercial activity between individuals interested in profiting from one another.

Beneath that veneer are lies, deceit, theft, swindling, corruption, crime and violence, all expressions of the subhuman in us. Even more revealing is the fact that unrelenting violence and frequent wars are the clearest sign of the disintegration of collective moral conscience.

Whenever we take the life of another human being, or when a military force destroys neighborhoods, towns, cities, regions or whole countries, we experience a sense of release from all moral restraint. All violence is a rebellion against conscience. It surges up from our prehistoric, predatory subconscience. This primeval power, associated with paranoid and homicidal instincts from our primitive past, can only be transformed and guided through a power superior to the persecuting and persecuted conscience of our religious past. That is, the only endowment capable of saving us from ourselves is humankind's evolving supraconscience.

Of course, the question is: How do we educate the supraconscience to transmute our lying, arrogance, and vengeful excesses into virtues, i.e., into mutual trust and understanding, empathy and humaneness?

In modern civilization, the pragmatic approach to solving this problem has been to ensure fundamental education in practical knowledge and skills so that all can take pride in the ability to make a living and to survive in a competitive world. The widespread building of primary and secondary schools as well as community colleges has greatly facilitated this basic level of mass education.

Yet, beyond such systems of education, humankind needs something more, something which will help cultivate the individual's prospects for the future. Over thousands of years, humankind's best minds have developed spheres of significance which have encouraged individuals to concentrate their creative curiosity, their instinct for discovery and exploration, and their search for a meaningful life. Humankind's natural aptitudes and talents have led to such major orbs of interest as the sciences, the humanities and the human sciences. And, of course, religion has always been one source of our humanization.

To be sure, this is not to imply that only the scientific, academic or religious provide the sole mental and emotional gratifications possible. Though many individuals are sufficiently endowed to become students, there are many sources of creative expression and mental fulfillment beyond academia. The subject of study is less important than the individual's dedication to what is to be learned or the skill to be mastered. The dedicated student not only advances his own knowledge but, in so doing, develops a new self-knowledge and pride in deciding how to live his own life.

The most important lesson learned from commitment to one's own education is the discovery that one can educate oneself. Though formal instruction under a skilled and wise teacher surely can accelerate the acquisition of general and specialized knowledge, the fact is that resourcefulness was what ensured humankind's survival; it even made it possible for us to thrive when exceptional individuals developed skills and knowledge never before seen in the world.

Never underestimate what you can learn or do better than anyone else. Self-competition is the ultimate means of evolution from basic survival to superiority as a resourceful individual.

In the past, ignorance and innocence were the reasons for our downfall. By contrast, today our pursuit of personal knowledge and wisdom can still lead humankind to mutual respect and to the survival of humane values.

Belief in the Afterlife Today

Present day ideas about the afterlife evoke opposing beliefs and responses. The tendency to defer to either the subconscience or the supraconscience reveals the attitudes of disbelievers and believers respectively.

Those individuals whose religion promises resurrection appear blessed in a sense. Yet, skeptics would insist that such persons are simply in denial of the ultimate truth of death. For the modern realist, there is no beyond where life's sorrows and suffering are healed, no ultimate consolation. For the individual dominated by the subconscience, life is spent in dread of death. The end of life is the end of everything. All that remains is the Void.

The religious fear to abandon the emotional assurance provided them by the religion of their parents. The philosophically inclined believe that a sound heart comes from knowing itself and has no fear of an afterlife. Others think to make life meaningful by dedication to a worthy cause. Even creating a plan gives life a direction and a degree of dedication. The realistic commit themselves to attainable ideals and so justify their destiny. In the end, they are prepared to pass a 'last judgment' on their own earthly lives.

In psyche's journey through time, there are those who fear that mankind is fated by the savage heritage of our subconscience. By contrast, optimistic individuals reveal faith in the supraconscience by contributing to the future.

Today, the orthodox among us argue that the afterlife provides sure punishment for our mortal sins, but religion seems to have little effect on controlling the crime rate or subduing acts of murderous violence in our everyday world. The impotence of moral law is exposed by the size of the criminal population. In free America, it has increased markedly for decades. In fact, the U.S.A. has more people in prison than the rest of the world combined. That means the subconscience is not only alive and well, but virulently active among us.

These statistics should awaken us to the danger that modern man can indeed destroy himself. The time has come to acknowledge our cultural ignorance. In America, we need to become aware of and take seriously the values of our minorities and ethnic groups. That is a task that all schools, colleges and universities should undertake in earnest. Some noteworthy contributions to the cultural education of the American citizen appear on television programs as CNN, PBS, the History and Discovery Channels.

It is time we learn what the rest of the world cherishes and holds sacred. Our ignorance of world cultures, and the assumption that ours is incomparably superior, is a very grave mistake and can lead to fateful miscalculations in international affairs. Our ignorance and arrogance are sure to be repaid in kind. In the eyes of the world, we are failing to live up to the promise of our democracy. How can America lead the world without knowing what world cultures represent and offer us?

We may still have time to befriend the antagonistic and those suspicious of our motives if we open our minds to the injustices they have suffered and to their present day need for honest understanding and aid. To be sure, we cannot be all things to all the world. Fortunately, many places have no need of us at all. They can take care of themselves very well and do not expect anything from us. So long as we respect their way of life, they will likely respect ours.

If we are open to others' cultural values, if we acknowledge the genius of other peoples, we will find ourselves enriched beyond all trade agreements or trillion dollar business deals. And, that way, what our young and immature nation has yet to offer the world will enjoy the benefits of reciprocal understanding from a world that is amazed at our new sense of neighborliness.

In the context of the psychic evolution of humankind, the way for all nations to gain mastery over the rebellious subconscience is to foster the cultural supraconscience of all humanity. When, at last, the conditions of life on earth are such that they provide a guarantee of mutual understanding and respect for the intelligence and good will of all races and religions, we will think less of the afterlife and live lives worthy of our practical and emotional acumen.

An Afterthought

An undue preoccupation with death can lead us to view life as meaningless. Yet, speculation about the afterlife can become a catalyst for the further evolution of our own supraconscience.

In fact, the mystery of the beyond continuously challenges our imagination, creativity and resourcefulness. Though the puzzle will never be solved till we meet death itself, the benefit of our having to constantly confront the enigma is that it accelerates the search for life's meaning. In effect, it is probable that reflections on death helped actualize human evolution over thousands of generations.

True, most minds despair of ever finding answers. Some are led to skepticism, cynicism or nihilism. However, beyond such surrender, our musing can lead us to a new wisdom of what life is meant to be. We may thereby rediscover those meaningful moments, hours, and events in this life which fulfilled us. In that fulfillment we find the significance of life and its ultimate purpose. As it turns out, life is for learning to live. But, each of us must decide how.

How Man and Woman Advanced Evolution

It is possible that man and woman evolved at different rates. Anthropological evidence reveals that the assertive, aggressive male concentrated on the development of skills in hunting, building shelters, protecting his territory and fighting those who sought to take what was his. Man developed greater physical strength, cleverness and a sense of co-operation in working together to accomplish common goals.

The habits and habitats of prehistoric man remind zoologists of the coordinated hunting techniques of dogs and wolves, or the ability of small animals to dig intricate tunnels as hideaways, or the use of caves as shelters by creatures of all kinds.

Thus men developed resourcefulness and the skills we associate with *Homo hablis*. By being innovative and using their powers of invention, early men activated their own mental evolution. What became moral evolution was the perfecting of their skills.

Women evolved in other ways. Anthropologists believe that, beyond foraging and food gathering, they conceived of and developed agriculture. They also invented pottery for the storage of water, grain, seed and oil. Ceramic vessels were used for cooking and serving food. Women also discovered the use of plants and herbs as medicines, and they made poultices to heal lesions and wounds. They learned to heal their husbands and children. They prepared edible foods. They cleaned meat and vegetables, roasted and boiled them to make them safer and easier to eat.

With their motherly skills, they clothed and nursed the family. In all these ways, women represented know-how in the stage of *Homo hablis*. And, they earned the respect of the tribe for their maternal skills.

Furthermore, they lived among other women and their children, their neighbors. Through child-rearing they developed a greater sympathy and understanding for growing boys and girls. Their humanity matured earlier than that of the men. With full motherhood, they evolved an innate compassion for all of their kind and even for the young of animals. In fact, their maternal understanding of life accelerated the moral evolution of humankind.

So, it may be that, while men greatly expanded and perfected practical knowledge and survival skills, woman grew more intuitive, subtle, gentle and creative in the skills of mutual agreement, thus assuring the survival of her family. In essence, she evolved further in the skills of love, which today we understand as compassion and charity.

The development of these survival skills actualized the human potential for further evolution. They became the basis for defining successive stages of human culture. Thus, man's practical know-how and woman's emotional intelligence made possible the transformation of our species into truly human beings.

The Supraconscience of Woman

Evolutionary biology describes mammalia as warm-blooded, higher vertebrates that nourish their young with milk released from the female's mammary glands. This necessity to mother the young must have influenced human evolution. Indeed, the difference between female and male character has had a marked influence on human history. It appears that woman was created to bring understanding and love into the savage male world of competition and conflict.

Our study of prehistoric and ancient religions revealed that female worshippers prayed for benign protection and guidance from their fertility goddesses. Indeed, it is likely that the humanization of our species was largely due to the compassionate, intelligent commitment of womankind. Moreover, her steady affection, tolerance, and loving presence stimulated the warm-hearted and forgiving centre of our evolving supraconscience.

In our tradition, ancient Law was expressed in the *Pentateuch* of the Old Testament and in terms of patriarchal authority. A stern and unforgiving father ruled the universe. So, on earth, law was the province of the male. Thus this legalistic, authoritarian and judgmental character typified the emerging supra-conscience of the male.

However, beyond laws carved in stone, a new ethic finally arose to transcend this legalistic approach to determining right and wrong. The new morality insisted on rightness, fairness and equity for men, women and slaves. That meant justice based on natural rights. Eventually the concept of law and order included judgment freed from prejudice and the illegal use of power.

Woman's wifely, motherly, daughterly and sisterly nature inspired the gentler, intuitive side of religion and law. She taught us that kindness and understanding were superior to male severity and assertiveness. Foremost, woman believes in loving relationships--first, last, and always.

In raising and protecting the young, she embraces the intimate, life-giving processes of nature. She has more important things to do than to waste life in senseless acts of aggression. Her role on earth is to guide and guarantee the future of humanity--the children of the world.

Angels of Earth?

In a theological context, it is possible that the belief in angels might be the outcome of real events in human history. It is likely that angels were actually humankind 'in the beginning'.

According to recent evolutionary research, at one time in our history, a devastating, worldwide disaster reduced humankind to only a few thousand survivors. So, in prehistoric times, was the mass of humanity cast down by toxic gases which drastically reduced breathable oxygen? Or did continent-wide epidemics occur? Surely the survivors did not understand such an event as a natural phenomenon caused by volcanic eruptions or earthquakes. They probably imagined that it was the punishment of irate gods.

Nevertheless, across the globe a few thousand people were spared extinction. These survivors had to have had the physical strength and mental resourcefulness to enable humanity to endure and to evolve in spite of these drastic changes. At least, they had the courage to start anew—and, in so doing, they may made possible our existence.

As religions evolved beyond fear and anxiety of unforeseeable catastrophes, people grew mentally and morally. By practicing rituals to propitiate the invisible powers in nature, by seeking to live in greater harmony with nature and among themselves, they undertook to show the gods that humankind were worthy of survival. Eventually, humans learned not to worship harmful demons and false saviors, i.e., magicians and tricksters.

Gradually, they came to trust in benevolent gods. In recent millennia, they came to believe in one and only one Supreme Being. Islam is a good example of the Muslim rejection of wicked spirits or *jinn* and surrender wholly to the omnipotent Allah.

The superior health and immunity of the early, prehistoric survivors must have enabled them to live through the worst of times. Later generations also steadily faced crises and disasters. They not only endured the unpredictable conditions associated with geological transformations, but also evolved mentally through these recurrent challenges.

Periods of disaster would have activated man's capacity for innovation and invention as well as his ability to expect the unexpected. Such surges in learning and creativity were followed by long periods of calm during which the pace of cerebral evolution would have steadied. During such quiescent stages, the mind probably integrated what had been learned from past experiences. As a consequence of its having learned lessons of survival and mutual co-operation, humanity likely matured a form of natural conscience based on the benign laws of nature.

Through misty memories, descendents recalled those who had survived past disasters. They became angels among humankind who had saved their people. In successive generations, imaginative and innovative leaders seemed at times evidence of angelic powers among us. They had not fallen to earth, but rather evolved to lead their people into the future.

The Reality of Human Evolution

Is it not probable that humankind's idea of God fostered human evolution?

Judging from recorded history, it appears that a new stage of ingenuity and cognition emerged when we developed a moral conscience. Indeed, mutual cooperation, the development of settlements, agriculture, irrigation, sanitation and communication between separated groups all contributed to the development of the human mind. Humankind was maturing with regard to practical, social and innovative intelligence.

As survival and domestic skills became second nature, there came hours when one was free to think and imagine. Long dry seasons and cold winters led men and women to mull over the hardness and brevity of life. In such periods, they pondered what the next year would bring or where they would be ten years hence. Over the changing seasons, such musing gave concern for the future of the yet-to-be-born.

At other times, the mystery of life and death gave them pause to wonder how the world came to be: What made the rivers flow? What drove the winds, made storm clouds gather and swallow an entire village, and even the land itself in darkness? When the clouds vanished, the sun shone again and the sky turned azure once more, they felt gratitude to the power that brought life to the earth.

Those who tilled the land learned that a spirit dwelled in each small seed. Once buried in the soil, that tiny life awakened, took root and reached slender, green fingers toward the warm sunlight. From a single seed came a plant, a shrub, a tree--finally an immense forest.

One day a dreamer wondered if there could be one, endless, invisible power in the stars that accounted for the magical transformations on earth. And, could it be that each living thing had its own destiny?

As time went on, some mystic sensed a spirit behind all things, a soul, a guardian guiding the life of every good being. When a thinker envisioned the Supreme Being, a new stage of human evolution began.

Till then, the creative conscience in nature had fostered humanity's own creative conscience. But, eventually when man came to believe in the reality of a divinity, our psyche was empowered to transcend its subhuman past.

That belief was a seed destined to create new forms of self-realization. It revealed to us our potential to develop superior conscious powers. That revelation illumined the path of our metamorphosis from prehistoric hominid to human being. That electric intuition, given us by a power greater than death, showed humankind was evolving a purpose to life.

So, existence had a sense beyond survival. We began to sense that life's meaning was an enduring one--it would outlive us. When we came to believe the Supreme Being was immanent in human life, our evolution was transformed into a destiny.

Belief in the deity's omniscience inspired the exponential metamorphosis of psyche's powers. Across time, that omniscience motivated mankind to collate an encyclopedic vision of reality. Over the millennia, this knowledge was refined and experience was converted into wisdom, a transformation which revealed humankind's natural religion. In psyche's journey through time, the Supraconscience of the universe has been guiding intelligent men and loving women to consummate the unfolding of the supraconscience of humanity.

Glossary

Author's Note

Evolution is the vital, universal process in nature which has animated human history, culture and civilization. Darwin's original, nineteenth century theory of evolution has itself also evolved. Twentieth century investigations in ecology, microbiology and genetics update our understanding of the world and human nature. Introspection into man's evolving self reveals that the interaction between our inner and outer worlds proceeds dialectically.

Third millennium biology also argues that nature itself is actuated by two interacting processes: creativity and integration. This interaction set in motion the creative conscience of living nature. In turn, because man emerged out of nature, he also evolved a nature-born creative conscience.

In other words, our biological evolution formed our biogenetic intelligence. This is the scientific basis for describing the evolution of the psyche from prehistoric times till today. By creating cultures and civilizations, the human psyche realized its own evolution.

Inspired by many forms of religion and the need for continual improvement in mental skills, man eventually acquired both secular knowledge and religious wisdom. These interacting processes eventually eclipsed the practical needs of conscience and produced a supraconscience beyond anything imagined or conceived in our past.

The dimensions of psyche are measured by our exoteric and esoteric understanding of how humankind traditionally came to terms with our earthly existence.

The Swiss psychologist, C.G. Jung, made modern man aware of the archetypes underlying the cultural experiences which formed humankind's collective unconscious. On the other hand, the French motivational psychologist, Paul Diel, wrote that psyche's *subconscious* and *superconscious* are evident in mythology, the Bible, and the concept of the Divinity. His key insights prepare the reader to better understand the breadth and depth of psyche.

These biological and psychological theories serve as scientific prelude and introduction to the cultural, psychological, historical and rational argument presented in *The Supraconscience of Humanity*.

Beginning with our prehistoric state of being, psyche's evolution is presented via key terms which help illuminate the influences and stages of its metamorphosis. In prehistory, we originally survived by the instinctive resourcefulness our *subconscience* and the emergence of our our nature-.born conscience.

Slowly, a greater self-understanding developed with belief in an afterlife; it enabled us to judge the value of this life. Through our myths and rituals, cosmologies and theisms, we intuitively imagined a Supreme Being. However, we were not yet conscious that we were evolving a supraconscience in imitation of a Cosmic Supraconscience. Over the course of history, there arose archetypes of sane and moral behavior as well as theological and philosophical understandings of the world and universe. With the appearance of the Old and New Testament, a segment of humanity gained a clearer comprehension of mankind's relationship with the Supreme Being.

Our identification with the sublime nature of the Divinity inspired us to visualize what superior intelligence and self-perfection could mean to personal evolution.

Mysticism gave expression to our *religious supraconscience*, and man's ingenuity and accumulated knowledge made clear we have acquired a *secular supraconscience*. As these two cultural powers unite in a self-surpassing dynamic, they will forge a future for humanity worthy of our faith in the existence of a Cosmic Supraconscience.

Introduction

The concept of the supraconscience draws on knowledge of evolutionary biology, ecology and microbiology. Contrary to the 19th and 20th century theories of evolution, a third millennium theory visualizes nature as inherently a dialectical process which empowers the creation and integration of all forms of life and effects the evolution of species.

On the other hand, to comprehend man's evolved psyche, we are required to delve into its heritage of exoteric perception and esoteric intuitions. Its self-created archetypes reveal characteristic patterns of human destiny. Beyond twentieth century psychological theories, *The Supraconscience* examines how psyche has been evolving over millennia. It initiated its own processes of self-realization and self-transformation through the creation of cultures and the integration of civilization.

What follows is a glossary of the terms essential to understanding the confluence of natural, historical and cultural forces which fostered the supraconscience of humanity.

I.. **Successive Concepts of Evolution**
    A. Darwin's Theory of Evolution
    B. Twentieth Century Ecology, Microbiology, and Genetics
    C. Third Millennium Biology
        (Based on *The Creative Conscience as Human Destiny*)

II. **Dimensions of Psyche**
    A. Exoteric and Esoteric
    B. C.G. Jung's Archetypes
    C. P. Diel's *Subconscious* and *Superconscious*

III. **Key Terms for Understanding the Evolution of Humanity's Supraconscience**
    A. Prehistoric **psyche** as *subconscience* and later as **nature-born** conscience
    B. Evolution of humankind's religious and secular conscience
    C. Evolution of humanity's religious and secular Supraconscience

Key Terms For Understanding Darwin's
The Origin of Species by Means of Natural Selection (1859).

Evolution
Darwin's theory of evolution presented a solid, scientific argument that nature's various types of plants and animals had their origin in pre-existing archetypes and that the generation of species explained their distinguishable characteristics, variations and mutations. Among his concepts were the following:

The Struggle for Existence
Species compete for food, space and mates. Those individuals less capable of survival, **those with limited** capacities or ineffective strategies, tend to be eliminated by their competitors. Moreover, those **who** do survive pass on their successful traits to offspring and descendants.

Natural Selection
Those individuals or groups in nature **who are** best adapted to their environment have the greatest chance of survival and of reproducing their own kind. This allows them to perpetuate the genetic characteristics best suited to that environment.

Survival of the Fittest
The expression is synonymous with natural selection.

Variation
Divergence from characteristics which are typical of an organism led to variation. The variety of species in the world is partly a consequence of their adaptation to various climates and environments.

On the other hand, Darwin thought species underwent a process of convergence as they evolved similar physical traits, structures and habits due to the fact that they occupied the same environment.

Key Terms Used in Twentieth Century Ecology and Microbiology

Ecology
As a branch of the biological sciences, ecology studies the relationship between organisms and their environment. Its aim is to achieve a holistic description of their relations and patterns of existence.

Microbiology

Microbiology is a relatively recent branch of biology which studies microscopic forms of life, namely, cells and genes. Although it was once unseen by the naked eye, the activity of single cells is now understood to be responsible for integrating all multi-cellular organisms through a process of ever increasing complexity of organization. Indeed, the process of consolidation effects the growth of tissue, muscle, and bone and also regulates all intra-somatic processes that characterize a life form.

Genetics

A new branch of microbiology is genetics or the study of the gene. As a sequence of nucleotides in DNA and RNA located in the germ plasm, the gene transmits our traits and characteristics from generation to generation. Obviously, this new science extends our understanding of the natural processes inherent in all life forms.

Geneticists have discovered genes evolve more quickly than imagined. Rather than "modern" men having the same DNA as people 50,000 years ago, our genes seem "10,000 years younger" due to dramatic, environmental changes. (June 29, 2009, Newsweek. "Don't' Blame Darwin, by Sharon Begley with Jeneen Interland)

That knowledge corroborates the argument of *The Supraconscience* that human evolution has accelerated over the last ten millennia as is evident in the creation of our cultures and the integration of our civilizations.

Key Terms Used in E.H. Strauch's
The Creative Conscience as Human Destiny (2004)

Third Millennium Biology
Morphogenesis

Scientifically speaking, morphogenesis is the formation and differentiation of tissues and organs. In other words, the process is responsible for the origin and development of bodily organs, tissue and bone.

However, morphogenesis can also be seen as encompassing much larger aspects and processes in nature, especially as nature has directly influenced the evolution of humankind. Morphogenesis not only activates and actualizes the embryonic development of the individual human being, but it also directs the ontogenesis of all human life through the stages of infancy, childhood, adolescence, and adulthood into advanced age. By extension, the morphogenetic nature of our species is shown in humankind's creativity. The principle can be extended to explain mankind's creation of worldwide cultures and civilizations.

Symbiosis

The usually accepted definition of symbiosis emphasizes the ecological relationship between organisms. Figuratively speaking, it describes the tolerant associations and living together of two dissimilar organisms. In other words, they are mutually dependent on each other. In the biological sciences, this phenomenon is called mutualism, an important concept needed to understand man's moral evolution.

A microbiological interpretation of any evolved lifeform makes clear that symbiosis is manifest in the arrangement, organization and integration of cells into multi-cellular tissues, organs, and entire life-support systems.

However, as morphogenesis itself, symbiosis plays a vital role not only in the development of the individual human being but also in human evolution. Closer examination of symbiosis reveals it is responsible for the design and form evident throughout animate nature. Moreover, it explains the emergence in humankind of a nature-born conscience. Indeed, it may be called a symbiotic conscience—that which propels us to complete and perfect whatever we undertake to do. It also explains our capacity for compassion for the distressed, the oppressed, the sick, the needy, and the helpless.

In sum, morphogenesis and symbiosis constitute the basis for humankind's biogenetic intelligence. Over time, these natural processes have interacted dialectically to produce the creative conscience of the human race.

The Exoteric vs. the Esoteric

The term *exoteric* is associated with the common sense understanding of the real world, and also with the physical, chemical and biological investigation of the empirical properties of reality. In the main, exotericism is preoccupied with outer appearances rather than the inward reality of the human being. Since it is largely indifferent to the mind's inner preoccupations, it basically focuses on existence. In simplistic terms, the exoteric is not concerned with the truths intrinsic or essential to the ageless needs of the psyche.

Although the esoteric is supposedly understood only by the initiated few, it offers more than a limited, subjective truth. Contrary to common views of it, the esoteric opens up archetypal, existential, metaphysical and perhaps eschatological conceptions of reality. These represent evolutionary stages of psyche's perception of the intricate relationship between a finite fact and a universal truth.

Such esoteric perceptions point to the extra-spatial and extra-temporal experiences which may conceivably enlighten the individual thinker to the vast dialectical processes in nature, in human cultures and possibly in the cosmos itself.

The Archetype

In C.G. Jung's *The Archetypes of the Collective Unconscious*, the Swiss analytical psychologist affirms that archetypes well up from humankind's *collective unconscious*, which contains latent dispositions from man's animal inheritance and ancestral heritage. A person is born with certain patterns of perceiving, feeling and thinking and these are actualized by individual experiences. An archetype is a pattern, process or form which focuses human emotional energy. Birth, death, rebirth, the culture hero, the wise old man, demons and God are all archetypes that are present in dreams, myths, folktales and religions.

One's archetype strives to unify the character into a coherent, integrated whole. As it is the center of the personality, recognition of it is the goal of one's life. Exemplified in such figures as Christ and Buddha, the *self* motivates the individual to seek out a destiny that unifies and integrates his life into a meaningful whole worthy of one's highest humanity. This archetype of the self is usually sought out in middle age after personality has become fully developed and individuated.

Jung acknowledges that the psyche is an arena of a struggle between rational and irrational forces. However, they not only oppose each other, but certain psychic powers attract each other and unite to enable the individual to survive. Jung identifies this tendency of psyche to integration as the *transcendental function.* It operates to balance and synthesize contrary systems into an integrated self.

In *Complex/Archetype/Symbol in the Psychology of C.G. Jung,* Jolande Jacobi explains that to Jung a complex can be a stimulus to greater effort. Because of his fundamentally teleological world view, Jung sees the complex as able to take a positive and prospective direction. The reintegration of a complex into the total personality heals the psyche and releases positive energies. Hence, archetypes have a transcendental function: They prompt the unconscious to reach beyond consciousness.

Archetypes in mythology, religion and poetry exhibit the creative power to synthesize experience, integrate personality, and synchronize energies through spiritual goals. Acknowledging an archetype's presence in one's soul has an effect not unlike that which we feel when we recognize the efficacy of a law of nature. Doing so leads to maturation and self-transformation, it causes one to move from a limited self to a larger one, from an inferior to a superior self-awareness.

Paul Diel's
Subconscious and Superconscious

In his *Psychologie de la Motivation* (1969), the French psychologist Paul Diel described how psyche displays the interaction between opposing psychic forces. The *subconscious* tends to cause the personality to disintegrate whereas the *superconscious* undertakes to transform, heal and integrate the personality into a definite identity with a purposeful destiny.

The subconscious commits a *vital sin* when the individual's personality degenerates as a result of giving in to noxious motives. Its *exalted imagination* deforms psyche, urges it to pursue senseless desires, and to surrender to an inane life of banalities. We become a victim of it when we fail ourselves, neglect to acknowledge the deeper value of life, and do not pursue a meaningful, personal destiny.

It is a *vital sin* to ignore our evolutionary instinct to fulfill a superconscious ideal. Vain pursuits endanger one's whole life in so far as they cause moral disintegration. The cause of human suffering is neglect of the inner, evolutionary intuition. Apathy also turns life into a meaningless banality.

The primary assumption in Diel's major work *The Divinity. The Symbol and Its Signification* (1971), is that soma and psyche form a biogenetic unity, and that it developed as the human species evolved. Thus, he takes life's evolutionary goal to be to find and fulfill the essential desire of one's destiny. Diel believes the symbolism in Greek mythology, the Holy Bible, and the Divinity Itself are manifestations of the divine in Scripture, literature and the arts. **All of these** reflect man's higher nature and developing superconscious.

Key Terms for Understanding the Evolution of Humanity's Supraconscience

The hypothesis underlying *The Supraconscience of Humanity* is that psyche generated its own evolution through the creation of cultures and civilizations. These manifestations of superior intelligence attest to humanity's evolution over 5000 generations. Our primeval origins, pre-history and recorded history evince identifiable stages of psyche's evolution.

I. The Primal and Pre-historic Stages of Psyche
Subconscience

The earliest stage of evolution of the human mind is best described by the term *subconscience*. It is apt because the primal and pre-historic psyche were consciously committed to survival. Its will to live gave it a clear sense of purpose. In human-like primates, the subconscience reached decisions which enabled it to stay alive.

Nature-born conscience

From other creatures, man learned watchfulness and ways to deal with predators. Sharpened powers of perception and skill at detection became essential to survival. Conscience developed basic human traits. The male became protective and heroic, the female, resourceful, patient and caring. Honor and valor defined man; constancy, trust and maternal love was natural to woman.

A second form of primal conscience involved bartering among groups. Trade and give-and-take encouraged mutual understanding. The survival of the family was the central goal of prehistoric life.

II. The Evolution of Conscience

Viable traditions established a communal ethic, yet often commandments warned transgressors of the fact that punishment might be brought upon either their family or the entire community. Common folk took greater pride in skills, down-to-earth knowledge and individual accomplishments. Gradually, conscience evolved into a clearer understanding of rightness, justice and common law.

However, recorded history has shown that the tendency to moral strictness and laxity respectively alternated between generations. Savagery and persecution often became habitual. Our subconscience still lived in the mental world of prehistoric terror, hatred and self-preservation at-all-costs.

Hence, periodically the primal subconscience rebelled against the conscience and overwhelmed human sanity. The ensuing subhuman savagery horrified all who survived, but taught mercy and compassion for friend and foe.

Family values also acted as a counterforce in so far as they fostered emotional maturity between man and woman as parents. Social codes were more or less obeyed. Both the religious and secular commitment to viable ideals nurtured the nobler side of humankind.

Though the cyclical conflict between the vengeful subconscience and an evolving religious conscience continued throughout history, the conscience of religion did instill responsibility, decision and a sense of honor in human relationships: Conscience taught us commitment to our word.

Fortunately, secular education began to effect transformations in the human species. Earthy common sense and secular knowledge offered the promise that we could gain some control over primitive human nature and so have improved prospects for the future. Eventually, conscience would metamorphose into the secular supraconscience of humankind.

III. The Evolution of the Supraconscience

Negative and positive conceptions of the afterlife appeared throughout antiquity. Ancient myths were imaginative projections of life after death. Rituals sought to invoke a supernatural entity for protection and guidance and endeavored to prove the soul superior to fate. Consolidating life's experiences into personal meaning allowed one to tap into the emotional intelligence at the heart of ritual and so cultivated humanity's supraconscience.

Ancient cosmologies also influenced the evolution of the supraconscience. Though fatalist religions revealed the ever-present power of the subconscience, Greek myths expressed the faith that death would be followed by a rebirth. The cosmology of the ancient Hebrews signaled, in their commitment to their God, spiritual evolution and development of a superior conscience.

Theism also had its effect on evolving the religious supraconscience. It affected the psyche's overall evolution as is evident from ancient Egypt's self-created gods and ancient Judaic monotheism. In sum, theism teaches us the exponential empowerment which derives from personal commitment. Such consolidation of mental powers is the incarnation of an individual's supraconscience.

Hence through successive stages of human evolution, the supraconscience came into being via: a) belief in an afterlife, b) ritual dedicated to diverse divinities, c) the working out and refinement of cosmologies, and d) the development of theism in diverse regions of the world.

IV. Four Archetypes of the Emerging Supraconscience

Over time, there arose four archetypes which gave evidence of the conscious emergence of both a religious and secular supraconscience evolving in humankind.

Archetype One: *Sōphrosynē (*Temperance)

In ancient Greece, the concept of knowing oneself and avoiding excesses in thought and behavior were inspired by historic legends of families who suffered terrible fates, and so also by the great Greek tragedies. Tragedy was a consequence of extremes of vanity, arrogance or uncontrolled passion. Such *hybris* was often accompanied by blindness (*hamartia*) to the consequences of violence. Sōphrosynē taught the individual to know oneself and to strive for self-mastery.

Archetype Two: The "Great Chain of Being"

This concept took the world to be self-sufficient and perfect, and the universe itself, self-transcending. Aristotle's was a special version of this vision in so far as he saw life as created on a scale of perfection from the inferior to superior levels of being. There was also the perception that a life force accounted for the transformation evident throughout nature. By the Renaissance, this archetype conceived of nature as the world's eternal state of Being, and, at the same time, life's eternal potential for Becoming.

Archetype Three: The Bible's Four Levels of Meaning

Biblical Scripture revealed four strata of significance: 1) the literal or historical, 2) the metaphorical or allegorical, 3) the moral and 4) the mystical. The Bible taught there was both an outer and an inner sense to our lives. Each individual should realize a plan in life. By studying the Bible at different stages in life, one could aspire to experience all four levels of life's meaning.

Archetype Four: The Divinity

This archetype expressed belief in an omniscient, omnipotent Being. Such religious belief was to have a pervasive influence on the religious creation of cultures and the secular evolution of civilizations. The idea of God inspired humankind's noblest ideals and achievements. It accelerated the growth of both religious and secular knowledge.

V. A Secular Interpretation of the Old Testament

The Old Testament is itself historical evidence of how faith solidifies into a cultural conscience and how belief in a Supreme Being can lead a community to interpret historical events in the light of their faith. Judaism integrated the Jews not only into a spiritual affiliation, but also a communal supraconscience.

Furthermore, the ethical essence of Judaism is not the sole evidence for the evolution of people's collective conscience. The body of historical fact that their most devout scholars devoted many centuries to finalizing and perfecting the Old Testament into its ultimate form itself shows a fantastic constancy of purpose. This sustained commitment surely fostered the superior mental powers of psyche and actualized the powers of man's still evolving supraconscience.

This same assertion can be made about Christian scholars of the New Testament and about Islamic scholars about the Holy Qur' an.

VI. A Secular Interpretation of the New Testament

Christ's role was to make clear the laws and prophecies of the Old Testament. Yet, he found it necessary to reinterpret the traditional understanding of the Father. Indeed, He came to teach a new way of thinking about God.

The Savior promised the faithful an afterlife with God. Jesus taught the sacredness of love, forgiveness, courage and resoluteness. Thus He inspired humankind's superior nature. He taught that each of us should realize his or her own potential for salvation. He taught mankind to be unafraid of tomorrow. He counseled Christians to attend to our need for each other and to learn the eternal truths that life itself teaches. Faith in ourselves and in others can thus become a self-fulfilling prophecy of good fortune for humankind. In and of itself, His life was a revelation. In our own lives, we should learn to be true to the wisdom of the heart. We should act on the faith that the purpose of humanity's future evolution will be revealed to us by our endeavors. The Cosmic Supraconscience is awaiting us on the other side of infinity.

VII. How Mysticism and Heresy Created Humankind's Supraconscience
Mysticism as Supraconscience

Religion fosters mankind's emotional and intuitive intelligence, which have contributed to the evolution of the supraconscience. Historically, mystics aimed at transcending their imperfections and sought perfection by commitment to their idea of God. This vow led some to achieve moral wholeness at different stages of life.

The medieval poet, Dante Alighieri, portrayed existence as a *Divine Comedy*: The good or evil one did in life would end in divine retribution, either heaven or hell. In the eighteenth century, G.E. Lessing defined the essence of the pure Jew, Christian and Muslim. Their conduct in life proved which possessed the true religion. In the nineteenth century, the poet Walt Whitman foresaw a grand destiny for humankind and praised life's experiences as eternity *now*. Perhaps most remarkable in this connection is the ancient Roman, Lucretius, who scorned fear of the afterlife. For him, there was nothing to fear because, at death, we simply disintegrated into atoms. Nevertheless, when humans use their superior potentials, they realize their natural destiny on earth. Hence those who put their trust in their intuitive intelligence helped evolve psyche's supraconscience.

Heresy and the Secular Supraconscience

The heretics' search for ultimate truth mirrored the devotion of mystics and mysticism. However, the heretics trusted their intelligence rather than their emotions. They embraced all forms of knowledge that would expand their own understanding of Truth. This started with believing that God's Word and His Love were greater than the orthodox teaching of any religion. Heretics came to regard evil as insane. Heaven and hell were delusions of the mind.

In time, they undertook the dispassionate and objective study of man's cultural history. Slowly, they developed a deeper appreciation of humankind's secular achievements. The countless forms of knowledge that we have developed, the impressive fact of the creation of rich cultures and advanced civilizations led them to a secular conclusion. These accomplishments were due to the evolution of our nature-born conscience. Since prehistoric times, mankind had

The Third Millennium Supraconscience

Both mysticism and heresy have contributed to the creation of the world we live in. Historically intertwined, they both sought universal verity. Mysticism led to the development of our religious supraconscience, and heresy, to humanity's secular supraconscience. What is important in this realization is that modern man and woman now know they can create a future based on the accumulated wisdom of our human supraconscience.

Bibliography

I. The Human Body and Mind

Achterberg, Jeanne. *Imagery in Healing. Shamanism and Modern Medicine.* Boston, MA. Shambala Publ.. 1989.

Ackerman, Diane. *A Natural History of the Senses.* New York, NY. Random House Publ, 1990.

Asimov, Isaac. *The Human Brain. Its Capacities and Functions.* New York, NY. New American Library, 1964.

Bateson, Gregory. *Mind and Nature--A Necessary Unity.* New York, NY Bantam Books, 1980.

Baumgart, Ernest. *Les mecanismes de la Vision.* Paris, France. Presses Universitaires de France, 1952.

Bouthoul, Gaston. *Les Mentalités.* "Que Sais-je?" Paris, France. P.U. de France,1971.

Brunschvicg, Leon. *Les âges de l'intelligence.* Paris, France. P.U. de France. 1947.

Bucke, R.M. *Cosmic Consciousness. A Study of the Evolution of the Human Mind.* Secaucus, NJ. Citadel Press,1977.

Donald, Merlin. *Origins of the Modern Mind. Three Stages in the Evolution of Culture and Cognition.* Cambridge, MA. Harvard UP, 1991.

Ferguson, Marilyn. *The Brain Revolution. The Frontiers of Mind Research.* New York, NY. Bantam Publ., 1975.

Gardner, Howard. *The Quest for Mind. Piaget, Levi-Strauss, and the Structuralist Movement.* New York, NY. Vintage Books. 1974.

Gazzaniga, M.S. *Mind Matters. How Mind and Brain Interact to Create our Conscious Lives.* Cambridge, MA. Houghton Mifflin/MIT Press. 1988.

Ghandi, Kishore. *The Evolution of Consciousness.* New York, NY. Paragon House. 1986.

Langer, Ellen J. *Mindfulness.* New York, NY. Addison-Wesley Publ. 1989.

Leahey, T.H. *A History of Psychology. Main Currents in Psychological Thought.* Upper Saddle River, NJ. Pearson/Prentice Hall, 2004.

Litvak, S. & Senzee, A.W. *Toward a New Brain: Evolution and the Human Mind.* Upper Saddle River, N.J. Prentice Hall, 1986.

Lloyd, Dan, *Simple Minds.* Cambridge, MA. MIT Press. 1989.

Piaget, *Biologie et Connaissance.* Paris, France: Gallimard, 1967.

Pickering, J. & Skinner, M., Eds. *From Experience to Symbols. Readings on Consciousness.* Toronto & Buffalo: University of Toronto Press. 1990.

Pool, J. Lawrence, M.D. *Nature's Masterpiece. The Brain and How It Works.* New York, NY, Walker, Publ. 1987.

II. Creativity and Conscience

Bernes, Jeanne. *L'Imagination*. Paris, France: P.U. de France, 1975.
Boirel, Rene. *L'Invention*. Paris, France: P.U. de France, 1961.
Bolton, Neil. *The Pyschology of Thinking*. London: Methuen, 1972.
Bridoux, Andre. *Le Souvenir*. Paris, France: P. U. de France, 1961.
Charpentier, Raymond. *La connaissance d'autrui*. Paris, France: P. U. de France, 1968.
D'Arcy, Philippe. *La Reflexion*. Paris, France: P. U. de France, 1972.
Davy, Marie-Magdeleine. *La connaissance de soi*. Paris, France: P. U. de France, 1971.
De Bono, Edward. *New Think. The Use of Lateral Thinking in the Generation of New Ideas*. New York, NY. Avon Press, 1971.
Dimnet, Ernest. *The Art of Thinking*. Greenwich, CT. Fawcett. 1956.
Granger,Gilles-Gaston. *La Raison*. Paris, France: P. U. de France. 1974.
Hawkes, Terence. *Metaphor*. London: Methuen Publ. 1977.
Jackson, K.F. *The Art of Solving Problems*. London: Heinemann, 1975.
Jung, C.G. *The Archetypes and the Collective Unconscious*. Trans. R.F.C. Hull, Princeton, NJ: Princeton UP. 1959.
Khatena, Joe. *Imagery and Creative Imagination*. Buffalo, NY. Bearly/ Creative Education Foundation, 1984.
Koestler, Arthur. *The Act of Creation*. New York, NY. Macmillan, 1964.
Luthi, Max. *Märchen*. Stuttgart, Germany. Metzler. 1964.
Muecke, D.C. *Irony*. London. Methuen. 1970.
Parnes, Sidney J. *Creativity: Unlocking the Human Potential*. Buffalo, N.Y. D.O.K. Publ.. 1972.
Rouquette, Michel-Louis. *La Creativité*. Paris, France. P U de France, 1973.
Ruthven, K.K. *Myth*. London. Methuen. 1976.
Veraldi, Gabriel & Brigitte. *Psychologie de la création*. Paris, France. Centre d' Etude de promotion de la lecture .1972.

III. Philosophy

Adler, M.J. & Gorman,W., Eds. *The Great Ideas. A Syntopicon of Great Books of the Western World*. Volume I & II. Chicago. Encyclopedia Britannica, Inc. 1952.
Boschenski, J.M. *Introduccion al Pensamiento Filosofico*. Barcelona, Spain. Herder, 1985.
Bouthol, Gaston. *Les Mentalités*. "Que Sais-je?" Paris, France. P.U. de France. 1971.
Brunschvig, Leon. *Les âges de l'intelligence*. Paris, France. PU de France. 1947.
Carper, J. *Your Miracle Brain*. N.Y. Harper Collins, 2000.

Dilthey, Wilhelm. *Theories des Conceptions du Monde. Essai d'une Philosophie de la Philosophie*. Trans. L. Sauzin. Paris, France. PU de France, 1946.
Donner, M., Eble, K.E., & Helbing, R.E., eds. *The Intellectual Tradition of the West.* Glenview, IL. Scott, Foresman & Co., 1967.
Foster, David. *The Philosophical Scientists*. New York, NY. Dorset Press. 1991.
Greenstein, G. *The Symbiotic Universe. Life and Mind in the Cosmos*. New York, NY. William Morrow, 1988.
Gutmann, J. & A. Diemer, Eds. *Philosophy A to Z*. Trans. S. Attanasio. New York, NY. Grosset & Dunlap. (Universal Reference Library)., 1963.
Kasla, D.S. & Stauth, C. *Brain Longevity. The Breakthrough Medical Program that Improves your Mind and Memory*. New York, NY. Time Warner, 1999.
Lasbax, Emile. *La dialectique du rhythme de l'univers*. Paris, France. Librairie Philosophique J. Vrin, 1925.
Magill, Frank N., Ed. *Masterpieces of World Philosophy in Summary Form*. New York, NY. Harper Collins. 1961.
Makreel, Rudolf A. *Dilthey, Philosopher of Human Studies*. Princeton, N.J. Princeton University Press, 1975.
Morot-Sir, Édouard. *La Pensée Negative*. Paris, France: Aubier, 1947.
Parain, B. Ed. *Histoire de la Philosophie 1.Orient-Antiquite-Moyen-Age.* L'Encyclopedie de la Pléiade. Paris, France. Edition Gallimard, 1969.
Rohmann, C. *A World of Ideas. A Dictionary of Important Theories, Concepts, Beliefs, and Thinkers*. New York, NY. Ballantine Books. 1999.
Rothacker, Erich. *Logik und Systematik der Geisteswissenschaften*. Bonn, Germany: Bouvier, 1947.
Wiener, Philip P. Ed. *Dictionary of History of Ideas/4. Psychological Ideas in Antiquity to Zeitgeist*. New York, NY. Charles Scribner & Sons. 1973.
Windelband, W. *A History of Philosophy I. Renaissance and Modern*. New York, NY. Harper Torchbooks, 1958. Trans. J.H. Tufts

IV. History of Humankind and Religion

Armstrong, K. A. *The History of God. The 4,000 Year Quest of Judaism, Christianity, and Islam.* New York, NY. A. Knopf Publ. 1993.
_____*The Great Transformation. The Beginning of Our Religious Traditions*. N.Y.: Alfred A. Knopf, 2006.
Benoist, Luc. *L'Esoterisme*. Paris, France: PU de France, 1965.
Borchert, Bruno. *Mysticism. Its History and Challenge*. York Beach, ME. Samuel Weiser. 1994.
Diel, Paul. *Le symbolisme dans la mythologie grécque; étude psychoanalytique*. Paris, France. Petite Bibliotheque Payot, 1966,
_____*La divinité; le symbole et sa signification*. Paris, France, Petite Bibliotheque Payot, 1971

_____ *Le symbolisme dans la bible; l'universalité de language symbolique et sa signification psychologique.* Paris, France. Petite Bibliotheque Payot, 1975.

Eliade, Mircea. *A History of Religious Ideas: from Stone Age to the Eleusinian Mysteries.* Trans. Willard F. Trask. Chicago: University of Chicago Press. 1978

Forde, C. Daryll & James, W. *African Worlds. Studies in the Cosmological Ideas and Social Values of African Peoples.* Great Britain: Oxford UP, 1999.

Gregoire, F. *L'Au Dela.* Paris, France. PU de France, 1970.

Herberger, Charles F. *The Thread of Ariadne. The Labyrinth of the Calendar of Minos.* N.Y. Philosophical Library, 1972.

Howells, William W. *Back of History. The Story of our own Origins.* Garden City, NY. Anchor Books, 1969.

Hutin, Sergei. *Les Gnostiques.* Paris, France.: PU de France, 1970.

James, E.O. *The Ancient Gods.* Edison,NJ. Castle Books, 2004.

James, William. *The Varieties of Religious Experience. A Study in Human Nature.* New York, NY. Barnes & Noble Classics, 2004.

King, Frank P. *A Chronicle of World History from 130,000 Years Ago to the Eve of A.D. 2000.* Lanham, MD. University Press of America, 2002.

Lewis, H.D. *Philosophy of Religion.* London: English Universities Press. 1965.

Murray, G. *Five Stages of Greek Religion.* Garden City, N.Y. Doubleday, 1951.

Nigg, W. *The Heretics. Heresy Through the Ages.* Trans. Winston, R & C. New York, NY. Dorset Press, 1962.

Peuche, D 'H-C. *Histoire des Religions II.* L'Encyclopedie de la Pléiade. Paris, France. Edition Gallimard. 1972.

Robertson, Roland, Ed. *Sociology of Religion.* Harmondworth, Middlesex, England: Penguin Books, 1972.

Thomson, Oliver. *A History of Sin.* N.Y.: Barnes & Noble, 1995.

Verenne, J. *Zarathustra et la tradition mazdèene.* Maîtres Spirituels. Paris, France. Editions de Seuil, 1966.

Index

A

A Philosophy of Literary Criticism 127
Abelard, Peter 147
    and heresy 191
Abraham 95-97
Achterberg, Jeanne
    and myth of Osiris 48, 131
Aeneid 36
afterlife, 4, 11, 14
    and conscience 15
    modern belief in 245
afterlife as worldview 22
    Ancient Egypt 22, 27
    Ancient Greece 28
    Ancient Persia 28
    Aristotle on 6
    Celts 37
    Christianity 39ff
    Etruscans and Romans 35
    Gauls 37
    Germans 37
    Gnostics 11
    Neoplatonism 34
Ahriman 28-29, 167
Akhenaton 5, 68
Amenemope,
    Egyptian sage 54
ancient cosmologies 50ff
angels,
    belief in 248
Apocalypse, the 139
    in modern media 236
apocalypticism 119-120, 173
    and media 236
arêté (excellence) 31
Aristotle,
    act and potency 61, 159
    and mysticism of nature 159
    De Anima 77
    logical works 61
    notion of entelechy 61, 159
    on afterlife 32-33
    on sōphrosynē 76
    soul as intelligence (*nous*) 33
    Poetics 6, 220
Atum (-Re),
    self-creator god 67
Aton, sun god 68

B

Babylonian myth 52
Bernard of Clairvaux 191
bipolarity of human nature 232
Blake, William 155
bodhi consciousness 97
Book of Chronicles 104
Book of the Covenant, 61, 99, 103
    and Hammurabi's Code 52, 61
    as basis for law 101
    as foundation of Judaism 102
Book of Daniel 119
Book of Ecclesiastes 19-20, 70
    and subconscience 114
Book of Exodus 102
Book of Genesis 95
Book of Genesis (Diel) 86
Book of Job 108
Book of Joshua 5
Book of Judges 103
Book of Kings 104
Book of Leviticus 101
Book of Proverbs 112
Book of Psalms 110
Book of Revelation 80, 139ff, 204
    and human spiritual evolution 139ff
    and prophecy of Daniel 121
    and subconscience 141
Book of the Seven Seals 140
Brethren of the Free Spirit 148-149
Bruno, Giordano 196
Bucke, R.M. 177

C

Catharism 191
catharsis 220-221
co-evolution,
    of inferior and superior human nature 222
collective sin 4
conscience,
    and guilt 52
    and self-purification 47
    and Truth 21
    incarnation of 18, 22

ancient Egyptian cult of
dead as source of 22
as battleground between good and
evil 18
conscience (vs. subconscience) 3
and American media 9
and Egyptian religion, 3-4
Akenhaton
and moral virtue 5
divine judgment of
deceased 4
Maat, Egyptian goddess of
justice 4, 52
Osiris 4
Ramses II,
and Hebrew slaves 5
and Aztecs 3
and early man 7
and Hebrew prophets 5
Joshua 5
Moses 5
and Minoan Golden Age 4
Homer,
heroic conscience 6, 30ff
Job,
and divine justice 6
role of women in evolution of 8-9
Copernicus 196
Cosmic Consciousness (Bucke) 177
cosmology,
Ancient Greek 55ff
Ancient Egyptian 53ff
Ancient Hebrew 61ff
and supraconscience of humanity,
tenets of 65-66
subconscience and supraconscience in antiquity 65ff

D
Daniel, 70, 119ff
A King's Punishment 121
Final Vision 123
The Fiery Furnace 121
The Handwriting on the
Wall 122
The Lion's Den 122
David,
King of Israel 104
Dante 152ff

De Anima 77
death,
as equalizer 42
Demeter 55
Deuteronomy 102
Diel, Paul 86
contrasted to Strauch 87
theory of motivation 86
superconscious/ subconscious
and Freud 86
divination 21
Donatism 188
dualism
and subconscience 238

E
Eastern Orthodox Church 169
Ecclesiastes, Book of 19, 70, 114
Egypt, ancient,
afterlife 4
Asiatic invasion of 54-55
Aton, sun god 68
Atum(-Re),
self-creator god 67
Maat, goddess of justice
68-69
Middle Kingdom 4, 53
Ptah,
Creator god 67
Thoth,
god of omniscience 68
Egyptian *Book of the Dead* 28, 54, 103
entelechial time 159
entelechy,
defined 61
development of 159
Erigena, Scotus 190
Eros/Thanatos,
modern psychology 58
evolutionary biology 33, 64, 247
exorcism 234
Ezekiel 118-119

F

G
good and evil,
struggle between
in primeval imagination 218

Index

in modern consciousness 219
Gospel of John 137
Gospel of Luke 136
Gospel of Mark 133
Gospel of Matthew 129
Gottschalk 190
Gnosticism, ancient 11ff
    Marcion 11
    and human intuition 12
Great Chain of Being, the
    as archetype 77
    interpretation of 77ff
    and supraconscience 77

H

hamartia 6, 74
Hammurabi,
    Code of Laws 52, 61
Hebrew prophets,
    Daniel 70, 116
    Joshua 5
    Ezekiel 118-119
    Isaiah 115
    Jeremiah 116
heresy,
    and modern psyche 199
    historical effect of 196ff
Hesiod,
    and creative force of Eros 58
Hippocrates 131
History of Sin 215
Homo hablis 126, 247
Homo sapiens 126, 179, 232
Hugo, Victor 156
human supraconscience,
    in modern era 22
human psyche,
    entelechial growth of 16-17
hybris 62
    Aristotle on 6
    in *Oresteia* 74
    vs. *sōphrosynē* 74

I

Imagery in Healing 48, 131
Inquisition, the 192
Irenaeus,
    and heresy 187
irony 107,

in biblical context 108
Isaiah 115
Isis 48

J

Jacob's Ladder 97
James, William 17-18, 177
Jeremiah 116
Joachim of Flores 148
Job 6, 51, 108
Joseph,
    premonitory powers 97
Judaism,
    ancient 70
    and creation 61
    and Messiah 70
    trust in divine protection 61, 70
Jungian analysis,
    and prayer 214
    animus/anima 163
    collective unconscious 127
    human spiritual evolution 151

K

karma,
    and human destiny 12-13
    and reincarnation 22

L

Leaves of Grass 156 ff
Lessing 154
Lucretius 159
Luther, Martin 195-96

M

Maat, Egyptian goddess of justice 4, 53-54, 68, 98
    and Hebrew exile 101
Manichaeism,
    and early Christianity 14, 139
    dualism in 14, 222
Marcion, 11
    and heresy 186

martyrdom, 156, 185ff
    of women 194
Mazdaism 28-29, 167
Meister Eckhart 149-150
Mithra, Persian god of light 50
Mithraic ritual 50

Mithraism,
    and Roman Army 50-51
    competitor to early Christianity 51
    Emperor Aurelian on religion 50
monotheism,
    in ancient Egypt 69
    truth of 164ff
    vs. polytheism 165
Montanist movement 187-188
Moses, 5
    Farewell Speech 103
    prophetic powers of 99ff
    revelation of Ten
    Commandments 100ff
mutualism 229
mysticism 17
    and heresy 198ff
    and number 80, 150
    Aristotelian 159
    modern, 147ff
        effect on psyche 199
    Pythagorean 83, 150
    third millennium, 18, 160ff
        emotional intelligence 162
        understanding of self 162
        visualization of soul 163
myth,
    Ancient Greek 45ff
    and ancient conscience 46ff

N
Nathan the Wise 154
Neoplatonism,
    rebirth of 34-35
Noah 95
Nun,
    and primitive subconscience 64

O
Odyssey 30
Olympian gods, the 55
On the Nature of Things 159
Oresteia 74
Origen 186-187
    and heresy 172
Orpheus, myth of 59
Orphic initiation rites 59
Osiris, myth of 4, 48-49

P
Pascal, Blaise 50, 153ff, 226
    and Jansenism 154
    and mysticism 154
Pelagianism 188-189
Penseés (Pascal) 154
Pentateuch 99, 248
Persephone 45
Plato,
    on sōphrosynē 75
    on the soul 31
    Theory of Forms 31, 60
    Republic 31
Poetics 6, 220
principle of continuity 77
principle of gradation 78
principle of plenitude 77
Proem (Lucretius) 159
prophecy, 80-81, 99, 107
prophetic intuition,
    and supraconscience 124
Proverbs of Solomon 113
Psalm 23 111
Psalm 51 112
Psalm 100 112
psyche,
    and idea of God 160ff
Ptah,
    Egyptian Creator god 67ff

Q

R
religion,
    and mystical experience 161ff
    and supraconscience 161ff
religious conversion,
    and human psychic evolution 164
Republic (Plato) 31, 60, 75
Revelation, Book of 80, 133
    and evolution 140
    and secular sciences 204
    and subconscience 134
Rhetoric 76
ritual,
    and human evolution 47ff
    Babylonian 52ff
    secular vs. religious 47ff

Index

Robinet, J.B., 78

S
Scripture,
    esoteric/exoteric readings 82-83
Second Coming of Christ
    139, 202
secular conversion,
    and fate 224
secular sciences, the 200
Sheol 70
Sic et Non (Yes, But Also No) 147, 191
Socrates,
    human supraconscience in
        antiquity 31-32
*Song of Solomon
    (Song of Songs)* 115
Solomon,
    King of Israel 105ff
Sophocles 75
sōphrosynē 6, 74
    and Christianity 76
    and Roman culture 76
    and supraconscience 75ff
    as archetype 73-74
    Plato on 75
    Aristotle on 76
    vs. *hybris* 74
Stoicism,
    afterlife 34-35
subconscience,
    confrontation with
        death 40
    and crucifixion 132-135
    and human spiritual
        evolution 222, 237
    and religion 167
    and Roman era 9, 132-135
    in media and global economy 235
subconscience vs. supraconscience,
    and ancient Egyptian culture 53
    and Babylonian myth 52
    and exorcism 234
    and Hebrew prophets 61
    and human spiritual evolution 226
    dialectic between 222
    historic antagonism 36
*subconscience/conscience/
    supraconscience* vii

Supraconscience, Cosmic 88-89, 230
    and archetypes 89-90
    and ancient religious faith 100
    and psyche's journey through time
        226ff, 250
    as understood in antiquity 100
supraconscience,
    evolution of subconscience 168,
        238
    effect of mysticism on 168ff, 182
    journey from subconscience 237
    mysticism and heresy 180
    religious 206
    secular 206
superconscious/ subconscious (Diel)
    contrasted to Freud 86
Supreme Being,
    and human destiny 18, 214, 226ff
    birth of idea of 212
syncretism 50
    in modern era 223

T
Tertullian 39
Ten Commandments,
    revelation of 99
Thanatos,
    and subconscience 58
*The Creative Conscience as Human
    Destiny* 87, 232
The Divine Comedy 152ff
*The Divinity, the Symbol and its
    Signification* (Diel) 86
The Heretics 180
theism,
    and evolution of human psyche
        66ff
Thoth,
    Egyptian god of omniscience 68
    as Supreme Deity 68
time lag,
    and human evolution 239
Tintern Abbey (Wordsworth) 156
Toba,
    eruption of 63
tragedy,
    Ancient Greek, 60
    and hybris 74-75
    and subconscience 75

U

V
Varieties of Religious Experience 17, 177
Virgil 36
Vision of the Seven Trumpets 147
Vita Nuova (The New Life) 152ff

W
Waldensians 178
Whitman 146
witchcraft,
    and subconscience 194
women,
    contribution to evolution 246ff
    supraconscience of 247
Wordsworth 156
Wycliffe, John 194

X

Y
Yahweh,
    and creation 61
    in early Judaism 14
    divine vs. human law 61
    conquest of Baal 61-62
Yom Kippur (Day of Atonement) 101

Z
Zoroastrianism,
    afterlife 28-29
    Ahriman,
        primitive subconscience 28
    and Christianity 14, 155-156
    and Judaism 14, 155-156
    dualism 14, 222
    good and evil in 222
    Ormazd, 29